# World Geography

by
Marcel Lewinski

American Guidance Service, Inc.
Circle Pines, Minnesota 55014-1796
800-328-2560

## About the Author

**Marcel Lewinski** is currently Associate Professor of History Education at Illinois State University. Previously, he was an award-winning high school social studies teacher. He has taught a wide range of subjects, including world history, United States history, geography, political science, economics, sociology, and contemporary problems. Lewinski is professionally active in many organizations and has given presentations at many state, regional, and national conferences. He has conducted numerous workshops for social studies teachers and has traveled all over the world. As author of several books in social studies, Mr. Lewinski acts as a consultant to school systems and has served as a frequent contributor to educational publications.

### Content Reviewers

Lois Barnes
Brentwood, TN

Janet L. Wolden
St. Paul, MN

### Publisher's Project Staff

Director, Product Development: Karen Dahlen
Senior Editor: Patrick Keithahn
Copy Editor: Dee Ready
Assistant Editor: Karen Anderson
Development Assistant: Bev Johnson
Designer: Julie Tilka
Design Manager: Nancy Condon
Desktop Publishing Manager: Lisa Beller
Desktop Publishing Specialist: Linda Peterson
Purchasing Agent: Mary Kaye Kuzma
Executive Director of Marketing: Matt Keller
Marketing Manager: Brian Holl

Printed in the United States of America

ISBN 0-7854-2436-9

Product Number 91500

A 0 9 8 7 6 5 4 3

# Contents

How to Use This Book: A Study Guide . . . . . . . . . . . . . . . . . . . . . 16

Introduction . . . . . . . . . . . . . . . . . . . . . . . . . . . . . . . . . . . . . . . . 24

**Unit 1**  **The United States and Canada** . . . . . . . . . . . . . . . . . . . . . . . . . 30

Chapter 1  The United States . . . . . . . . . . . . . . . . . . . . . . . . . 32

Section 1  The United States . . . . . . . . . . . . . . . . . . 34

Section 2  Physical Features and Climate . . . . . . . . 37

Section 3  The People . . . . . . . . . . . . . . . . . . . . . . . 42

Section 4  Economy and Environment . . . . . . . . . . 46

Chapter Summary . . . . . . . . . . . . . . . . . 51

Chapter Review . . . . . . . . . . . . . . . . . . . 52

Chapter 2  Canada . . . . . . . . . . . . . . . . . . . . . . . . . . . . . . . . . . 54

Section 1  Canada . . . . . . . . . . . . . . . . . . . . . . . . . . 56

Section 2  Physical Features and Climate . . . . . . . . 60

Section 3  The People . . . . . . . . . . . . . . . . . . . . . . . 64

Section 4  Economy and Environment . . . . . . . . . . 67

Chapter Summary . . . . . . . . . . . . . . . . . 71

Chapter Review . . . . . . . . . . . . . . . . . . . 72

| | | |
|---|---|---|
| **Unit 2** | **Latin America** . . . . . . . . . . . . . . . . . . . . . . . . . . . . . . . . . . . . **76** | |

| | | |
|---|---|---|
| Chapter 3 | Mexico . . . . . . . . . . . . . . . . . . . . . . . . . . . . . . . . . . . . | 78 |
| | Section 1  Mexico  . . . . . . . . . . . . . . . . . . . . . . . . . . . | 80 |
| | Section 2  Physical Features and Climate. . . . . . . . | 83 |
| | Section 3  The People. . . . . . . . . . . . . . . . . . . . . . . . | 86 |
| | Section 4  Economy and Environment . . . . . . . . . | 90 |
| | Chapter Summary . . . . . . . . . . . . . . . . | 95 |
| | Chapter Review. . . . . . . . . . . . . . . . . . . . | 96 |

| | | |
|---|---|---|
| Chapter 4 | Central America and the Caribbean . . . . . . . . . . . . | 98 |
| | Section 1  Central America and the Caribbean. . . | 100 |
| | Section 2  Physical Features and Climate. . . . . . . | 103 |
| | Section 3  The People. . . . . . . . . . . . . . . . . . . . . . . . | 106 |
| | Section 4  Economy and Environment . . . . . . . . . | 111 |
| | Chapter Summary . . . . . . . . . . . . . . . . | 115 |
| | Chapter Review. . . . . . . . . . . . . . . . . . . . | 116 |

| | | |
|---|---|---|
| Chapter 5 | South America  . . . . . . . . . . . . . . . . . . . . . . . . . . . . . | 118 |
| | Section 1  South America . . . . . . . . . . . . . . . . . . . . | 120 |
| | Section 2  Physical Features and Climate. . . . . . . | 123 |
| | Section 3  The People. . . . . . . . . . . . . . . . . . . . . . . . | 127 |
| | Section 4  Economy and Environment . . . . . . . . . | 130 |
| | Chapter Summary . . . . . . . . . . . . . . . . | 135 |
| | Chapter Review. . . . . . . . . . . . . . . . . . . . | 136 |

| **Unit 3** | **Europe** | | ........ **140** |
|---|---|---|---|
| | Chapter 6 | The British Isles | ........ 142 |
| | | Section 1 The British Isles | ........ 144 |
| | | Section 2 Physical Features and Climate | ........ 148 |
| | | Section 3 The People | ........ 150 |
| | | Section 4 Economy and Environment | ........ 154 |
| | | Chapter Summary | ........ 159 |
| | | Chapter Review | ........ 160 |
| | Chapter 7 | Western Europe | ........ 162 |
| | | Section 1 Western Europe | ........ 164 |
| | | Section 2 Physical Features and Climate | ........ 167 |
| | | Section 3 The People | ........ 170 |
| | | Section 4 Economy and Environment | ........ 173 |
| | | Chapter Summary | ........ 179 |
| | | Chapter Review | ........ 180 |
| | Chapter 8 | Southern Europe | ........ 182 |
| | | Section 1 Southern Europe | ........ 184 |
| | | Section 2 Physical Features and Climate | ........ 187 |
| | | Section 3 The People | ........ 190 |
| | | Section 4 Economy and Environment | ........ 194 |
| | | Chapter Summary | ........ 199 |
| | | Chapter Review | ........ 200 |
| | Chapter 9 | Northern Europe | ........ 202 |
| | | Section 1 Northern Europe | ........ 204 |
| | | Section 2 Physical Features and Climate | ........ 208 |
| | | Section 3 The People | ........ 211 |
| | | Section 4 Economy and Environment | ........ 215 |
| | | Chapter Summary | ........ 219 |
| | | Chapter Review | ........ 220 |

| | | | |
|---|---|---|---|
| **Unit 4** | **Eastern Europe and Russia**................................**224** | | |
| | Chapter 10 | Eastern Europe and the Balkan Countries ..... 226 | |
| | | Section 1 | Eastern Europe and the Balkan Countries ................... 228 |
| | | Section 2 | Physical Features and Climate........ 231 |
| | | Section 3 | The People........................ 234 |
| | | Section 4 | Economy and Environment ........ 238 |
| | | | Chapter Summary ................ 243 |
| | | | Chapter Review.................. 244 |
| | Chapter 11 | Russia and the Independent Republics ........ 246 | |
| | | Section 1 | Russia and the Independent Republics........................ 248 |
| | | Section 2 | Physical Features and Climate........ 251 |
| | | Section 3 | The People........................ 254 |
| | | Section 4 | Economy and Environment ........ 258 |
| | | | Chapter Summary ................ 265 |
| | | | Chapter Review.................. 266 |

| Unit 5 | **Africa and the Middle East** .......................... **270** |
|---|---|

Chapter 12   West Africa................................. 272
             Section 1   West Africa ...................... 274
             Section 2   Physical Features and Climate........ 276
             Section 3   The People........................ 279
             Section 4   Economy and Environment ......... 284
                         Chapter Summary ................ 289
                         Chapter Review................... 290

Chapter 13   Southern Africa ........................... 292
             Section 1   Southern Africa................... 294
             Section 2   Physical Features and Climate........ 296
             Section 3   The People........................ 299
             Section 4   Economy and Environment ......... 303
                         Chapter Summary ................ 309
                         Chapter Review................... 310

Chapter 14   Central and East Africa...................... 312
             Section 1   Central and East Africa ............. 314
             Section 2   Physical Features and Climate........ 316
             Section 3   The People........................ 320
             Section 4   Economy and Environment ......... 324
                         Chapter Summary ................ 329
                         Chapter Review................... 330

Chapter 15   North Africa and the Middle East ............. 332
             Section 1   North Africa and the Middle East  .... 334
             Section 2   Physical Features and Climate........ 336
             Section 3   The People........................ 340
             Section 4   Economy and Environment ......... 346
                         Chapter Summary ................ 349
                         Chapter Review................... 350

| | | |
|---|---|---|
| **Unit 6** | **Central and East Asia** . . . . . . . . . . . . . . . . . . . . . . . . . . . . . . **354** | |
| | Chapter 16 China . . . . . . . . . . . . . . . . . . . . . . . . . . . . . . . . . . . . 356 | |
| | Section 1 China . . . . . . . . . . . . . . . . . . . . . . . . . . . . . 358 | |
| | Section 2 Physical Features and Climate . . . . . . . 360 | |
| | Section 3 The People . . . . . . . . . . . . . . . . . . . . . . . 363 | |
| | Section 4 Economy and Environment . . . . . . . . 367 | |
| | Chapter Summary . . . . . . . . . . . . . . . 373 | |
| | Chapter Review . . . . . . . . . . . . . . . . . . 374 | |
| | Chapter 17 Japan and the Koreas . . . . . . . . . . . . . . . . . . . . . . . . 376 | |
| | Section 1 Japan and the Koreas . . . . . . . . . . . . . 378 | |
| | Section 2 Physical Features and Climate . . . . . . . 380 | |
| | Section 3 The People . . . . . . . . . . . . . . . . . . . . . . . 384 | |
| | Section 4 Economy and Environment . . . . . . . . 389 | |
| | Chapter Summary . . . . . . . . . . . . . . . 393 | |
| | Chapter Review . . . . . . . . . . . . . . . . . . 394 | |
| **Unit 7** | **South Asia, Southeast Asia, and the Pacific** . . . . . . . . . . . . . . **398** | |
| | Chapter 18 South Asia . . . . . . . . . . . . . . . . . . . . . . . . . . . . . . . . 400 | |
| | Section 1 South Asia . . . . . . . . . . . . . . . . . . . . . . . 402 | |
| | Section 2 Physical Features and Climate . . . . . . . 404 | |
| | Section 3 The People . . . . . . . . . . . . . . . . . . . . . . . 407 | |
| | Section 4 Economy and Environment . . . . . . . . 412 | |
| | Chapter Summary . . . . . . . . . . . . . . . 417 | |
| | Chapter Review . . . . . . . . . . . . . . . . . . 418 | |
| | Chapter 19 Southeast Asia . . . . . . . . . . . . . . . . . . . . . . . . . . . . 420 | |
| | Section 1 Southeast Asia . . . . . . . . . . . . . . . . . . . 422 | |
| | Section 2 Physical Features and Climate . . . . . . . 424 | |
| | Section 3 The People . . . . . . . . . . . . . . . . . . . . . . . 427 | |
| | Section 4 Economy and Environment . . . . . . . . 432 | |
| | Chapter Summary . . . . . . . . . . . . . . . 437 | |
| | Chapter Review . . . . . . . . . . . . . . . . . . 438 | |

Chapter 20    The Pacific World . . . . . . . . . . . . . . . . . . . . . . . . 440
              Section 1    The Pacific World . . . . . . . . . . . . . . . . 442
              Section 2    Physical Features and Climate. . . . . . . 444
              Section 3    The People. . . . . . . . . . . . . . . . . . . . . 448
              Section 4    Economy and Environment . . . . . . . . 452
                           Chapter Summary . . . . . . . . . . . . . . . 457
                           Chapter Review. . . . . . . . . . . . . . . . . . 458

Chapter 21    Geography and Today's World. . . . . . . . . . . . . . 462
              Section 1    Geography Today . . . . . . . . . . . . . . . . 464
              Section 2    Environmental Issues  . . . . . . . . . . . . 466
              Section 3    The Condition of Human
                           Geography  . . . . . . . . . . . . . . . . . . . . 470
              Section 4    The Global Economy . . . . . . . . . . . . . 473
                           Chapter Summary . . . . . . . . . . . . . . . 477
                           Chapter Review. . . . . . . . . . . . . . . . . . 478

World Atlas . . . . . . . . . . . . . . . . . . . . . . . . . . . . . . . . . . . . . . 480

Glossary . . . . . . . . . . . . . . . . . . . . . . . . . . . . . . . . . . . . . . . . 490

Index. . . . . . . . . . . . . . . . . . . . . . . . . . . . . . . . . . . . . . . . . . . 500

Acknowledgments. . . . . . . . . . . . . . . . . . . . . . . . . . . . . . . . . 511

Willis Carrier . . . . . . . . . . . . . . . . . . . . . . . . . . . . . . . . . . . . 45

Ujjal Dosanjh . . . . . . . . . . . . . . . . . . . . . . . . . . . . . . . . . . . . . 66

Octavio Paz . . . . . . . . . . . . . . . . . . . . . . . . . . . . . . . . . . . . . . 87

Fidel Castro . . . . . . . . . . . . . . . . . . . . . . . . . . . . . . . . . . . . . 107

Chico Mendes . . . . . . . . . . . . . . . . . . . . . . . . . . . . . . . . . . . 133

Anita Lucia Roddick . . . . . . . . . . . . . . . . . . . . . . . . . . . . . . 157

Jacques Cousteau . . . . . . . . . . . . . . . . . . . . . . . . . . . . . . . . 173

Galileo Galilei . . . . . . . . . . . . . . . . . . . . . . . . . . . . . . . . . . 193

Roald Amundsen . . . . . . . . . . . . . . . . . . . . . . . . . . . . . . . . 213

Marie Curie . . . . . . . . . . . . . . . . . . . . . . . . . . . . . . . . . . . . 230

Vladimir Putin . . . . . . . . . . . . . . . . . . . . . . . . . . . . . . . . . . 256

Abd al-Rahman Ibrahima . . . . . . . . . . . . . . . . . . . . . . . . . 281

Nelson Mandela . . . . . . . . . . . . . . . . . . . . . . . . . . . . . . . . . 302

Tegla Loroupe . . . . . . . . . . . . . . . . . . . . . . . . . . . . . . . . . . 321

Princess Basma Bint Ali . . . . . . . . . . . . . . . . . . . . . . . . . . 344

Dalai Lama . . . . . . . . . . . . . . . . . . . . . . . . . . . . . . . . . . . . . 360

Akio Morita . . . . . . . . . . . . . . . . . . . . . . . . . . . . . . . . . . . . 391

Mother Teresa . . . . . . . . . . . . . . . . . . . . . . . . . . . . . . . . . . 411

Aung San Suu Kyi . . . . . . . . . . . . . . . . . . . . . . . . . . . . . . . 427

Cathy Freeman . . . . . . . . . . . . . . . . . . . . . . . . . . . . . . . . . 450

Bill Gates . . . . . . . . . . . . . . . . . . . . . . . . . . . . . . . . . . . . . . 465

## Geography in Your Life

**Careers**

Meteorologists Predict the Weather . . . . . . . . . . . . . . . . . 40
Urban Planners . . . . . . . . . . . . . . . . . . . . . . . . . . . . . 152
Tourism . . . . . . . . . . . . . . . . . . . . . . . . . . . . . . . . . 305
Volcano Expert . . . . . . . . . . . . . . . . . . . . . . . . . . . . . 319
Park Ranger . . . . . . . . . . . . . . . . . . . . . . . . . . . . . . . 455

**Economics**

Rice . . . . . . . . . . . . . . . . . . . . . . . . . . . . . . . . . . . . 433

**Fine Arts**

Diego Rivera's Fresco Murals in Mexico . . . . . . . . . . . . . 89
The Influence of Greek and Roman Architecture . . . . . . 185
The Arts in Japan . . . . . . . . . . . . . . . . . . . . . . . . . . . 385

**Health**

Medicinal Plants from Rain Forests . . . . . . . . . . . . . . . 132
Insects in West Africa . . . . . . . . . . . . . . . . . . . . . . . . 274

**Math**

The Ancient Islamic World's Influence on Math . . . . . . 340
The Richter Scale . . . . . . . . . . . . . . . . . . . . . . . . . . . 406

**Science**

Acid Rain . . . . . . . . . . . . . . . . . . . . . . . . . . . . . . . . . 69
Global Warming . . . . . . . . . . . . . . . . . . . . . . . . . . . . 241
The Chernobyl Nuclear Power Plant Accident . . . . . . . 263
Research at the South Pole . . . . . . . . . . . . . . . . . . . . . 467

**Technology**

The Building of the Panama Canal . . . . . . . . . . . . . . . . 104
The Chunnel . . . . . . . . . . . . . . . . . . . . . . . . . . . . . . 172
How Computers Help the Study of Geography . . . . . . . 207
The Building of the Three Gorges Dam in China . . . . . . 371

The Barn: A Fading Symbol of Urban America . . . . . . . . 50
The St. Lawrence Seaway . . . . . . . . . . . . . . . . . . . . . . . . . 70
Chocolate: The Drink of the Gods! . . . . . . . . . . . . . . . . 94
"Beisbol"—A Big Hit in Central America
and the Caribbean. . . . . . . . . . . . . . . . . . . . . . . . . . . . . . 114
The Galápagos. . . . . . . . . . . . . . . . . . . . . . . . . . . . . . . . . 134
The Canals of England . . . . . . . . . . . . . . . . . . . . . . . . . 158
The Iceman . . . . . . . . . . . . . . . . . . . . . . . . . . . . . . . . . . 178
The History of Pizza . . . . . . . . . . . . . . . . . . . . . . . . . . . 198
What's in a Name?. . . . . . . . . . . . . . . . . . . . . . . . . . . . . 218
The Legend of Dracula . . . . . . . . . . . . . . . . . . . . . . . . . 242
The Fabergé Easter Eggs . . . . . . . . . . . . . . . . . . . . . . . . 264
Songhai: The Last Great Empire of West Africa . . . . . . 288
Diamonds: Southern Africa's Best Friend . . . . . . . . . . 308
Africa: The First Home of Humans? . . . . . . . . . . . . . . . 328
Graffiti Is Nothing New . . . . . . . . . . . . . . . . . . . . . . . . 348
The Secret of Silk. . . . . . . . . . . . . . . . . . . . . . . . . . . . . . 372
Sumo—An Ancient Tradition . . . . . . . . . . . . . . . . . . . . 392
India's Bollywood . . . . . . . . . . . . . . . . . . . . . . . . . . . . . 416
The War in Vietnam . . . . . . . . . . . . . . . . . . . . . . . . . . . 436
The 2000 Olympics. . . . . . . . . . . . . . . . . . . . . . . . . . . . 456
The 100-Person World . . . . . . . . . . . . . . . . . . . . . . . . . 476

## Writing About Geography

Writing a Brochure . . . . . . . . . . . . . . . . . . . . . . . . . . . . . . . 46
Writing About a Mental Map. . . . . . . . . . . . . . . . . . . . . . 61
Writing an Opinion . . . . . . . . . . . . . . . . . . . . . . . . . . . . . . 90
Writing a Speech. . . . . . . . . . . . . . . . . . . . . . . . . . . . . . . . 112
Writing a Personal Letter . . . . . . . . . . . . . . . . . . . . . . . . 122
Writing Definitions of Words . . . . . . . . . . . . . . . . . . . . 155
Writing an Opinion . . . . . . . . . . . . . . . . . . . . . . . . . . . . . 166
Writing a Travel Article . . . . . . . . . . . . . . . . . . . . . . . . . 189
Writing an Opinion . . . . . . . . . . . . . . . . . . . . . . . . . . . . . 212
Writing an Opinion . . . . . . . . . . . . . . . . . . . . . . . . . . . . . 229
Writing a Research Report . . . . . . . . . . . . . . . . . . . . . . . 253
Writing an Action Plan. . . . . . . . . . . . . . . . . . . . . . . . . . 286
Writing an Opinion . . . . . . . . . . . . . . . . . . . . . . . . . . . . . 294
Writing a Personal Letter . . . . . . . . . . . . . . . . . . . . . . . . 325
Writing About a Current Event . . . . . . . . . . . . . . . . . . . 334
Writing a List. . . . . . . . . . . . . . . . . . . . . . . . . . . . . . . . . . 362
Writing a Poem . . . . . . . . . . . . . . . . . . . . . . . . . . . . . . . . 383
Writing an Opinion . . . . . . . . . . . . . . . . . . . . . . . . . . . . . 413
Writing to Solve a Problem . . . . . . . . . . . . . . . . . . . . . . 430
Writing About Culture. . . . . . . . . . . . . . . . . . . . . . . . . . 449
Writing a List. . . . . . . . . . . . . . . . . . . . . . . . . . . . . . . . . . 473

## Skill Builders

Maps. . . . . . . . . . . . . . . . . . . . . . . . . . . . . . . . . . . . . . . . . . 74
Compare and Contrast. . . . . . . . . . . . . . . . . . . . . . . . . . 138
Graphs and Charts . . . . . . . . . . . . . . . . . . . . . . . . . . . . . 222
Understanding Political Maps . . . . . . . . . . . . . . . . . . . . 268
Understanding Physical Maps . . . . . . . . . . . . . . . . . . . . 352
Understanding Special-Purpose Maps . . . . . . . . . . . . . 396
Analyzing Aerial Photographs. . . . . . . . . . . . . . . . . . . . 460

## Graph Studies

How Americans Spend Their Money (bar graph)......47

Life Expectancy in Central America and the Caribbean (bar graph)...................................108

The Ten Most Popular Places to Travel (bar graph) ...175

Production in Northern Europe (circle graphs) ......217

Nations That Rely on Nuclear Energy the Most (bar graph)...................................259

Major Religions of the World (circle graph) .........409

World Carbon Dioxide Emissions from Fossil Fuels (circle graph)...................................435

Growth of the World's Population (line graph).......471

## Chart Studies

Provinces and Territories of Canada.................59

Active Volcanoes in Mexico .......................83

Major Rivers of the World ........................124

Territories of the United Kingdom .................144

Economy of Southern Europe .....................194

Mountain Ranges in Eastern Europe and the Balkans . 232

African Refugees ...............................283

Major Deserts of the World .......................296

Major Lakes of the World .........................317

World Oil Trade ...............................347

Languages of the World .........................364

Most Populated Cities in the World ................388

States and Territories of Australia ..................442

## Map Skills

The United States . . . . . . . . . . . . . . . . . . . . . . . . . . . . . . . . 33
Canada . . . . . . . . . . . . . . . . . . . . . . . . . . . . . . . . . . . . . . . . 55
Mexico . . . . . . . . . . . . . . . . . . . . . . . . . . . . . . . . . . . . . . . . 79
Central America and the Caribbean . . . . . . . . . . . . . . . . . 99
South America . . . . . . . . . . . . . . . . . . . . . . . . . . . . . . . . . 119
The British Isles . . . . . . . . . . . . . . . . . . . . . . . . . . . . . . . . 143
Western Europe . . . . . . . . . . . . . . . . . . . . . . . . . . . . . . . . 163
Southern Europe . . . . . . . . . . . . . . . . . . . . . . . . . . . . . . . 183
Northern Europe . . . . . . . . . . . . . . . . . . . . . . . . . . . . . . . 203
Eastern Europe and the Balkans . . . . . . . . . . . . . . . . . . . 227
Russia and the Independent Republics . . . . . . . . . . . . . . 247
West Africa . . . . . . . . . . . . . . . . . . . . . . . . . . . . . . . . . . . 273
Southern Africa . . . . . . . . . . . . . . . . . . . . . . . . . . . . . . . . 293
Central and East Africa . . . . . . . . . . . . . . . . . . . . . . . . . . 313
North Africa and the Middle East . . . . . . . . . . . . . . . . . . 333
China . . . . . . . . . . . . . . . . . . . . . . . . . . . . . . . . . . . . . . . . 357
Japan and the Koreas . . . . . . . . . . . . . . . . . . . . . . . . . . . 377
South Asia . . . . . . . . . . . . . . . . . . . . . . . . . . . . . . . . . . . . 401
Southeast Asia . . . . . . . . . . . . . . . . . . . . . . . . . . . . . . . . . 421
Australia and New Zealand . . . . . . . . . . . . . . . . . . . . . . . 441
Urban Population of the World . . . . . . . . . . . . . . . . . . . . 463

## Map Studies

Physical Features of the World . . . . . . . . . . . . . . . . . . . . . 26
Physical Features of the United States . . . . . . . . . . . . . . . 37
Physical Features of South America . . . . . . . . . . . . . . . . 126
France and Surrounding Countries . . . . . . . . . . . . . . . . 168
Spain and Portugal . . . . . . . . . . . . . . . . . . . . . . . . . . . . . 187
Average Annual Rainfall in Europe . . . . . . . . . . . . . . . . 210
Ethnic Diversity in Eastern Europe and the Balkans . . . 237
Physical Features of Africa . . . . . . . . . . . . . . . . . . . . . . . 278
Where Muslims Live . . . . . . . . . . . . . . . . . . . . . . . . . . . . 343
Agriculture and Industry of China . . . . . . . . . . . . . . . . . 368
Vegetation of Australia and New Zealand . . . . . . . . . . . 447

# How to Use This Book:
# A Study Guide

Welcome to a study of world geography. You may be asking yourself, "Why do I need to know about people and places other than those in the United States?" When we study geography of the world, we learn more about how the world is today. Many countries are very important to the U.S. They provide us with goods and services. In turn, the U.S. sells its goods and services to other nations. It is important that we know our world and the people who inhabit it. Everyone is responsible for making the world a better place to live.

As you read the units, chapters, and sections of this book, you will learn about the important places and people of our world.

## How to Study

◆ Plan a regular time to study.

◆ Choose a quiet desk or table where you will not be distracted. Find a spot that has good lighting.

◆ Gather all the books, pencils, and paper you need to complete your assignments.

◆ Decide on a goal. For example: "I will finish reading and taking notes on Chapter 1, Section 1, by 8:00."

◆ Take a five- to ten-minute break every hour to keep alert.

◆ If you start to feel sleepy, take a short break and get some fresh air.

## Before Beginning Each Unit

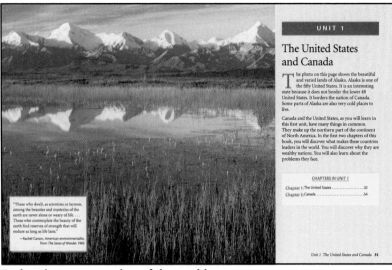

**Each unit covers a region of the world.**

◆ Read the unit's title.

◆ Read the opening paragraphs.

◆ Study the picture. Do you recognize anything in the picture?

◆ Read the quotation. Try to connect the ideas to the picture.

◆ Read the titles of the chapters in the unit.

◆ Look at the headings of the sections. They will help you locate main ideas.

◆ Read the Chapter and Unit Summaries to help you identify the key ideas.

## Before Beginning Each Chapter

◆ Read the chapter title.

◆ Study the Goals for Learning. The Chapter Review and tests will ask questions related to these goals.

◆ Study the Geo-Stats, which give information about the place or places in the chapter.

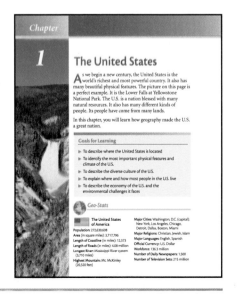

## Before Beginning Each Section

Read the section title and rephrase it in the form of a question. For example:

| Section | 1 | The United States |
|---------|---|-------------------|

Write: *What is the United States?*

Look over the entire section, noting . . .

◆ pictures
◆ graphs or charts
◆ maps
◆ boldface words
◆ text organization
◆ boxed stories

Wooden barns are not as common as they once were in the U.S.

**Physical Features of the United States**

**MAP STUDY**

This map shows the main physical features of the United States. What large mountain range covers most of the West? What river extends from the northern United States to the Gulf of Mexico? The Great Lakes lie in the Midwest near the Canadian border. What are the names of these five lakes?

| Biography | WILLIS CARRIER: 1876–1950 |
|-----------|---------------------------|

In 1915, American engineer Willis Carrier discovered how to control humidity in a print shop. Next, he dealt with the heat of moving parts in a textile factory. Air conditioning followed! At first, only hotels and movie theaters used it. But after World War II, people began installing air conditioning in their offices and homes.

Today, Carrier's invention cools people and keeps ancient books from falling apart. It enables miners to go deep into the earth. It keeps computers from breaking down. Without air conditioning, many hot regions of the world would be very uncomfortable places to live.

## As You Read the Section

**Section 1**

◆ Read the major headings. Each subhead is in the form of a question, as shown below:

### How Does Geography Affect People in the U.S.?

◆ Read the paragraphs that follow to answer the question.

◆ Before moving on to the next heading, see if you can answer the question.

◆ If you cannot, reread the section to look for the answers. If you are still unsure, ask for help.

◆ Answering the questions in the Section Review will help you see if you know the key ideas in the section. For example:

**SECTION 2 REVIEW** On a separate sheet of paper, write answers to these questions.

1) What are the names of three mountain ranges located in the U.S.?

## Using Vocabulary

**bold type**
*Words seen for the first time will appear in bold type*

**glossary**
*Words listed in this column are also found in the glossary*

Knowing the meaning of all the boxed words will help you understand what you are reading.

These words will appear in **bold type** the first time they appear in your text and will usually be defined in the paragraph.

A **basin** is a low area of land surrounded by higher land, often mountains.

Remember, all of the words in the side column are also defined for you in the **glossary** at the back of the book.

**Basin** (bā´ sn) A low area of land surrounded by higher land, often mountains (p. 37)

## What to Do With a Word You Do Not Know

When you come to a word you do not know, ask yourself these questions:

◆ Is the word a compound word? Can you find two words within the word? This could help you understand the meaning. For example: *Rustbelt*.

◆ Does the word have a prefix at the beginning? For example: *multicultural*. The prefix *multi-* means 'many,' so this word refers to many cultures, or people. A multicultural society has many cultures.

◆ Does the word have a suffix at the end? For example: *industrialize, -ize*. This means to become industrial, or to develop industry.

◆ Can you identify the root word? Can you sound it out in parts? For example: *Mid west*.

◆ Are there any clues in the sentence that will help you understand the word?

◆ Look for the word in the margin box, glossary, or dictionary.

◆ If you are still having trouble with a word, ask for help.

## Word Study Tip

◆ Start a vocabulary card file with index cards to use for review.

　◆ Write one word on the front of each card. Write the chapter number and the definition on the back.

　◆ You can use the flash cards in a game by yourself or with a study partner to test your knowledge.

Sea level

Chapter 1

The level at the surface of the ocean

## Taking Notes in Class

As you read, you will be learning many new facts and ideas. Writing these key ideas down will help you remember. Your notes will be useful when preparing for class discussions and studying for tests.

There are many ways to take notes. You may want to try several methods to decide which one works best for you.

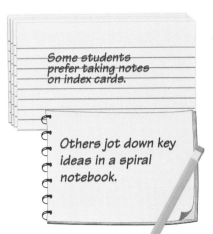

*Some students prefer taking notes on index cards.*

*Others jot down key ideas in a spiral notebook.*

- ◆ Always write the main ideas and supporting details.
- ◆ Using an outline format will help save you time.
- ◆ Keep your notes brief. You may want to set up some abbreviations to speed up your note-taking. For example: *with=w/ and=+ dollars=$*
- ◆ Use the same method all the time. Then when you study for a test, you will know where to go to find the information you need to review.

- ◆ Use your own words.
- ◆ Do not try to write everything the teacher says.
- ◆ Write down important information only.
- ◆ Do not be concerned about writing in complete sentences. Use phrases.
- ◆ Be brief.
- ◆ Rewrite your notes to fill in possible gaps as soon as you can after class.

## Using an Outline

You may want to outline the section using the subheads as your main points. An outline will help you remember the major points of the section. The Student Study Guide with this textbook will help you outline the sections.

## Listening in Class

- ◆ Plan to listen to remember.
- ◆ Concentrate on the topic. Do not allow your mind to wander.
- ◆ If you do not understand, raise your hand and ask a question.

- ◆ Listen for these key phrases: this is important..., do not forget..., the first reason..., because of this..., in conclusion..., you need to know this... .

## Getting Ready to Take a Test

The Summaries and Reviews will help you get ready to take tests. Getting information about the test ahead of time and having a study plan will help you do well on the test.

◆ Ask what type of test it will be. For example: true/false, multiple choice, short answer, matching, essay.

◆ Keep current on your reading assignments. Do not put off reading the chapter until the night before the test.

◆ A couple of days before the test, gather all of your notes, vocabulary lists, corrected worksheets, answers to questions in the book, and your textbook.

## Use the Summaries

◆ Read the summaries from your text to make sure you understand the main ideas that you will be reviewing.

◆ Make up a sample test of items you think may be on the test. You may want to do this with a classmate and share your questions.

◆ Review your notes and test yourself on vocabulary words and key ideas.

◆ Practice writing about some of the main events from the chapter.

## Use the Reviews

◆ Answer the questions under Identifying Facts.

◆ Answer the questions under Multiple Choice.

◆ Answer the questions under Understanding Main Ideas.

◆ Write what you think under Write Your Opinion.

◆ Answer the questions under Applying the Five Themes of Geography.

## Use the Test-Taking Tips

◆ Read the Test-Taking Tips with each Chapter Review from your text.

 **Test-Taking Tip** Prepare for a test by making a set of flash cards. Write a word on the front of each card. Write the definition on the back. Use the flash cards in a game by yourself or with a partner to test your knowledge.

## When Taking a Test

◆ Arrive well rested and alert.

◆ Look over the entire test before you start.

◆ Plan so you will have time to complete each section.

◆ If you have trouble with a question, mark it and come back to it later. This will save you time.

◆ Proofread your essay answers for errors. Double-check to see that you answered the question that was asked.

◆ If time allows, read over all of your answers. Make sure your writing is readable.

Remember to save your corrected test when it is returned. Use it to study for future tests. Identify the types of errors you made. For example: Were most of your errors in a certain section? Perhaps you could study ways to improve in that area.

## Begin Your Journey . . .

This section has been included as a study tool that you can refer to later. You are now ready to begin your journey into world geography.

You may not know it, but you use geography every day. It affects you in many ways, such as when you read a map, take a trip, or read a newspaper.

# *Introduction*

## What Is the Study of Geography?

Geography
*The study of the planet Earth and its people*

Physical environment
*The natural world in which a person lives*

**Geography** is the study of the planet Earth and its people. As you study geography, you will learn about the world around us. You will learn answers to many questions: What form does the land have? Was it originally covered by forests or grasses? Is the weather hot or cold?

You will also learn answers to questions about the people of the world: Where did they come from? Why did they settle in some places and not in others? What do they eat? What languages do they speak? How have they changed their **physical environment**, or the natural world in which they live?

Believe it or not, you use geography every day. When you look at a map to find the location of a shopping mall, you use geography. When you learn about events taking place in other countries, you use geography. Geography influences your choice of what to wear. It also influences what you eat.

## How Does Geography Link the Global Society?

Today the people of the world are more closely linked than at any other time in history. The United States ships products and services to distant parts of the world. For example, U.S. farmers sell their products all over the world. Likewise, people in the United States buy products from many other countries. Workers in other countries make most new televisions or microwaves sold in the U.S. Much of the way we live depends on energy **resources** transported from lands around the world. A resource is a thing of value that we can use to do or make something.

Probably the biggest change of the last 100 years has been the development of a global society. We are all members of this society. We share the same home—spaceship Earth. In the future, we will be more and more dependent upon each other.

## What Are the Two Different Branches of Geography?

The two main branches of geography are **physical geography** and **human geography**. With the first, you mainly study Earth's physical features, the natural world. With the second, you study how people live on Earth.

Physical geography looks at Earth itself. What does the land look like? Is it mountainous? Is it flat? What kind of soil does it have? What is the weather like? What plants and animals does the land support? Physical geography looks at the natural features of Earth. Nature, not people, make these features.

Human geography studies how people live on Earth. It looks at everything people do. How do they make a living?

What jobs do they do? These things influence the **economy**. We call them economic factors. An economy is a system of building, using, and distributing wealth and resources.

Human geography also studies the **culture** of people around the world. Culture includes their languages, religions, customs, art, and dress. Finally, human geography studies the **political** factors, such as countries and governments, of people around the world.

## How Do Geographers Organize Geographic Information?

Organizing all this geographic information is not easy. To help with organization, geographers have developed five basic themes. These five themes help to answer the questions you have read so far in this introduction.

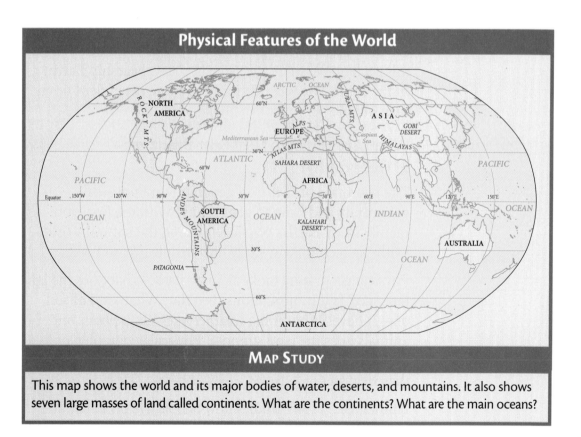

### Physical Features of the World

### MAP STUDY

This map shows the world and its major bodies of water, deserts, and mountains. It also shows seven large masses of land called continents. What are the continents? What are the main oceans?

As seen from outer space, Earth is a large mass of land and water. Geographers use five themes to organize geographic information about our planet.

**Absolute location**
*The exact spot or area of a place*

**Interaction**
*How people settle, use, live on, and change the land*

**Location**
*The place on Earth where something is*

**Place**
*The physical and human features that make an area special*

**Relative location**
*A place described in relationship to another place*

### What Question Does "Location" Answer?

The first theme is **location.** It answers the question "where." Location is the place on Earth where something is. For example, you know where your school is and where you live. An address tells you their exact or **absolute location.** But we can also describe locations in relation to other things. For example, we might describe Mexico as the country located on the southern border of the United States. This is its **relative location**.

### What Questions Does "Place" Answer?

**Place** is the second theme. All places have special features that make them different from other places. Place answers questions like "What place is this?" or "How does this place differ from other places?" Geographers describe places by both their physical and their human features. For example, we could describe the city of New Orleans, Louisiana, by its location at the mouth of the Mississippi River. Or we could describe it by its plants or weather. But we could also describe New Orleans by its special buildings, music, and food.

### What Questions Does "Interaction" Answer?

A third theme for geographers is human-environmental **interaction**. This theme examines what people have done to the place they settled. It answers questions such as "How do people use this land?" "How do they live in this place?" and "How have they changed this place?"

Ships bringing goods from one place to another is an example of the theme of movement.

Movement
*How people, ideas, and products move between places*

People interact with their environment and try to change it to their advantage. For example, early colonists to the United States cut down forests to build homes. They started farming. They introduced some plants that they had brought from Europe.

### What Question Does "Movement" Answer?

People often move from place to place. **Movement** is a theme that geographers use to organize this information. The key question it answers is "Why and how do people, products, and ideas move between places?"

Every place on Earth has advantages and disadvantages. People often move to take advantage of what a place might offer. For example, many retired people in the United States move from their homes in cold-weather states to warm-weather states. People also move because another place may offer a better job. Many of us enjoy traveling. This is another example of the movement of people.

Goods and ideas also move. The United States sells many goods and services to other countries. It also buys goods and services from other countries. Most people in the United States believe so strongly in their government system that they support other countries who have the same kind of government.

Region

*An area on the earth's surface that geographers define by certain similar characteristics*

## What Question Does "Region" Answer?

**Region** is the fifth and final theme that geographers use to study Earth. A region is an area on the earth's surface that geographers define by certain similar characteristics. Region answers the question "How are places on Earth alike and different?"

Many different types of regions exist on Earth. Sometimes, physical features define a region. An example would be the Rocky Mountains or the Sahara Desert. Sometimes, a common feature sets a region apart from other areas. An example would be the farmlands of the American Midwest.

Another way of looking at regions is historically. For example, a geographer might study the history of the six states that make up New England. These states were among the first places in what came to be known as the United States.

This book uses political regions most of the time. Political regions have set boundaries and a common system of government. The United States is an example of a political region. The state you live in is another.

These five themes—location, place, interaction, movement, and region—will help you study Earth and its people.

Enjoy your study of world geography.

**An area in which farming is common is an example of a region. Regions can also be political, historical, or based on a physical feature.**

"Those who dwell, as scientists or laymen, among the beauties and mysteries of the earth are never alone or weary of life. . . . Those who contemplate the beauty of the earth find reserves of strength that will endure as long as life lasts."

—Rachel Carson, American environmentalist, from *The Sense of Wonder*, 1965

# The United States and Canada

The photo on this page shows the beautiful and varied lands of Alaska. Alaska is one of the fifty United States. It is an interesting state because it does not border the lower 48 United States. It borders the nation of Canada. Some parts of Alaska are also very cold places to live.

Canada and the United States, as you will learn in this first unit, have many things in common. They make up the northern part of the continent of North America. In the first two chapters of this book, you will discover what makes these countries leaders in the world. You will discover why they are wealthy nations. You will also learn about the problems they face.

### CHAPTERS IN UNIT 1

**Chapter 1:** The United States ....................32
**Chapter 2:** Canada .............................54

*1*

# The United States

As we begin a new century, the United States is the world's richest and most powerful country. It also has many beautiful physical features. The picture on this page is a perfect example. It is the Lower Falls at Yellowstone National Park. The U.S. is a nation blessed with many natural resources. It also has many different kinds of people. Its people have come from many lands.

In this chapter, you will learn how geography made the U.S. a great nation.

## Goals for Learning

▶ To describe where the United States is located

▶ To identify the most important physical features and climate of the U.S.

▶ To describe the diverse culture of the U.S.

▶ To explain where and how most people in the U.S. live

▶ To describe the economy of the U.S. and the environmental challenges it faces

 ## Geo-Stats

 **The United States of America**

**Population:** 272,639,608

**Area** (in square miles): 3,717,796

**Length of Coastline** (in miles): 12,373

**Length of Roads** (in miles): 4.08 million

**Longest River:** Mississippi River system (3,710 miles)

**Highest Mountain:** Mt. McKinley (20,320 feet)

**Major Cities:** Washington, D.C. (capital); New York, Los Angeles, Chicago, Detroit, Dallas, Boston, Miami

**Major Religions:** Christian, Jewish, Islam

**Major Languages:** English, Spanish

**Official Currency:** U.S. Dollar

**Workforce:** 136.3 million

**Number of Daily Newspapers:** 1,500

**Number of Television Sets:** 215 million

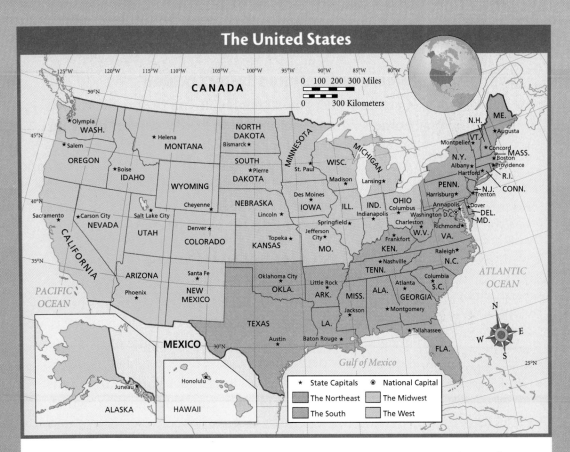

# The United States

CANADA

0 100 200 300 Miles

0 300 Kilometers

WASH. ★Olympia
★Salem
OREGON
★Boise
IDAHO
MONTANA ★Helena
WYOMING
Cheyenne ★
NEVADA ★Carson City
Sacramento ★
Salt Lake City ★
UTAH
Denver ★
COLORADO
CALIFORNIA
ARIZONA
Phoenix ★
Santa Fe ★
NEW MEXICO
NORTH DAKOTA
Bismarck ★
SOUTH DAKOTA
★Pierre
NEBRASKA
Lincoln ★
KANSAS
Topeka ★
OKLAHOMA
Oklahoma City ★
TEXAS
Austin ★
MEXICO
MINNESOTA
St. Paul ★
IOWA
Des Moines ★
MO.
Jefferson City ★
ARK.
Little Rock ★
LA.
Baton Rouge ★
WISC.
Madison ★
ILL.
Springfield ★
MISS.
Jackson ★
MICHIGAN
Lansing ★
IND.
Indianapolis ★
OHIO
Columbus ★
KEN.
Frankfort ★
TENN.
Nashville ★
ALA.
Montgomery ★
GEORGIA
Atlanta ★
N.H.
Montpelier ★ VT.
ME.
★Augusta
Concord ★
MASS.
★Boston
N.Y.
Albany ★
Hartford ★
Providence ★
R.I.
PENN.
Harrisburg ★
CONN.
N.J.
Trenton ★
W.V.
Charleston ★
VA.
Richmond ★
DEL.
MD.
Washington D.C. ⊛
Annapolis ★
Dover ★
N.C.
Raleigh ★
S.C.
Columbia ★
FLA.
Tallahassee ★

PACIFIC OCEAN

ATLANTIC OCEAN

Gulf of Mexico

ALASKA
Juneau ★

HAWAII
Honolulu ★

★ State Capitals  ⊛ National Capital

The Northeast
The South
The Midwest
The West

*Map Skills*

The United States has 50 states and four basic regions. The Pacific Ocean separates Hawaii from the rest of the states. Canada separates Alaska from the 48 states that border one another. The United States borders Canada in the north and Mexico in the south. It is part of North America.

Use this map to find the state in which you live. To what region does it belong? What states border it? Continue studying the map, then answer the following questions:

**1)** What are the four regions on this map?

**2)** What oceans border the United States?

**3)** What is its national capital?

**4)** Which countries border the U.S.?

**5)** Why do you think that most of the states in the West are large and most in the Northeast are small?

**Continent**
*One of the seven large areas of land on Earth*

**Equator**
*An imaginary line that goes around the middle of Earth; it lies halfway between the North and the South Poles*

**Latitude**
*How far north or south of the equator a place is*

**Longitude**
*How far east or west a place is from the Prime Meridian*

**Prime Meridian**
*A fixed point that is zero degrees longitude and runs through Greenwich, England*

## Where Is the United States Located?

Canada borders the United States on the north; Mexico borders it on the south. These three countries make up most of what geographers call North America. North America is a **continent.** It is one of seven large areas of land on Earth. The United States lies between two oceans. The Atlantic Ocean forms the east coast of the United States. The Pacific Ocean forms the west coast.

## In What Latitudes Is the U.S. Located?

Geographers use **latitude** and **longitude** to describe locations on the earth's surface. Latitude explains how far north or south of the **equator** a place is. The equator is an imaginary line that goes around the middle of Earth. Longitude explains how far east or west a place is from a fixed point at zero degrees longitude. This fixed point is called the **Prime Meridian.** It runs through the town of Greenwich, England.

The United States is located in the middle latitudes. Its climate is neither too hot nor too cold. Being in the middle latitudes also means that people can earn a living in many different ways.

## What Are the Four Regions of the United States?

The United States government collects a lot of information about the way its people live. It collects facts about their jobs, what they do with their free time, and where they live. The government groups the nation into four regions: the Northeast, the South, the Midwest, and the West. Geographers define these regions according to their physical, economic, and historic features. They also divide each of these four regions into smaller ones called subregions.

## What Is the Northeast Region?

The Northeast has many people and large cities, but it is still the smallest region of the U.S. It extends southward

Industry
*A business that makes or puts together things to sell*

Plain
*A low-lying, usually flat area*

and westward from the Atlantic Ocean and includes nine states. It was the first region to build **industries,** or businesses that make or put together things. It has some of the oldest factories in the U.S.

New York City, which is in the Northeast region, is the nation's biggest city. Many of the nation's biggest and most important businesses have headquarters there. Boston, Massachusetts; Philadelphia, Pennsylvania; and Baltimore, Maryland, are other important cities in the Northeast region. The nation's capital, Washington, D.C., is also in this region.

## What Is the Southern Region?

South of the Northeast region lies the region geographers call "the South." It contains 16 states. Its broad, coastal **plain** borders the Atlantic Ocean and the Gulf of Mexico. Plains are low-lying, usually flat areas. Further inland, the land becomes hilly. Forests cover the ground. Miami, Florida, and New Orleans, Louisiana, are important port cities in the South.

The South today differs from what it was in the past. At one time, it was the world's largest cotton-growing area. Today, farming remains, but other industries are more important. The South is home to major factories where workers put together automobiles. The South also contains 90 percent of the U.S. cloth-making industry. The South attracts factory owners because of its mild climate and its lower cost of labor.

## What Is the Midwest Region?

The Midwest region borders all three of the other regions. It contains 12 states and stretches onward as one large plain. Its rich soil is especially good for growing grain. Bakers use grain to make bread. For this reason, geographers sometimes call

**New York City is the nation's largest city. It is also the business center for the U.S.**

Desert
*A dry area in which few or no people live*

the Midwest America's breadbasket. In fact, most of the grain produced in the U.S. comes from the Midwest. Farmers also grow corn and soybeans. Many raise pigs.

Besides its farms, the Midwest also has several large cities. Chicago—the third largest city in the U.S.—is an important manufacturing, business, and transportation center in Illinois. Other key business centers are Minneapolis, Minnesota; Omaha, Nebraska; Kansas City and St. Louis, Missouri; and Detroit, Michigan.

### What Is the Western Region?

The largest of the four regions in area is the West. It has 13 states, including Alaska, the largest of the 50 states. Alaska has large stretches of land on which no trees can grow. Only grasses and mosses grow on some of this land. The West also includes the Rocky Mountains, whose peaks reach as high as 14,000 feet. The biggest and driest **deserts** of the U.S. stretch across areas of the West. A desert is a dry area in which few or no people live.

Many people live in the coastal area of California. In fact, two-thirds of the population of the West live in California. It has more people than any other state. But huge areas of the West have few people.

| WORD BANK |
| --- |
| South    Northeast |
| West    Mexico |
| regions |

**SECTION 1 REVIEW** On a separate sheet of paper, write the word from the Word Bank that completes each sentence.

1) Most of North America is made up of three countries: Canada, the United States, and _____.

2) To study areas better, geographers divide them into _____.

3) The largest of the four regions of the U.S. is the _____.

4) The region with the largest city in the U.S. is the _____.

5) The region with a broad coastal plain is the _____.

**What do YOU think?**

If you had a choice, in which region of the U.S. would you like to live? Why? Give three reasons with your answer.

Basin
*A low area of land
surrounded by
higher land, often
mountains*

## What Are the Main Physical Features of the U.S.?

In the United States, the Appalachian Mountains stretch from Maine to Alabama. The Rocky Mountains stretch from Alaska to New Mexico. These two mountain ranges frame the Central Plains.

To the west, the Cascade Mountains have several high peaks: Mount Rainier, Mount Shasta, Mount Saint Helens, and Mount Hood. Between the Rockies and the Cascades lies the Great **Basin.** A basin is a low area of land

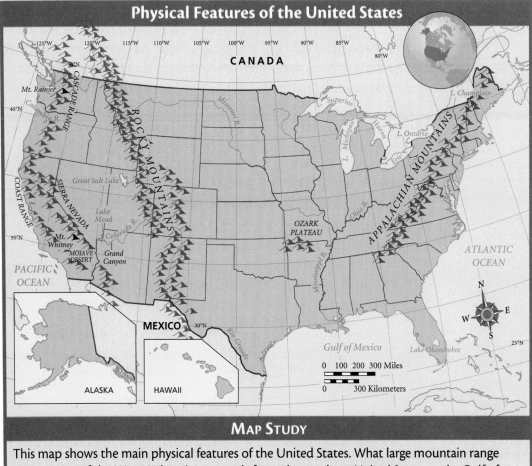

**Physical Features of the United States**

**MAP STUDY**

This map shows the main physical features of the United States. What large mountain range covers most of the West? What river extends from the northern United States to the Gulf of Mexico? The Great Lakes lie in the Midwest near the Canadian border. What are the names of these five lakes?

**St. Louis, Missouri, is one of many cities the Mississippi River system passes through.**

surrounded by higher land, often mountains. The Great Basin contains Death Valley—the lowest place in all of North America. This California valley lies 282 feet below **sea level**. Sea level is the level at the surface of the ocean.

### How Did the Ice Age Affect the U.S.?

North America has more lakes than any other continent. During the last ice age thousands of years ago, huge **glaciers** covered much of it. Glaciers are large, slow-moving sheets of ice. As these glaciers moved, they dug deep craters in the earth. When the ice melted, lakes formed in these craters. The last ice age created the five Great Lakes. They hold the largest freshwater supply in the world.

### How Did the Ice Age Create the Mississippi River?

Long ago, the great glacier ice sheets melted. Water ran off in large streams that became great rivers. They formed the Mississippi **River system.** A river system is a group of rivers that are joined together. The Mississippi River, with its many **tributaries,** drains the middle of the United States. A tributary is a smaller river that flows into a larger one.

One major river in the United States is the Missouri River. It is one tributary of the Mississippi River system. Another tributary is the Ohio River. It joins the Mississippi at Cairo, Illinois.

The Mississippi empties into the Gulf of Mexico near New Orleans, Louisiana. There, the Mississippi has created a **delta.** A delta is an area of rich land at the mouth of a river. A river carries dirt downstream to form the delta.

Delta
*An area of rich land at the mouth of a river; new land formed by dirt carried downstream by a river*

Glacier
*A large, slow-moving sheet of ice*

River system
*A group of rivers that are joined together*

Sea level
*The level at the surface of the ocean*

Tributary
*A smaller river that flows into a larger one*

## How Else Does Water Affect the U.S.?

Almost every state in the U.S. has lakes and rivers. They are important sources of freshwater. Often, they supply cities with freshwater. People use them for recreation. Sometimes workers dam rivers to create **hydroelectric** power, or power created by running water.

Many of the goods the U.S. buys from other countries come by ocean transport. The oceans supply fish, lobsters, crabs, and other seafood. More importantly, oceans (in addition to plants) are a major source of oxygen on which all human life depends. They are also responsible for much of our **weather.** Weather refers to the condition of the air at a given time or place.

## What Influences Climate?

**Climate** is the average of weather conditions over a period of time. Earth is tilted as it rotates in space. Its position to the sun determines climate. The equator lies halfway between the North Pole and the South Pole. The **Tropic of Cancer,** an imaginary line, lies 23.5 degrees north of the equator. The **Tropic of Capricorn,** also an imaginary line, lies 23.5 degrees south of the equator.

The **Tropics** is the area between the Tropic of Cancer and the Tropic of Capricorn. They receive the most direct rays of sunlight. They tend to have warmer climates than other areas on Earth. Areas north of the Tropic of Cancer and south of the Tropic of Capricorn sometimes get only indirect sunlight. These areas tend to have colder climates.

The sun is the most important influence on Earth's climate. But temperature and **precipitation** also influence it. Precipitation means how much rain, snow, or sleet falls from the sky. Temperature makes a region hot or cold. Precipitation makes a region dry or wet. Being near water or being locked in by land can influence climate, too. Water can keep an area cool in the summer and somewhat warmer in the winter.

---

**Climate**
*The average of weather conditions over a period of time*

**Hydroelectric**
*Power created by running water*

**Precipitation**
*How much rain, snow, or sleet falls from the sky*

**Tropic of Cancer**
*An imaginary line that lies 23.5 degrees north of the equator*

**Tropic of Capricorn**
*An imaginary line that lies 23.5 degrees south of the equator*

**Tropics**
*The area between the Tropic of Cancer and the Tropic of Capricorn*

**Weather**
*The condition of the air at a given time or place*

## Glossary

**Highland climate**
*The varying climate of a mountainous area*

**Humid**
*Very moist*

**Humid continental climate**
*A climate with long, cold winters and hot, wet summers; a climate with four different seasons*

**Leeward**
*The side away from the wind*

**Steppe climate**
*A climate with very hot summers and very cold winters, with little precipitation*

**Subtropical climate**
*A climate with hot and humid summers and mild winters*

**Windward**
*The side from which the wind is blowing*

# What Climates Can Be Found in the U.S.?

The United States has many climates. The Northeast and Midwest regions have a **humid continental climate**. They have four seasons, with long, cold winters and hot, wet summers. The area between the western edge of the Midwest and the mountains has a **steppe climate.** It has very hot summers and very cold winters, with little precipitation. The land is covered with wild grasses and few trees.

The South has a **subtropical climate.** Subtropical areas border on the Tropics. Summers are hot and **humid,** or very moist. Winters are mild.

The West has many climates. In mountain areas there is a **highland climate,** in which temperatures change. Generally, the higher up the mountain, the cooler the temperature. The **windward** side of the mountains—the side from which the wind is blowing—receives larger amounts of rain. The **leeward** side—the side away from the wind—often receives less rain.

---

*Geography In Your Life*

**CAREERS**

## Meteorologists Predict the Weather

Since ancient times, people have tried to predict the weather. Farmers want to know if the sun will shine on their crops. Travelers want to know if they need to pack a heavy winter coat for a journey to another city. Meteorologists who have become radio and television weather forecasters help both the hopeful farmer and the worried traveler.

Since 1959, modern meteorologists have used satellites that circle Earth to collect weather information. These satellites provide a view of cloud patterns. Meteorologists use this information to predict natural disasters before they happen. Their warnings help people move to safety.

Meteorology is really the study of Earth's atmosphere. Meteorology students in universities around the world study computer models, graphs, charts, satellites, and weather balloons. They study pressure patterns to predict highs and lows in the atmosphere. They also study the interaction between Earth's ocean and its atmosphere. Many of these students will predict this century's weather!

---

**Marine west coast climate**
*A climate from Southeast Alaska to California that has mild, cloudy summers and wet winters*

**Mediterranean climate**
*A climate like that of countries near the Mediterranean Sea: mild, wet winters and hot, dry summers*

Also in the West is the **marine west coast climate.** It runs down the coast from Southeast Alaska to Northern California. This area has mild and often cloudy summers with wet winters. Southern California has a **Mediterranean climate.** This climate is like that of countries near the Mediterranean Sea in Europe. It has mild, wet winters and hot, dry summers.

## How Does Geography Affect People in the U.S.?

People adapt to their physical environment. For example, people in hot climates such as Florida do not need winter coats. People in cold climates such as North Dakota do. In hot and humid parts of the United States, people consider air conditioning necessary.

The Northeast has thin, rocky soil and a short growing season. Few people farm. But the Midwest has rich soil, a lot of flat land, and good growing conditions. More people farm in that region. Many people once worked as fishermen along the coastal waters of the North Atlantic. Where many trees grew, workers used lumber to build ships and made furniture.

From early in U.S. history, people changed the places in which they lived. They cut forests, plowed fields, and built huge cities. They thought they could control the environment. However, weather and other parts of nature cannot be controlled.

**SECTION 2 REVIEW** On a separate sheet of paper, write answers to these questions.

1) What are the names of three mountain ranges located in the U.S.?

2) How were the Great Lakes formed?

3) What river system drains the middle of the U.S.?

4) What is a major source of oxygen on which all human life depends?

5) What do geographers call the average of weather conditions over a period of time?

**What do YOU think?**

What effect do you think a large lake like Lake Michigan would have on the weather of that region?

Cultural diffusion
*The borrowing of language, customs, and religion among cultures*

Multiculturalism
*A blend of many cultures*

## What Cultures Are There in the United States?

Culture is the way of life of a group of people. The United States blends many cultures. This is called **multiculturalism.** Some parts of this culture are like England's because many of the early colonists were English. Other colonists came from other parts of Europe. Some people came from Africa. There are also many American Indian cultures. In recent years, many people have come from Asia and Latin America. All these people have their own language, religion, and customs.

Sometimes cultures change. They do this by borrowing from one another. This is called **cultural diffusion.** For example, today most people in the United States enjoy foods like pizza, tacos, and egg rolls. Different cultures brought all these foods to the U.S. Music played in the United States also comes from many different cultures. Jazz is rooted in African-American music. Salsa comes from Latin America. Rap and hip-hop reflect both African-American and Latin-American roots.

**The United States is a mix of many cultures. People who have come to the U.S. have brought their languages, religions, and customs.**

## What Religions Are There in the United States?

More than 272 million people live in the United States. About 92 percent are **Christians**. They believe in the teachings of Jesus. His early followers believed that he was the Son of God.

**Christianity**, the religion of Christians, has many branches. The largest branch is the **Roman Catholic** Church. The head of this branch is the pope. All other Christians are **Protestants.** They have many of the same beliefs as Catholics.

**Judaism** is much older than Christianity. About 4 percent of all Americans are Jews. They were among the first people to believe in one God as the all-powerful creator and ruler of the universe.

Followers of nearly every religion live in the U.S. However, some are much more common in other regions of the world. You will learn about them in later chapters.

## What Languages Do People in the U.S. Speak?

A culture has to have a language because language allows people to talk with one another. Language also allows them to pass learning from older people to younger people. Most people in the United States speak English. Over 31 million people use Spanish as their first language. The number of people coming to the U.S. from Spanish-speaking countries—especially Mexico—is increasing.

Throughout most of its history, the U.S. has welcomed **immigrants**—people from other countries. They have adopted the culture and language of the majority of people living in the United States. But many immigrants keep their native culture and language. Because of this, some U.S. cities have immigrants who do not speak English. Instead, they speak the language of their native countries.

## Where Do Most People Live in the United States?

In the past, most people in the United States lived in small farm communities. Places away from the city like farm

**Megalopolis**
*A vast city made up of many cities, one right next to another*

**Metropolitan area**
*A city and its suburbs*

**Rural**
*An area away from the city, such as a farm community*

**Suburb**
*An area next to a city*

**Trend**
*A way in which something is headed*

**Urban**
*Having to do with a city*

communities are called **rural** areas. Today, the U.S. is a nation of cities. Nearly 80 percent of its citizens live in **metropolitan areas.** A metropolitan area includes the city and the **suburbs.** The suburbs are areas next to a city.

Each of the 40 largest metropolitan areas in the United States has more than a million people. But most of these people live in suburbs. Some cities and their suburbs have grown so large that they have absorbed nearby cities. All together, they create one large city. For example, a person can drive from Boston, Massachusetts, all the way to Washington, D.C., and never leave an **urban,** or city, area. In the 1960s, geographers began to use the name **megalopolis** to describe that area of the U.S. The word means "a very large city." Today, about one-sixth of the people in the United States live in a megalopolis.

Many cities in the United States developed because of changes in transportation. The colonists first settled along the Atlantic Ocean. They built the port cities of Boston, Massachusetts; New York City; and Baltimore, Maryland.

Soon, however, the country expanded westward. Settlers used rivers as early highways. Many cities developed along these rivers or where two rivers met. New Orleans, located at the mouth of the Mississippi River in Louisiana, is one example. St. Louis, Missouri, developed where the Missouri, Illinois, and Mississippi Rivers come together. The coming of the railroads also helped the growth of other cities. Chicago sits near the center of the United States. This Illinois city became a railroad center.

## What Trends Are Affecting the United States Today?

A **trend** is a way in which something is headed. Two important trends affect the U.S. today. First, the population is becoming different. At one time, most people in the United States were alike. They were mostly white and Christian. They spoke English and shared the same culture. Over time the United States has attracted many immigrants from other countries. They have their own religion, language, and culture.

## Biography | WILLIS CARRIER: 1876–1950

In 1915, American engineer Willis Carrier discovered how to control humidity in a print shop. Next, he dealt with the heat of moving parts in a textile factory. Air conditioning followed! At first, only hotels and movie theaters used it. But after World War II, people began installing air conditioning in their offices and homes.

Today, Carrier's invention cools people and keeps ancient books from falling apart. It enables miners to go deep into the earth. It keeps computers from breaking down. Without air conditioning, many hot regions of the world would be very uncomfortable places to live.

**Rustbelt**
*Industrial states that are growing slowly or losing population*

**Sunbelt**
*The states of California, Arizona, Texas, and Florida*

Second, the population of the South and Southwest are growing faster than the rest of the country. The **Sunbelt** states—California, Arizona, Texas, and Florida—are the fastest growing states. The **Rustbelt** states—older, industrial states—are growing more slowly or losing population.

**SECTION 3 REVIEW** On a separate sheet of paper, write *True* if the statement is true or *False* if the statement is not true. Make each false statement true by changing the underlined word.

1) American <u>culture</u> is a blend of Native Americans and cultures from Europe, Africa, Asia, and Latin America.

2) Cultures <u>never</u> change.

3) <u>Christians</u> were the first people to believe in one single God as the all-powerful creator and ruler.

4) Most people in America live in <u>metropolitan</u> areas.

5) In the U.S., people are moving to the <u>Rustbelt</u>.

**What do YOU think?** Do you think cities in the U.S. will continue to grow or will more people choose to live in smaller towns? Give two or three reasons for your answer.

Natural resource
*A raw material from nature*

Pulp
*A wood product used in the making of paper*

Renewable resource
*A resource that can be used but then replanted or replaced*

## What Are Two Important Natural Resources in the U.S.?

The United States is the fourth largest country in the world and the richest. Why do U.S. citizens live better than people in many other countries? One reason is their rich **natural resources,** which are raw materials from nature.

One such resource is its rich farmland. U.S. farmers produce enough food for everyone in the United States with a lot left over to sell to other countries. Water is a second important natural resource. The U.S. has water for crops and hydroelectric power. Its many rivers serve as highways for transporting goods. Ocean water provides seafood. Many people along the coasts fish for a living.

## What Are Two Other Important Natural Resources?

Forests are a third natural resource. Forests cover much of the U.S. With careful management, they are a **renewable resource.** They can be replaced. In the Southeast, logging is a key industry. Workers in the huge forests of the Pacific Northwest make lumber and **pulp** from wood. Pulp is a wood product used in the making of paper.

A fourth natural resource in the U.S. includes minerals such as coal, natural gas, and oil. Deep below the surface of Earth lie huge deposits of coal. In fact, the U.S. owns about one-third of all the known coal deposits on Earth. Most mining areas are in the Appalachian Mountains of the South. Mines have recently opened in the Rocky Mountains and northern Great Plains.

Alaska, California, and the Texas and Louisiana coasts of the Gulf of Mexico contain oil and natural gas. People who search for other minerals have discovered many in the western mountains of the U.S. There, miners dig gold, silver, copper, zinc, platinum, tin, and iron ore.

Writing About Geography

A brochure is a small, folded advertisement for something. Choose a place in the United States that many tourists visit each year. Research this place. Then write your own brochure about it. Explain why people would want to visit it.

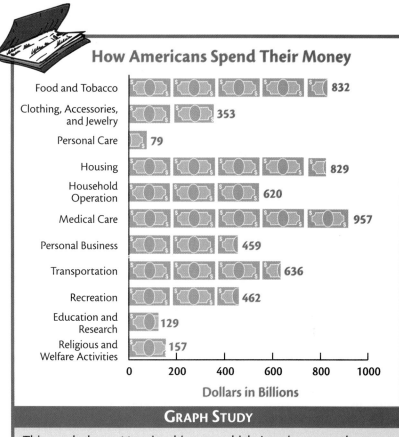

## How Americans Spend Their Money

| Category | Dollars in Billions |
| --- | --- |
| Food and Tobacco | 832 |
| Clothing, Accessories, and Jewelry | 353 |
| Personal Care | 79 |
| Housing | 829 |
| Household Operation | 620 |
| Medical Care | 957 |
| Personal Business | 459 |
| Transportation | 636 |
| Recreation | 462 |
| Education and Research | 129 |
| Religious and Welfare Activities | 157 |

Dollars in Billions

**GRAPH STUDY**

This graph shows 11 major things on which Americans spend money each year. According to this graph, on what do Americans spend the most money? the least money? How much do they spend on food and tobacco? on education and research?

## What Natural Resources Helped the U.S. Build Its Industries?

**Import**
*A product from another country; to bring a product from another country into one's own country*

Many natural resources helped the United States build its industries. Using natural resources in the U.S. was cheaper than using **imports,** or goods from another country. One important product for an industrialized country is steel. Workers used iron ore from Minnesota and coal from the Appalachians to make steel. Huge steel mills developed around Pittsburgh, Pennsylvania; Cleveland, Ohio; and near Chicago, Illinois. These mills helped the U.S. become an industrial giant in the late 1800s.

There are many cars in the United States. These add to air pollution problems.

## What Important U.S. Industry Uses Steel?

Detroit, Michigan, is the home of the automobile industry, which uses a lot of steel. It was in Detroit that Henry Ford first introduced the **assembly line.** An assembly line is a group of workers in a line who put parts together to make a product quickly.

Nearly one-fourth of all working people in the United States are involved in manufacturing. U.S. industries are world leaders in many areas. For example, they manufacture more than half of the world's aircraft. Among its fastest growing industries are computer and electronic manufacturing.

## What Is a Service Industry?

Manufacturing is important to the U.S. economy. But most people today work in **service industries.** A service industry is a business that provides a service. Restaurants, tourism, garages, and shops provide service. People from other countries like to visit the United States. In many areas, the service industry of tourism is a major source of jobs and money.

## What Environmental Challenges Exist?

People in the United States produce more garbage than anyone else on Earth. This garbage badly affects the physical environment. Every day people throw out tons of garbage—plastic, glass, newspapers, and aluminum cans. Then workers bury or burn the garbage. Yet it may contain valuable materials! **Recycling,** or making new products from the old, is one answer to this problem. However, the U.S. recycles only a small percentage of what it uses.

To **pollute** is to make something dirty, impure, or unhealthy. Air pollution—or impure and unhealthy air—is another big environmental problem. Pollution can cause serious diseases like asthma. Air pollution is a bigger problem around cities than in rural areas. However, winds can carry pollution from one area to another.

**Assembly line**
*A group of workers who put parts together to make a product quickly*

**Pollute**
*To make something dirty, impure, or unhealthy*

**Recycle**
*To make new products from old ones*

**Service industry**
*A business that provides a service*

Sometimes, dangerous chemicals end up in rivers and lakes. These cause water pollution. Often, industries are the source of water pollution. Sometimes cities dump untreated human waste into the sea. Then pollution makes seafood unsafe to eat. Water pollution can also cause serious health problems in people and animals.

**SECTION 4 REVIEW** Choose the letter of the answer that correctly completes each sentence. Write your answers on a separate sheet of paper.

**1)** One of the most important reasons why the U.S. is a rich nation is that it _____.

    a. is the largest country

    b. has the largest population

    c. has rich natural resources

    d. borders on two oceans

**2)** _____ are renewable resources.

    a. Coal mines        c. Natural gas

    b. Forests             d. Oil fields

**3)** Most mining for minerals in the U.S. is done in the Appalachian Mountains of the _____.

    a. Northeast        c. South

    b. Midwest          d. West

**4)** _____ is not a service industry.

    a. Repairing cars      c. Manufacturing cars

    b. Medical services    d. Tourism

**5)** _____ is an environmental problem for the U.S.

    a. Air pollution       c. Too much garbage

    b. Water pollution    d. All of the above

**What do YOU think?** Why might water be a more valuable resource in the future?

# The Barn: A Fading Symbol of Rural America

The barn has been a symbol of rural America for a long time. During the 1800s, farmers often had barn-raising parties. People from all over the area gathered and helped to build a new barn. Farmers kept animals in barns. They also used barns to store tools and farm machinery like plows.

Farmers usually painted their barns red. The stain they used for this color

**Wooden barns are not as common as they once were in the U.S.**

was cheap and lasted a long time. Farmers mostly built barns in the shape of a rectangle. But in the 1870s, they built many round and eight-sided barns. These were usually the biggest buildings on the farm. Farm neighbors danced in them. Children played hide and seek in them. Farm workers gathered in them to get out of the hot sun and to plan their day.

But the wooden barn is disappearing. In 1900, about 50 percent of all the people in the United States lived or worked on a farm. Today, less than one percent do. The United States has fewer farms, but these farms are bigger. A large number of barns became unnecessary. Also, today's large farm machinery no longer fits in wooden barns. Some farm equipment is 16 feet tall and 20 feet wide.

Experts on farm life say that farmers are replacing wooden barns with metal storage buildings. These are cheaper and bigger than the old wooden barns. But some people want to save the remaining wooden barns. (More than half are gone now.) They believe that the barn is an important symbol of an American way of life that deserves to be saved.

## Spotlight Story Wrap-Up

1) How did barns help build a rural community?

2) Why were barns usually painted red?

3) What are three things farmers used barns for?

4) What is one reason why the wooden barn is disappearing?

5) Why do some people want to save wooden barns?

◆ The United States, Canada, and Mexico are the three largest countries in North America.

◆ Geographers use regions to study different areas on the globe. They define regions according to physical environments, their history, and their economy.

◆ Geographers usually divide the United States into four regions: the Northeast, the South, the Midwest, and the West.

◆ The United States has a varied landscape. It is relatively flat along the Atlantic coast. A large mountain range in the East is the Appalachian range. The middle of the U.S. is also relatively flat. The West has many high mountains, including the Rocky Mountains.

◆ Huge, slow-moving sheets of ice called glaciers formed many lakes and rivers when they melted. Among these were the five Great Lakes and the Mississippi River system.

◆ Average weather is called climate. The U.S. has many climates. The Northeast and Midwest regions have four seasons, with long, cold winters and hot, wet summers. The South has a subtropical climate with hot and humid summers and mild winters. Because of its mountains and coastline, the West has several climates.

◆ U.S. culture blends cultures from many other lands. The cultures of American Indians and people from Europe, Africa, Latin America, and Asia have influenced U.S. culture.

◆ Almost all major religions of the world are represented in the U.S., but most people in the United States are Christians.

◆ Nearly 80 percent of the population in the U.S. lives in metropolitan areas. It is an extremely urbanized country.

◆ The U.S. is rich in natural resources including soil, water, forests, and minerals.

◆ Many people in the U.S. work in manufacturing industries, such as steel, automobiles, computers, and electronics. The largest percentage of workers work in service industries.

◆ The U.S. faces several environmental problems, such as air and water pollution and what to do with garbage.

## Comprehension: Identifying Facts

On a separate sheet of paper, write the words from the Word Bank to complete each sentence.

**WORD BANK**

culture

glaciers

North America

Tropic of Cancer

West

1) The United States, Canada, and Mexico are the three largest countries in the continent of _____.

2) The largest region in the U.S. is the _____.

3) The five Great Lakes and many of the rivers of the U.S. were created when _____ melted.

4) The imaginary line 23.5 degrees north of the equator is called the _____.

5) Language and religion are two parts of _____.

## Comprehension: Multiple Choice

On a separate sheet of paper, write the letter of the answer that correctly completes each sentence.

1) _____ is a measure of how far north or south of the equator a place is.

   a. Location        c. Longitude
   b. Latitude        d. Distance

2) The region with the largest city in the U.S. is the _____.

   a. Northeast       c. Midwest
   b. South           d. West

3) Borrowing things from other cultures and making them a part of your own is called cultural _____.

   a. stealing        c. acquisition
   b. diffusion       d. birth

4) Nearly 80 percent of the people of the U.S. live in _____ areas.

   a. country         c. metropolitan
   b. small town      d. mountain

**5)** Coal, water, forests, natural gas, and oil are examples of
_____.

a. manufacturing
b. imports

c. service industries
d. natural resources

## Comprehension: Understanding Main Ideas

On a separate sheet of paper, write the answer to each question. Use complete sentences.

**1)** What is the climate like in each of the four regions of the United States?

**2)** Why does the United States have so many cultures?

**3)** What are some environmental challenges the U.S. faces?

## Critical Thinking: Write Your Opinion

On a separate sheet of paper, write your opinion about each question. Use complete sentences.

**1)** Imagine you were given the task of locating a new manufacturing plant somewhere in the U.S. In what region would you build the plant? Give two or three reasons.

**2)** How have people in the United States changed their physical environment? Give two or three examples.

 ## Applying the Five Themes of Geography

 *Location*

How did the location of the Northeast region affect its growth?

> **Test-Taking Tip**  Prepare for a test by making a set of flash cards. Write a word on the front of each card. Write the definition on the back. Use the flash cards in a game by yourself or with a partner to test your knowledge.

# 2

# Canada

Canada is the second largest country in the world. It has many things in common with its neighbor to the south, the United States. It has much land and open space, as the picture on this page shows. Canada is highly industrialized, and its people enjoy a high standard of living. Canada has far fewer people than the United States. However, the two countries share a similar culture and economy.

## Goals for Learning

▶ To describe where Canada is located

▶ To identify the most important physical features and climates of Canada

▶ To describe the cultures of Canada

▶ To explain where and how most people in Canada live

▶ To describe the economy of Canada and its environmental challenges

 *Geo-Stats*

 **Canada**

**Population:** 30,589,000
**Area** (in square miles): 3,849,670
**Length of Coastline** (in miles): 151,394
**Length of Roads** (in miles): 634,040
**Longest River:** Mackenzie (2,635 miles)
**Highest Mountain:** Mt. Logan
  (19,524 feet)

**Major Cities:** Ottawa (capital), Toronto, Montreal, Vancouver, Edmonton, Calgary
**Major Religion:** Christian
**Major Languages:** English, French
**Official Currency:** Canadian Dollar
**Workforce:** 15.3 million
**Number of Newspapers:** 108
**Number of Television Sets:** 19.4 million

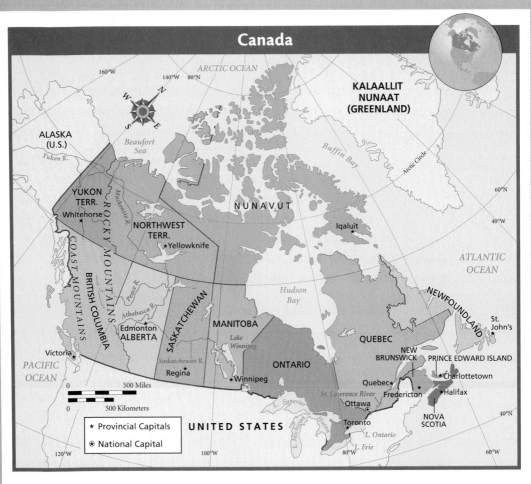

## Canada

**Map Skills**

Canada is a large nation north of the United States. Like the United States, it is part of North America. It has ten large provinces, or states, and three territories. It is a nation with a wide range of temperatures and many prairies, lakes, and mountains.

Study the map and answer the following questions:

**1)** What is the largest province in Canada?

**2)** What large body of water does much of Canada surround?

**3)** What mountain ranges can be found in western Canada?

**4)** What is Canada's capital?

**5)** Why do you think Canada is such a cold place to live?

**Bedrock**
*The solid rock under the loose material and soil of Earth's surface*

**Province**
*A state*

**Territory**
*An area of land that is part of a country, but is not officially a province or state of a country*

**Tundra**
*A plain with no trees*

## Where Is Canada Located?

Canada, the largest country in North America and the second largest in the world, stretches 3,987 miles from east to west. This is almost one-quarter around the world! The Atlantic Ocean borders it on the east, the Pacific Ocean on the west.

Canada has the longest coastline of any country in the world. Its northern-most point is Cape Columbia on Ellesmere Island, which is only 477 miles from the North Pole. From this point to Canada's farthest point south is over 2,000 miles. Canada's border with the U.S. is the longest undefended border in the world.

## What Physical Regions Exist?

Canada has six physical regions. The Canadian Shield is the first and largest physical region. Located in eastern Canada, it covers nearly half of the nation. Its name came from the hard **bedrock** beneath the soil. Bedrock refers to the solid rock under the loose material and soil of Earth's surface.

West of the Canadian Shield lies the second physical region, the Central Plains. A huge range of mountains in the far west makes up a third region. The Arctic region is the fourth physical region. It lies in the far north and is made up of hundreds of islands in the Arctic Ocean. This area also has **tundra.** Tundra is a plain with no trees.

In eastern Canada, the Appalachian Mountains make up its fifth physical region. Ancient glaciers wore down these old mountains. Today the area has gently rolling hills with fertile valleys in between. The sixth and smallest physical region in Canada is the Great Lakes-St. Lawrence lowlands. This region sits between the Appalachian Mountain region and the Canadian Shield region.

## What Political Regions Exist?

Geographers also divide Canada into six political regions. These include ten **provinces,** or states, and three **territories.**

**Toronto is the largest city in Canada. It is located in the province of Ontario.**

A territory is an area of land that is part of a country, but is not officially a province or state of that country.

## What Are the Maritime Provinces?

Maritime
*Bordering on or near the sea*

The first political region includes the four **Maritime Provinces**. Maritime means bordering on or near the sea. New Brunswick, Nova Scotia, Newfoundland, and Prince Edward Island make up the Maritime Provinces. They border the Atlantic Ocean. These were the first places that Europeans settled.

The Maritime Provinces are a rugged area of low, forested mountains. Only Prince Edward Island has any large areas of flat farmland. Because of this, most people in these provinces depend on the forests and the sea to make a living. Geographers call the shallow waters off the eastern shore of Newfoundland the Grand Banks. They have some of the best commercial fishing in the world.

## What Is Quebec?

To the west and north of the Maritime Provinces is the second political region of Quebec. It is Canada's largest province. About one out of every four Canadians lives in this province. Its most famous cities are Montreal and Quebec City. Both cities are located on the St. Lawrence River. Quebec is an important center of manufacturing.

Inuit
*The native people of
Canada*

## What Is Ontario?

West of Quebec sits the industrial heartland of Canada, the province of Ontario. It is the third political region. Great forests cover northern Ontario. But southern Ontario is different. Most of the region's people live there. The United States buys most of the things this region produces. Ontario is one of the fastest growing business centers in the world. Toronto, the biggest city in Canada, is located in Ontario. Canada's capital city of Ottawa is also in Ontario.

## What Are the Prairie Provinces?

At one time, the Prairie Provinces region was a large prairie covered with tall grasses. European settlers plowed the grasses under and planted grain crops. Today, the Prairie Provinces produce much of the world's wheat. Manitoba, Saskatchewan, and Alberta make up the Prairie Provinces. Manitoba's chief industries are manufacturing and agriculture. Saskatchewan is mostly agricultural. Alberta produces natural gas and oil. Its mountains are beautiful, so tourism is also important in Alberta. Some of the main cities in this region are Winnipeg in Manitoba and Calgary and Edmonton in Alberta.

## What Is British Columbia?

The fifth political region in Canada is British Columbia. Mountains separate it from the rest of the country. These mountains are the Brooks Range, an extension of the Rocky Mountains. Thick forests and salmon-rich waters make British Columbia famous. The largest city in British Columbia is Vancouver. It is the third largest city in Canada. It is Canada's major port city on the Pacific Ocean.

## What Is the Arctic North?

The sixth political region in Canada is the Arctic North. It covers more than a third of the country. The Arctic North includes three territories: the Yukon Territory, the Northwest Territories, and Nunavut, which is Canada's newest territory. The Canadian government created this new territory for the **Inuit,** the native people who live

## Provinces and Territories of Canada

| Province/Territory | Area in Square Miles | Population |
|---|---|---|
| Alberta | 255,287 | 2,696,826 |
| British Columbia | 365,948 | 3,724,500 |
| Manitoba | 250,947 | 1,113,898 |
| New Brunswick | 28,355 | 738,133 |
| Newfoundland | 156,649 | 551,792 |
| Nova Scotia | 21,425 | 909,282 |
| Ontario | 412,581 | 10,753,573 |
| Prince Edward Island | 2,185 | 134,557 |
| Quebec | 594,860 | 7,138,795 |
| Saskatchewan | 251,866 | 990,237 |
| Northwest Territories | 503,951 | 39,672 |
| Yukon Territory | 186,661 | 30,766 |
| Nunavut | 818,959 | 24,730 |

### CHART STUDY

This chart lists information about Canada's 13 provinces and territories. Which has the highest population? the lowest? How many square miles is Quebec? Alberta?

there. People once called them Eskimos. This Arctic North region is a desert because it is dry, but it is a cold desert. Geographers predict that life will soon change in the Arctic North. Miners have discovered huge mineral deposits there.

**SECTION 1 REVIEW** On a separate sheet of paper, write the word from the Word Bank that completes each sentence.

### WORD BANK

Canada

Canadian Shield

Grand Banks

Inuit

Toronto

1) The native people of Canada are the _____.

2) Canada's biggest city is _____.

3) Some of the best commercial fishing in the world is on the _____.

4) _____ is the second largest country in the world.

5) The largest physical region of Canada is the _____.

**What do YOU think?** Why is it good that Canada and the United States are good friends and trading partners and what is it that has made them this way?

Cordillera
*The Spanish word for mountain range*

Geologist
*A person who studies Earth's physical structure and history*

## What Are Some Physical Features of Canada?

Glaciers once covered much of Canada. They shaped its land. Glaciers also wore down the high mountains that once stood in eastern Canada.

**Geologists** study physical features of Earth. They say that these eastern Canadian mountains formed about 280 million years ago. As time passed, glaciers, wind, and running water wore them down. Today, these old mountains range in height from 500 feet to about 4,000 feet. These give the Maritime Provinces gently rolling land.

The melting glaciers left behind many lakes and rivers. In fact, Canada has more lakes than any other country in the world. About 30 percent of the world's freshwater is located in Canada.

## What Did Glaciers Do Beyond Eastern Canada?

The central plains of Canada also owe much to glaciers. Their melting left behind rich topsoil for growing crops. To the west of these plains rise the peaks of the **cordillera.** This Spanish word means mountain range.

The Canadian Rocky Mountains are a part of the same range as the Rocky Mountains found in the U.S. Some of these mountains reach 12,000 feet. The western cordillera includes the Coast Mountains in British Columbia and the St. Elias Mountains in the Yukon. The tallest mountain in Canada is Mt. Logan in the St. Elias Mountains. It is 19,524 feet tall. Even today, glaciers cover much of these mountains.

Glaciers also created Canada's many islands. (It has over 50,000 of them!) Three large islands include Baffin, Ellesmere, and Victoria. Together, these islands are larger than the European countries of Norway, Sweden, and Denmark combined.

## What Major Bodies of Water Lie in Canada?

Canada's biggest water feature is Hudson Bay. The entire state of Texas would fit into it! Few people live along the flat, swampy lowlands of its southern shore. The northern portions of Hudson Bay are frozen much of the year.

Canada's longest river is the Mackenzie. Located in the Northwest Territories, it flows 2,635 miles. Like Hudson Bay, the Mackenzie is frozen much of the year. A smaller but far more important river is the St. Lawrence. About 16 million people—more than 60 percent of Canada's people—live in the St. Lawrence lowlands. Many of Canada's industrial centers are located there.

Canada and the United States share four of the five Great Lakes. Lakes Superior, Huron, Erie, and Ontario border both countries. Only Lake Michigan lies completely within the U.S. These countries also share Niagara Falls. This huge waterfall is 158 feet high and 2,600 feet wide on the Canadian side.

## What Is a Subarctic Climate?

Most of Canada has a **subarctic climate.** This cold climate is the area immediately outside the **Arctic Circle,** or 66.5° north of the equator. Because of this, Canada is one of the coldest countries in the world. Its average temperature is 22°F.

In the Arctic North, the ground is always frozen. Geographers call it **permafrost,** or permanently frozen ground. The Arctic North receives less snowfall than the rest of Canada. But the Arctic is so cold that the snow that does fall never melts. Many other parts of Canada have long and cold winters, too. However, even in the Northwest Territories and the Yukon, summer temperatures can reach 80° F, but summers are short.

## Which Part of Canada Has a Maritime Climate?

Canada's West Coast has a **maritime climate.** Being close to water influences this climate. Rain falls more frequently than snow during the winter. On the windward side of the coastal mountains, some places receive as much as 195 inches of rain a year.

**Writing About Geography**

Think about what Canada looks like. Then draw a picture of the map based only on your memory. Compare your drawing to an actual map of Canada. Write about how your drawing compares to the actual map. Which parts are similar? Which parts are different?

The Rocky Mountains cover much of western Canada. This photo shows Lake Louise and the Canadian Rockies in Alberta, Canada.

**Chinook**
*A hot, dry wind along the eastern slopes of the Rocky Mountains*

**Continental climate**
*The climate in landlocked areas far from oceans; a climate of short, warm summers and long winters*

**Drought**
*A long period of dry weather*

**Landlocked**
*Surrounded by land and little water*

## Which Part of Canada Has a Continental Climate?

The **landlocked** Prairie Provinces have a **continental climate.** Land surrounds a landlocked area. It is far from an ocean. In a continental climate, people experience short, warm summers and long winters. In Canada, there are short, warm summers because it is in the higher latitudes. The Prairie Provinces of Manitoba, Saskatchewan, and Alberta lie on the leeward side of the western mountains. They do not receive much rain.

Sometimes a hot, dry wind called a **Chinook** blows down from the Rocky Mountains. In winter, it provides a break from the cold temperatures. If the Chinook comes in summer, it can cause long periods of dry weather. This is called a **drought.**

## Where Is Canada's Humid Continental Climate?

Canada's southernmost point, Point Pelee in Ontario, is farther south than some parts of California. Southern Ontario has Canada's mildest climate, a humid continental climate. With this climate, people enjoy four different seasons with short winters and long summers.

## How Does Geography Affect the Canadians?

The Inuit have always lived in balance with nature. Their language reveals the respect they have for it. For example, they have 100 names for snow because of its importance to their life. Many of these native people live by hunting and fishing.

Fish and other seafood are plentiful in the coastal waters of Canada. Many commercial fishermen work there. Salmon fishing is especially important on the Pacific Coast. Many freshwater fish swim in Canada's rivers and lakes. These fish provide food and attract tourists.

Agriculture is big business in Canada's fertile valleys and central plains. Canada also has vast mineral deposits and huge forests. These resources provide work for many Canadians.

**SECTION 2 REVIEW** On a separate sheet of paper, write answers to these questions.

1) What created most of Canada's physical features?
2) What is the highest mountain in Canada?
3) What is Canada's most important river even though it is not the longest?
4) What do geographers call ground that is permanently frozen?
5) What kind of climate does most of Canada have?

 **What do YOU think?** If you could choose any part of Canada to live in, where would it be? Give two or three reasons.

## What Was the First Canadian Culture?

The oldest Canadian cultures are those of its native peoples, like the Inuit. About 370,000 non-Inuit natives live in Canada. In 1997, the Canadian government set aside a new territory called Nunavut for the Inuit to govern themselves.

**Bilingual**
*Speaking two languages*

The Inuit have their own language and culture. However, their way of life is changing. In the past, many lived in ice or snow houses called igloos. They traveled with dog sleds or in small, covered canoes called kayaks. Today, many live in wooden or brick homes. They use snowmobiles and watch television, because other cultures are influencing their lives.

People of native cultures celebrate their way of life in Canada. Here an Ottawa girl performs a traditional dance.

## What Cultures Exist in Canada?

Canada is a country of immigrants. When it was founded in 1867, only 3.4 million people lived there. Today, the population is about 30 million. People from European countries have given Canada a European flavor. Since the 1970s, many immigrants have come from Asia. Many settled in the western city of Vancouver, British Columbia. Asians now make up well over 3 percent of Canada's population.

## What Languages Are Spoken?

Most Canadians speak English. However, in Quebec, most people speak French. Canada is a **bilingual** country because it has two official languages: English and French. Throughout Canada, road signs and other messages appear in both languages. Besides English and French, many other languages are spoken.

## What Religions Do Canadians Practice?

Almost 82 percent of Canadians are Christians. But many of the immigrants have brought their native religions to Canada. Most big cities have people who follow other world religions.

## Where Do Most Canadians Live?

About 23 percent of Canadians live in rural areas; 6 percent live on farms. Most people live in urban areas. Three main areas are Toronto, Montreal, and Vancouver.

Toronto is the center of culture, industry, and **finance.** Finance is the use and management of money by banks and businesses. Toronto has Canada's largest stock exchange. The city is **cosmopolitan** because its people come from all over the world. It is a lot like New York City in the United States.

Montreal is the center of French-Canadian culture. In fact, it is the second largest French-speaking city in the world. Montreal is the center for French-speaking theater and for French-language newspapers. It has two French-Canadian universities and is a major financial and industrial center.

Vancouver is much younger than Toronto or Montreal. It developed after the completion of the Canadian Pacific railroad. Then Vancouver became the industrial, business, and financial center of British Columbia.

## What Trends Affect Canada Today?

Three important trends affect Canada today: **diversity,** dependence on the U.S., and language division. Diversity is a variety of people living in one place. More and more immigrants are moving there. Its government has passed laws that recognize their different and varied cultures.

Canada depends a lot on the U.S. Three out of four Canadians live within 200 miles of Canada's border with the United States. Canada **exports,** or sells, raw materials to the U.S. and imports finished goods. U.S. firms control much of Canadian industry. The United States also produces much of what Canadians read and see on television.

In February 2000, British Columbia elected Ujjal Dosanjh its head of government. He is the first Indo-Canadian to hold this position. Dosanjh was born in a small village in India in 1947. When he was 17, he moved to England. There, he worked in a crayon and an auto parts factory for four years.

In 1968, Dosanjh settled in Vancouver, British Columbia, and worked in a mill until he hurt his back. Afterward, he studied political science and law. Dosanjh won his first political election in 1991. Since that time, he has spoken out against violence and spoken for education.

**Quebecois**
*The French-speaking people of Quebec*

The growing division between French-speaking and English-speaking Canadians is causing problems. **Quebecois** are the French-speaking people of the province of Quebec. Many of them want greater independence from the Canadian government.

The Quebec government has taken over some businesses in the province. It insists that all business be conducted in the French language. Some Quebecois even want to make Quebec an independent nation from Canada. Canada's future may depend on its ability to knit these two groups into one.

**SECTION 3 REVIEW** On a separate sheet of paper, write *True* if the statement is true or *False* if the statement is not true. Make each false statement true by changing the underlined word.

1) Canada is a country of <u>immigrants.</u>
2) Canada has two official languages: English and <u>Italian.</u>
3) Canada is a mostly <u>urban</u> country.
4) The largest city in Canada is <u>Toronto.</u>
5) The Quebecois want to create an independent <u>English-speaking</u> country.

**What do YOU think?**

The U.S. has a large Spanish-speaking population in some places. Should the U.S. recognize Spanish as an official language like Canada recognizes French? Why or why not?

## What Are Some of Canada's Natural Resources?

Canada is rich in natural resources. It has much rich farmland. Water is another important resource. Its rivers provide hydroelectricity. Its lakes and rivers provide seafood. Commercial fishing is one of Canada's biggest industries. Canada has about 10 percent of the world's forests. These cover almost one-quarter of the country.

Canada leads the world in zinc and uranium production. British Columbia contains some of North America's largest coal deposits. Huge reserves of oil and natural gas lie in the province of Alberta, the Northwest Territories, and off the coast of Newfoundland.

## What Are Some Major Canadian Industries?

Manufacturing is important to the Canadian economy. Ontario and Quebec produce more than 75 percent of all the manufactured goods in Canada. Every major U.S. automaker operates factories in Canada. Only Japan and Germany export more motor vehicles than Canada.

Forest products are Canada's single largest export. Canada sells paper and paper products all over the world. Canadian trees provide about one-fourth of all the paper used for newspaper around the world. Pulp, the raw material used in making newsprint, is another big export. Canada exports large amounts of its lumber to Asia, especially Japan.

## How Is Mining Important?

Mining is another industry tied to Canada's great resources. Few people work in mining, but it plays an important role in the economy. For example, many people sell and distribute Canadian minerals.

Forest land is an important natural resource in Canada. Products made from wood make up Canada's leading export. This photo shows a pulp and paper mill.

Deforestation
*The clearing or destruction of forests*

Erosion
*The process by which running water, wind, or ice break down rock or soil*

Wetland
*Land covered with water some or most of the time, but where plants continue to grow*

As with mining, few people work in agriculture. However, farm products account for 3 percent of the Canadian economy. A typical farm is large and uses lots of machinery. Canada is one of the world's biggest wheat producers. Farmers also produce oats, barley, and dairy products.

As in most advanced nations, most Canadians work in service industries. About 80 percent of them work in tourism, banking, and restaurants.

## What Environmental Problems Does Canada Face?

Canada's environmental problems are similar to those of the United States. Canadians produce a lot of garbage. The cost of burying or burning all that garbage is expensive. Air and water pollution are also problems. Air pollution has decreased in Canada, but it is still a big problem. The paper industry is a major source of water pollution.

Soil **erosion** is a problem in Canada's central plains. Erosion is the process by which running water, wind, or ice breaks down rock or soil. This has happened because farmers sometimes use poor methods of farming.

**Deforestation,** the clearing or destruction of forests, is another problem in Canada. This large country seems to have an unlimited supply of forests. The truth is, loggers have destroyed many valuable forests. Canadians must soon find ways to renew these forests.

A similar problem is the destruction of **wetlands.** A wetland is land covered with water some or most of the time, but where plants continue to grow. Acting as sponges, wetlands absorb water that might otherwise flood surrounding land. When people destroy wetlands, flooding becomes a problem. Also, many birds breed and feed in wetlands. People who drain these wetlands to create farmland threaten the lives of the birds.

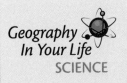
**Acid Rain**

Scientists use the term *acid rain* for rain, snow, or sleet that harmful acids have polluted. How do these acids get into rain? Factories, power plants, and automobiles burn fuels for energy. Three of these fuels—coal, gasoline, and oil—put sulfur dioxide and nitrogen oxide into the atmosphere. When these oxides mix with water vapor, sulfuric acid and nitric acid result.

Acid rain pollutes lakes, rivers, and streams. Fish and other wildlife die. It damages buildings, statues, and bridges. It harms land and forests. Of course, it can get into human drinking water and affect food.

Acid rain especially affects Canada, the United States, and western Europe. In the 1980s, Canada accused the U.S. of polluting its waters and forests. In 1990, the U.S. Congress set new standards to reduce the amount of acid rain in Canada and the United States.

**SECTION 4 REVIEW** Choose the letter of the answer that correctly completes each sentence. Write your answers on a separate sheet of paper.

1) Forests cover about _____ of Canada.

   a. one tenth      c. two-thirds

   b. one quarter    d. half

2) Canada is the world's leading producer of _____.

   a. gold and silver    c. oil and natural gas

   b. copper and lead    d. zinc and uranium

3) Most Canadian workers work in _____.

   a. manufacturing    c. banking

   b. service industries   d. mining

4) Farming accounts for _____ of the Canadian economy.

   a. 3 percent      c. 30 percent

   b. 20 percent    d. 40 percent

5) A major environmental problem related to soil and farming is _____.

   a. deforestation      c. erosion

   b. destruction of wetlands  d. all of the above

**What do YOU think?** Why do you think deforestation is a problem? How could it be prevented?

# The St. Lawrence Seaway

Canadians once had a dream about the St. Lawrence River. They wanted to use it to bring ocean-going ships to their inland ports on the Great Lakes. The dream took a long time to happen.

The problem was that the Great Lakes are much higher than the Atlantic Ocean. Workers built a series of locks. A lock is a waterway with gates at each end. The lock "locks in" water between the gates.

**Ships are used on the St. Lawrence Seaway to carry raw materials to and from inland ports.**

Ships heading up the St. Lawrence had to be raised. The engineers filled the locks with water. This raised the ship to the level of the next waterway. A ship traveling the seaway now goes through 15 locks to reach Lake Superior. By then, the locks have raised a ship over 600 feet above sea level. To help ships get back to the Atlantic Ocean, engineers let the water out of the locks.

The seaway was a joint U.S. and Canadian project. Its construction began in 1954 and ended in 1959. Now ocean-going ships could travel thousands of miles into the interior of North America. Ships from Europe could reach over 50 port cities of the Great Lakes. Toronto, Windsor, and Thunder Bay—port cities in Ontario, Canada—would enjoy more business. The port cities of Detroit, Michigan; Toledo, Ohio; Chicago, Illinois; and Duluth, Minnesota, in the U.S. would, too.

But the seaway disappointed everyone. Shipping did not increase as much as expected. The seaway was out of date almost by the time it was completed. New technology changed ocean-going ships. They became so big that they did not fit in the locks! Also, for three months a year, the waterway was frozen over. No ships could travel through its locks during these months. Today, ships use the seaway mostly to carry raw materials like coal, iron ore, and wheat.

## Spotlight Story Wrap-Up

1) What was the dream of Canadian and U.S. port cities along the Great Lakes?

2) How long did it take to build the St. Lawrence Seaway?

3) What does a lock in a waterway do?

4) How many locks are in the St. Lawrence Seaway?

5) Why did the seaway disappoint people?

- Canada is the second largest country in the world.

- Like the U.S., Canada is highly industrialized.

- Canada has six physical regions: the Canadian Shield, the Central Plains, the western mountainous region, the Arctic, the Appalachian Mountain region of the east, and the Great Lakes-St. Lawrence lowlands.

- Canada has six political regions: the Maritime Provinces, Quebec, Ontario, the Prairie Provinces, British Columbia, and the Arctic North.

- Canada has a varied landscape. Glaciers wore down mountains in the east. The Maritime Provinces have gently rolling hills. The middle of Canada is relatively flat with rich farmland. The west has many high mountains, including the Canadian Rocky Mountains.

- Glaciers also left behind many islands. Ellesmere Island, Baffin Island, and Victoria Island are larger than Norway, Sweden, and Denmark combined. Canada has more lakes than any other country in the world. About 30 percent of the world's freshwater is located there.

- Most of Canada has a subarctic climate. It is one of the coldest countries in the world. Its West Coast has a maritime climate; the Prairie Provinces have a continental climate; and southern Ontario has a humid continental climate.

- The Inuit, the native people of Canada, have their own language and culture. Immigrants from Europe have given Canada a European flavor. Asian immigrants now make up over 3 percent of the population.

- Almost all major religions of the world are represented in Canada. Most Canadians are Christians.

- Canada has two official languages: English and French.

- Much of the Canadian population lives in urban areas.

- Canada is rich in natural resources including farmland, water, forests, and minerals.

- Most people work in Canadian service industries. Some work in manufacturing industries. Forest products, mining, and agriculture are tied to Canada's great natural resources.

- Canada faces several environmental problems: air and water pollution, too much garbage, farmland erosion, deforestation, and the destruction of wetlands. Many of the problems also exist in the U.S.

## Comprehension: Identifying Facts

On a separate sheet of paper, use the words from the Word Bank to complete each sentence.

| WORD BANK |
| --- |
| Canadian Shield |
| forest |
| subarctic |
| United States |
| urban |

1) The largest physical region in Canada is the _____.

2) Canada borders the _____ on the south.

3) Most of Canada has a(n) _____ climate.

4) Like the U.S., Canada is a(n) _____ society.

5) Canada's single biggest export is _____ products.

## Comprehension: Multiple Choice

On a separate sheet of paper, write the letter of the answer that correctly completes each sentence.

1) _____ is a plain with no trees.

  a. Tundra      c. Desert

  b. Pine forests  d. Savanna

2) Canada is the _____ largest country in the world.

  a. second      c. third

  b. fourth      d. fifth

3) Canada's two official languages are English and _____.

  a. Greek      c. Inuit

  b. French     d. Spanish

4) _____ has the greatest influence on most Canadians.

  a. Great Britain  c. The United States

  b. France     d. Russia

5) Most Canadians work in _____ industries.

   a. manufacturing    c. mining

   b. fishing         d. service

## Comprehension: Understanding Main Ideas

On a separate sheet of paper, write the answer to each question. Use complete sentences.

1) What physical features of Canada help make it a major trading nation?

2) What are Canada's natural resources and what is their importance to its economy?

3) What are the major industries of Canada?

## Critical Thinking: Write Your Opinion

On a separate sheet of paper, write your opinion to each question. Use complete sentences.

1) Is Canada's cultural diversity a strength or a weakness? Explain your answer.

2) Why do you think Canadians chose Ottawa as their capital instead of Toronto or Montreal?

## Applying the Five Themes of Geography

### *Interaction*

Find magazine or newspaper pictures or draw a series of pictures that show the effects of human interaction and environment in Canada.

**Test-Taking Tip**    When studying for a test, write your own test based on the chapter goals for learning. Have a partner do the same. Then complete each other's test. Double-check your answers together.

# Maps

To read a map, you need to understand its symbols. Most maps have a key, or legend, that explains these symbols. Sometimes the key is simple to understand; sometimes it is more difficult.

0        100        200 Miles

0      100     200 Kilometers

Artists draw some maps to scale. You can use the scale to find the actual distances on a map.

Most maps show direction. A compass rose shows at least the four major directions: north, east, south, and west. Some compass roses also include northeast, southeast, northwest, and southwest. To show north, some maps use an arrow and the letter *N*.

Many maps show lines of longitude and latitude. Vertical (north and south) lines are longitude. Horizontal (east and west) lines are latitude. The line for zero degrees (0°) longitude goes through Greenwich, England. This line is called the Prime Meridian. The 0° latitude is at the equator, the widest part of the globe.

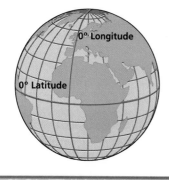

You can read many different kinds of maps. Each map provides different information. Here are five examples:

**Physical Map**—This map shows the roughness of Earth's surface, including mountains, rivers, and plains.

**Elevation Map**—This map shows different heights of land above sea level.

**Political Map**—This map shows borders between countries.

**Climate Map**—This map shows different kinds of climates.

**Natural Resources Map**—This map shows the location of natural resources, such as minerals, oil, and natural gas.

Choose the kind of map you would use to answer each question.

1) Where in the United States can you find the mineral iron ore?

2) How tall is Mount Whitney?

3) What part of Canada has the coldest average temperature?

4) What are the names of two Canadian rivers?

5) What states form the border between the United States and Canada?

◆ The United States, Canada, and Mexico are the three largest countries in North America. Canada is the second largest country in the world.

◆ The United States has four physical regions. Canada has six.

◆ Both Canada and the U.S. have high mountains, vast prairies, long rivers, and big lakes.

◆ When the glaciers melted, they formed many lakes and rivers. Among these was the Mississippi River system and the Great Lakes in the United States. Canada shares four of the Great Lakes with the United States. Canada has more lakes than any other country in the world.

◆ The U.S. has many climates. The Northeast and Midwest regions have four seasons, with long, cold winters and hot, wet summers. The South has a humid subtropical climate. Because of its mountains and coastline, the West has several climates.

◆ Most of Canada has a subarctic climate, making it one of the coldest countries in the world.

◆ Both the U.S. and Canada blend cultures from many other lands. The American Indian cultures and cultures of Europe, Africa, Latin America, and Asia have influenced U.S. culture. Europeans, Asians, and the Inuit (native people of Canada) have influenced the Canadian culture.

◆ English and French are the two official languages of Canada. English is the official language of the U.S.

◆ People in Canada and the U.S. practice almost all the major religions of the world. Most people in these countries are Christians.

◆ Both the U.S. and Canada are urbanized.

◆ Both Canada and the U.S. are rich in natural resources including soil, water, forests, and minerals.

◆ In both the U.S. and Canada, many people work in manufacturing industries. The largest percentage of people work in service industries.

◆ Both Canada and the U.S. face air and water pollution and produce too much garbage. The destruction of wetlands and deforestation challenge Canada.

"Today we all speak, if not the same tongue, the same universal language. There is no one center, and time has lost its former coherence: East and West, yesterday and tomorrow exist as a confused jumble in each one of us."

—Octavio Paz, Mexican poet and essayist, from
*Alternating Current*, 1967

# UNIT 2

# Latin America

In this unit, you will travel south of the United States to Latin America. Here you will study Mexico and the many countries of Central America, the Caribbean, and South America.

These nations have many things in common, especially the language. Most people speak Spanish or Portuguese. Some of the earliest cities also started in these places thousands of years ago. These countries also have many important rivers, deserts, and mountains. The picture to the left is Iguazú Falls in Brazil. This huge waterfall is on the Paraná River in South America. How is it different from the rivers near where you live? In this unit, you will see how Latin America is very different from the United States and Canada.

**CHAPTERS IN UNIT 2**

**Chapter 3:** Mexico . . . . . . . . . . . . . . . . . . . . . . . . . . . . . . .78
**Chapter 4:** Central America and the Caribbean  . .98
**Chapter 5:** South America . . . . . . . . . . . . . . . . . . . . . . .118

# 3

# Mexico

Mexico has a long and colorful history. Over 500 years ago, people from Europe sailed to Mexico. Long before that, however, it had some of the world's greatest civilizations. Today, Mexico is a highly industrialized country. It is also an important source of workers, resources, and food for its northern neighbor, the United States.

## Goals for Learning

▶ To describe where Mexico is located

▶ To identify the most important physical features and climate of Mexico

▶ To describe the diverse cultures of Mexico

▶ To explain where and how people in Mexico live

▶ To describe the economy and the environmental challenges Mexico faces

## Geo-Stats

### Mexico

**Population:** 99,734,000

**Area** (in square miles): 754,120

**Length of Coastline** (in miles): 5,794

**Length of Roads** (in miles): 155,250

**Longest River:** Río Grande/Río Bravo del Norte (1,900 miles)

**Highest Mountain:** Pico de Orizaba (18,700 feet)

**Major Cities:** Mexico City (capital), Guadalajara, Puebla, Monterrey

**Major Religions:** Roman Catholic, Protestant Christian

**Major Languages:** Spanish, native languages

**Official Currency:** New Mexican nuevo peso

**Workforce:** 36.6 million

**Number of Daily Newspapers:** 309

**Number of Television Sets:** 13.1 million

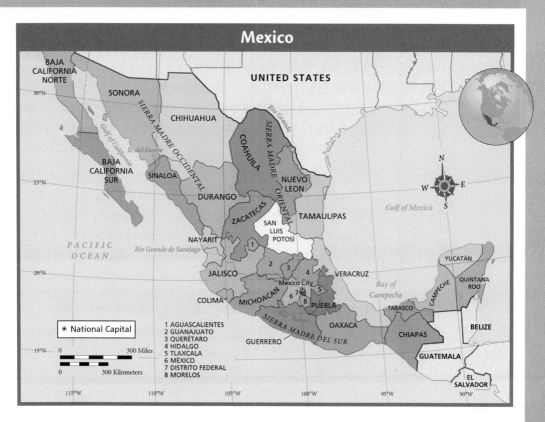

# Mexico

**BAJA CALIFORNIA NORTE**

30°N

**SONORA**

**UNITED STATES**

**CHIHUAHUA**

*Rio Grande*

*Gulf of California*

*R. del Fuerte*

**SIERRA MADRE OCCIDENTAL**

**COAHUILA**

**SIERRA MADRE ORIENTAL**

**BAJA CALIFORNIA SUR**

25°N

**SINALOA**

**NUEVO LEON**

**DURANGO**

**ZACATECAS**

**SAN LUIS POTOSÍ**

**TAMAULIPAS**

*Gulf of Mexico*

**NAYARIT**

*Rio Grande de Santiago*

1

N

W  E

S

**PACIFIC OCEAN**

20°N

**JALISCO**

2

3

4

**VERACRUZ**

*Bay of Campeche*

**YUCATÁN**

Mexico City

5

**QUINTANA ROO**

**COLIMA**

**MICHOACAN**

6 7

8

**PUEBLA**

**CAMPECHE**

**TABASCO**

**BELIZE**

*Rio Balsas*

**OAXACA**

**CHIAPAS**

⊛ **National Capital**

**SIERRA MADRE DEL SUR**

**GUERRERO**

**GUATEMALA**

15°N

0      300 Miles

1 AGUASCALIENTES
2 GUANAJUATO
3 QUERÉTARO
4 HIDALGO
5 TLAXCALA
6 MÉXICO
7 DISTRITO FEDERAL
8 MORELOS

**EL SALVADOR**

0      300 Kilometers

115°W    110°W    105°W    100°W    95°W    90°W

*Map Skills*

Mexico lies south of the United States in North America and north of Central America. This beautiful country has 31 states and a growing economy. Its economy makes it an important trading partner for the United States.

Study the map and answer the following questions:

**1)** Which oceans, gulfs, and bays surround Mexico?

**2)** What is the capital of Mexico?

**3)** Which river separates much of Mexico from the United States?

**4)** What are three mountain ranges in Mexico?

**5)** Why do you think Mexico has a warm climate?

Irrigate
*To pipe in or channel water to fields that get little rain*

Isthmus
*A narrow strip of land connecting two larger land areas*

Plateau
*An area of level highland*

Valley
*A stretch of lowlands between mountains*

## Where Is Mexico Located?

Mexico, the nation just south of the United States, is shaped like a triangle. It is widest in the north where it borders the United States. This border is 1,429 miles long. In the south, Mexico borders the Central American countries of Belize and Guatemala.

The Pacific Ocean borders Mexico on the west. The Gulf of Mexico borders it on the east. The narrowest part of Mexico, the **Isthmus** of Tehuantepec, is only 134 miles wide. An isthmus is a narrow strip of land connecting two larger land areas.

## Where Is Mexico's Central Plateau Region?

Mexico has four physical regions. The Central **Plateau** is its largest region. Like all plateaus, the Central Plateau is an area of level highland. This plateau has two parts. The northern half is generally dry. Farmers must **irrigate** to raise crops. That is, they bring water to fields rather than depend on natural rainfall. They use pipes to channel the water.

The southern half of the Central Plateau is higher than the northern half. Because the southern half gets more rain, more crops can be grown there than in the northern half. Farmers grow corn, which is Mexico's favorite and most important crop. Geographers describe this part of the Central Plateau as Mexico's heartland.

The heartland of the Central Plateau is the richest part of Mexico. Most of Mexico's people live in this southern part. Within it is the **Valley** of Mexico. It is a stretch of lowlands between Mexico's mountains. The Valley of Mexico is almost 50 miles long and 40 miles wide. Mexico City, the capital of Mexico, sits in this large valley.

**Earthquake**
*The shaking of Earth's surface from plate movement*

**Lava**
*Hot, liquid rock*

**Plate tectonics**
*The idea that there is slow movement of Earth's plates*

**Volcano**
*A mountain formed when hot liquid rock comes from deep within Earth to its surface*

Scientists believe that Earth's crust is broken up into several huge slabs called plates. These plates move slowly underneath Earth's surface. Physical geographers call their movement **plate tectonics**. Sometimes these plates crash into one another. Then the edge of one plate may slide beneath that of another. This is one way in which mountains form.

Mountains can also form from hot liquid rock that comes from deep within the earth. It rises to Earth's surface and forms **volcanoes**. Geographers call this liquid rock **lava**. Mexico has many active volcanoes.

Popocatépetl, an active volcano in Mexico, means "smoking mountain."

The Central Plateau region has many **earthquakes.** They happen whenever Earth's plates shift. Four important tectonic plates come together in Mexico. This creates a great deal of shifting, which causes earthquakes. These earthquakes have killed people and destroyed property.

## Where Is Mexico's Coastal Plains Region?

The second region in Mexico is its coastal plains. They form a rim around Mexico's great central region of plateau and mountains. The eastern coastal plain runs along the Gulf of Mexico. The plain extends from the Texas border to the Yucatán Peninsula. The western coastal plain along the Pacific is more narrow and dry than the gulf coastal plain. Farmers there use irrigation to grow cotton, wheat, and other crops.

Jungle
*A thick growth of trees and vines*

Peninsula
*A strip of land surrounded on three sides by water*

Geographers divide the coastal plains into two subregions. The northern half of the plain is warm, but receives little rainfall. **Jungle,** a thick growth of trees and vines, covers the rainy southern half.

## Where Is the Desert Region in Mexico?

The northwestern part of Mexico is a desert region. Its largest desert is the Sonoran. In the most western part of Mexico lies another desert. Geographers call it Baja California. This desert is a **peninsula,** or a strip of land surrounded on three sides by water. Few people live in this empty desert region.

## Where Is the Yucatán Peninsula Region?

The Yucatán Peninsula is the fourth and final region of Mexico. Because this region is part of the eastern coastal plain, it is somewhat flat. Limestone rock formed most of it. This soft rock dissolves in water. Sometimes this creates huge underground caves. The Yucatán Peninsula is not very good for farming. Because of this, the region has a small population.

**Section 1 Review** On a separate sheet of paper, write the word from the Word Bank that completes each sentence.

**WORD BANK**

Central Plateau

irrigation

plate tectonics

Sonoran

United States

1) The country that lies on Mexico's northern boundary is the _____.

2) Mexico's largest region is the _____.

3) Farmers in Mexico use _____ to bring water to their crops.

4) Many mountains form because of _____.

5) The largest desert in Mexico is the _____.

**What do YOU think?** How might Mexico's geography help explain why many Mexicans come to the U.S. to live?

Deciduous
*A type of tree that drops its leaves*

Rain forest
*A thick forest in the Tropics where a great deal of rain falls*

## What Mountains Exist in Mexico?

Mexico's main physical feature is its mountains. High mountain ranges rise on the east, west, and south of the Central Plateau. Geographers call all these mountain ranges the Sierra Madre.

The Sierra Madre Oriental, the Eastern Sierras, is the southern part of the same mountain range that makes up the U.S. Rocky Mountains. The Sierra Madre Occidental, the Western Sierras, continues in California as the Sierra Nevada range. **Deciduous** forests cover the dry northern part of the Sierra Madre Occidental. In a deciduous forest, trees drop their leaves. The Southern Sierras, the Madre del Sur, extend down to the Isthmus of Tehuantepec. A narrow plain there separates these mountains from the Pacific Ocean. Tropical **rain forests** cover the Southern Sierras. This type of dense forest grows in the Tropics where a great deal of rain falls.

## What Is Mexico's Tallest Mountain?

Mexico's tallest mountain is Pico de Orizaba, which is an old volcano. It is 18,700 feet high. The people of Mexico City can see two snow-covered mountains from their homes. One is Popocatépetl, which means "Smoking Mountain." The other is Ixtacihuatl, which means "White Woman."

### Active Volcanoes in Mexico

| Volcano | Last Eruption Date | Height of Volcano |
|---|---|---|
| Pico de Orizaba | 1687 | 18,700 |
| Popocatépetl | 1999 | 17,930 |
| Colima | 1999 | 12,361 |
| El Chichon | 1982 | 7,300 |

**CHART STUDY**

This chart shows active volcanoes in Mexico. An active volcano may erupt, or overflow with lava, at any time. What is the highest active volcano? Which two volcanoes erupted in 1999? Which one erupted in 1982?

## What Are Some Famous Coast Resorts in Mexico?

Mexico has a long coastline with some of the world's most beautiful beaches. The government has developed some beaches into resorts. On the eastern coast, the government created Cancun out of a part of the Yucatán Peninsula. Acapulco, Puerto Vallarta, and Mazatlan lie on the western, or Pacific, coast. Each of these cities has a beautiful beach.

## What Are the Major Bodies of Water in Mexico?

Mexico is mountainous, and many parts of it have little rain. Because of this, no major river systems cross Mexico. Most of its rivers are short. They drop quickly from the high mountains to the coast. Sometimes they drain into large lakes.

The largest lakes in Mexico are Lake Chapala in the state of Jalisco and Lake Pátzcuaro in Michoacan. The Río Bravo del Norte forms part of the border between Mexico and the United States. People in the U.S. call this river the Río Grande. It is so shallow that people can walk across it in some spots.

## What Is the Climate Like in Mexico?

Much of Mexico has a steppe climate. This is the dry climate usually found near deserts. The Mexican deserts have a little more rain than many deserts in other parts of the world. Still, some parts of these deserts receive little rain because of the high mountains that stand beside them.

The steppe can get both very hot and very cold. Juarez, on Mexico's northern border, provides an example of this. The temperatures in this city can be below 32° F in the winter and above 90° F in the summer.

Some of Mexico's coastal areas have a **tropical savanna climate.** They are hot all year around. These coastal areas receive a lot of rain but have a drier season during the winter. Common savanna plants include tall grasses with a few trees.

**The Catavinea Desert is in Baja Mexico.**

**Altitude**
*The height of something above sea level*

**Tierra caliente**
*An area of land in a low altitude with a hot average temperature*

**Tierra fría**
*An area of land in a high altitude with a cold average temperature*

**Tierra templada**
*An area of land that is neither too hot nor too cold*

## How Do Mountains Affect Mexico's Climate?

Without mountains, Mexico would be hot most of the time. Temperatures usually get hotter the closer a place is to the equator. However, **altitude,** the height a place is above sea level, affects climate. A high altitude brings with it cooler temperatures. Usually, rainfall also increases at high altitudes. Because mountains cover Mexico, its climate can be both hot and cold.

## What Are Mexico's Three Altitudinal Zones?

The European country of Spain ruled Mexico for 300 years. The Spanish recognized how the mountains influenced Mexico's climate. They picked out three altitudinal zones to show this. Geographers still use the Spanish names for these three zones. They call the hot areas at lower altitudes **tierra caliente.**

Higher altitudes of about 3,000 to 6,000 feet are **tierra templada.** These areas are neither too hot nor too cold. Much of the Central Plateau, where most of Mexico's people live, is tierra templada. Mexico City's average temperature in January is 54° F. Its average temperature in July is 64° F.

Mexico's higher altitudes of over 8,000 feet is **tierra fría,** or cold lands. Temperatures are colder there and frost may form. Few people live above 10,000 feet.

**Section 2 Review** On a separate sheet of paper, write answers to the following questions.

1) What is the main physical feature of Mexico?

2) Why does Mexico not have a river system that crosses the country?

3) What climate does much of Mexico have?

4) Generally, what happens to rainfall the higher up a place is from sea level?

5) Generally, what happens to temperatures at higher altitudes?

**What do YOU think?**

If you were living in Mexico, why would you probably prefer to live in tierra templada?

**Empire**
*A nation that rules a large area of land*

**Descendant**
*A person who is related to a certain group of people*

**Isolated**
*Separated from other areas or people*

**Mestizo**
*A person of mixed native and European ancestry*

## What Cultures Does Mexico Have?

Before Europeans came to Mexico, many native groups lived there. Some groups were small. They lived in villages and farmed the land. Others developed large **empires.** An empire is a nation that rules a large area of land. The Mayas built a great empire in Yucatán and Guatemala. The Toltecs and Aztecs formed empires in the Valley of Mexico.

At one time, millions of native people lived in Mexico. Then the Europeans brought diseases, such as measles and smallpox. These killed many native people. Perhaps 90 percent of them died by the end of the 1500s. **Descendants,** people related to a certain group, still make up about 10 percent of Mexico's population.

Many towns in Mexico are rural. Some are **isolated,** or separated from other areas. Native people there have kept much of their culture, such as religious beliefs and languages.

## Who Are the Mestizos?

In 1519, a Spaniard named Hernando Cortés sailed to Mexico. There he met the Aztecs, the native people of the area. Cortés also met some smaller native groups. Because Aztec rule made these smaller groups unhappy, they helped Cortés defeat the Aztecs.

Soon more Spaniards arrived in Mexico. Some married native women. Historians call their descendants **mestizos.** They are people of mixed native and European ancestry. About 75 percent of the Mexican people are mestizos. The culture of the mestizos is a blend of native and European people. However, their beliefs and values are often more European than native. Great differences exist among them. Some mestizos are wealthy landowners. Others are poor.

About 15 percent of the Mexican people are neither native people nor mestizos. This 15 percent is made up of immigrants. Most of them came from countries in Central America. Some came to Mexico to escape political troubles.

Words written by Octavio Paz begin Unit 2 of this book. Throughout the world, people read his poetry. The culture of the native people of Mexico, especially the Aztecs, influenced his poetry. In fact, an enormous stone Aztec calendar inspired him to write his most famous poem, "The Stone." In 1990, Paz won the Nobel Prize for literature. He was the first Mexican author to receive this prize. From 1962 to 1968, Paz served as Mexico's ambassador to India. In 1968, Paz gave up that post because he wanted to protest Mexico's treatment of rebellious students back home.

Others came because they hoped to find better jobs there. People from Japan, Canada, Spain, and the United States also live in Mexico. Most of them are business people who work for Mexico's trading partners.

## What Languages Do the Mexican People Speak?

Because Spain ruled Mexico for many years, Spanish is its official language. The government, businesses, and schools use Spanish. Many native people, however, speak their native languages. A visitor to Mexico may hear as many as 50 native languages being spoken!

Over a million native people speak only their native languages. They do not know Spanish. They have given the world words such as *tortilla* and *tamale*. These words come from Nahuatl, the language of the Aztec people.

## What Is the Main Religion in Mexico?

The Spanish brought both their language and their religion to Mexico. More than 90 percent of its people are Roman Catholic. Some of the poor, however, have turned away from Catholicism and become Protestant Christians. They have done this because the Roman Catholic Church sometimes sides with the small group of wealthy landowners. In some rural areas, up to one-third of the population is Protestant. Most of them are poor native people.

## What Are the Population Trends in Mexico?

In the last 100 years, Mexico's population has exploded. In 1900, Mexico had about 13 million people. Today its population is close to 100 million! Nearly one-third of this number is under 15 years of age. That is an important fact. The more people under 15, the more likely the population will continue to grow.

The big increase in Mexico's population has caused problems. For example, unemployment is high. Also, the government does not have enough money for schools and medical care for all its people. To slow the rate of population growth, the government teaches people about family planning. However, the Catholic Church is against this.

## Where Do Most Mexicans Live?

In 1900, most Mexicans lived in small farming villages. Today, over two-thirds of Mexico's people live in urban areas. People have moved from villages to cities, since farming in parts of Mexico is hard. Many **campesinos,** or poor farmers, thought they could find a better and easier life in the cities. This **migration** of people from rural areas to cities is a big trend all over the world.

Mexico City is one of the biggest cities in the world. Some 22 or 23 million people live in its metropolitan area. That is more than one out of every five Mexicans! The Mexican people built this city on the ruins of the old Aztec capital of Tenochtitlán.

Mexico's capital is a city of differences. For example, it has beautiful tree-lined streets and tall buildings. It also has some of the worst **slums** in the world. These are poor, overcrowded areas. Mexico City has fine places to shop. It also has noisy city markets. A visitor to Mexico City may see people traveling on horseback. That same visitor might also experience horrible traffic jams. These are far worse than in U.S. cities.

Guadalajara is Mexico's second largest city. Like Mexico City, it is located on the Central Plateau. It is an important

## Geography In Your Life

**FINE ARTS**

### Diego Rivera's Fresco Murals in Mexico

Fresco painting was popular in the 1400s and 1500s. Then, in the 1920s, Diego Rivera made frescoes popular again in Mexico. Creating frescoes is hard work. A painter first draws a picture. Then a worker applies damp plaster to a wall. Next, the artist places the picture against the plaster and draws around it. Finally, the painter mixes dry pigments with water and applies them to the wet plaster.

Rivera was born in Guanajuato, Mexico, in 1886. He studied art in Paris. Returning to Mexico City in 1921, Rivera began to create large fresco murals on the walls of public buildings, such as the National Palace. In these murals, the artist showed the history of his people. He also showed the problems they faced. His fresco murals, done in rich earth colors, show farmers, workers, costumes, and the famous people of Mexico's history.

and growing industrial center. Monterrey is the largest city in northern Mexico. Its workers produce most of Mexico's steel and iron.

Tampico and Vera Cruz are Mexico's two biggest ports. Both sit on the Gulf side of Mexico. Vera Cruz is a major rail center. Trains from there carry products to and from southern Mexico. Acapulco, on the Pacific coast, is also an important port.

**Section 3 Review** On a separate sheet of paper, write *True* if the statement is true or *False* if the statement is not true. Make each false statement true by changing the underlined word.

1) <u>Native people</u> make up the largest percentage of the Mexican people.

2) <u>Mestizos</u> are people of mixed native and European ancestry.

3) <u>Spanish</u> is the official language of Mexico.

4) Over two-thirds of the Mexican people live in <u>rural</u> areas.

5) <u>Acapulco</u> is an important rail center that links southern Mexico and the Central Plateau.

**What do YOU think?**

To reduce air pollution in Mexico City, the government has told car owners that they cannot drive one day a week. Do you think this is an effective way to reduce pollution? Why or why not?

**Land reform**
*The taking of land from the wealthy and giving it to the poor people who have worked on it*

**Offshore**
*In water rather than on land*

**Revolution**
*The overthrowing of a government*

**Technology**
*The use of science and machines to improve ways of doing things*

## How Important Is Oil to Mexico?

Mexico is rich in natural resources. Its most important is oil. Workers first discovered oil on the coast of the Gulf of Mexico in 1901. Mexico soon became a leading oil exporter.

In the 1970s, workers discovered large new oil and natural gas fields. Most of these are located **offshore**. They are in water rather than on land. Mexico's economy has grown to depend greatly on oil. Mexico supplies gas and oil for itself and exports the rest. Its best customer is the United States.

## What Are Mexico's Other Natural Resources?

Besides oil and natural gas, Mexico has many other mineral resources. Workers mine uranium, mercury, iron ore, coal, zinc, copper, lead, and silver. Mexico is the world's leading producer of silver. The most important mining regions lie in the Central Plateau and the Sierra Madre Occidental. Mexico also has large forest resources.

## How Did Land Reform Change Mexico?

People can farm only about 12 percent of Mexico's total land. Nevertheless, more than one-fourth of its people farm. At one time, a few rich landowners owned almost all the land. However, this changed in 1910 when Mexico had a **revolution**. A revolution is the overthrowing of a government.

One important result of the revolution was **land reform.** The government took land from the wealthy and gave it to poor farmers. New **technology,** better seeds, irrigation, and training have now increased crop growth. For example, irrigation in northern Mexico has made it an important cotton-growing region. As a result, Mexico produces enough cotton for its own needs and to sell.

However, land reform and technology have created a problem for Mexico. Machines have decreased the need for workers. Many workers have left the country to find work in the city. This is true for many countries around the world.

**Writing About Geography**

Why do you think the economy of Mexico is so important to the United States? Write a paragraph about this. Include details from this section to support your opinion.

Shops like these are common in many parts of Mexico. They are important to Mexico's economy.

## What Are Some Manufacturing Industries in Mexico?

The Mexican government hopes the extra farmers will find manufacturing jobs. It adds more to Mexico's economy than farming. The largest industry is metal products, which employs the most workers. Other important industrial products are cars, textiles, chemicals, food products, electrical goods, glass, and paper.

## How Do Foreign-Owned Assembly Plants Help Mexico?

A growing part of the Mexican economy is the **maquiladoras**. Most of these foreign-owned assembly plants are located near the border between Mexico and the United States. In these plants, Mexican workers assemble products. Companies in the U.S. sell the products using their own brand names.

The main maquiladoras make cars, electrical goods, furniture, and chemicals. Big car producers operate maquiladoras in Mexico. These companies have their headquarters in the United States. However, they build plants in Mexico because manufacturing is cheaper there than in the U.S. The maquiladoras help U.S. companies and provide jobs for Mexican workers.

## What Is Mexico's Biggest Service Industry?

Service industries are a big part of Mexico's economy. The biggest service industries are tourism, banking, and insurance. Tourists come to Mexico for its sunshine, beautiful beaches, and scenery. They also visit the remains of Mexico's ancient cultures.

## What Is NAFTA?

Mexico, the United States, and Canada signed the **North American Free Trade Agreement (NAFTA).** It took effect in 1994. It created one large **free-trade** area in North America. This means that the three countries got rid of

**trade barriers.** A barrier divides one thing from another. Trade barriers divide countries because they limit imports or put special taxes on them.

Now products from the three members of NAFTA cross international borders as easily as they cross state borders. Mexico already does more than two-thirds of its trade with the U.S. It hopes that NAFTA will increase that trade even more. It also hopes that more U.S. businesses will invest their money in Mexico. This would lead to more jobs and a higher standard of living for more of Mexico's people.

## How Does Poverty Challenge Mexico?

Mexico faces several important challenges today. One is the growing gap between wealthy and poor people. At least 40 percent of Mexico's population today lives in poverty. New reforms like NAFTA have helped some people become richer. However, rural areas, especially in the south, lag far behind. Millions of **peasants,** Mexico's small farmers and farmworkers, remain poor. The poorest people in Mexico are its native people.

In 1994, a group of native peasants rebelled against the government. They raised an army in the southern state of Chiapas and called themselves **Zapatistas.** The peasants demanded that the government help the poor and end NAFTA.

To feed their families, some poor Mexican people have turned to crime. The drug trade has become a big business. The U.S. and the Mexican governments have tried to stop the flow of drugs. This is not easy. These **illegal** drugs (those that are against the law) provide some poor people with their only income.

**Foreign debt** is the money a country owes to other governments. In the 1970s and 1980s, Mexico borrowed huge sums of money to pay for industrial development. Soon Mexico owed about $100 billion. Because of this, the government cut back on imports, medical care, education, and care for the aged.

# What Environmental Problems Does Mexico Face?

Air pollution is serious in Mexico City. It may cause up to 100,000 deaths a year. Water pollution is another problem. Millions of tons of untreated human waste flow into rivers each year. Industry and agriculture poison Mexico's rivers with chemicals. Garbage is a also a problem. Mexico City produces 11,000 tons of garbage every day, but only about 75 percent of it is collected! Deforestation and soil erosion are also big problems.

**Section 4 Review** Choose the letter of the answer that correctly completes each sentence. Write your answers on a separate sheet of paper.

1) Mexico's most important natural resource is _____.
   - a. coal
   - b. uranium
   - c. oil
   - d. copper

2) Mexico is the world's leading producer of _____.
   - a. silver
   - b. mercury
   - c. gold
   - d. oil

3) _____ refers to a government taking land from large landowners and giving it to those who worked on it.
   - a. Maquiladora
   - b. Peasant
   - c. Land reform
   - d. Zapatista

4) _____ is the free-trade agreement that took effect in 1994 among Mexico, Canada, and the United States.
   - a. NATO
   - b. NAFTA
   - c. NFL
   - d. ASF

5) In 1994, some poor native people in Mexico rebelled against the government in the state of _____.
   - a. Jalisco
   - b. Durango
   - c. Michoacán
   - d. Chiapas

**What do YOU think?** Why might you choose to visit Mexico?

*Spotlight Story*

# Chocolate: The Drink of the Gods!

Chocolate is made from cacao beans. A tree bears these beans. The tree's Latin name is *Theobroma cacao*. Theobroma means "drink of the gods."

When Cortés arrived in Mexico in 1519, he met Montezuma, the king of the Aztecs. Montezuma was drinking a cacao drink from a gold cup. The Aztecs used the cacao beans as money. Drinking a cacao drink showed Montezuma's wealth.

**These workers are drying cacao beans on a plantation in Tabasco, Mexico.**

Cortés tried the drink, but it seemed bitter to him. Nevertheless, he decided to take some cacao seeds back to Spain. He thought Spaniards could grow cacao trees. Then they would have beans with which to trade with the Aztecs.

People in Spain experimented with Montezuma's recipe. They added hot water and sugar to the ground-up beans and created a hot chocolate drink. People still drink it today. As the years passed, people began pressing the beans and removing a fat called cacao butter. Then they added sugar, heated the mixture, and cooled it. In 1828, someone used this recipe to create the first chocolate bar.

Today, farmers grow cacao trees on plantations in Mexico, Central America, the Caribbean Islands, and West Africa. Chocolate is no longer just for kings. People around the world enjoy it.

## Spotlight Story Wrap-Up

1) What does the Latin word for the cacao tree mean?

2) How did the Aztecs use cacao beans?

3) What did Spaniards add to Montezuma's drink to make it taste better?

4) In what year did people begin buying chocolate bars?

5) In what places do farmers grow cacao trees today?

◆ Mexico has four physical regions: the Central Plateau, the coastal plains, the desert, and the Yucatán Peninsula.

◆ Mexico's main physical feature is its mountains, the Sierra Madre. Because of them, it has no major river system. Mexico's long coastline features some of the world's most beautiful beaches.

◆ Much of Mexico has a steppe climate, which is the dry climate found near deserts. Some coastal areas have a tropical savanna climate.

◆ Before the arrival of Europeans, Mexico had many native groups, such as the Maya, Toltecs, and Aztecs. Descendants of these native people make up 10 percent of Mexico's population. Spanish conquerors married many native women. Their descendants, the mestizos, make up about 75 percent of the Mexican people. Immigrants from Central America and other countries make up the final 15 percent of the population.

◆ Roman Catholicism is Mexico's main religion. However, in Mexico's rural areas, up to one-third of the people are now Protestant Christians.

◆ Mexico's official language is Spanish.

◆ Over two-thirds of Mexico's people live in urban areas. Mexico City is one of the biggest cities in the world.

◆ Mexico's main natural resource is oil. Workers also mine uranium, mercury, iron ore, coal, zinc, copper, and lead. Mexico is the world's leading producer of silver.

◆ Because of land reform after the 1910 revolution, more than one-fourth of Mexico's population farms. However, manufacturing adds more to the national economy than farming. The largest industry in Mexico is metal products. Other important industrial products are textiles, chemicals, food products, electrical goods, glass, and paper. Some big car producers from other countries operate maquiladoras, or assembly plants, in Mexico. The biggest service industry is tourism.

◆ Because of the North American Free Trade Agreement (NAFTA), Mexico now conducts more than two-thirds of its trade with the U.S.

◆ Mexico faces several problems: the gap between the poor and the wealthy; the drug trade; rebellion by some native people; and the environment challenges of air and water pollution, deforestation, soil erosion, and garbage.

## Comprehension: Identifying Facts

On a separate sheet of paper, write the words from the Word Bank to complete each sentence.

**WORD BANK**

irrigation

mestizos

mountains

plateau

Spanish

**1)** A _____, such as the one that covers much of Mexico, is an area of level highland.

**2)** In areas that do not receive enough rainfall, farmers often use _____.

**3)** Mexico's main physical feature is its _____.

**4)** The largest percentage of the Mexican people are the _____.

**5)** The official language of Mexico is _____.

## Comprehension: Multiple Choice

On a separate sheet of paper, write the letter of the answer that correctly completes each sentence.

**1)** The largest physical region of Mexico is the _____.

  a. Yucatán Peninsula   c. Sonoran Desert

  b. Central Plateau     d. coastal plains

**2)** The steppe climate is usually found near _____.

  a. deserts          c. lakes

  b. mountains      d. oceans

**3)** Some native people living in Mexico have been able to keep their own culture because they live in _____.

  a. Mexico City     c. urban areas

  b. the Sierra Madre   d. isolated rural communities

**4)** About _____ of Mexico's people live in urban areas.

  a. one-quarter     c. one-third

  b. two-thirds      d. one-half

5) _____ are foreign-owned assembly plants built close to the border between Mexico and the United States.

   a. Maquiladoras      c. Campesinos

   b. Zapatistas        d. Mestizos

## Comprehension: Understanding Main Ideas

On a separate sheet of paper, write the answer to each question. Use complete sentences.

1) What are three of the industries on which Mexico's economy depends?

2) What are some environmental problems that face Mexico today?

3) What are two ways in which Spain's long rule influenced Mexican culture?

## Critical Thinking: Write Your Opinion

On a separate sheet of paper, write your opinion to each question. Use complete sentences.

1) Should the U.S. make it easier for Mexican workers to come to the United States? Why or why not?

2) What is the connection between rapid population growth and poverty?

## Applying the Five Themes of Geography

### *Movement*

Give at least two examples of the theme of movement as it applies to Mexico and the U.S.

**Test-Taking Tip**

When a teacher announces a test, listen carefully. Write down the topics that the teacher will include on the test. Write down the items that the teacher says to review. Ask any questions you have about what the test will include.

# Central America and the Caribbean

**M**any small countries make up Central America and the Caribbean. Much of this area is remote and isolated. The picture of a beach in the Dominican Republic on this page is an example of this. Much of the land is tropical, so tourism is important. As you will learn in this chapter, the United States is also very important to these countries.

## Goals for Learning

▶ To describe where Central America and the Caribbean are located

▶ To identify the most important physical features and climate of Central America and the Caribbean

▶ To describe the cultures of Central America and the Caribbean

▶ To explain where and how most people of the area live

▶ To describe the economy of the countries of Central America and the Caribbean and the environmental challenges they face

## Geo-Stats

### Key Nations of Central America and the Caribbean

**Nation:** Cuba
**Population:** 11,178,000
**Area** (in square miles): 42,804
**Major Cities:** Havana (capital), Santiago de Cuba, Camagüey, Guantánamo

**Nation:** Honduras
**Population:** 5,901,000
**Area** (in square miles): 43,277
**Major Cities:** Tegucigalpa (capital), San Pedro Sula, La Ceiba, El Progreso

**Nation:** Haiti
**Population:** 7,751,000
**Area** (in square miles): 10,714
**Major Cities:** Port-au-Prince (capital), Hinche, Saint-Marc, Léogane

**Nation:** Panama
**Population:** 2,809,000
**Area** (in square miles): 29,157
**Major Cities:** Panama City (capital), Colón, David, Penonomé, Santiago

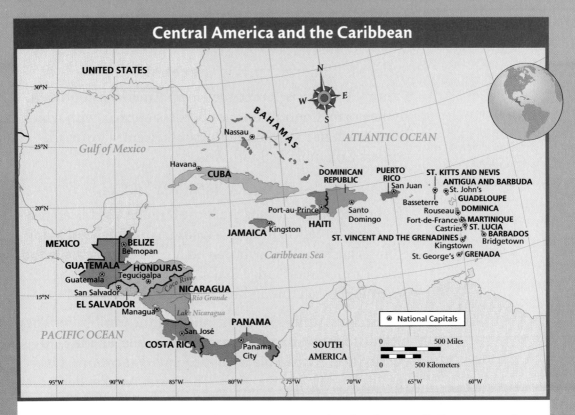

# Central America and the Caribbean

UNITED STATES

30°N

Gulf of Mexico

25°N

BAHAMAS

Nassau

ATLANTIC OCEAN

Havana

CUBA

20°N

Port-au-Prince

JAMAICA  Kingston

HAITI

DOMINICAN
REPUBLIC

Santo
Domingo

PUERTO
RICO

San Juan

ST. KITTS AND NEVIS

ANTIGUA AND BARBUDA

St. John's

GUADELOUPE

Basseterre

Rouseau  DOMINICA

Fort-de-France  MARTINIQUE

Castries  ST. LUCIA

ST. VINCENT AND THE GRENADINES

BARBADOS
Bridgetown

Kingstown

MEXICO

BELIZE

Belmopan

GUATEMALA  HONDURAS

Guatemala  Tegucigalpa

San Salvador

EL SALVADOR

Managua

Coco River

NICARAGUA

Rio Grande

Lake Nicaragua

PACIFIC OCEAN

San José

COSTA RICA

Panama
City

PANAMA

Caribbean Sea

St. George's  GRENADA

SOUTH
AMERICA

15°N

⊛ National Capitals

0          500 Miles

0     500 Kilometers

95°W    90°W    85°W    80°W    75°W    70°W    65°W    60°W

*Map Skills*

This map shows the two areas that this chapter will discuss: Central America and the Caribbean. Central America, a region that is south of Mexico and north of South America, includes seven countries. The Caribbean is a group of islands in the Caribbean Sea. The largest island is Cuba, which lies just off of the southern tip of Florida in the United States.

Study the map and answer the following questions:

**1)** Which oceans and seas touch Central America?

**2)** What lake can be found in Central America?

**3)** What is the capital of Honduras? Nicaragua? Haiti? Cuba?

**4)** What island is directly south of Cuba?

**5)** Which nation in Central America is the farthest south? the farthest north?

Archipelago
*A group of islands*

Mainland
*A continent or part of a continent that is not an island*

## Where Is Central America Located?

Central America is part of the North American continent. In the north, Central America borders Mexico, with which it has much in common. In the south, Central America borders Colombia in South America.

## Where Are the Caribbean Islands Located?

All the Caribbean islands are located in the Caribbean Sea. Geographers call a group of islands an **archipelago.** Many of the islands in the Caribbean archipelago are actually the tops of a mountain range that sit on the bottom of the sea. Geographers call this archipelago the Antilles.

The Greater Antilles lie to the north of the Caribbean. They include four big islands: Jamaica, Cuba, Hispaniola, and Puerto Rico. Hispaniola is divided into two nations: Haiti and the Dominican Republic. The Lesser Antilles lie farther south. They form the eastern boundary of the Caribbean Sea. Geographers often call the Greater and Lesser Antilles the West Indies.

A third island group is the Bahamas. They lie farther north than the rest of the Caribbean islands. The entire area, except for the Bahamas, lies in the Tropics, the area between the Tropic of Cancer and the Tropic of Capricorn. As you know, the Tropic of Cancer lies north of the equator. The Tropic of Capricorn lies south of it.

## What Two Subregions Exist?

Geographers usually divide Central America and the Caribbean into two subregions. The first is the **mainland.** A mainland is a continent or part of a continent that is not an island. The mainland of Central America includes its seven countries. They are Guatemala, Belize, Honduras, El Salvador, Nicaragua, Costa Rica, and Panama.

**Many people in Central America live in small villages. This is a village in the Central American nation of Belize.**

**Hacienda**
*A large, self-sufficient farm in a Spanish-speaking country*

**Rimland**
*The land, often islands and coastal plains, around the edge of an area*

Geographers call the second subregion the **rimland.** The rim of something is its edge. A rimland is the land, often islands and coastal plains, around the edge of an area. The islands and the coastal plains of Central America are its rimland.

Important geographical and cultural differences exist between the two subregions. Most mainland people are mestizos. Like most Mexicans, they are of mixed Spanish and native ancestry. People of the mainland live mostly in the highlands rather than on the coast.

Most rimland people are of Spanish and African ancestry. Until recently, European countries ruled many of the Caribbean islands. On some, the way people live and the language they speak show this European influence.

## How Did Geography Shape This Area's History?

Spanish soldiers conquered Central America and the Caribbean hundreds of years ago. On the mainland, they divided the land into large farms called **haciendas.** These farms often had much land. Spanish landlords owned the land. The native people and mestizos did most of the work to make money for the landlords.

**Cash crop**
*A crop raised to be sold by those who grow it*

**Plantation**
*A large farm on which the owner grows only one crop*

**Self-sufficient**
*Able to take care of one's needs without help from someone else*

Haciendas were often almost **self-sufficient.** This means that the people living and working there took care of most of their needs without outside help. The haciendas could be self-sufficient because they grew many different types of crops. They grew their own food, made their own clothing, and made their own tools.

The Spanish took the best land for their haciendas. The people who did not work for the Spanish had only poor land to farm. This pattern continues today. Foreigners own the best land, while most of the people remain poor and landless.

On the islands, the Spanish introduced a different use of land. They divided it into large **plantations.** One important difference existed between these large farms and the haciendas on the mainland. The plantations grew only one crop; the haciendas grew many. Many plantations grew only sugarcane or bananas. Instead of eating or using these crops, the plantation owners sold them. For this reason, these crops are called **cash crops.**

**Section 1 Review** On a separate sheet of paper, write *True* if the statement is true or *False* if the statement is not true. Make each false statement true by changing the underlined word.

1) Cuba is part of the <u>Lesser</u> Antilles.
2) <u>The Bahamas</u> is the only country in this area that is not located in the Tropics.
3) The countries of Central America are part of the <u>rimland</u> subregion.
4) <u>Haciendas</u> are large, self-sufficient farms.
5) <u>Plantations</u> are large farms that usually grow only one crop.

**What do YOU think?** Why do foreigners continue to own the best land in Central America and the Caribbean?

Atoll
*A chain of islands made up of coral*

Coral
*A tiny sea animal*

Dormant
*The state a volcano is in when it is not likely to erupt*

Geothermal
*Heat from the interior of the earth*

## What Are the Mainland's Physical Features?

Like Mexico, the mainland area of Central America has high mountains. Some rise more than 13,000 feet. Many are active volcanoes. Some, however, are **dormant,** or not likely to erupt.

The mountains give way to lowlands along the coasts. These coastal lowlands differ from one another. On the eastern side of Central America, thick rain forests cover the land. The heavy rainfall washes away good minerals from the soil. Without these minerals, the soil is not good for farming. Because the Pacific coastal lowlands receive less rain, its soil is rich. Farmers there grow many different crops.

## How Did Volcanoes Make Islands on the Rimland?

Most islands in the Caribbean are actually the mountain tops of dormant volcanoes. This is especially true of the Greater Antilles. The highest point of each volcanic island is generally near its center. At the water's edge, the land often flattens into a small, coastal plain.

Some islands in the Caribbean are still active volcanoes. The lava from them can both harm and help people. It harms by destroying life and property. It helps because it sometimes holds important minerals. When lava breaks down, it forms good soil for farming. Also, volcanoes are hot. People can use their heat to make electricity. This is called **geothermal** power. Costa Rica is a Central American country that uses geothermal power.

## How Does Coral Make Islands?

Some islands in the Caribbean are not volcanic. Geographers call these low, nonvolcanic islands **atolls.** Tiny sea animals called **corals** created these islands. As the corals die, their remains slowly build up a coral reef. These atolls are usually just a few feet above sea level. The soil is thin and not good for growing crops. Most people who live on atolls earn their living by fishing.

## What Are the Mainland's Major Bodies of Water?

Most of the rivers in Central America are short and not **navigable.** This means that larger ships cannot travel up or down them. The mainland has only a few lakes. The most important one is Lake Nicaragua. Central America has one extremely important human-made waterway. It is the Panama Canal, which connects the Atlantic Ocean with the Pacific Ocean. It makes it possible for ships to travel through Central America rather than around South America.

## What Is the Climate Like?

The mountain areas of Central America have a highland climate. As in Mexico, the area between 3,000 and 6,000 feet, the tierra templada, has a climate that is neither too hot nor too cold. Most of the people live in this climate zone. The climate higher up in the mountains is generally too cold for farming most crops.

*Geography In Your Life*
TECHNOLOGY

### The Building of the Panama Canal

For many years, the United States dreamed of a faster way to sail from its East Coast to its West Coast. At that time, ships had to sail around the tip of South America. The journey was long and dangerous. This would change if the U.S. built a canal in Central America.

**The Panama Canal allows ships to travel through Central America rather than around South America.**

In 1903, the United States paid Panama $10 million, plus yearly rent, for a ten-mile wide strip of land. The U.S. chose Panama because it was the most narrow country in Central America. In 1906, workers began to build a 51-mile-long canal there. They worked for eight years and completed it in 1914. Today the waterway saves time and money. A ship traveling from New York City to San Francisco can save 7,800 miles by using the canal.

From 1914 to 1977, the United States owned the Panama Canal. Between 1977 and 2000, the U.S. and Panama owned it together. Now Panama owns and runs it alone. A 1979 treaty promises that the canal will be neutral during a war.

The Caribbean lowlands have a tropical climate. Most of the time, the weather is hot and damp. Some inland areas, like parts of Guatemala and Costa Rica, have tropical rain forests. It rains almost daily. The Pacific lowlands have a tropical savanna climate. There it is warm and sunny much of the time.

Most Caribbean islands also have tropical savanna climates. Soft winds keep the heat from becoming too uncomfortable. Rain falls often, but usually not for long. However, during the **hurricane** season, this changes. These tropical storms bring heavy rainfall, strong winds, and huge waves. The hurricanes are worst during August and September. When a hurricane hits, it usually leaves behind millions of dollars of damage.

## How Does the Physical Environment Affect the People?

As in Mexico, most people in Central America choose to live in highland areas. The climate in these areas is milder than on the coasts. Farmers have cleared much of the coastal lowlands to plant cash crops like bananas and sugarcane. The almost constant sunshine and warmth attract millions of tourists from around the world.

**Section 2 Review** On a separate sheet of paper, write answers to these questions.

1) What is the main physical feature of the Central American mainland?

2) What are two ways that the Caribbean islands were formed?

3) What is geothermal power?

4) In what climate zone do most people in this area live?

5) What are hurricanes?

---

**What do YOU think?** In the year 2000, the U.S. gave Panama total control of the Panama Canal. Do you think this was a wise decision? Why or why not?

---

**Mulatto**
*A person whose ancestors were African and European*

**Slave**
*A person who is held against his or her will and forced to work for free*

## What Cultures Exist in Central America?

Central America and the Caribbean have many cultures. As in Mexico, the native people have lived in the area the longest. Most of them are poor farmers. Their numbers are largest in Guatemala. There, about half the population is native people.

Spain influenced Central American culture more than any other European country. Shortly after the Spanish came to Mexico, they traveled south into Central America. As in Mexico, Spanish soldiers often married native women. As a result, many of the people in Central America are mestizos. In some countries such as Honduras, about 90 percent of the people are mestizos. In still other countries such as Costa Rica, almost all the people are of European background.

The Spanish did not conquer all of Central America. Great Britain set up colonies in some parts of it. Belize, on the Caribbean coast of the Yucatán Peninsula, was a British colony. It has a large population descended from Africans. Some of them married Europeans. Geographers call their descendents **mulattos.**

## What Cultures Exist in the Caribbean?

Most people living on the Caribbean islands are descended from Africans. Europeans brought millions of Africans to the islands to work as **slaves** on sugarcane plantations. Some African slaves had children with Europeans, so the mulatto population on the islands is high.

Great Britain used to rule some of the Caribbean islands. Britain also ruled India. Many East Indians, which is the name given to people from India, came to the Caribbean. They settled on islands such as Trinidad.

## What Are Some Signs of the Cultural Blend in This Area?

Many people migrated from the Caribbean islands to the mainland of Central America to work. The resulting

**Creole**
*A mixture of French and African languages*

**Voodoo**
*A belief that good and evil spirits influence a person's daily life*

culture brought together many languages. For example, in some places the language blends African languages with European ones. Music in the Caribbean blends Spanish and African music. Reggae music first developed in Jamaica.

## What Religions Do the People Practice?

Usually, a place with many cultures also has many religions. Most people of Central America and the Caribbean are Christians. However, many of the native people practice their own religions. Some people of African descent believe in **voodoo.** Followers of voodoo believe that good and evil spirits affect daily life. Voodoo is strongest in Haiti.

## What Languages Do the People Speak?

A place with many cultures also has many languages. Many of the native people speak only their native languages. However, Spain once ruled most of Central America. Because of this, Spanish is the language spoken most often.

On the Caribbean islands, tourists often hear the language of the Europeans who once ruled there. For example, the British ruled Jamaica and the Bahamas, so the people there speak English. The people of Haiti, Guadeloupe, and Martinique speak mostly French. In many places the language blends two or more languages. For example, Haitians speak a language called **creole.** It mixes the French language with African languages.

---

**Biography**   FIDEL CASTRO: 1926–

In 1953, a leader named Fulgencio Batista ruled Cuba. Fidel Castro, who was a lawyer at the time, opposed this strong and harsh ruler. For six years, Castro and his followers fought against Batista's army. On January 1, 1959, Castro won. The Cubans rejoiced! Castro then took land from the wealthy and gave it to the poor. He took away businesses from people who had come to Cuba from other countries. Cubans began to run these businesses. In 1961, Castro made Cuba a Communist country. Today he is Cuba's president.

---

**Population density**
*The average number of people living in each square mile of an area*

## Where Do Most People of This Area Live?

Most people of Central America and the Caribbean live in rural areas. Geographers use the term **population density** to describe the average number of people living in each square mile of an area. The only country in Central America with a high population density is El Salvador. The entire Central American and Caribbean area has only two cities with more than a million people. They are Guatemala City in Guatemala and San Salvador in El Salvador.

## What Problems Does This Area Face?

Central America faces many problems. Great differences exist between the rich and the poor. In most countries, a small group of rich people controls most of the wealth. However, most people are poor. Many rich people look down on native people.

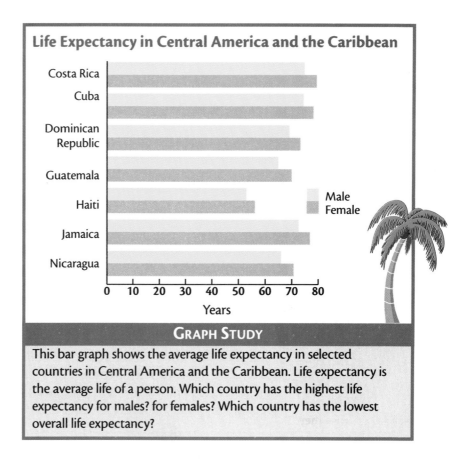

### Life Expectancy in Central America and the Caribbean

Male
Female

Years

#### GRAPH STUDY

This bar graph shows the average life expectancy in selected countries in Central America and the Caribbean. Life expectancy is the average life of a person. Which country has the highest life expectancy for males? for females? Which country has the lowest overall life expectancy?

In some countries, this unequal treatment of the poor has led to fighting. El Salvador experienced a bitter **civil war** throughout most of the 1980s. A civil war is a war fought by people within a single country or state against each other. Because of this war, as many as 20 percent of the people left their homeland and moved to the United States.

For over 30 years, Guatemala fought its own civil war. It ended in 1993. Nicaragua had a revolution in 1979 and set up a government based on **communism.** Communism is a government in which there is no private property. The government controls and owns the land and goods. The United States was against this new government.

In 1987, Oscar Arias Sánchez, the president of Costa Rica, offered a plan. The leaders of Costa Rica, El Salvador, Guatemala, Honduras, and Nicaragua signed it, and ended the fighting. This earned Arias the Nobel Peace Prize, one of the world's highest honors.

Another problem is industry. Many countries in Central America and the Caribbean grow the same crops. People tend to compete rather than cooperate. To live better, the countries must develop new industries. Recently, countries like the United States have built manufacturing plants in the area. These companies pay the workers less than they

**Many people try to leave some Caribbean countries in search of a better life in the U.S. These people are often called "boat people" because they travel by boat.**

Birthrate
*The number of births over a given period of time*

pay workers in the U.S. However, workers still earn more than they did before. The rising **birthrate** and population growth are also problems. The more people, the greater the effect on natural resources. Already much of the rain forests have been destroyed to make farmland.

Some say that the biggest challenge for Central America and the Caribbean is how to get along with the United States. The U.S. has great power over the area. Its government has often sent soldiers to Cuba, Haiti, and Nicaragua. Relations with Cuba have been especially bad, because the U.S. does not get along with the Cuban government.

The U.S. controls Puerto Rico. Puerto Ricans are U.S. citizens. Many live well, but many are poor. Puerto Ricans will have to decide whether to remain U.S. citizens, become the 51st state, or become a free nation.

**Section 3 Review** Choose the letter of the answer that correctly completes each sentence. Write your answers on a separate sheet of paper.

1) _____ strongly influenced Central America.
   a. Great Britain          c. France
   b. Spain                  d. India

2) Africans were brought to the Caribbean as _____.
   a. explorers              c. rulers
   b. soldiers               d. slaves

3) Descendants of European and African marriages are _____.
   a. mulattos               c. mestizos
   b. Creoles                d. voodoo

4) Most Central Americans and Caribbeans speak _____.
   a. English                c. French
   b. Spanish                d. creole

5) _____ proposed a plan to end fighting in Central America.
   a. Fidel Castro           c. Bill Clinton
   b. Oscar Arias            d. Daniel Ortega

**What do YOU think?**

Why do you think Central America and the Caribbean have only two cities with over a million people?

Subsistence farming
*Growing crops mainly to meet the needs of a family*

## What Are the Natural Resources in This Area?

Good weather and much sunshine are the major resources of the Caribbean islands. Because of this, many tourists visit the beautiful beaches and clear waters of the Caribbean islands. They scuba dive, snorkel, fish, and sail in these waters. Cruise ships often stop at the islands. Some of these islands have many hotels for tourists.

Forests are a great resource of Central America. Once they covered more than half of its land. These forests provide many kinds of wood. One kind of tree provides chicle, the basic part of chewing gum.

However, Central America and the Caribbean do not have great mineral resources. Workers have mined some gold and silver in the mountains of Nicaragua. They have also discovered small amounts of lead, nickel, iron, zinc, and copper. The island of Jamaica has a large supply of bauxite. Aluminum is made from this mineral.

## What Are Some Major Industries in Central America?

The economies of most Central American countries depend on farming. More than half the people of Guatemala and Honduras farm. Most of them do **subsistence farming.** That is, the farmers own only enough land to grow crops for themselves. They have no crops to sell to earn extra money. Subsistence farming provides only for the basic needs of a farmer's family. If a crop fails, the health and the lives of the family members may be in danger.

A small group of rich people and foreign businesses own much of the land in Central America. They have divided this land into huge plantations that grow bananas, cotton, or coffee. The landowners export most of these cash crops either to the United States or Europe. The crops account for most of Central America's export income.

Tourism is a major industry in the Caribbean. This photo shows Luquillo Beach in Puerto Rico.

## What Are Some Major Industries in the Caribbean?

Most people on the Caribbean islands also work in agriculture. Some work on plantations that grow sugarcane, cacao, coconuts, and bananas. Others work in plants that process the crops. For example, some factories turn sugarcane into table sugar. Still other island people work on ships or on the docks. There, businesses package farm goods and prepare them for sale.

A big part of the economy, especially in the Caribbean, depends on tourism. Tourism brings in millions of dollars every year. However, people from other countries own most of the hotels and resorts. Few of the local people share in the wealth. Tourism provides many jobs, but most of these jobs require little skill or education. Because of this, the foreign owners do not pay the workers much money.

## What Environmental Challenges Exist?

The biggest challenge to this area of the world is **overdevelopment.** People from other countries have built tourist hotels and other things with little thought for the natural environment. They have cut down native trees and plants. Many new people have moved into the area. In

**Extinct**
*No longer existing anywhere*

some places, the government has not created enough ways to keep the water clean. This has caused water pollution.

Another serious problem in Central America is the destruction of the rain forests. Many animals and plants found only in Central America live in these forests. Scientists believe that these plants hold the secret for curing some diseases. If workers cut down the rain forests, many animals and plants will become **extinct.** That is, they will no longer exist anywhere.

**Section 4 Review** On a separate sheet of paper, write the word from the Word Bank that completes each sentence.

**WORD BANK**

agriculture

mineral

rain forests

subsistence

tourism

1) Central America and the Caribbean do not have great _____ resources.

2) Most Central American countries have an economy based on _____.

3) In _____ farming, a farmer is able to grow only those crops that provide for the basic needs of life.

4) A big part of the economy on the Caribbean islands is _____.

5) The _____ support many animals and plants found only in Central America.

 **What do YOU think?** Should the United States accept some responsibility for the environmental problems of Central America and the Caribbean? Give a reason for your opinion.

# "Beisbol"—A Big Hit in Central America and the Caribbean

Americans often think of baseball as America's game. Actually, the sport is played all over the world. Many players from other countries also play baseball in the United States. Today, players from other countries play for every American major league baseball team. In 1977, close to 11 percent of the baseball players came from other countries. By 1997, the percentage had grown to 20.4. In other words, one out of every five baseball players in the major leagues was from another country.

In 1997, these players came to the United States from 17 different countries. Many of these were Latin American countries. The small Caribbean country of the Dominican Republic sent 89 players to the United States. This was the most of any country. Puerto Rico sent 42 players. Even tiny Panama sent 9. If you add up all the 1997 Latin American players in the major leagues, you get a grand total of 206.

As these numbers show, baseball is popular in Central America and the Caribbean. The people do not have good playing fields and equipment, but they do have talent. Most U.S. baseball teams send scouts to the area. These scouts search for good players who want to play ball in the United States.

The major baseball leagues in the U.S. have set up camps in Central America and in the Caribbean. The Dominican Republic, Puerto Rico, and Mexico all have camps. These camps develop the talent of the players in this area of the world.

**Baseball is played all over the world, including Central America and the Caribbean.**

The young men who reach the major leagues are lucky. Some of them become stars and earn a lot of money. A few of these players, like Sammy Sosa of the Chicago Cubs and Edgar Renteria of the Florida Marlins, return to their homeland each year. There, they have built schools and hospitals to help their people.

## Spotlight Story Wrap-Up

1) In what Latin American countries is baseball played?

2) What was the percentage of major league baseball players from other countries in 1997?

3) Which Caribbean country had the most major league players in 1997?

4) How do the major leagues discover and develop baseball players from Central America and the Caribbean?

5) Who are two famous major league players from this area?

◆ Central America is part of the North American continent. The Caribbean islands, or West Indies, are an archipelago in the Caribbean Sea. Except for the Bahamas, the entire area is located in the Tropics.

◆ Central America and the Caribbean have two regions: the mainland and the rimland. The mainland includes the seven Central American countries. The rimland includes the Caribbean islands and the coastal plains of Central America.

◆ The mainland has high mountains. Thick rain forests cover the eastern side of Central America, so the land is not good for farming. The Pacific coastal lowland has rich soil. Most Caribbean islands are inactive volcanic mountain tops.

◆ Most rivers in Central America are short and not navigable. The Panama Canal, a human-made waterway, is its main water feature.

◆ The mountain areas of the mainland have a highland climate. The Caribbean lowlands have a tropical climate. The Pacific lowlands and the Caribbean islands have a tropical savanna climate.

◆ Descendants of native people live in Central America and the Caribbean. Many countries have a large population of mestizos, descendants of the Spanish and the native people. Belize has a large population whose ancestors came from Africa.

◆ Christianity is the main religion of the area. However, many native people have kept their own religions. Some people of African descent practice voodoo.

◆ Tourists most often hear Spanish spoken in this area, but they also hear native languages, English, French, and creole.

◆ Most of the people live on farms or in small towns. Only two cities have more than a million people.

◆ The chief natural resources are forests, good weather, sunshine, and beaches. The area has few mineral resources.

◆ The economies of Central America and the Caribbean depend on agriculture.

◆ Central America and the Caribbean face the environmental problems of overdevelopment by foreign investors, water pollution, and the destruction of rain forests.

◆ The nations of this region also face the social problems of poverty, economic development, a rising birthrate, and the task of getting along with the United States.

## Comprehension: Identifying Facts

On a separate sheet of paper, write the words from the Word Bank to complete each sentence.

<table>
<tr><td>

**WORD BANK**

Central America

Panama Canal

rural

Spanish

volcanic

</td></tr>
</table>

1) _____ is part of North America.

2) Most of the Caribbean islands are really _____ mountain tops.

3) The most important water feature of Central America is probably the _____.

4) Most people of Central America and the Caribbean live in _____ areas.

5) The language spoken most often in Central America is _____.

## Comprehension: Multiple Choice

On a separate sheet of paper, write the letter of the answer that correctly completes each sentence.

1) The Caribbean islands and the coastal plains of Central America are part of the _____ subregion.

   a. mainland      c. rimland

   b. archipelago   d. atoll

2) The Caribbean lowlands have a _____ climate.

   a. continental   c. tropical

   b. highland      d. maritime

3) The heat of volcanoes creates _____ power.

   a. geothermal    c. hydroelectric

   b. nuclear       d. volcanic

4) Tropical storms called _____ bring strong winds, heavy rainfall, and huge waves.

   a. tornadoes     c. floods

   b. blizzards     d. hurricanes

5) Among the languages spoken in Central America and the Caribbean are _____.

   a. native and English     c. creole and Spanish

   b. English and French    d. all of the above

## Comprehension: Understanding Main Ideas

On a separate sheet of paper, write the answer to each question. Use complete sentences.

1) How do most people in Central America and the Caribbean earn a living?

2) What are the two subregions of Central America and the Caribbean?

3) What is probably the most important natural resource in Central America and the Caribbean?

## Critical Thinking: Write Your Opinion

On a separate sheet of paper, write your opinion to each question. Use complete sentences.

1) Should businesses from other countries invest or spend money in Central America and the Caribbean? Give a reason for your opinion.

2) What would you do about the environmental problems in Central America and the Caribbean?

## Applying the Five Themes of Geography

### Location

Why did engineers select the location they did for the building of the Panama Canal, which connects the Atlantic Ocean to the Pacific Ocean?

**Test-Taking Tip**    When studying for a test, learn the most important points. Practice writing or saying the material out loud. Have a partner listen to check to see if you are right

# Chapter

## 5

# South America

South America is one of the world's seven continents. Much of it is covered with rain forests like the picture on this page shows. South America is home to over 300 million people. In 1498, Christopher Columbus became the first European to see South America. Today, great differences exist among South America's countries and people.

---

## Goals for Learning

▶ To describe where South America is located

▶ To identify the most important physical features and climates of South America

▶ To describe the many cultures of South America

▶ To explain where and how the people of South America live

▶ To describe the economy of South America and the environmental challenges it faces

---

### 🌐 Geo-Stats

**Four Largest Nations of South America**

**Nation:** Argentina
**Population:** 36,568,000
**Area** (in square miles): 1,068,302
**Major Cities:** Buenos Aires (capital), Córdoba, Rosario, Mendoza

**Nation:** Colombia
**Population:** 38,581,000
**Area** (in square miles): 439,737
**Major Cities:** Bogotá (capital), Cali, Medellín, Barranquilla, Cartagena

**Nation:** Brazil
**Population:** 167,988,000
**Area** (in square miles): 3,286,488
**Major Cities:** Brasília (capital), São Paulo, Rio de Janeiro, Salvador

**Nation:** Peru
**Population:** 26,624,000
**Area** (in square miles): 96,225
**Major Cities:** Lima (capital), Arequipa, Trujillo, Callao

## South America

CENTRAL AMERICA

Caribbean Sea

Caracas ⊛

**VENEZUELA**

Georgetown ⊛
Paramaribo ⊛ Cayenne
⊛

Bogotá ⊛

**COLOMBIA**

**GUYANA**

**FRENCH GUIANA**

**SURINAME**

Equator 0°

Quito ⊛

**ECUADOR**

**B R A Z I L** 10°S

P
E
R
U

Lima ⊛

Brasília
⊛

**BOLIVIA**
⊛ La Paz

20°S

⊛ Sucre

**PARAGUAY**

PACIFIC OCEAN

Asunción ⊛

A
R
G
E
N
T
I
N
A

**URUGUAY** 30°S

Santiago ⊛

Buenos ⊛
Aires

⊛ Montevideo

ATLANTIC OCEAN

C
H
I
L
E

40°S

⊛ National Capitals

0          1000 Miles
0          1000 Kilometers

Falkland Islands (U.K.)
Strait of Magellan

50°S

100°W    90°W    80°W    70°W    60°W    50°W    40°W    30°W

10°N

N
W    E
S

*Map Skills*

South America is the fourth largest continent in the world. It has many big cities and the huge nation of Brazil. Study the map and answer the questions:

**1)** What is the largest country in South America? the smallest?

**2)** Along which coast is Chile located?

**3)** Which oceans and seas surround South America?

**4)** What is the capital of Argentina? Uruguay? Colombia?

**5)** Which country covers most of the east coast of South America?

## Where Is South America Located?

Most people think that South America lies directly south of North America. Actually, it is quite a bit farther east. Santiago, Chile, on the western side of South America, is almost directly south of Boston, Massachusetts, on the eastern coast of North America. Much of South America is in the Tropics. The equator runs through the countries of Brazil, Colombia, and Ecuador.

South America has three long coastlines. One is on the Atlantic Ocean. Another is on the Pacific Ocean. The shortest coastline is on the Caribbean Sea. Being so close to large bodies of water has affected South America's trade, economy, and climate.

## What Is Continental Drift?

Look at the world map in the Atlas at the back of this textbook. Note the shape of South America and the shape of Africa. They seem to fit together. Geographers suggest that one huge piece of land, which they call **Pangaea,** once sat in Earth's ocean. Over millions of years, Pangaea broke apart. It became the seven different continents.

Geographers give the name **continental drift** to this idea. Experts believe that some time in the far past, Pangaea divided and the continents drifted apart around the globe. **Fossils** support this idea. Fossils are molds or parts of ancient plants or animals. Scientists have found fossils of the same plants and animals in places many thousands of miles apart. This suggests that land once connected these areas of Earth.

## What Countries Make Up Caribbean South America?

Geographers divide South America into three regions that are based on location: Caribbean South America, Atlantic South America, and Pacific South America. The first region to which Europeans came was Caribbean South America. It includes the countries of Colombia, Venezuela, Guyana,

**South Americans celebrate during a cultural festival.**

and Suriname. French Guiana, a territory of France, is also part of this region.

Caribbean South American has highlands over 7,000 feet high as well as plains. The largest plain stretches across Venezuela. The region has several large cities. Bogotá, Colombia, has over five million people. Caracas, Venezuela, has almost two million. However, most people in the region live in rural areas and small towns.

## What Countries Make Up Atlantic South America?

Four countries make up this region. Uruguay and Paraguay are small. Brazil and Argentina are giants. In fact, Brazil is the largest country in South America. It is almost as large as the United States. This South American country is so large that geographers divide it into four parts.

Most Brazilians live in the southeastern part of Brazil. Its biggest cities, Rio de Janeiro and São Paulo, are located there. The northeastern part of Brazil is poorer than the southeastern.

Geographers call the central west of Brazil *campo cerrado* because of the plants that grow there. Until recently, the area had few people. However, in 1960, Brazil built its new capital, Brasília, there. Now the area is developing quickly; its population is growing.

The fourth and final part of Brazil is Amazonia. Geographers give it this name because the Amazon River flows through it. Amazonia covers 42 percent of Brazil. The world's largest rain forests grow in this part of Brazil. Its thick forests and hot, damp climate make living and moving about hard.

## What Countries Make Up Pacific South America?

Pacific South America is different from Atlantic South America. The Andes Mountains rise on the western side of South America. They stand more than 20,000 feet high. That is more than 6,000 feet higher than the Rocky Mountains in the United States! The Andes form the backbone of the western side of South America. This backbone makes traveling between the countries of eastern South America and western South America hard. It also affects communication.

The countries in this region are Ecuador, Peru, Bolivia, and Chile. In Peru and Bolivia, a high, broad plateau sits between two mountain ranges that stretch southward. Geographers call this high plain by its Spanish name of *Altiplano*. Bolivia is the only country of the four that is landlocked. Because land surrounds it, Bolivia has no gateway to the sea. Chile is shaped like a snake. It is 2,650 miles long, but only about 265 miles wide.

**Section 1 Review** On a separate sheet of paper, write *True* if the statement is true or *False* is the statement is not true. Make each false statement true by changing the underlined word.

1) The theory of <u>Altiplano</u> explains how seven continents came to be on Earth.

2) Europeans first settled in <u>Caribbean</u> South America.

3) <u>Brazil</u> is the largest country in South America.

4) <u>Bolivia</u> is a snake-shaped country in Pacific South America.

5) The <u>Andes Mountains</u> stand on the western side of South America.

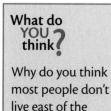

**Writing About Geography**

Choose one of the regions of South America. Imagine that you live there. Then write a personal letter to a friend in the United States. Describe the region in South America in which you live.

**What do YOU think?**

Why do you think most people don't live east of the Andes Mountains?

**Foothill**
*A hill at the base of higher hills or a mountain range*

**Loess**
*A fine and fertile soil that the wind deposits on the ground*

**Pampa**
*The grass-covered plain of Argentina*

## What Are South America's Physical Regions?

South America has three big physical regions. The Andes Mountains form the first region. They begin at Tierra del Fuego, an archipelago at the southern tip of South America. The Andes stretch northward for more than 4,500 miles to Venezuela on the Caribbean coast of South America.

The Andes are the longest mountain system in the world. Some rise more than four miles above sea level. They are like a wall between the eastern and western parts of South America. In Peru and Bolivia, they are almost 500 miles wide. The few people who live in the valleys of the Andes are mostly native people. The mountains separate one village from another.

The plains form the second physical region. They stretch from the **foothills** of the Andes eastward to the Atlantic Ocean. A foothill is a hill at the base of higher hills or a mountain range. The plains cover much of Argentina and Paraguay. In Argentina, geographers call these plains the **pampas.** Rich **loess** soil covers the pampas. Loess is a fine and fertile soil that the wind leaves on the ground. The plains are one of the richest farm areas in the world.

A large area of lowlands and plateaus in Brazil is the third physical region. The Amazon River flows through a huge area of mostly flat land. A wide coastal plain stretches along the Atlantic coast. It is here that Europeans set up the first sugarcane plantations. After they planted sugarcane year after year, the land wore out. Today, what was once a rich part of Brazil is its poorest part.

## What River Systems Exist?

Three large river systems flow through South America. The largest is the Amazon. No river in the world carries

**The Andes Mountains spread along the western coast of South America.**

Estuary
*A flooded river valley at the mouth of a river where saltwater from a sea mixes with freshwater from a river*

more water than the Amazon. It begins in the ice-covered Andes Mountains in Peru. About 4,000 miles later, the Amazon empties into the Atlantic Ocean. The Amazon has over 1,000 tributaries. The most important of these rivers are the Río Negro, Xingu, Putumayo, and Juruá. Each is over 1,000 miles long.

The second largest river system in South America is the Rio de la Plata. The many rivers of this system drain an area of more than 1,500,000 miles! The river is important to Argentina, Paraguay, and Uruguay. Because of this, geographers often call them the Rio de la Plata countries.

The Rio de la Plata is really a huge **estuary.** An estuary is a flooded river valley at the mouth of a river. There, saltwater from the sea mixes with freshwater from the river. The three chief rivers that form the Rio de la Plata estuary are the Paraná, the Paraguay, and the Uruguay. Each of these rivers is more than 1,000 miles long.

## Major Rivers of the World

| River | Location | Length in Miles |
|---|---|---|
| Nile | Africa | 4,160 |
| Amazon | South America | 4,083 |
| Yangtze | China | 3,915 |
| Mississippi/Missouri/Red Rock | United States | 3,741 |
| Huang (Yellow) | China | 3,395 |
| Ob/Irtysh | China/Kazakhstan/Russia | 3,362 |
| Amur/Shilka | Asia | 2,744 |
| Lena | Russia | 2,734 |
| Congo/Zaire | Africa | 2,718 |
| Mackenzie/Peace/Finlay | Canada | 2,635 |
| Mekong | Asia | 2,597 |
| Niger | Africa | 2,548 |
| Yenisei | Russia | 2,548 |
| Paraná | Brazil | 2,450 |
| Murray/Darling | Australia | 2,331 |

### CHART STUDY

This chart shows the 15 largest rivers in the world. The Amazon and the Paraná are both in South America. How much longer is the Nile than the Amazon? How long is the Mississippi/Missouri/Red Rock river system?

**Temperate climate**
*A climate that is neither very hot nor very cold and has warm and cool seasons*

The third important river system in South America is the Orinoco. The Orinoco River drains an area of about 360,000 miles, mostly in Venezuela.

## What Are Some Other Important Bodies of Water?

An area with many rivers is likely to have many waterfalls. One of the most beautiful is Angel Falls in Venezuela. It is the world's tallest waterfall. The water drops more than 3,000 feet! It is 19 times higher than Niagara Falls in the United States. The two biggest lakes in South America are Lake Maracaibo in Venezuela and Lake Titicaca in Peru and Bolivia.

Except for the land bridge at its northwest corner, water surrounds South America. Many people in Chile and Peru fish for a living. All three coasts—the Caribbean, the Atlantic, and the Pacific—have port cities. From these ports, companies ship many products to other parts of the world.

## What Climates Does South America Have?

Most of South America falls between the Tropics. However, high mountains stretch from north to south. As a result, South America has nearly every kind of climate. Temperature and rainfall differ greatly.

From the base of the Andes Mountains to their peaks, there are three climates: a tropical climate, a mild one, and a cold one. The Atacama Desert of Chile is one of the world's driest deserts. The Amazon River Valley is one of the wettest tropical rain forests.

Much of South America has either a rain forest climate or a savanna climate. Rain forests are hot and wet all year; savannas are dry. Some areas have a humid subtropical climate. Other areas have dry winters and wet summers. The southern tip of South America is called Patagonia. This area lies in Chile and Argentina. It is dry and cold.

In the middle latitudes of South America's Atlantic Coast, people live in **temperate climates.** This means that the weather is neither very hot nor very cold. Temperate climates have warm and cool seasons.

## Physical Features of South America

Where is the Atacama Desert located? In what part of South America does the Amazon River flow? What strait sits at the southern tip of South America?

CENTRAL AMERICA

Caribbean Sea

Orinoco R.

10°N

Equator 0°

Negro R.

Amazon R.

Amazon R.

Tapajos R.

Xingu R.

Tocantins R.

Sao Francisco R.

10°S

SOUTH AMERICA

Lima

Brasilia

Paraguay R.

Parana R.

20°S

Rio de Janeiro

PACIFIC OCEAN

ATACAMA DESERT

Uruguay R.

30°S

Santiago

ATLANTIC OCEAN

40°S

Negro R.

0        1000 Miles

0        1000 Kilometers

Falkland Islands (U.K.)

50°S

Strait of Magellan

100°W    90°W    80°W    70°W    60°W    50°W    40°W    30°W

**Section 2 Review** On a separate sheet of paper, write answers to these questions.

1) What are the three physical regions of South America?

2) What was the first plantation crop that Europeans grew on the plain of northeast Brazil?

3) What are the three great river systems of South America?

4) Name a major desert and a major rain forest in South America.

5) What are three kinds of climates in South America?

**What do YOU think?** Should people cut down the trees in the huge Amazon rain forest or should they save it as a national park? Explain your answer.

**Alpaca**
*An animal similar to a llama with silky hair*

**Llama**
*An animal related to the camel and used to carry things*

## What Are the Three Cultures of South America?

The countries of South America have much in common, but they differ, too. They can be divided into three cultural regions: Indo-America, Afro-America, and Euro-America.

## Where Is the Indo-American Region?

Indo-America includes large parts of Bolivia, Peru, Ecuador, and part of Colombia. The native people who live here have influenced the region's culture. Most people still speak their own native languages rather than Spanish or Portuguese. They also keep their own customs and ways of dressing.

The native people in this region are subsistence farmers. They plant the same crops and use many of the same tools that those who lived before them did. They raise sheep, **llamas,** and **alpacas.** Llamas are related to the camel. When people travel, they pack things on the llama's back. Alpacas are similar to llamas. People use its silky hair to make sweaters. Most native people are the poorest people in South America. They live much as their ancestors did hundreds of years ago.

## Where Is the Afro-American Region?

Afro-America includes the coastal areas of Colombia, Venezuela, the Guianas, and the east coast of Brazil. People from Africa influence this region. Years ago, Europeans came to this region and settled. They set up plantations and dug mines. Much of the native population died from European diseases. The Europeans then turned to Africa for the many workers they needed.

From 1500 to the mid-1800s, European ships brought millions of African slaves to South America. A large percentage of today's population in this region is descended from these African slaves. The music of Brazil and some popular foods show the influence of Africa.

South America is a mix of big cities and small villages. This is a village in Colombia near the Andes Mountains.

**Death rate**
*The number of deaths over a given period of time*

**Gaucho**
*A cowhand of the pampas*

## Where Is the Euro-American Region?

European influence is strongest in Euro-America. This region covers most of southern Brazil, Paraguay, Uruguay, Argentina, and Chile. Euro-America has fewer people than the rest of South America.

The few native people who once lived in this region mixed with Europeans. People began to raise cattle on the pampas of Argentina. Cowhands called **gauchos** developed their own culture, based on fine horsemanship and courage. After the 1880s, millions of Europeans settled in this region. The new settlers came from Italy, Poland, France, Russia, Germany, and the Middle East. They liked the good weather and the rich land. Their culture gradually replaced the gauchos.

## What Languages Are Spoken?

People from Spain settled much of South America, so Spanish is the most common language. However, people from Portugal settled in Brazil, so Portuguese is its official language. The native people speak their own languages. As in the United States, immigrants often speak their native languages. Because of this, people speak Italian, German, Russian, and many other languages in larger cities.

## What Religion Do Most People Practice?

Most people in South America are Christians. However, followers of every major world religion live in South America. Often the native religions have blended with Christianity. Some descendents of the African slaves still follow their African religions.

## What Are the Population Trends?

South America has one of the highest birthrates in the world. Geographers expect its population to double in the next 25 years. In the past, South America had a high birthrate, but it also had a high **death rate.** However, today the death rate has fallen because of new medicines and better health conditions. Many people believe South America will lower its birthrate. If it does not do this, too many people will continue to be poor.

## Where Do Most South Americans Live?

Most South Americans live in rural areas. However, every year thousands of poor peasants leave the countryside and migrate to cities. They hope to find better jobs, schools, and health care. Most of the time the city disappoints them, but still they stay.

Their migration has created big problems for the cities. Many of these poor people live in slums. Whole towns spring up next to garbage dumps. People must beg for food. Three of the largest urban areas in the world are in South America: São Paulo and Rio de Janeiro in Brazil and Buenos Aires in Argentina.

**Section 3 Review** On a separate sheet of paper, write the word from the Word Bank that completes each sentence.

| WORD BANK |
| :---: |
| Indo-America |
| Afro-America |
| Euro-America |
| Portuguese |
| Spanish |

1) The influence of the native people of South America is strongest in _____.

2) The influence of the European culture in South America is strongest in _____.

3) The influence of African culture in South America is strongest in _____.

4) The language most South Americans speak is _____.

5) The language most Brazilians speak is _____.

**What do YOU think?** Should South American countries do more to try to keep native cultures alive? Explain your answer.

Agribusiness
*The business of farming with large farms and lots of machines and chemicals*

Invest
*To give or loan money to something in the hope of getting more money back in the future*

## What Is Agribusiness?

Agriculture is important to the economy of South America. In the mountain valleys of the Andes, native people still do subsistence farming. However, in other parts of South America, farming has become big business, or **agribusiness.** That is, farmers use many big machines on large farms. They use science and chemicals. They grow large crops and ship fruits and vegetables to other countries such as the United States.

Plantations also use lots of machines. Plantation farmers grow sugarcane, bananas, and cacao. In Colombia and Brazil they grow coffee. Brazil also ships oranges to other countries. In fact, it is now the world's largest exporter of oranges and orange juice.

## What Industries Are Important?

Some South American countries have many industries. This leads to better living for the people in these countries. Brazil, Argentina, Chile, and Venezuela developed large industries in the 1940s and 1950s after World War II.

Making cars is a big industry in Brazil. At first, workers there made cars for use only in Brazil. Then they began

selling cars to other countries. Next, many foreign-owned car companies **invested** millions of dollars in Brazil. That is, they spent money on business there in the hope of getting more money back in the future. Investing money in Brazil's car companies created thousands of jobs for the people there. The steel-making factories needed more workers to produce steel for the car makers. The automobile factories needed more workers to put the cars together.

Coffee is an important cash crop in Brazil and Colombia.

## How Do Multinationals Help South America?

Today, South American factories make many kinds of goods. Their economies are growing because **multinational corporations** invest in them. These multinationals are large companies that do business in more than one country.

As in most countries, service industries are also growing in South America. More than one-third of the working people of Brazil work in service jobs. Many work for the government. Others work in offices, shops, or restaurants.

## What Are the Natural Resources of South America?

South America is rich in oil. Venezuela has a lot of it. In recent years, workers have also found oil off the coasts of Chile, Colombia, Brazil, and Argentina. South America is also rich in minerals. For example, Chile is the world's leading exporter of copper. Brazil is the second largest producer of iron ore and tin in the world. Almost every known mineral has been found in South America.

Good weather, rich farmland, water, and rain forests are also important resources in South America. Its many rivers provide water for irrigation and hydroelectric power. Its rain forests provide lumber. The lumbering industry has created many jobs. It has brought much money to some South American countries.

However, the lumber industry has also brought problems. Workers often **clear-cut** the rain forests. That is, they cut down every tree in an area. Then poor people move onto the treeless land and begin to grow crops. However, the soil of a rain forest is thin. In a few years, the farmers can no longer grow crops on this poor soil. The clearing of the rain forests also leads to a second problem. Many animals and plants that lived and grew on the land become extinct.

## What Problems Does South America Face?

Cutting down the rain forest is one problem that affects people everywhere. The rain forest takes in a lot of the **carbon dioxide** in the air. Carbon dioxide is a gas made up

Global warming
*A rise in Earth's temperature caused by too much carbon dioxide in the air*

of carbon and oxygen. People breathe it out; plants breathe it in. If workers cut down the rain forest, Earth loses many of the trees that breathe in the carbon dioxide. The gas remains in the air. Some scientists believe that this leads to **global warming.** They say that more carbon dioxide in the air leads to warmer temperatures on Earth. Global warming might lead to the melting of the ice at the North Pole and the South Pole. All this new water would flood the coastal lowlands of all the continents.

The selling and buying of illegal drugs is also a problem that affects the whole world. Many South American farmers know that they can make more money growing these drugs. Tons of these drugs are shipped to the United States, Canada, and Europe. The drug trade has caused corruption and violence in South America.

Another problem is the military. Members of the military are taking more power for themselves. South America has had a history of weak governments. Often, the military opposes the elected government. When that happens, military leaders sometimes take over. Early in the year 2000, the military in Ecuador overthrew the elected government. The military is also gaining strength in Colombia.

*Geography In Your Life*
HEALTH

## Medicinal Plants from Rain Forests

The Amazon Rain Forest is the greatest natural resource on Earth. It takes in much of the carbon dioxide in the air and turns it into oxygen. It also provides the world with many natural resources, including plants that people use for medicine.

Among the rain-forest medicines are ipecac, quinine, pilocarpine, and curare. Doctors use ipecac, which is a plant in the madder family, to treat accidental poisoning. Quinine comes from the bark of the cinchona tree. Doctors use this drug to treat the fever of the disease malaria.

Scientists get pilocarpine from the leaves of a rain-forest shrub. Doctors use it to treat glaucoma, an eye disease. Curare comes from a rain-forest vine. It relaxes a person's muscles when doctors set broken bones. Doctors also use curare to treat some mental disorders. Scientists believe that other rain-forest plants might cure AIDS, diabetes, arthritis, cancer, and Alzheimer's disease.

Born in Ecuador, Chico Mendes worked in the rubber industry. When ranchers began to clear-cut the rain forest for their cattle, it left workers without jobs. No longer could they gather Brazil nuts and collect rubber from trees.

Mendes organized the workers. They tried to bring an end to clear-cutting. Mendes asked South American countries to protect parts of the rain forest. When leaders began to listen to him, the ranchers got angry. They murdered Mendes on December 22, 1988. Since that time, many groups have protested the deforestation of the Amazon Rain Forest.

**Section 4 Review** Choose the letter of the answer that correctly completes each sentence. Write your answers on a separate sheet of paper.

1) _____ is the growing of crops for money on large farms with many machines.
   a. Subsistence farming
   b. Hacienda farming
   c. Agribusiness
   d. Regionalism

2) The world's largest exporter of oranges is _____.
   a. the United States
   b. Brazil
   c. Argentina
   d. Colombia

3) One of Brazil's biggest manufacturing industries is the making of _____.
   a. textiles
   b. books
   c. computers
   d. cars

4) The world's leading exporter of copper is _____.
   a. Colombia
   b. Argentina
   c. Chile
   d. Ecuador

5) _____ in South America affects people everywhere.
   a. Cutting down the rain forest
   b. A powerful military
   c. Population growth
   d. Farming overproduction

**What do YOU think?**

What do you think is the best way for the U.S. to discourage the producing of illegal drugs in South America?

# The Galápagos

On February 23, 1535, the bishop of Panama set sail for Peru. The strong ocean currents drove his ship off course. On March 10, his sailors saw an island that was different from any they had ever seen.

The bishop's sailors rowed a small boat to the strange island. There, they found water for themselves and grass for their horses. They also found seals and huge land turtles that could carry people on their backs! Large snake-like lizards crawled over the island's black rocks. These animals had no fear of the sailors. This island, with its few trees and unusual animals, was part of the Galápagos Islands.

**The Galápagos Islands are hundreds of islands off the coast of Ecuador. This photo shows Pinnacle Rock.**

Hundreds of islands make up the Galápagos. They lie about 600 miles off the coast of Ecuador. Volcanoes formed them millions of years ago. Today, many tourists visit the Galápagos Islands. In 1968, the islands became a national park. However, people did a lot of harm before 1968. They killed thousands of the turtles. Early settlers brought different animals to the islands. These new animals killed many native animals. They also destroyed many native plants.

In September 1835, English Scientist Charles Darwin visited the islands. He wanted to study its plants and animals. He found that the turtles on each island were different. He also saw many different kinds of small birds called finches. Some of them were large; others were small. Some ate flowers and plants; others ate insects.

Darwin wondered why the finches had developed so differently. He came to believe that animals and plants must adapt, or change, to fit their environment. Plants and animals that adapt best continue to live. They evolve, or change, over time. Those that cannot adapt die off.

When Darwin returned to England, he wrote a book called *The Origin of the Species.* Many scientists read his book. It changed the way they looked at the world.

## Spotlight Story Wrap-Up

1) How were the Galápagos Islands discovered?

2) What formed the Galápagos Islands?

3) Where are the Galápagos Islands located?

4) How have humans changed the environment of the islands?

5) How did Darwin explain the differences he found in the finches of the Galápagos Islands?

◆ South America is one of the world's seven continents.

◆ South America has three regions based on location: Caribbean South America, Atlantic South America, and Pacific South America.

◆ South America has three physical regions. The Andes Mountains are a series of high mountain ranges on its western side. Plains stretch eastward from the foothills of the Andes to the Atlantic coast. Brazil has lowlands and plateaus.

◆ South America has three large river systems: the Amazon, the Rio de la Plata, and the Orinoco. No river in the world carries more water than the Amazon River in South America. It has over 1,000 tributaries.

◆ Because of the Andes Mountains, South America has many climates. Much of it has a tropical climate that is either rain forest or savanna. The east coast has a temperate climate. Patagonia has a dry, cold climate.

◆ South America has three cultural regions: Indo-America, Afro-America, and Euro-America. Many descendants of native people live in Bolivia, Peru, Ecuador, and Colombia (Indo-America). Many descendants of African slaves live on the coastal areas of Colombia, Venezuela, the Guianas, and the east coast of Brazil (Afro-America). Many descendants of Europeans live in southern Brazil, Paraguay, Uruguay, Argentina, and Chile (Euro-America).

◆ Christianity is South America's main religion. However, many native people have kept their own religions. Other people practice all the main religions of the world.

◆ People from Spain settled in much of South America, so Spanish is the most common language. However, people also speak native and European languages. Portugal sent settlers to Brazil, so its people speak Portuguese.

◆ Most South Americans live on farms or in small towns. However, many are now migrating to urban areas.

◆ South America's economy depends on agriculture and industry.

◆ South America's chief natural resources are oil, minerals, rich farmland, and rain forests.

◆ The cutting down of the rain forests is an environmental problem for South America. Its social problems are poverty, slums, a rising birthrate, the selling of unlawful drugs, and the growing power of the military.

## Comprehension: Identifying Facts

On a separate sheet of paper, write the words from the Word Bank to complete each sentence.

**WORD BANK**

Amazon
Andes
Brazil
Pangaea
Spanish

1) At one time, one huge land mass called _____ sat in Earth's ocean.

2) The _____ Mountains are the longest mountain system in the world.

3) The _____ River carries more water than any other river in the world.

4) Many people in South America speak _____.

5) Rio de Janeiro and São Paulo are the two largest cities in _____.

## Comprehension: Multiple Choice

On a separate sheet of paper, write the letter of the answer that correctly completes each sentence.

1) The largest country in South America is _____.

   a. Argentina          c. Colombia

   b. Peru               d. Brazil

2) The middle latitudes of South America's Atlantic Coast has a _____ climate.

   a. tropical           c. temperate

   b. steppe             d. arctic

3) The tallest waterfall in the world is _____ Falls in Venezuela.

   a. Victoria           c. Niagara

   b. Angel              d. Mtarazi

4) Most of the Africans brought to South America came as _____.

   a. slaves             c. immigrants

   b. settlers           d. sailors

5) The poorest people in South America are the _____.

   a. U.S. Americans    c. Euro-Americans

   b. Afro-Americans    d. Indo-Americans

## Comprehension: Understanding Main Ideas

On a separate sheet of paper, write the answer to each question. Use complete sentences.

1) What are some main physical features of South America?

2) What are the major cash crops grown in South America?

3) Why does South America have several cultures?

## Critical Thinking: Write Your Opinion

On a separate sheet of paper, write your opinion to each question. Use complete sentences.

1) Why do you think Brazil is the most industrialized country in Latin America?

2) Why do you think that multinational corporations like to invest in companies in South America?

## Applying the Five Themes of Geography

### Interaction

How have people harmed the natural environment of the Galápagos Islands?

**Test-Taking Tip**  When studying for a test, review any worksheets, tests, quizzes, Section Reviews, or Chapter Reviews you completed that cover the same information.

# Compare and Contrast

When you write, you often compare or contrast people, ideas, and events. When you read, you often have to look for comparing and contrasting. To compare is to show how things are alike. To contrast is to show how things are different. As you read, ask questions to see if you are reading a comparison or a contrast. Look for words that show comparing and contrasting.

> To compare, ask: "How are these things alike?"
>
> To contrast, ask: "How are these things different?"

* To decide if things are being compared, look for words such as

> also    both    like    similar
>
> *Like* the United States and Canada, people came to Mexico from other countries.

* To decide if things are being contrasted, look for words such as

> but       however    instead
> not       only       while
>
> The difference between plantations and haciendas was that plantations grew *only* one crop.

Decide whether each sentence compares or contrasts.

1) Both Mexico and Brazil are large nations.

2) Mexico is one nation, while many nations make up South America.

3) Central America is south of Mexico but north of South America.

4) Two nations of South America are landlocked; however, all the Caribbean nations are islands surrounded by water.

5) Like the nations of Central America, Mexico has economic problems.

Compare and contrast Mexico and South America by writing one sentence for each of the words below. Write a comparing sentence or a contrasting sentence for each word. Be sure to use words that compare or contrast.

6) mountains

7) climate

8) religion

9) people

10) economy

◆ Latin America includes Mexico, Central America, the Caribbean, and South America. Mexico is south of the United States. Central America is south of Mexico. Central America and Mexico belong to the continent of North America. The Caribbean includes island nations south of the eastern United States. South of Central America is South America, one of Earth's seven continents.

◆ Mexico has four physical regions. Central America and the Caribbean have two. South America has three regions.

◆ The main physical feature in Mexico is its mountains, the Sierra Madre. The Andes Mountains are the main physical feature in South America. The mainland of Central America also has high mountains. Most Caribbean islands are inactive volcanic mountain tops.

◆ Much, but not all, of the climate in Latin America is tropical. Its mountain ranges have many different climates.

◆ Descendants of native groups make up part of the population of Latin America. The mestizos, descendants of Spaniards and native people, make up 75 percent of Mexico. Mestizos also live in Central America and the Caribbean. Descendants of native groups, European settlers, and African slaves live in South America.

◆ Roman Catholicism is Mexico's main religion. Christianity is practiced in Central America, the Caribbean, and South America. However, many native people have kept their own religions.

◆ Mexico's official language is Spanish. Many people also speak Spanish in Central America, the Caribbean, and South America. However, they also speak native and European languages or a mixture of the two, such as creole.

◆ Over two-thirds of Mexico's people live in urban areas. However, most people of Central America, the Caribbean, and South America live in rural areas.

◆ Mexico's chief resource is oil. Central America and the Caribbean have forests, good weather, sunshine, and beaches. South America is rich in minerals, farmland, and rain forests.

◆ The economies of Central America and the Caribbean depend on agriculture and tourism. However the economies of Mexico and South America depend mostly on farming and manufacturing.

◆ Mexico, Central America, the Caribbean, and South America face many environmental problems. Mexico faces air and water pollution and deforestation. Central America and the Caribbean also face water pollution. Both of these areas and South America face the cutting down of rain forests.

"If we go on the way we have, the fault is our greed. If we are not willing to change, we will disappear from the face of the globe, to be replaced by the insect."

—Jacques Cousteau,
French marine explorer, 1971

# UNIT 3

# Europe

In this unit, you set sail for Europe, a continent that is a mixture of old and new ways of life. The photo on this page shows London, England. This is a fine example of a European city with much history, but all of the parts of a modern society.

In this unit, you will tour the British Isles where London is located. Then you will cross the English Channel and see France and other great nations of western Europe. Next, you will visit the ancient city of Rome in southern Europe. Then you will cross over to Greece and ancient Athens. Finally, you will travel north to the mountains of Norway and Sweden. All of these places and more make Europe a very interesting and diverse place on Earth.

**CHAPTERS IN UNIT 3**

**Chapter 6:** The British Isles ........................142
**Chapter 7:** Western Europe .......................162
**Chapter 8:** Southern Europe .....................182
**Chapter 9:** Northern Europe .....................202

# The British Isles

The British Isles are made up of two large islands and many small ones. From the largest island, the British Empire once stretched around the globe. This empire greatly influenced the history of the world. It gave the world ideas about how governments should rule people. The British Empire was once so great that people said "the sun never set" on it. The British Isles are a part of Europe. However, the history and the culture of the British Isles differ from the rest of Europe. The photo on this page shows an English countryside.

## Goals for Learning

▶ To describe where the British Isles are located

▶ To identify the most important physical features and climate of the British Isles

▶ To describe the culture of the British Isles

▶ To explain where most people in the British Isles live

▶ To describe the economy of the British Isles and the environmental challenges it faces

## Geo-Stats

 **The United Kingdom**
Population: 59,364,000
**Area** (in square miles): 94,248
**Length of Coastline** (in miles): 7,718
**Major Cities:** London (capital), Birmingham, Glasgow, Liverpool
**Major Religions:** Anglican, Roman Catholic
**Major Languages:** English, Welsh, Gaelic
**Number of Television Sets:** 20 million

 **Republic of Ireland**
Population: 3,734,000
**Area** (in square miles): 27,137
**Length of Coastline** (in miles): 899
**Major Cities:** Dublin (capital), Cork, Limerick, Galway, Waterford
**Major Religion:** Roman Catholic
**Major Languages:** English, Irish (Gaelic)
**Number of Television Sets:** 1 million

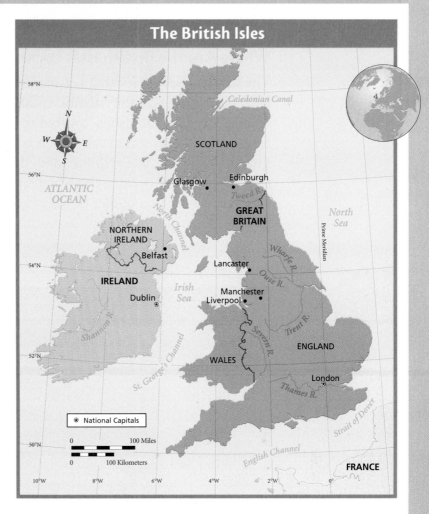

## The British Isles

Caledonian Canal

SCOTLAND

Glasgow • • Edinburgh

Tweed R.

GREAT
BRITAIN

North
Sea

ATLANTIC
OCEAN

North Channel

Prime Meridian

NORTHERN
IRELAND

• Belfast

Wharfe R.

Lancaster •

Ouse R.

IRELAND

Irish
Sea

Manchester •
Liverpool •

Dublin ⊛

Shannon R.

Trent R.

Severn R.

St. George's Channel

WALES

ENGLAND

London ⊛

⊛ National Capitals

Thames R.

Strait of Dover

English Channel

FRANCE

58°N  56°N  54°N  52°N  50°N
10°W  8°W  6°W  4°W  2°W  0°

0          100 Miles
0          100 Kilometers

*Map Skills*

The British Isles include several islands off the coast of western Europe. The Republic of Ireland covers most of one of the large islands. Northern Ireland sits at the northern part of that island. England, Scotland, and Wales make up Great Britain, the largest island. Northern Ireland, the island of Great Britain, and many small islands make up the United Kingdom.

Study the map and answer the following questions:

**1)** Which channel flows between England and France?

**2)** Which sea lies to the east of Great Britain?

**3)** Which sea runs between Ireland and England?

**4)** What are some major cities in England?

**5)** Which river passes through London, England?

## Where Are the British Isles Located?

The British Isles are located between 50° and 60° north latitude. They lie on the Atlantic coast of western Europe. At one time, a great glacier covered the continent of Europe. Land connected the British Isles to the rest of Europe. However, as Earth warmed, the ice melted. Then the run-off water became the North Sea and the English Channel. These two bodies of water now separate the British Isles from the European mainland.

### Territories of the United Kingdom

| Territory | Location | Area in Square Miles | Population |
|-----------|----------|----------------------|------------|
| Anguilla | Caribbean Sea (Leeward Islands) | 60 | 10,700 |
| Bermuda | North Atlantic Ocean off of the coast of North Carolina | 21 | 60,144 |
| British Virgin Islands | Caribbean Sea (Greater Antilles chain) | 59 | 17,000 |
| Cayman Islands | Caribbean Sea | 100 | 31,900 |
| Channel Islands | English Channel | 75 | 135,300 |
| Falkland Islands | South Atlantic Ocean off of the coast of Argentina | 5,700 | 2,600 |
| Gibraltar | Strait of Gibraltar | 2.5 | 28,100 |
| Isle of Man | Irish Sea | 221 | 72,700 |
| Montserrat | Caribbean Sea | 40 | 8,000 |
| Pitcairn Island | Pacific Ocean | 2 | 50 |
| St. Helena | South Atlantic Ocean | 47 | 1,500 |
| South Georgia and South Sandwich Islands | South Atlantic Ocean | 1,580 | no permanent population |
| Turks and Caicos Islands | North Atlantic Ocean | 192 | 12,350 |

#### CHART STUDY

This chart shows the many territories (not including England, Wales, Scotland, and Northern Ireland) that are part of the United Kingdom. Some are part of the British Isles, but many are not. What is the population of the Channel Islands? What is the largest territory? Where are most of the territories located?

**Loch**
*A Scottish lake*

The larger of the two main islands in the British Isles is Great Britain. It has three political parts. Its largest part is England, which lies in the south. Wales and Scotland make up the two smaller parts. Wales lies in the west; Scotland is to the north. Wales, Scotland, England, northern Ireland, and many smaller territories make up the nation of the United Kingdom.

The smaller of the two big islands is Ireland. It has two political parts. The Republic of Ireland, an independent country, is the southern part. Northern Ireland is the northern part.

## What Physical Regions Exist in the British Isles?

There are two physical regions in the British Isles. The first is the lowlands. When the ice sheet melted, the English Channel divided this lowland from the plains that cover much of France and Germany. These lowlands are part of the North European Plain. The lowlands cover much of southern and eastern England.

The second physical region is the highlands. They lie on the west and north of Great Britain. They include the old, worn-down mountains of Scotland and Wales and the Pennine Chain. Geographers call this mountain range the backbone of England.

## What Political Regions Exist?

The British Isles can also be divided into four political regions. The first of these is the island of Ireland. People sometimes called this island the "Emerald Isle" because the countryside is so green. The island is the second farthest point west in all of Europe. It contains Ireland and Northern Ireland. The Shannon River, the longest river in the British Isles, is in Ireland.

## Where Is Scotland?

The second political region of the British Isles is Scotland. It occupies the northern half of the island of Great Britain. Scotland's land is rough, yet beautiful. Glaciers shaped Scotland. They carved out deep **lochs,** or lakes. Some people believe that the Loch Ness monster, a giant sea creature, lives in one of these deep lakes! Only a small number of people live in many parts of Scotland. Scottish farmers have raised sheep for hundreds of years.

## Where Is England?

The third political region of the British Isles is England. It lies south of Scotland on the island of Great Britain. No place in England is more than 100 miles from the sea. Like Scotland, northern England has many beautiful lakes. They sit in beautiful mountain valleys.

The English Midlands occupy the center of the island of Great Britain. The **Industrial Revolution** started in these midlands. This revolution, which began in the late 1700s, changed the way people worked. Inventors found new ways to make better machines and to create iron and steel. Because of this, England became the strongest country in the world.

**Great Britain has a long history of kings and queens who once ruled large empires. This drawing shows a British king in India.**

Southern England has few highland areas. Instead, forests cover much of its rolling hills. Farmers work the rest of the land not covered by towns and cities. London, the capital and leading city of Great Britain, is located in the southern part of England. It is one of the world's greatest cities and is more than 2,000 years old! London is famous for its art, buildings, museums, fashion, and popular music.

## Where Is Wales?

Wales is the fourth political region of the British Isles. It lies on the western part of the island of Great Britain. Like Scotland in the north, Wales has a small population. It has rough highlands with wooded hills. Wales used to be an important coal mining area, but many of its mines have closed. Farming and sheep herding are important to the economy of northern Wales. Cardiff and Swansea, the two biggest cities of Wales, are located in its southern part.

**Section 1 Review** On a separate sheet of paper, write *True* if the statement is true or *False* if the statement is not true. Make each false statement true by changing the underlined word.

1) The British Isles are located in the <u>Pacific Ocean</u>.

2) <u>Glaciers</u> formed many of the physical features of the British Isles.

3) The island of <u>Ireland</u> has two political parts.

4) Workers first used new machines and technology in <u>Scotland</u> to create iron and steel.

5) <u>London</u> is the capital and leading city of the island of Great Britain.

**What do YOU think?** Are all islands created by the melting of glaciers? Explain your answer. Hint: Remember what you learned about islands in Chapter 4.

Bog
*A low-lying swampy area that water covers for long periods of time*

Peat
*Decayed plants that have grown in bogs; material burned for heat*

## What Are the Main Physical Features?

The British Isles have no tall mountains. The highest mountain is Ben Nevis. This Scottish mountain stands 4,406 feet tall. It is part of the Grampian Hills.

Most parts of England are fairly flat. Scafell Peak, which is only 3,210 feet high, is England's highest peak. The Pennines mountain range extends from Scotland south into England. The large industrial cities of Manchester and Liverpool are located on the slopes of the Pennines.

A special feature of the British Isles are its **bogs.** Water covers these low-lying swampy areas for long periods of time. The plants that grow there become **peat** when they die. In the past, people burned peat to heat their homes. The bogs are important for wildlife, especially birds. Ireland and Great Britain contain large areas of bogs.

## What Bodies of Water Exist?

England's longest river is the Thames. It is short, but one of the most famous rivers in the world. It begins in the hills of southwestern England and flows to the capital city of London.

The British Isles have many beautiful coastlines. This shows the Cliffs of Dover on the eastern coast of England.

The British Isles also have many lakes. Glaciers formed most of them. Many tourists visit the Lake District of England. Lake Windermere is the largest lake there.

The people who live in the British Isles have a long history of going to sea. Many explorers who traveled the world began their journey from the British Isles. People from Great Britain are also great traders. Goods from all parts of the world flow in and out of its ports. Also, the sea provides the people with a steady supply of seafood.

## What Is the Climate Like in the British Isles?

The British Isles lie as far north as parts of Canada. However, the British Isles enjoy cool to mild weather. It has a marine west coast climate with warm summers and cool winters. About the same amount of rain falls every month of the year. The ocean is the main influence on the climate.

The **Gulf Stream** touches the western shores of Great Britain. The Gulf Stream is a warm ocean current that begins in the western Caribbean Sea of the Tropics. It travels northward through the Atlantic Ocean. The water of this current is warmer than the surrounding water, so it warms the air above it. In winter, the Gulf Stream warms the cold westerly winds that blow toward Europe. Because of the Gulf Stream, the weather is almost always mild along the western shores of Great Britain. In fact, palm trees grow in some parts. Summer temperatures are usually below 90° F. Winter temperatures average around 42° F.

Rain is heaviest in the western upland areas of the British Isles. The weather changes quickly. Rain falls year around. Strong winds, called **gales,** often blow there in the winter months.

**Section 2 Review** On a separate sheet of paper, write the word from the Word Bank that completes each sentence.

**WORD BANK**

bog

Gulf Stream

marine west coast

peat

Thames

1) A low-lying swampy area that water covers for long periods of time is a _____.

2) People burned _____, the decayed plants of a bog, for warmth.

3) England's longest and most important river is the _____.

4) The climate of the British Isles is called _____.

5) The _____ touches the western shores of the island of Great Britain and brings a mild climate.

 **What do YOU think?** What connection do you see between the United Kingdom's location and the fact that it became a world power?

## What Cultures Are There in the British Isles?

Like many nations, Great Britain is a mixture of different people. Many of them are the descendants of people who settled in the British Isles throughout history. Among the first were the Celts. These warlike people took over western Europe around 500 B.C. Today, their descendants live in Ireland, Scotland, Wales, and some parts of England.

Roman armies from southern Europe sailed to England between A.D. 77 and A.D. 407. Then people from northern Europe invaded England and settled there. These people were members of several tribes. The most important tribes were the Angles, the Saxons, and the Jutes. They became the English people. The Vikings and the Normans also invaded the British Isles and influenced the culture.

Before the 1950s, most immigrants came to Great Britain from Ireland and other parts of Europe. However, since the 1950s, many immigrants have come from countries that were once part of the British Empire. The largest number

People of the British Isles are proud of their culture. Here girls perform a traditional Scottish dance in Glasgow, Scotland.

has come from India, Pakistan, and the Caribbean. Today, these people make up about 5 percent of the population.

## What Religions Are Practiced?

Most people of the British Isles are Protestant Christians. The Church of England is the largest Protestant group in England and its official church. The queen or the king of the United Kingdom of Great Britain and Northern Ireland is the head of the Church of England. In the United States, followers of the Church of England are called Anglicans.

John Knox founded the Church of Scotland in 1560. It is separate from the Church of England. In the United States, followers of this Protestant church are called Presbyterians. Other Protestant groups in the British Isles include the Methodists and the Baptists.

Almost 93 percent of the people in the Republic of Ireland are Roman Catholic Christians. In fact, over 5 million Roman Catholics live in the British Isles. Members of other religions also live there. They include Jews, Buddhists, Hindus, Sikhs, and about 1.5 million Muslims. The Muslim religion is strongest among Pakistani immigrants.

## What Language Do People Speak?

English is the official language of the British Isles. The English language is a blend of words from many languages. Each group that invaded the British Isles gave some of its words to the English language. About half of the words in English come from the language of the Angles and the Saxons. The other half of the English language comes from **Romance languages,** such as French, Spanish, and Italian. These languages came from Latin, the language spoken long ago in the Roman Empire. Latin was the language of the Roman armies that once ruled England.

Most people in Ireland, Scotland, and Wales speak English. However, some speak Celtic languages as well. Gaelic and Welsh, which about 500,000 people speak, are Celtic languages. Of course, many of the newly-arrived immigrants to the British Isles speak their own languages.

## Where Do Most People Live in the British Isles?

The island of Great Britain is crowded. Its population is about 58 million people. That gives it a high population density. On the average, many people live on each square mile of land. The average population density for Great Britain is 600 people per square mile. Most of these people live in England. Nearly half of them live in a band that runs across England from the northwest to the southeast.

Mountains and farmland make up about 90 percent of the total land area of the British Isles. Cities, towns, and suburbs make up the remaining 10 percent. Yet 90 percent of the population lives in this 10 percent area.

Great Britain is an urbanized country; it has many big cities. Its largest and most important city is London. Other areas with a lot of people are Manchester, Birmingham, Leeds, and Sheffield in England, and Glasgow in Scotland.

## How Has Prejudice Affected the People?

One big problem for the people of the British Isles is **prejudice.** That is, some people form an opinion about other people before getting to know them. They look down on people and judge them unfairly because of their color, religion, or race.

---

*Geography In Your Life*

CAREERS

### Urban Planners

Since ancient times, people have planned how to make cities beautiful and easy to live in. The Industrial Revolution led to slums. Urban planners then tried to bring a good water supply and waste system to these areas. They built parks and playgrounds so people had some beauty in their lives.

Today, urban planners look at the whole city and try to make it more livable for everyone. They think of the flow of traffic. They set aside areas for the building of factories, tall buildings, apartments, and stores. They think of the height of a building, which might block out the sun for the people below.

Urban planners study the needs of people. They study how people live and work in an urban area. They study how people get to work and get home. They also plan new cities. Some urban planners have planned totally new cities in India, Israel, and South America.

---

Many immigrants are coming to Great Britain. Some people, especially the poor of the inner cities, dislike these new immigrants. Many workers fear that immigrants will take jobs away from them. They fear that immigrants will work for less money. They think this will lower the pay rates, so all workers will end up earning less money. The government of Great Britain is taking strong steps to try to correct this situation.

## Why Can a Low Birthrate Be a Problem?

Great Britain has a low birthrate. As you know, a high birthrate can cause problems. It can keep a country from having a higher standard of living. A low birthrate brings its own set of problems. Fewer babies are being born in Great Britain, but the number of older people is increasing. They no longer work, and taking care of them is costly. With fewer workers, Great Britain's economy might slow down. This could cause many problems for such an industrialized country.

**Section 3 Review** On a separate sheet of paper, write answers to these questions.

1) Where do the descendants of the Celts live in the British Isles?

2) What three tribes from northern Europe influenced British culture?

3) What is the official language of the British Isles?

4) What does high population density mean?

5) Why is too low a birthrate a problem?

---

**What do YOU think?** What is the best way to stop prejudice? Explain your answer.

## What Is a Free-Market Economy?

A **free-market economy** has **producers** and **consumers.** The producers are manufacturers and farmers. They compete for the business of consumers. The consumers are the people who buy and use the producers' goods and services. The British Isles and all the countries you have studied up to now have free-market economies.

If the free-market producers are right about what people want and need, they make money. If the producers are wrong, they may go out of business. In a free-market economy, the government usually lets producers make or grow what they like. However, the government may make a few rules for the producers. In this way, the government makes sure that the producers are fair.

There are several ways to tell how rich a country is. **Per capita income** is one way. This is found by dividing total income in a country by the number of people who live there. Based on per capita income, Great Britain is one of the richest countries in the world.

## What Industries Exist?

In the past, Great Britain's economy depended on manufacturing. The largest number of workers made a living in its steel, heavy machinery, shipbuilding, and car industries. This is called **heavy industry.** Many of these heavy industries have fallen behind in recent years. However, several British-owned multinational corporations are among the world's largest industrial businesses.

Service industries create about two-thirds of all jobs in Great Britain. London has more banks than any other city in the world. It also has the largest insurance market. Great Britain is a leading developer of computer and software services. Many tourists visit the British Isles each year. Because of this, many people in the British Isles work in the tourist industry.

**Consumer**
*A person who buys and uses goods and services*

**Free-market economy**
*An economy in which producers compete for the business of consumers*

**Heavy industry**
*Steel, heavy machinery, and other such industries*

**Per capita income**
*A way to measure how rich a country is by dividing total income by the number of people*

**Producer**
*A manufacturer or farmer who makes a product to sell*

**Tourists visit the British Isles to see its beauty and history. Stonehenge is an ancient site that many people visit in Salisbury, England. No one knows what these stones were once used for.**

Agriculture is also important in the British Isles. Farmers there are using new technology. That is, they are using science to make farming easier. With this new technology, they waste little time and energy. Because of this, the farmers of the British Isles are able to produce about two-thirds of the food the people there need. The other one-third comes from other countries.

## How Does Trade Affect the Economy?

Trade is important to the people of the British Isles. The countries there import and export many products and services. Great Britain exports about one-third of everything that it produces. Major exports include chemicals, electronics, aircraft parts, and computer-related products. London's Heathrow Airport is one of the busiest airports in the world. Close to 500 million tons of goods pass through 300 British seaports every year. The United States and Germany are Great Britain's biggest trading partners.

## What Natural Resources Do the British Isles Have?

Coal led to the rise of Great Britain as a great industrial power. It still has more coal than any other country in Europe. Most of this coal is underground. However, coal mines cost a lot to run, so many of them are closed down. The British Isles have few other mineral resources. The people import the minerals they need for industry.

Until 1975, Great Britain had to import most of the oil it needed. Then workers found oil under the North Sea. The largest oil fields lie to the east of mainland Scotland. Now, Great Britain has enough oil to meet its needs. Natural gas is another important energy resource. Workers also found it under the North Sea.

## What Are Some Environmental Problems in the British Isles?

The British Isles face the same environmental problems that other industrialized countries face. Many people worry about air and water pollution. In recent years some people have begun to worry about modern farming. They think that the chemicals farmers use affect the environment badly.

Great Britain used to depend on manufacturing companies much like this airplane plant in Derby, England. Now the economy includes other forms of income.

Born in England, Anita Lucia Roddick traveled to less industrialized countries when she was in her twenties. In her travels, she met native women with wonderful skin and hair. They used only natural plants and fruits. This gave Roddick an idea. In 1976, she opened her first shop in England. There she sold skin and hair products made from natural ingredients. She put these products in simple packages and refillable bottles. The shop was a success! Now, Roddick uses her profits to help native people in the rain forests of Brazil. She works to help the environment, not harm it.

**Section 4 Review** Choose the letter of the answer that correctly completes each sentence. Write your answers on a separate sheet of paper.

1) _____ is one measure of how rich a country is.
   a. Number of televisions  c. Per capita income
   b. Technology             d. Number of computers

2) The making of steel is an example of a _____.
   a. light industry      c. consumer
   b. natural resource    d. heavy industry

3) Most people in Great Britain work in _____ jobs.
   a. manufacturing    c. mining
   b. service          d. transportation

4) Great Britain's biggest trade partners are the United States and _____.
   a. Germany    c. Canada
   b. France     d. China

5) Great Britain has always had lots of _____, the mineral resource that helped it become an industrial power.
   a. oil       c. natural gas
   b. iron ore  d. coal

**What do YOU think?**

Why do you think tourists from the United States like to travel to the British Isles?

# The Canals of England

The British Isles have one of the world's best transportation systems. Great Britain was one of the first countries to develop a railroad system. In the 1900s, workers built a network of highways. These help people travel quickly around Great Britain and Ireland. Modern airports serve every major city in the British Isles and throughout the world.

All these are important. However, many people do not know about another means of transportation: the canal. Canals are human-made rivers. They helped England become a great industrial power. Workers dug its earliest canal in 1571. By 1805, England had 3,000 miles of canals. These canals linked coal mines, factories, mills, and cities.

**Many of England's canals no longer exist. This is Regent's Canal in London, England.**

Travel on these early canals was faster than on the poor roads of the day. Because of this, canals lowered the cost of taking coal to factories and products to cities. An example of this is the Manchester canal, which workers built in 1761. It lowered the price of coal by 80 percent!

English workers built three main types of canals. The first type was large enough to handle seagoing ships. The second type was called a mainline canal, which was about 14 feet wide. The third type was called a narrow canal, which was about 7 feet wide.

Usually, canals were not deep. Special flat-bottomed boats called barges were made to float in the shallow water. These traveled up and down the canals. Often, entire families lived on these barges. Their work was hard.

The barges had no engines, so a person or a horse had to pull them. They did this by walking slowly along the banks of the canal. As they walked, they pulled a rope attached to the barge.

Today, many English canals are gone, but some are still in working order. Tourists take trips in them along the waterways. A canal trip gives visitors a look at a way of life that disappeared long ago.

## Spotlight Story Wrap-Up

1) Why do we say that the British Isles have one of the world's best transportation systems?

2) Why were canals built?

3) What happened to the price of coal in Manchester after a canal was built in 1761?

4) What are the three main types of canals?

5) What is a barge?

◆ Two big islands and many small ones make up the British Isles.

◆ The largest island is Great Britain. It has three political parts: Scotland, England, and Wales.

◆ The next largest island is Ireland. It has two political parts: the Republic of Ireland and Northern Ireland. Northern Ireland is part of the United Kingdom.

◆ Great glaciers once covered Europe. When these melted, their water formed the North Sea and the English Channel. These waterways divide the British Isles from mainland Europe.

◆ The British Isles have two physical regions: the lowlands and the highlands. The British Isles have many wetlands. These peat bogs are important for the people and for wildlife. Peat from these bogs were used for fuel.

◆ The climate of the British Isles is a marine west coast climate with mild weather. The main influence on the climate is the ocean waters and the Gulf Stream.

◆ Many people have invaded the British Isles and settled there. Each influenced the culture. Since the 1950s, immigrants have come from India, Pakistan, the Caribbean, and other places.

◆ Most people of the British Isles are Protestant Christians. The Church of England is the largest Protestant group. Over 5 million Roman Catholics and 1.5 million Muslims live in the British Isles. Jews, Buddhists, Hindus, and Sikhs also live there.

◆ English is the official language of the British Isles.

◆ Great Britain has a high population density. Ninety percent of the population live in urban areas.

◆ The British Isles have a free-market economy. Using the measurement of per capita income, Great Britain is one of the richest countries in the world.

◆ Great Britain has more coal than any other European country. In the 1970s, workers found oil fields and natural gas under the North Sea. Other than these, the British Isles have few mineral resources.

◆ Many people in the British Isles work in heavy industry. However, the largest percentage of workers work in service industries. Trade and tourism are important to the economy.

◆ The British Isles face the problem of prejudice against immigrants and the environmental problems of air and water pollution and the use of chemicals by farmers.

## Comprehension: Identifying Facts

On a separate sheet of paper, write the words from the Word Bank to complete each sentence.

**WORD BANK**

Christian

coal

Gulf Stream

London

Shannon

1) The capital and leading city of the United Kingdom of Great Britain and Northern Ireland is _____.

2) The warm ocean current responsible for the mild climate of the British Isles is the _____.

3) The longest river in the British Isles is the _____.

4) Most people in the British Isles practice the _____ religion.

5) The chief natural resource of the British Isles is _____.

## Comprehension: Multiple Choice

On a separate sheet of paper, write the letter of the answer that correctly completes each sentence.

1) The British Isles are located on Europe's _____ edge.
   a. northern        c. eastern
   b. southern        d. western

2) People sometimes call Ireland the _____ because its countryside is so green.
   a. Greenland       c. Iceland
   b. Emerald Isle    d. the pearl of the Atlantic

3) The highest point of the British Isles is in _____.
   a. Scotland        c. Wales
   b. England         d. Ireland

4) England's longest and most important river is the _____.
   a. Shannon         c. Thames
   b. Gulf Stream     d. Avon

**5)** The British Isles have a _____ economy.

   a. command        c. Communist

   b. democratic       d. free-market

## Comprehension: Understanding Main Ideas

On a separate sheet of paper, write the answer to each question. Use complete sentences.

**1)** Where are the British Isles located?

**2)** What cultures are there in the British Isles?

**3)** How does trade affect the economy of the British Isles?

## Critical Thinking: Write Your Opinion

On a separate sheet of paper, write your opinion to each question. Use complete sentences.

**1)** Will the British Isles become more powerful or less powerful in the future? Explain your answer.

**2)** Should the governments of the British Isles try to save languages like Welsh and Gaelic, which only a small number of people speak? Why or why not?

## Applying the Five Themes of Geography

### *Interaction*

How is the link between England's huge deposits of coal and its rise to an industrial power an example of the theme of interaction?

*Test-Taking Tip*    When studying for a test, use the titles and subtitles in the chapter to help you recall the information.

# 7

# Western Europe

Have you seen the Eiffel Tower before? This huge landmark is pictured on this page. It is located in Paris, France, which is in western Europe. Western Europe has been important to world history. It has influenced world culture, religion, and industry in many ways. Many of these nations' economies have been separate for many years. Today, however, the nations of western Europe are beginning to work together instead of apart.

## Goals for Learning

▶ To describe where western Europe is located
▶ To identify western Europe's most important physical features and climate
▶ To describe the diverse cultures found in western Europe
▶ To explain where and how most people in western Europe live
▶ To describe the economy of western Europe and the environmental challenges it faces

## Geo-Stats

### Key Nations of Western Europe

**Nation:** France
**Population:** 59,067,000
**Area** (in square miles): 210,026
**Major Cities:** Paris (capital), Marseille, Lyon, Toulouse, Nice

**Nation:** Netherlands
**Population:** 15,799,000
**Area** (in square miles): 16,023
**Major Cities:** Amsterdam (capital), Rotterdam, The Hague, Utrecht

**Nation:** Germany
**Population:** 81,950,000
**Area** (in square miles): 137,857
**Major Cities:** Berlin (capital), Hamburg, Cologne, Frankfurt

**Nation:** Switzerland
**Population:** 7,119,000
**Area** (in square miles): 15,941
**Major Cities:** Bern (capital), Zurich, Basel, Geneva, Lausanne

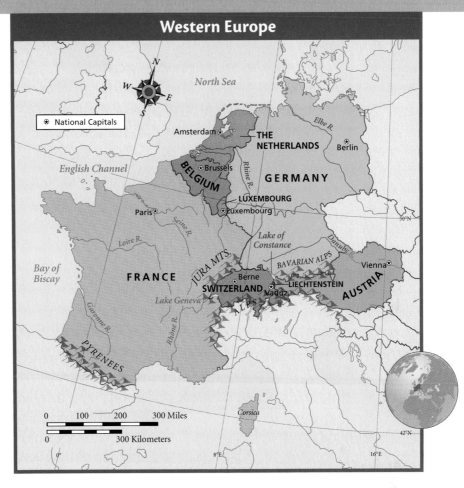

## Western Europe

North Sea

National Capitals

Amsterdam

THE NETHERLANDS

Berlin

Elbe R.

English Channel

BELGIUM

Brussels

Rhine R.

GERMANY

LUXEMBOURG

Paris

Luxembourg

Seine R.

50°N

Loire R.

Lake of Constance

Danube R.

Bay of Biscay

JURA MTS.

FRANCE

BAVARIAN ALPS

Vienna

Berne

SWITZERLAND

LIECHTENSTEIN

Vaduz

AUSTRIA

Lake Geneva

ALPS

Rhône R.

Garonne R.

PYRENEES

Corsica

0   100   200   300 Miles

0   300 Kilometers

0°   8°E   16°E   42°N

*Map Skills*

Western Europe is south of the North Sea, north of the Mediterranean Sea, and east of the Atlantic Ocean and the Bay of Biscay. These nations have a rich history and beautiful lands. Tourists come from all over the world to visit them.

Study the map and answer the following questions:

**1)** What bay is located off of the west coast of France?

**2)** What is the capital of Germany? Switzerland? The Netherlands?

**3)** What major rivers flow through western Europe?

**4)** What is the mountain range in southern Switzerland and southern Austria?

**5)** What mountain range can be found in southwestern France?

### Where Is Western Europe Located?

Western Europe is made up of seven countries: France, the Netherlands, Belgium, Luxembourg, Austria, Germany, and Switzerland. They are located in the middle latitudes, between 43° and 55° north.

The North Sea and the English Channel lie to the north of western Europe. The countries of Poland, the Czech Republic, Slovakia, and Hungary lie to the east of western Europe. The Mediterranean Sea and the countries of southern Europe lie to the south of western Europe. The Bay of Biscay and the Atlantic Ocean lie to the west of western Europe.

### Why Is Western Europe's Location Important?

Western Europe's location has helped it influence the world. It is near both Africa and some parts of Asia. For hundreds of years, people and goods have traveled to North and South America from western Europe's many ports. Explorers and settlers left these ports on long sea voyages around the world. These voyages spread European beliefs, cultures, and languages.

World War I, which was fought between 1914 and 1918, took place in western Europe. About 20 years later, World War II, which took place between 1939 and 1945, was also fought partly in western Europe. These two wars were the largest ones people have ever fought. Millions of people died.

Parts of western Europe are still recovering from World War II. In parts of Germany, for example, a huge wall once divided East and West Germany after the war. This was called the Berlin Wall. It finally came down in 1989, as this picture shows. Germany is now one country again.

## What Are the Three Physical Regions of Western Europe?

Western Europe has three physical regions. The largest region is the Central Lowlands. Geographers call it the Northern European Plain. This fairly flat area extends from southern England to the Ural Mountains in Russia. The region is almost totally flat in the Netherlands, but somewhat hilly everywhere else. Most Europeans live in this region. It has Europe's biggest cities and most of the industry. It also has the biggest transportation system, such as roads, highways, and railways.

The second physical region of western Europe is the Central Uplands. It lies between the Central Lowlands and the Alps Mountains. This region stretches from the Atlantic coast of Spain to Poland. It includes central and eastern France. It also includes the Black Forest and the Bohemian Forest areas of southern Germany.

The third physical region of western Europe is the Alps. These mountains stretch far beyond western Europe. When people think of the Alps, they think of Switzerland. However, the Alps also cover parts of southeastern France, northern Italy, southwestern Germany, Austria, and Slovenia. The region that contains the Alps has a low population density, except for some of its larger valleys.

## How Has Geography Shaped Western Europe's History?

Geography has played a big role in the history of western Europe. For example, Switzerland has mountains. These high mountains allowed Switzerland to stay out of wars. People who lived in mountain valleys developed their own culture because they were away from other people. The cultures often differed from that of the other people in their country. They often developed a different language. In fact, these people became more loyal to their region than to their country. That is one reason why Germany did not become one country until the late 1800s.

Having no mountains can also shape history. For example, **invaders,** or soldiers from other places, have often marched into the plains of the Central Lowlands. They took over the land from the people who lived there. These invaders used the many lowland rivers as highways. Of course, the people in the Central Lowlands have always used these rivers to ship goods and to travel.

## How Did Western Europe's Geography Influence World War I?

World War I is a good example of how geography influences history. In 1914, Germany declared war against France. However, the border between the two countries kept German soldiers from attacking France directly. Thick forests covered much of the border; the rugged Vosges Mountains formed the rest of the border.

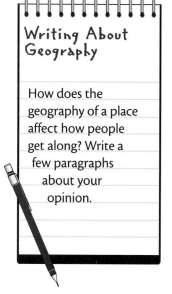

**Writing About Geography**

How does the geography of a place affect how people get along? Write a few paragraphs about your opinion.

Belgium, a small neighbor of the two countries, wanted to stay out of the war. This was impossible, however, because of the French-German dispute. To reach the French capital of Paris, German generals decided that the best way to reach Paris was to go through Belgium. They quickly took over nearly all of Belgium and the industrial area of northeastern France.

**Section 1 Review** On a separate sheet of paper, write answers to the following questions.

1) What seven countries make up western Europe?

2) How does the location of western Europe explain why it has influenced the world?

3) What are the three physical regions of western Europe?

4) In what region do most of the people in western Europe live?

5) Why did Germany choose to go through Belgium to get to France in World War I?

**What do YOU think?** Can mountains protect countries as much today as they did in the past? Explain your answer.

**Dike**
*A wall that prevents flooding and keeps back the sea*

**Eurasia**
*The world's largest land mass; the continents of Europe and Asia together*

**Pass**
*An opening in a mountain range*

**Peak**
*The top of a mountain*

**Polder**
*A piece of land that was once part of the sea*

## What Are the Main Physical Features?

The biggest physical feature of western Europe is the Alps. This range of young mountains is about 700 miles long and stretches across several countries. Mont Blanc, which stands 15,771 feet tall, is the highest of all the Alps. It is also the tallest mountain in western Europe. Snow covers many of the **peaks,** or tops, of the Alps. Tourists can see huge glaciers, large waterfalls, and many streams in these mountains. They contain many **passes,** or openings.

France has other large upland areas. The Massif Central is located in the southeast-central part of France. This area of low, worn-down mountains and newer peaks covers about one-sixth of the country. France's other mountain ranges are the Vosges in the northeast; the Jura in the east; and the Pyrenees in the south on the Spanish border.

Huge, sandy plains cover northern France and northern Germany. They stretch for hundreds of miles. In the Netherlands, the Dutch people have created **polders** by taking back land from the sea. For hundreds of years, the people of the Netherlands have built **dikes,** or walls, to prevent floods. They use huge electric pumps to keep the seawater from returning to the polders. Half of the Netherlands is made up of polder land.

## What Bodies of Water Exist?

Some people describe Europe as a giant peninsula because water surrounds it on three sides. The peninsula is on the western part of **Eurasia,** which is the world's largest piece of land. Eurasia includes the continents of Europe and Asia. Water surrounds western Europe on the north, the south, and the west.

**The Alps stretch across several countries in the southern part of western Europe.**

The North Sea to the north is somewhat shallow. The Mediterranean Sea touches the southern coast of France. The Bay of Biscay forms the western shore. This bay is part of the Atlantic Ocean.

Rivers are important to western Europe. The four most important rivers of France are the Loire, the Seine, the Garonne, and the Rhône. The Loire is its longest river. It flows from the Massif Central to the Bay of Biscay. Paris, the capital of France, is located on the Seine, which flows north. The Garonne flows from the Pyrenees to the Atlantic. The Rhône starts in the Swiss Alps and flows into the Mediterranean.

The three important rivers of Germany are the Rhine, the Danube, and the Elbe. The Rhine links northern and southern Europe. It is Germany's most important waterway. Every year, thousands of large barges carry goods

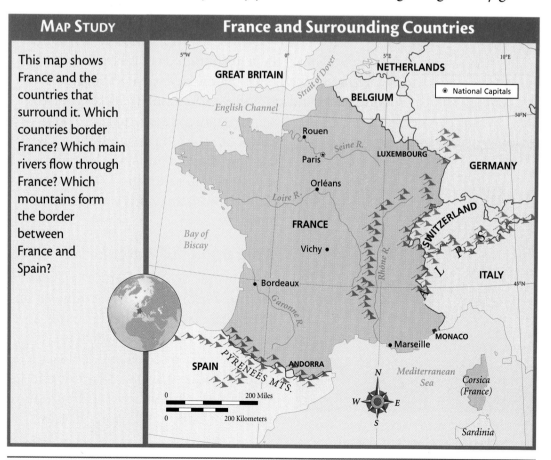

**MAP STUDY**

**France and Surrounding Countries**

This map shows France and the countries that surround it. Which countries border France? Which main rivers flow through France? Which mountains form the border between France and Spain?

**Mistral**
*A strong, cold, dry northerly wind from the Alps that blows across southern France*

on this river. The Danube begins in Germany and flows nearly 800 miles eastward through seven other countries. Then it reaches the Black Sea. The Elbe flows from the southeast to the northwest. The great German harbor of Hamburg is located where the Elbe meets the North Sea.

## What Is the Climate Like in Western Europe?

Western Europe has at least three climates. The main climate is marine west coast. Northern France, Belgium, the Netherlands, Luxembourg, and Germany share this climate with the British Isles. The Gulf Stream makes it neither too hot nor too cold. However, cold air from the north may cause temperatures to drop well below freezing. This is especially true in Germany.

The southern part of western Europe, near the Mediterranean, has a different climate. The French Riviera borders the Mediterranean Sea. It has mild winters and dry, hot summers. Of course, the mountain areas of western Europe have their own climate. Southern France has **mistrals,** which can blow over 100 miles per hour! These strong, cold, dry winds blow down from the Alps. They cause temperatures in southern France to drop quickly.

**Section 2 Review** On a separate sheet of paper, write the word from the Word Bank that completes each sentence.

**WORD BANK**

Alps

Eurasia

marine west coast

Massif Central

Rhine

1) The biggest physical feature of western Europe is the _____.

2) The _____ covers about one-sixth of France.

3) Europe forms a peninsula on the western part of _____, which is the worlds' biggest piece of land.

4) Germany's most important waterway is the _____ River.

5) Most of western Europe has a _____ climate.

**What do YOU think?** The Mediterranean Sea is warm. Why do you think its warmth does not affect more of western Europe?

Dialect
*A different form of a language*

## What Cultures Does Western Europe Have?

Each country in western Europe has its own rich culture. The people are proud of their language and of their influence on world civilization. What is surprising about western Europe is how much the seven countries share in common. The day-to-day life of the people is much the same. All the children go to school. Their parents work. Most people live in cities. These cities mix the old with the new. Some parts look the same as they did hundreds of years ago. Other parts have tall buildings and fast highways.

Europeans share an interest in music, art, and books. Most larger cities have many theaters, opera houses, art museums, and dance companies. In nice weather, people sit outside in sidewalk cafes. There they share meals and talk. Western Europe has a long history of making and enjoying delicious food. Western Europeans also enjoy sports. Soccer is a popular sport. However, in Europe, soccer is called football. In mountain areas, skiing is also popular.

## What Languages Are Spoken?

Each country in western Europe has its own language. Some of these languages are related. For example, German and Dutch, the language of the Netherlands, are Germanic languages. People in some parts of Switzerland, Austria, and Belgium speak a German **dialect.** That is, they speak different forms of the German language.

The people of southern Belgium and France speak French. This Romance language grew out of Latin, the language of the ancient Romans. Switzerland has four official languages. Most people there speak a German dialect. Smaller

Western Europe has a rich culture. In this photo, people wear wooden masks during a festival in Germany.

groups speak French and Italian. The fourth language is Romansh, a language also based on Latin. Many people in western Europe speak several languages, including English.

## What Religions Do the People Practice?

Most western Europeans are Christians. The largest number are Roman Catholics. The rest are Protestants. These two groups have sometimes fought one another. The Thirty Years War (1618–1648) was a religious war between the Catholics and the Protestants. Most European powers fought in this war.

Immigrants have come to all the countries of western Europe. Many of these immigrants brought with them a different culture, language, or religion. Because of this, all the major world religions can be found in western Europe.

## Where Do Most Western European People Live?

Most western Europeans live in urban areas in the Central Lowlands. In fact, western Europe has one of the highest population densities in the world. People have been moving to the cities since the beginning of the Industrial Revolution. More than a million people live in several western European cities. The largest city in western Europe is Paris, France. In Germany, Hamburg, Berlin, and Munich have more than a million people each. Amsterdam, the capital of the Netherlands, is also large. Brussels, the capital of Belgium, is its biggest city. The region in which most of these cities are located forms a huge megalopolis of 4 million people.

## What Problems Do the People Face?

Western Europe has an aging population. Its population is growing slowly. People are living longer because of new technology in medicine. This means that more older people will need care in the future. Most governments believe that they have a duty to take care of the health and well-being of the elderly. In the future, this aging population could be a burden for younger people.

## The Chunnel

For over 200 years, people in England and France wanted to build a tunnel beneath the English Channel. This body of water separates the two countries. In 1986, work began. In 1994, the Chunnel opened! It connects Folkestone, England, with Coquelles, France.

The Chunnel is a 31-mile-long tunnel beneath the waters of the English Channel. (Channel + tunnel = Chunnel.) About 24 of its 31 miles are 130 feet beneath the channel's seabed. The Chunnel has three tubes built side by side. The two outer tubes carry people and vehicles. The inner tube supplies fresh air. It also provides space for workers to do repair on the outer tubes.

Trains speed through the two outer tubes. One tube carries cars, buses, trucks, and their drivers. The second tube carries goods. The trip under the English Channel takes about 35 minutes.

---

**Foreigner**
*A person from another country*

A second problem is the economy. Economic growth in many of the countries has slowed down. France and Germany have a lot of unemployment. In the 1960s and 1970s, factories had lots of work but not enough workers. Because of this, they hired **foreigners,** or people from other countries.

Now, some unemployed workers in France and Germany dislike these foreigners. They say that the foreigners are taking jobs away from them. Political parties in many western European countries have spoken out against new immigration.

**Section 3 Review** On a separate sheet of paper, write *True* if the statement is true or *False* if the statement is not true. Make each false statement true by changing the underlined word.

1) The cultures of western Europe share <u>much</u> in common.

2) The favorite sport of most western European countries is what Europeans call football and North Americans call <u>soccer</u>.

3) Switzerland has <u>two</u> official languages.

4) The largest city in western Europe is <u>Berlin, Germany</u>.

5) One big issue facing western Europe is its <u>aging</u> <u>population</u>.

**What do YOU think?**

Why is knowing and speaking more than one language a good thing?

---

Currency
*A system of money*

European Union
*A group of European nations that agreed to rid trade barriers and use a common currency*

Tariff
*A tax that countries put on goods they import*

## What Is Western Europe's Economy Like?

All the countries of western Europe have successful free-market economies and a large manufacturing base. Many western European countries have high-tech industries, such as airplane and space technology.

After World War II, France, Italy, West Germany, Belgium, the Netherlands, and Luxembourg wanted closer ties with one another. To do this, they agreed to get rid of **tariffs** and some trade barriers. A tariff is a tax that countries put on goods they import. In 1957, these countries created the European Economic Community, also known as the Common Market.

During the 1980s and 1990s the European Economic Community grew. In 1992, it became the **European Union**. The members agreed to reduce trade barriers even more. They also agreed to create a common European **currency,** or system of money. The new Euro will replace the currency that each country has now.

In 2000, the European Union had 15 member nations. More than 12 other countries in eastern and southern Europe may join soon. Slowly, the people are taking steps to unite Europe.

---

### Biography  JACQUES COUSTEAU: 1910–1997

During the 1960s and 1970s, television carried the series "The Undersea World of Jacques Cousteau." Viewers watched Cousteau and his crew aboard *Calypso*, his research ship. They saw this famous French oceanographer explore the oceans around the world. His work helped people begin to take care of ocean life.

In 1943, Cousteau invented the aqualung. It helps divers move freely under water for long periods of time. He also developed the bathyscaphe. Within it, oceanographers move about in deep water. Cousteau is also famous for his books, such as *The Silent World*. His movies about the ocean won three Academy Awards.

## How Does Trade Affect Western Europe?

Business people try to sell their goods and services for the highest price. They also try to find the cheapest way to make goods and deliver them to other countries. When they do this, they make more money. This explains why European explorers set sail to find new lands. Columbus was not looking for the Americas when he found them. He was looking for a better and faster way to get to Asia. Then Europe could more easily sell its goods to the people there. This is an example of **international trade.** It is the buying and selling of goods and services among people in different countries.

People around the world want the products made in western Europe. Germany exports machine tools, electrical equipment, chemical products, and cars. The Netherlands is the world's leading maker of machinery for food and chemical processing. Factories in the United States, England, Germany, and other industrialized countries depend on these machines. Perfumes, fashions, and wines from France are world famous.

## What Natural Resources Does Western Europe Have?

France, the largest western European country, has few resources. It does have large coal deposits, but many of its mines are closed. Importing coal from other countries is now cheaper than mining its own coal. France has only a little oil, so it imports oil from the North Sea, the Middle East, and Africa.

France does have lots of fast-running rivers. Workers have built dams on many of these rivers. They supply France with hydroelectric power. France has built the world's first power station that depends on **tides,** the regular daily rise and fall of ocean waters.

Like France, Germany also has large coalfields. Some of this coal is near the surface. Huge mines remove tons of coal at one time. Mining provides cheap energy, but it harms the environment. Like France, Germany must import oil.

Hydroelectricity is an important source of power in parts of southern Germany, where fast-moving rivers flow. Germany is also trying out wind and sun power.

The Netherlands is the only country in western Europe with large amounts of natural gas. The Netherlands uses about half of the natural gas it produces. It exports the rest to its European neighbors. The port of Rotterdam in the Netherlands is always busy. Many European exports and imports pass through this harbor.

## What Are Some of Western Europe's Industries?

People use much of western Europe's land for farming. European farmers are some of the most productive in the world. As their farms become bigger, they use a lot of machinery. They grow many grains, especially wheat. Another important crop is grapes, which they grow to make wine. France produces more wine than any other country in the world. Germany also produces wine. The Netherlands exports tulips and other flowers around the world.

Western Europe is one of the world's most important industrial areas. Only the United States produces more products. Most of the heavy industries are located in one

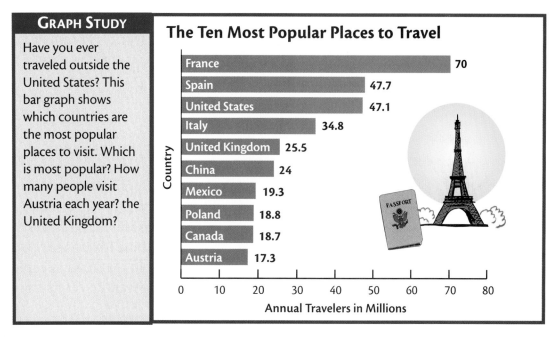

**GRAPH STUDY**

Have you ever traveled outside the United States? This bar graph shows which countries are the most popular places to visit. Which is most popular? How many people visit Austria each year? the United Kingdom?

**The Ten Most Popular Places to Travel**

| Country | Annual Travelers in Millions |
| --- | --- |
| France | 70 |
| Spain | 47.7 |
| United States | 47.1 |
| Italy | 34.8 |
| United Kingdom | 25.5 |
| China | 24 |
| Mexico | 19.3 |
| Poland | 18.8 |
| Canada | 18.7 |
| Austria | 17.3 |

area. It is made up of the **Benelux countries** of Belgium, Netherlands, and Luxembourg; the northeast corner of France; and northwest Germany. Its main industries are steel, automobiles, machines, textiles, and chemicals. However, most people work in service industries. For example, Switzerland is famous for its banks.

Millions of people work in tourism in western Europe. Some work in hotels and restaurants; others work as guides, bus drivers, or taxi drivers. The historical places, beautiful scenery, and cultural centers of western Europe appeal to many tourists. Most of them are other Europeans, but many come from the United States and Japan. Some like to hike or ski in the mountains. Others like to lie on the Mediterranean beaches.

## What Environmental Challenges Exist?

Western Europe faces the same environmental challenges as other industrialized countries. Among these are air and water pollution. Automobile traffic causes air pollution. Western Europe could build more roads, but that would hurt the environment. Because of this, the countries of western Europe have invested a lot of money in railroads. They have some of the world's fastest and most comfortable trains. Many cities do not let people drive cars in their central business areas.

**Western European nations have spent a lot of money on trains to cut down on the use of automobiles.**

The rivers of western Europe are badly polluted. As the population grows and river traffic increases, so does water pollution. The Rhine River is so polluted that many people do not want to eat its fish.

**Section 4 Review** Choose the letter of the answer that correctly completes each sentence. Write your answers on a separate sheet of paper.

1) The European Union is a group of _____.
   a. farmers
   b. steel workers
   c. industries
   d. countries

2) _____ is the buying and selling of goods and services among people in different countries.
   a. International trade
   b. Currency
   c. Trade barriers
   d. Tariffs

3) A major natural resource in western Europe is _____.
   a. silver
   b. coal
   c. gold
   d. bauxite

4) Western Europe's biggest producer of natural gas is _____.
   a. Germany
   b. France
   c. the Netherlands
   d. Belgium

5) French and German farmers grow grapes to make _____.
   a. fuel
   b. oil
   c. wine
   d. perfume

**What do YOU think?** Why is international trade important?

# The Iceman

On September 19, 1991, a German couple was hiking in the Alps. Suddenly, they saw what looked like a doll sticking out of the ice. Then they looked more closely and saw that it was a human body. They reported their find to officials. These officials called in experts.

The experts did tests that showed the body to be over 5,000 years old! They thought that this man must have been a hunter or a trader who lived in the mountains. For some reason, he lay down to rest. Maybe he was tired or sick. Then he fell asleep and froze to death. Soon snow and ice covered his body, protecting it so that it became like an Egyptian mummy. Because of this, the experts called him the Iceman.

The Iceman told the experts a lot about life in western Europe thousands of years ago. They found tattoo-like markings on his body. They think that these markings had something to do with the man's religious life. The remains of the Iceman's clothing told the experts that the people of his time could sew clothes together.

The Iceman carried things with him. These also told the experts about life in western Europe long ago. For example, the Iceman

**This picture shows what the Iceman may have looked like when he was alive.**

carried a fungus on a string. He may have used this for medicine. He also carried tiny pieces of wheat and a copper ax. This means the people in the Iceman's time knew how to mine copper. They also knew how to melt it and shape it into useful tools like an ax.

The Iceman taught us many things. We now know that people have lived in western Europe for thousands of years. These ancient people must have traveled from one mountain valley to another. They traded goods. They grew grains like wheat and barley. They made copper tools.

## Spotlight Story Wrap-Up

1) Who is the Iceman?

2) Where was the Iceman found?

3) What do some experts think was the meaning of the tattoos on the Iceman's body?

4) What does the Iceman's copper ax tell us?

5) What does the wheat that the Iceman carried tell us?

◆ Western Europe is made up of seven countries: France, the Netherlands, Belgium, Luxembourg, Austria, Germany, and Switzerland. They lie south of the North Sea, east of the Atlantic Ocean, and north of the Mediterranean Sea.

◆ Western Europe has three physical regions: the Central Lowlands, the Central Uplands, and the Alps.

◆ The biggest physical feature of western Europe is the Alps. This mountain chain is about 700 miles long. It covers parts of France, Italy, Germany, Austria, Switzerland, and Slovenia.

◆ Northern France and Germany are areas of vast plains. The people of the Netherlands have created land from the sea called polders.

◆ The climate of western Europe is a marine west coast climate. The main influence on the climate is cold air from the north and the Gulf Stream. The mountainous areas have their own climate.

◆ Each country in western Europe has its own language and culture. However, many of these languages are related because they are Germanic. Switzerland has four official languages: a German dialect, French, Italian, and Romansh. French is a Romance language.

◆ Most people of western Europe are Christians. The largest number are Roman Catholics; most of the rest are Protestants. However, immigrants have brought every major religion to the area.

◆ Most western Europeans live in urban areas. Western Europe has one of the highest population densities in the world.

◆ The seven countries of western Europe have successful free-market economies. The European Union is a group of countries that work together to get rid of trade barriers and tariffs. This community of countries is uniting Europe.

◆ The main natural resource of western Europe is coal. Both France and Germany use their rivers for hydroelectricity. The Netherlands is the only country in western Europe with large amounts of natural gas.

◆ Many people in western Europe farm. They raise grains, especially wheat, and grapes for wine. France produces more wine than any other country in the world. Western Europe is one of the world's main industrial areas. However, the largest percentage of workers work in service industries and tourism.

◆ Western Europe faces the environmental problems of air and water pollution.

## Comprehension: Identifying Facts

On a separate sheet of paper, use the words from the Word Bank to complete each sentence.

| WORD BANK |
| --- |
| Alps |
| Bay of Biscay |
| Germanic |
| Paris |
| Polders |

1) The _____ is part of the Atlantic Ocean.

2) The _____ are the highest mountains in western Europe.

3) The largest city in western Europe is _____.

4) _____ are lands that the people of the Netherlands made from the sea.

5) Except for the French, most people of western Europe speak a _____ language.

## Comprehension: Multiple Choice

On a separate sheet of paper, write the letter of the answer that correctly completes each sentence.

1) The largest country in western Europe is _____.

   a. Germany          c. Belgium

   b. France           d. Switzerland

2) The _____ River flows through Germany and links northern and southern Europe.

   a. Rhône            c. Rhine

   b. Seine            d. Loire

3) Most of western Europe has a _____ climate.

   a. marine west coast   c. continental

   b. tropical         d. highland

4) _____ is a Romance language based on Latin, the language of the ancient Romans.

   a. German           c. Dutch

   b. French           d. Russian

5) Western Europe faces the environmental problems of
_____.

    a. air and water pollution  c. soil erosion

    b. deforestation            d. none of the above

## Comprehension: Understanding Main Ideas

On a separate sheet of paper, write the answer to each question. Use complete sentences.

1) What are the three main physical regions of western Europe?

2) Why do geographers think of western Europe as a peninsula?

3) Where do most western Europeans live?

## Critical Thinking: Write Your Opinion

On a separate sheet of paper, write the answer to each question. Use complete sentences.

1) Imagine that you work for a U.S. company involved in international trade. Why might knowing French or German help you in your work?

2) Why might some western European countries be unwilling to join the European Union?

## Applying the Five Themes of Geography

### *Region*

Why might the European Union be considered a region?

> **Test-Taking Tip**
>
> Look over a test before you begin answering questions. See how many parts there are. Skim through the whole test to find out what is expected of you. Try to set aside enough time to complete each section.

# Southern Europe

Southern Europe is small, but it is an important area. It contains four countries: Portugal, Spain, Italy, and Greece. Spain and Portugal once had great empires. Millions of people around the world speak their languages. Ancient Greece gave the world many ideas about government. The building pictured on this page is the Parthenon, a building from ancient Greece. Rome, the capital of Italy, gave the world ideas about laws.

## Goals for Learning

▶ To describe where southern Europe is located

▶ To identify southern Europe's most important physical features and climate

▶ To describe the cultures of southern Europe

▶ To explain where most people live in southern Europe

▶ To describe the economy of southern Europe and the environmental challenges it faces

### *Geo-Stats*

**The Nations of Southern Europe**

**Nation:** Greece
**Population:** 10,539,000
**Area** (in square miles): 50,962
**Major Cities:** Athens (capital), Thessaloníki, Piraeus, Patras

**Nation:** Portugal
**Population:** 9,992,000
**Area** (in square miles): 35,672
**Major Cities:** Lisbon (capital), Porto, Vila Nova de Gaia, Amadora, Cascais

**Nation:** Italy
**Population:** 57,717,000
**Area** (in square miles): 116,324
**Major Cities:** Rome (capital), Naples, Milan, Turin

**Nation:** Spain
**Population:** 39,418,000
**Area** (in square miles): 194,897
**Major Cities:** Madrid (capital), Barcelona, Valencia, Seville, Zaragoza

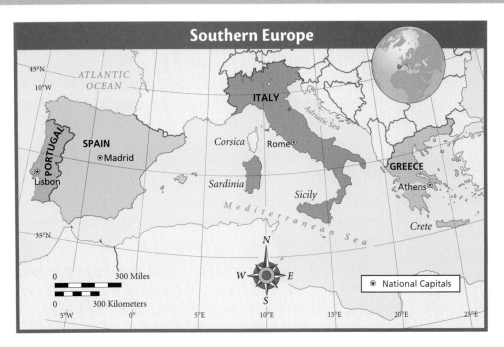

## Southern Europe

45°N
ATLANTIC
OCEAN
10°W

ITALY

PORTUGAL

SPAIN

⊛Madrid

⊛ Lisbon

Corsica

Rome⊛

Adriatic Sea

GREECE

Sardinia

Athens⊛

Sicily

Mediterranean Sea

Crete

35°N

N
W — E
S

0    300 Miles

0    300 Kilometers

⊛  National Capitals

5°W        0°        5°E        10°E        15°E        20°E        25°E

*Map Skills*

Southern Europe lies along the northern coast of the Mediterranean Sea. It is made up of the four countries of Spain, Portugal, Italy, and Greece. Ancient Greece and Italy's ancient Rome are two of the oldest civilizations in the world. Some buildings from these civilizations still stand today. Like western Europe, many tourists visit southern Europe for its beauty and history.

Study the map and answer the following questions:

**1)** What sea lies to the east of Italy?

**2)** What is the capital of Greece? Italy? Spain? Portugal?

**3)** Near what degrees of latitude and longitude is most of southern Europe?

**4)** Geographers often call southern Europe and northern Africa the Mediterranean Region. Why does this name fit?

**5)** Why is the Mediterranean Sea important to the countries of southern Europe?

Meseta
*The large plateau in Spain that is dry and hot with little vegetation*

Strait
*A narrow passage of water between two larger bodies of water*

## Where Is Southern Europe Located?

Southern Europe is located between 35° and 45° north of the equator. The area is sometimes called Mediterranean Europe because the countries of southern Europe are located on the Mediterranean Sea.

## What Physical Regions Exist in Southern Europe?

Three peninsulas make up southern Europe: the Iberian Peninsula, the Italian peninsula, and the Balkan Peninsula. These peninsulas are the three physical regions.

Spain and Portugal make up the Iberian Peninsula. Like all peninsulas, water surrounds it on three sides. The Bay of Biscay lies to the northwest. The Mediterranean Sea borders the east and south. The Atlantic Ocean touches the western coast of the peninsula. The **Strait** of Gibraltar links the Atlantic Ocean with the Mediterranean Sea. A strait is a narrow passage of water between two larger bodies of water.

Four seas, each a part of the Mediterranean Sea, surround the Italian peninsula. The Adriatic Sea lies to the east. The Ionian Sea separates Italy from Greece in the southeast. The Tyrrhenian Sea lies off Italy's southwestern coast. The Ligurian Sea borders the northwestern coast.

Greece is the most southern part of what geographers call the Balkan Peninsula. The Ionian Sea touches its western coast. The Aegean Sea lies to the east and south. This sea is another arm of the Mediterranean Sea. The Aegean stretches from northeastern Greece to Crete, the country's largest and southernmost island.

## What Political Regions Exist?

The four nations of southern Europe are Spain, Portugal, Italy, and Greece. Spain is the largest of the southern European countries. More than half of the country is a dry plateau that geographers call the **meseta** or tableland. The meseta receives little rainfall. Summers are hot. The region has little vegetation and is hard to farm. Most people in Spain live on coastal lowlands on the edge of the meseta. The Costa Brava, or Rough Coast, lies in the north of Spain. To the south is the Costa del Sol, or Coast of the Sun. Its year-round sunshine draws thousands of tourists.

Portugal's land looks a lot like Spain's. Much of it is a dry highland. Geographers call southern Portugal the Algarve. Northern Portugal receives more rain than the Algarve. Northern Portugal also has fertile soil and good farmland.

Mountains cover more than three-fourths of Italy and Greece. Most people in Italy live in mountain valleys or coastal plains. The western plains of Italy's Tyrrhenian coast are good for farming. In the south, the plains used to be swampy and marshy. However, Italian farmers drained the swamps and marshes to create new farmland. Since most Greeks live on the coast, Greek farmers also drained swampy areas to create farmland.

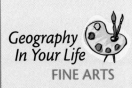

*Geography In Your Life*
FINE ARTS

### The Influence of Greek and Roman Architecture

Architecture is the art of designing and building places where humans live and work, worship, and do business. The ancient Greeks and Romans developed many styles of architecture and many ways to enclose space. Greek architects gave civilization three different kinds of columns. They used them to build their temples for worship. Romans perfected two more kinds of columns plus the arch, the dome, and the vault. These allowed them to cover large open spaces and to build bigger public buildings and baths.

Today, architects still use columns, arches, domes, and vaults in buildings. They use them to build banks, museums, colleges, government buildings, stock exchanges, railway stations, subways, and churches. When you visit Washington, D.C., look at the great dome on the capitol. The Romans gave us the idea for that! Look upward as you walk between its tall columns. Note the decorations. The Greeks gave the idea for those columns to us!

**The Erechtheion at the acropolis in Athens, Greece, is a good example of ancient Greek architecture.**

## How Did Geography Shape the History of Southern Europe?

Because of the rugged land in which they lived, the people of southern Europe have always looked to the sea. All four countries share a long history of sailing. The ancient Greeks were among the first people to trade with others by sailing the Mediterranean. During the 1300s and 1400s, Italian ships sailed this sea. Merchants brought silks and spices overland from India and China to the eastern end of the Mediterranean Sea. Then Italian ships carried them to Italy and sold them in cities like Venice, Pisa, and Genoa.

Soon Spain and Portugal began looking for their own trade routes. They wanted to have silks and spices to sell. During the 1400s, Portugal began to search for a sea route to India and China. Portuguese sailors sailed south down the Atlantic Ocean toward the tip of Africa. They were the first explorers to go around the tip of Africa to get to India.

Spanish sailors also tried to reach Asia by sea. However, they sailed west instead of south as the Portuguese had done. Christopher Columbus, an Italian sea captain, sailed from Spain. He tried to reach India and its spices by crossing the Atlantic Ocean. Instead, he reached the Americas.

**Section 1 Review** On a separate sheet of paper, write *True* if the statement is true and *False* if the statement is not true. Make each false statement true by changing the underlined word.

1) Another name for southern Europe is <u>Atlantic</u> Europe.

2) A <u>strait</u> is a narrow passage of water between two larger bodies of water.

3) The <u>Ionian</u> Sea separates Italy from Greece.

4) <u>Plains</u> cover more than three-fourths of Italy and Greece.

5) Explorers from Spain and Portugal took to the sea to find new trade routes to <u>India</u> and China.

**What do YOU think?** How might history be different if fertile farmland instead of mountains made up most of southern Europe?

## What Are the Main Physical Features?

When you think of southern Europe, think of mountains. The Pyrenees Mountains separate Spain from France and western Europe. Some of these mountain peaks are over 11,000 feet high. The Pyrenees separate Spain and Portugal from western Europe. The Cantabrian Mountains is another big range in Spain. While not as high as the Pyrenees, the Cantabrians are almost as long.

The Alps Mountains border northern Italy. Farther east, between Italy, Switzerland, and Austria, stand the Dolomite Mountains. Just south of the Po River valley, the Apennine Mountains form the backbone of Italy. They stretch from northern to southern Italy. The biggest mountain range in Greece is the Pindus Mountains.

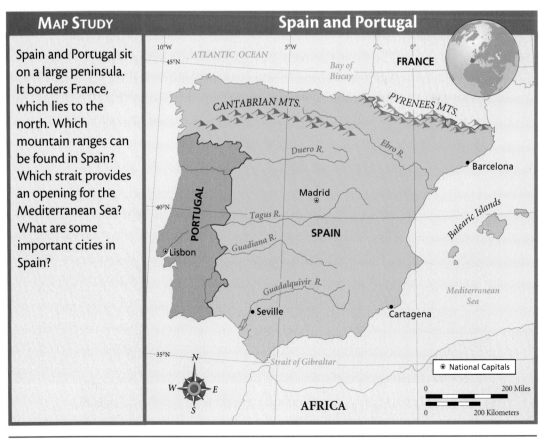

**MAP STUDY**

Spain and Portugal sit on a large peninsula. It borders France, which lies to the north. Which mountain ranges can be found in Spain? Which strait provides an opening for the Mediterranean Sea? What are some important cities in Spain?

**Spain and Portugal**

Southern Europe also has many islands. Greece includes an archipelago of hundreds of islands. In fact, islands make up about 20 percent of Greece. Its biggest islands are Crete, Corfu, and Rhodes in the eastern Mediterranean. The two largest islands in the Mediterranean are Sicily and Sardinia. They both belong to Italy. Spain also has some important islands off its coast. The Balearic Islands sit in the Mediterranean. The Canary Islands lie 800 miles southwest of Spain. They sit in the Atlantic Ocean and are only 70 miles from the northwestern coast of Africa. Grand Canary and Tenerife are the biggest of these islands.

## What Are the Main Bodies of Water?

As you know, many seas touch the coasts of southern Europe. However, this area also has many rivers. Most of them are shallow and short. Portugal's most important river is the Douro. Two important Spanish rivers rise out of the mountains. The Ebro and the Guadalquivir supply water for irrigation and hydroelectric power. Some of Spain's rivers dry up when rain does not fall.

The Po is the only navigable Italian river. The Po River valley has some of the best farmland in Europe. Italy's other important rivers are the Arno, the Tiber, the Dora, and the Taro. As in Spain, many of Italy's smaller rivers dry up in the hot summer months.

**The Mediterranean Sea is an important resource for the people of southern Europe.**

Greek rivers run short, winding courses from the highlands to the sea. None of them are navigable. Large ships cannot sail on any of them. The Achelous is Greece's longest river. It is only 137 miles from beginning to end.

The most famous lakes of southern Europe are in Italy. Glaciers in the Alps formed them thousands of years ago. They include Lake Como, Lake Maggiore, and Lake Garda.

## What Is the Climate Like?

Geographers usually describe the climate of southern Europe as Mediterranean. Summers are hot and dry; winters are short and mild. Rain usually falls in the winter. In fact, southern Europe has only two seasons: the dry season and the rainy season. However, some climate differences do occur in southern Europe. For example, more rain falls on its northern part than on its southern part. As a person travels farther south, temperatures remain about the same.

How high the land is also affects the climate. Mountain areas like the Alps receive more than 30 feet of snow a year. High up on the mountains, temperatures are generally lower than on the coastal plains. More precipitation falls in the mountains than on the coastal plains.

The best climate in southern Europe is probably on its islands. There, temperatures are almost the same throughout the entire year. Because of this, many tourists come to these islands every year.

**Section 2 Review** On a separate sheet of paper, write answers to the following questions.

1) What is the main physical feature of southern Europe?
2) What are the two biggest islands in the Mediterranean Sea?
3) What are the two main rivers of Spain?
4) What are the three most famous lakes in Italy?
5) What is the climate of southern Europe?

**Writing About Geography**

Imagine that you are a newspaper reporter for the travel section of a newspaper. Choose a city in southern Europe. Research your city, then write an article about it. Point out why a tourist would want to visit this place.

**What do YOU think?**

What would you like and dislike about living in southern Europe? Explain your answer.

Extended family
*An entire family,*
*including parents,*
*children,*
*grandparents, aunts,*
*uncles, cousins,*
*godparents, and*
*even close friends*

## What Cultures Exist in Southern Europe?

Each country in southern Europe has its own culture. Spain, Portugal, and Italy are a mix of many people. Their cultures reflect the different peoples who once ruled the land. For example, Spain has several cultures, each one different from the other. Northern Spaniards are descended from Celtic people. Southern Spain was strongly influenced by 700 years of Arab rule. Ancient Iberian tribes influenced the people of eastern Spain and Portugal. The Iberians were the first people in Portugal. Later the Celts and Romans arrived there. Still later, the Moors, Arab invaders from North Africa, overran Portugal and conquered the people there.

Most Italians are descended from the ancient Etruscans and Romans. During its long history, however, many different people have settled in Italy. Greeks sailed to the south of Italy and set up colonies. Later, Germanic and Norman people invaded Italy, defeated the people living there, and stayed.

The people of Greece call their country Hellas; they call themselves Hellenes. About 94 percent of the people of Greece have a Greek background. But people from other areas have also influenced Greece. Slavic people from the Balkans live in the northern part of the country. (You will learn about the Slavic people in Chapter 10.) About 4 percent of the people living in Greece are Turkish. This is because the Turks ruled Greece for many years.

## What Do the Cultures of Southern Europe Have in Common?

Southern European cultures share much in common. The people in Portugal, Spain, Italy, and Greece believe that the family is more important than anything else. They have **extended families.** That is, they believe that a family is made up of parents, children, grandparents, aunts, uncles, cousins, godparents, and even close friends.

**Tradition**
*The ideas, beliefs, and customs that people pass down to their descendants*

Religion, history, and **tradition** play a big part in the lives of the people of southern Europe. Traditions are ideas, beliefs, and customs that people pass down to their descendants. Meals are an important part of daily life because they are a time for families to get together. Southern Europeans like good food. In fact, people all over the world like their foods, especially those of Greece and Italy.

## What Religions Do Southern Europeans Practice?

Small groups of Protestants, Jews, and Muslims live in Southern Europe. However, most southern Europeans are Christians. Most people in Spain, Portugal, and Italy are Roman Catholics. Religious holidays are an important part of their culture. One of the biggest events in their year is Holy Week. This is the week that ends with the celebration of Easter.

The world center for Roman Catholics is Vatican City. It sits within the city of Rome, Italy. The pope, who is the head of the Roman Catholic Church, lives there. He runs Vatican City, which is an independent nation.

More than 95 percent of Greeks belong to the Greek Orthodox Church. Until about the eleventh century, it was part of the Roman Catholic Church.

**Vatican City is an independent nation within Rome. The pope lives there.**

## What Languages Do Southern Europeans Speak?

All southern European languages, except Greek, are Romance languages. Romance languages grew out of Latin. It was the language of ancient Rome. The people of Portugal speak Portuguese. Most people in Spain speak Spanish. However, in some parts of Spain, the people speak a local dialect. The language of Italy is Italian. Many people there also speak a local dialect. Sometimes, people who speak one dialect do not understand people who speak another dialect. In Italy's border areas, many people speak German or French.

## Where Do the People of Southern Europe Live?

Before the 1940s, most southern Europeans lived in rural areas. After World War II, people left their farms and went to the cities to work in factories. Today, both Spain and Italy are very urban. Of the four southern European countries, Italy has the most people. About 97 percent of Italians live in cities. In Spain, more than 90 percent live in cities. Portugal and Greece are more rural, but there too, over half of the people live in cities.

Southern Europe has many big cities. Madrid and Barcelona are the two largest cities in Spain. More than four million people live in the metropolitan areas of these two Spanish cities. Italy's largest cities are Rome, Napoli, Milan, and Turin. Lisbon, the capital of Portugal, has over two million people. Three out of every ten Greeks live in Athens.

## What Problems Do the People Face?

One problem facing Spain and Italy is **regionalism.** That is, people feel more loyal to their part of the country than to the whole country. One example of this is the Basques. They live in northern Spain. They speak their own language and have their own culture. Some Basques want to separate themselves from Spain. As for Italy, it has been united only since 1871. Regionalism is not as strong there as in Spain, but it does exist.

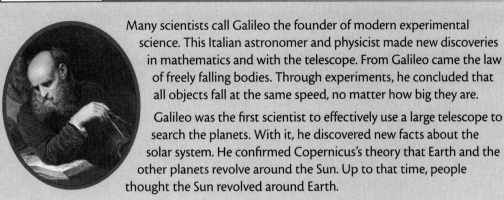
**Section 3 Review** Choose the letter of the answer that correctly completes each sentence. Write your answers on a separate sheet of paper.

1) Southern Spain was influenced by _____ rule.

   a. French          c. Roman
   b. Arab            d. Germanic

2) Southern Europeans believe that _____ is more important than anything else.

   a. food            c. religion
   b. holidays        d. family

3) The world center for Roman Catholics is Vatican City, which is located in _____.

   a. Rome            c. Madrid
   b. Lisbon          d. Athens

4) The most urbanized country of southern Europe is _____.

   a. Italy           c. Spain
   b. Portugal        d. Greece

5) Some Basque people want to separate themselves from _____.

   a. Vatican City    c. Spain
   b. Portugal        d. Greece

**What do YOU think?**

Which Italian foods do you like most and why?

Inflation
*A period of rising prices*

Unemployment
*The condition of people not being able to find jobs*

## What Is Southern Europe's Economy Like?

The economies of southern Europe differ. All four countries are members of the European Union. However, Italy is one of the richest countries in Europe; Greece is one of the poorest. Until World War II, all four countries had economies based on farming. Agriculture is still important in Greece and Portugal even though they do have some industry. Italy began to industrialize right after the war ended. Spain industrialized in the 1960s and 1970s. Its economy grew quickly.

In recent years, Spain has had many problems. One problem is **inflation,** which is a period of rising prices. During a time of inflation, money does not buy as much as it used to. Spain's second problem is **unemployment.** Many young people there cannot find jobs.

## What Are Southern Europe's Natural Resources?

None of the southern European countries are rich in natural resources. Italy has to import oil. It does produce some hydroelectric and geothermal power. Italy mines only three minerals in large amounts: mercury, sulfur, and marble. It is the biggest producer of marble in the world. People use Italian marble to build fine buildings.

### Economy of Southern Europe

| Country | People in the Workforce | Unemployment Rate | Exports (in billions) | Imports (in billions) | Key Industries |
|---------|------------------------|-------------------|----------------------|----------------------|----------------|
| Spain | 16.2 million | 21% | $94.5 | $118.3 | machinery, tourism, agriculture |
| Portugal | 4.53 million | 7% | $23.8 | $33.9 | textiles, footwear, paper products |
| Italy | 22.8 million | 12.2% | $250 | $190 | tourism, textiles, steel, agriculture |
| Greece | 4.1 million | 10% | $9.8 | $27 | tourism, agriculture |

#### CHART STUDY

This chart contains information about the economies of Spain, Portugal, Italy, and Greece. What is Spain's workforce? What is the unemployment rate in Italy? How much does Portugal export? How much does Greece import? What industries do these countries have in common?

**Olives are an important export for Greece.**

Spain also uses its fast-moving mountain streams to produce hydroelectric power. Like Italy, Spain must import oil for its energy needs. It does have some iron, coal, and zinc in the north. Small amounts of other minerals have been found in Spain's central highlands. Some mineral resources have been found in Portugal. These are difficult to mine, however, so few mines exist.

The most important mineral found in Greece is bauxite. Oil has been discovered near some Greek islands, but it has not been drilled for yet. The reason for this is that nearby Turkey also claims the waters in which the oil has been found.

## What Are Some Major Industries in Southern Europe?

Agriculture is still an important part of the economy of Portugal, Spain, and Greece. Portugal is the world's leading producer of cork, which comes from trees. Fruit is Spain's biggest agricultural export. Greece exports olives, grapes, and other fruits. The Portuguese and Greeks have always turned to the sea to make a living. Their fishing industries are important. Shipping is also important to the Greek economy.

Thousands of people in southern Europe leave the countryside each year and move to factory jobs in the big cities. Other European Union countries have started

Venice is a city in northern Italy that was built on the Adriatic Sea. The city has many canals. Boats called gondolas are used for transportation on these canals. Flooding is a problem in this city. A flood in 1966 caused a lot of damage in Venice.

manufacturing businesses in Spain. They have done this because Spanish people work for less money than German or French people.

Italy's largest, oldest, and most important industry is textiles. Workers produce silk, cotton, and wool cloth. An industry related to textiles is the making of clothes. People around the world buy Italian suits, dresses, purses, hats, and shoes. Italy also has a large chemical industry. Italian-made motorcycles and cars are sold everywhere, as are Italian-made tires, appliances, and electronic equipment.

Tourism is important to all four southern European countries. Tourists come to see the ruins of ancient marble buildings and other historical sites. They also enjoy the swimming, fishing, sailing, and wonderful weather in southern Europe.

## What Environmental Challenges Exist?

The most serious environmental problem for southern Europe is water. In some places like Spain and Greece, the problem is that they have too little water. In Italy, the problem is too much water. The government has spent millions of dollars to try to stop flooding. A flood in 1966 caused a lot of damage to the city of Venice. No other place like Venice exists on Earth. Workers built the city long ago on supports they sank into the Adriatic Sea. Years ago, Venice had been sinking into the sea.

Water pollution is also a problem for southern Europe. Some factories let deadly chemicals flow into the rivers. Farmers use chemicals that run off the land into the rivers. These chemicals, used by industry and agriculture, pollute the rivers.

Another environmental problem is soil erosion. Much of the soil in southern Europe has eroded because farmers have worked the land for so many years. They have also raised goats for thousands of years. These farm animals have added to the problem of soil erosion. Goats can live on land that is too rocky or too poor for farming. Unfortunately, they eat plants down to the roots. When that happens, nothing is left to hold the soil to the land. Because of this, heavy rains wash away much of the topsoil and strong winds blow it away.

**Section 4 Review** On a separate sheet of paper, write the word from the Word Bank that completes each sentence.

| WORD BANK |
| :---: |
| Greece |
| Italy |
| Portugal |
| Spain |
| Venice |

1) _____, which is built on supports in the Adriatic Sea, is different from any other city on Earth.

2) _____ is the world's leading producer of cork.

3) _____ is one of the poorest countries in Europe.

4) Textiles is the oldest and most important industry in _____.

5) Foreign investors build factories in _____ because its workers work for less money than workers in some other European countries.

**What do YOU think?** Which country in this chapter do you think will have the strongest economy in the future? Explain your answer.

# The History of Pizza

Pizza is probably the favorite food of most U.S. teenagers. Every day, people in the U.S. eat 100 acres of pizza. That is 350 slices of pizza per second! Where did this favorite food come from? No one knows for sure.

Some historians think that the ancient Roman soldiers first made pizza. The word itself comes from the Latin word *picea*. Picea describes the blackening of the crust by the fire underneath. The first pizza was simply a round bread with oil and spices on top. No cheese and no tomatoes topped it.

How did tomatoes become a topping for pizza? Columbus brought back tomato plants from the Americas. He discovered that the native people in the Americas grew a red, juicy fruit that tasted delicious. He carried tomato plants back to Europe. Europeans had never seen tomatoes. At first, some of them thought that this new fruit was poisonous. After a while, however, people came to like tomatoes, so they added them to their pizza.

In 1889, a famous pizza maker created a pizza for the queen of Italy. He wanted the pizza to show the red, green, and white of the new flag of Italy. He used tomatoes for the red. For the green, he used basil, an herb. The white came from mozzarella cheese. This pizza is now sold all around the world.

Pizzas were cheap and filling, so even poor people could have them. This made pizza a popular food. When Italian immigrants came to the United States, they brought their pizza recipe with them. In 1905, one of these Italian immigrants opened the first store that sold pizza in the United States. Today, over 3 billion pizzas are sold every year in the U.S.

**No one knows for sure how pizza came to be. It has become a very popular food in the United States.**

## Spotlight Story Wrap-Up

1) How much pizza do Americans eat every day?

2) The word *pizza* comes from the Latin word *picea*. What does this Latin word mean?

3) Why were there no tomatoes on the first pizzas?

4) Why did pizza end up having red, green, and white ingredients?

5) When did the first store selling pizzas open in the U.S.?

◆ Southern Europe is made up of four countries: Portugal, Spain, Italy, and Greece. They lie north of the Mediterranean Sea and south of western Europe.

◆ Three peninsulas make up southern Europe: the Iberian, the Italian, and the Balkan. Around and about these peninsulas are the Bay of Biscay; the Atlantic Ocean; the Strait of Gibraltar; and the Mediterranean, Adriatic, Ionian, Tyrrhenian, Ligurian, and Aegean Seas. The people of southern Europe have always taken to sailing and exploring.

◆ More than half of Spain is a dry plateau. Much of Portugal is a dry highland. Mountains cover more than three-fourths of Italy and Greece.

◆ Most rivers in southern Europe are shallow and short.

◆ The climate of southern Europe is Mediterranean. The mountainous areas have their own climate.

◆ Each southern European country has its own language and culture. Portugal, Spain, and Italy are a mix of people from other places. Southern Europeans believe that the family is more important than anything else.

◆ All southern European languages, except Greek, are Romance languages.

◆ Most people in Portugal, Spain, and Italy are Roman Catholics. More than 95 percent of Greeks belong to the Greek Orthodox Church, which used to be part of the Roman Catholic Church.

◆ Most Spaniards and Italians live in urban areas. More than half the Greeks and Portuguese live in cities.

◆ The four countries of southern Europe have different economies. They all belong to the European Union. Italy is one of the richest European countries; Greece is one of the poorest.

◆ None of the southern European countries are rich in natural resources. Italy is the world's biggest producer of marble. Bauxite is Greece's most important mineral.

◆ Many southern Europeans farm. Portugal exports cork; Spain exports fruit; Greece exports olives, grapes, and other fruit.

◆ Both Spain and Italy have become more industrialized since World War II. Italy's largest industry is textiles. One of Spain's biggest industries is cars. Tourism is a large industry for southern Europe.

◆ Southern Europe faces the environment problems of too little or too much water, water pollution, and soil erosion.

## Comprehension: Identifying Facts

On a separate sheet of paper, use the words from the Word Bank to complete each sentence.

| WORD BANK |
| :--- |
| Gibraltar |
| Ionian Sea |
| mountains |
| regionalism |
| western Europe |

1) _____ is located north of southern Europe.

2) The body of water that separates Italy from Greece is the _____.

3) _____ cover most of southern Europe.

4) The Strait of _____ links the Atlantic Ocean with the Mediterranean Sea.

5) _____ occurs when people feel more loyal to one part of a country than to the whole country.

## Comprehension: Multiple Choice

On a separate sheet of paper, write the letter of the answer that correctly completes each sentence.

1) _____ is not a Romance language.

   a. Portuguese     c. Spanish

   b. Italian         d. Greek

2) The most serious environmental problem in southern Europe is _____.

   a. air pollution     c. soil erosion

   b. deforestation    d. too much or too little water

3) The climate of much of southern Europe is _____.

   a. Mediterranean   c. subtropical

   b. continental      d. marine west coast

4) _____ conquered parts of Portugal and Spain and influenced their cultures.

   a. Germans      c. Arabs

   b. Russians     d. Greeks

5) _____ is the world's largest producer of marble.

   a. Spain             c. Italy

   b. Portugal       d. Greece

## Comprehension: Understanding Main Ideas

On a separate sheet of paper, write the answer to each question. Use complete sentences.

1) How do the economies of the countries of southern Europe differ from one another?

2) In what way were the countries of Portugal, Spain, and Italy a mix of many cultures?

3) What makes southern Europe so popular with tourists?

## Critical Thinking: Write Your Opinion

On a separate sheet of paper, write your opinion to each question. Use complete sentences.

1) Should the United States give countries like Greece and Italy money to save important ancient buildings? Explain your answer.

2) Some countries that do not have energy resources like oil and natural gas build nuclear power plants. Is this a good idea? Explain your answer.

## Applying the Five Themes of Geography

*Movement*

In the nineteenth and early twentieth centuries, many people left Italy and Greece and moved to the United States. Why do you think they did this?

Test-Taking Tip

Do not wait until the night before a test to study. Plan your study time so that you can get a good night's sleep the night before a test. Study in short sessions rather than one long session. In the week before the test, spend time each evening reviewing your notes.

# Northern Europe

Iceland, Norway, Sweden, Denmark, and Finland make up northern Europe. They could be called the Northlands because they are so far north. They have fewer people than any other part of Europe. In fact, all the countries together have only about 24 million people. However, even though so few people live in northern Europe, these five countries enjoy a high standard of living. The photo on this page shows Norway.

## Goals for Learning

▶ To describe where northern Europe is located
▶ To identify northern Europe's most important physical features and climate
▶ To describe the cultures of northern Europe
▶ To explain where and how most people live in northern Europe
▶ To describe the economy of northern Europe and the environmental challenges it faces

 *Geo-Stats*

### The Nations of Northern Europe

 **Nation:** Denmark
**Population:** 5,325,000
**Area** (in square miles): 16,638
**Capital:** Copenhagen

 **Nation:** Norway
**Population:** 4,462,000
**Area** (in square miles): 125,182
**Capital:** Oslo

 **Nation:** Finland
**Population:** 5,170,000
**Area** (in square miles): 130,558
**Capital:** Helsinki

**Nation:** Sweden
**Population:** 8,856,000
**Area** (in square miles): 173,732
**Capital:** Stockholm

 **Nation:** Iceland
**Population:** 277,000
**Area** (in square miles): 39,769
**Capital:** Reykjavík

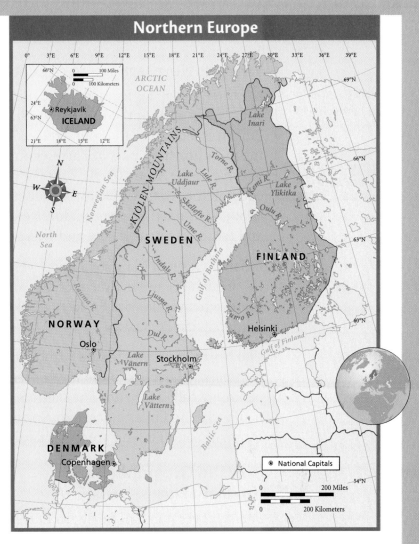

*Map Skills*

Northern Europe is north of western Europe. Four of the countries lie east of the North Sea and the Norwegian Sea. Much of northern Europe is mountainous and many islands are located in the nearby waters. One country, Iceland, is an island. It sits between the North Atlantic Ocean and the Greenland Sea. Have you ever heard of Vikings? These early explorers came from northern Europe.

Study the map and answer the following questions:

**1)** What five countries make up northern Europe?

**2)** Which two countries are side by side on a peninsula?

**3)** Where are the Kjölen Mountains located?

**4)** What are the main lakes in northern Europe?

**5)** What is the capital of Iceland? Denmark? Finland?

Arctic
*The cold area at the most northern part of Earth*

Scandinavia
*The five countries of northern Europe*

## Where Is Northern Europe Located?

Northern Europe is located in the north latitudes. It stretches from about 55° to 73° north. Much of northern Europe is located in the cold **Arctic.** This is the cold area at the most northern part of Earth. Some of northern Europe lies within the Arctic Circle. Like the two tropics and the equator, the Arctic Circle is an imaginary line of latitude about 66.5° north of the equator. Northern Europe is north and east of the British Isles and western Europe.

Iceland is a small island 645 miles west of Norway. The Norwegian Sea lies between Iceland and Norway. Norway shares a peninsula with Sweden. Geographers call this the Scandinavian Peninsula.

The North Sea separates the Scandinavian Peninsula from Denmark, which lies to the south. Denmark sits on its own peninsula called Jutland. The Baltic Sea lies between this peninsula and Finland. Iceland, Norway, Sweden, Denmark, and Finland are the **Scandinavian** countries.

## How Did Geography Shape Northern Europe's History?

Forests cover much of northern Europe. Mountains cover Norway and Sweden. For half the year, snow covers Finland. The climate there is harsh. Farming is also difficult.

Most people in northern Europe live close to the sea. They are descendants of fine sailors and boat builders. These early people used wood from the forests to build long boats. The boats were strong enough to carry them across the Atlantic Ocean. They were shallow enough to travel Europe's rivers.

In the past, farmers in northern Europe could not grow enough food for all its people. Because of this, many sailors took to the sea. They became great explorers, traders, and warriors.

Vikings lived long ago in Scandinavia. They were fine sailors and shipbuilders. Some of their largest ships could hold over 100 men. The Vikings explored much of Europe, and even traveled as far as North America in their ships.

## Who Were the Vikings?

A thousand years ago, people from Scandinavia were called Vikings. Many people feared them. They left Scandinavia and sailed to other parts of the world. They invaded the British Isles. From the Atlantic coast, they sailed and marched inland until they controlled much of Europe. In their great wooden ships, they sailed across the Atlantic to Iceland, Greenland, and North America. They did this 500 years before Columbus set sail from Spain in southern Europe. A group of Vikings called "the Rus" reached the Middle East and Central Asia. They left behind the name *Russia,* which, of course, is the name of the country there today.

## What Four Regions Exist in Northern Europe?

The four regions in northern Europe include Iceland, Denmark, the Scandinavian Peninsula, and Finland. These regions are political regions and physical regions.

**Most people in northern Europe live close to the sea. This photo shows Bergen Harbor, in Bergen, Norway.**

Rift
*A crack in the earth*

Volcanoes formed Iceland millions of years ago. It is located on a great **rift,** or crack in the earth. This rift lies in the deep waters of the Atlantic Ocean. In this area of Earth, volcanoes create new islands all the time. Earthquakes happen often. Because of this, the Icelandic people build concrete houses. These are harder for earthquakes to damage.

Denmark extends northward from the European plain that covers much of western Europe. It is one of the flattest countries in the world. Its highest point is only 531 feet. It has many islands.

Mountains cover much of the Scandinavian Peninsula. As you know, it is made up of the two countries of Norway and Sweden. Norway is almost one long chain of mountains. Most of its people live along the coast. Sweden is the largest country in northern Europe. The Swedish highlands are in the north. The land becomes less rugged as a person travels south. Southern Sweden is a plain with

## How Computers Help the Study of Geography

Like most people today, geographers use computers often. Computers help geographers do things faster, cheaper, more accurately, and in greater depth than by hand. Geographers use computers called Geographic Information Systems (GIS). They are used to collect and store information about Earth and its people. This information is then used to answer questions or to solve problems. Geographers can see patterns in society or how the land has changed over time. They can also create models to predict what could happen to the land or people in the future.

People other than geographers use computers to study geography. Meteorologists, for example, use computers to study the weather. Many businesses, schools, and government groups also use them. For example, someone in the restaurant business could use a GIS to find out the best place to build a restaurant. A computer could find the cheapest place to build a new restaurant that has the most people nearby to become its customers. This saves time and prevents poor business decisions.

rolling hills. This is where most Swedes live and where the biggest cities are located.

Finland, which lies to the northeast of Sweden, is mainly a plain. It is the most northerly country in the world. Glaciers formed most of the land features of northern Europe. They formed Finland's plain.

**Section 1 Review** On a separate sheet of paper, write the word from the Word Bank that completes each sentence.

| WORD BANK |
| --- |
| Arctic Circle |
| Denmark |
| Glaciers |
| Norway |
| Scandinavian |

1) The imaginary line around Earth at 66.5° north latitude is the _____.

2) Norway and Sweden occupy the _____ Peninsula.

3) _____ is one of the flattest countries in the world.

4) _____ is almost one large chain of mountains.

5) _____ formed many of the land features of northern Europe.

**What do YOU think?** Do you think geography or something else was the reason for the Vikings leaving their homelands and setting sail? Explain your answer.

Fjord
*A long, deep, narrow, ocean inlet that reaches far inland*

Geyser
*A hot spring that throws out jets of water and steam*

## What Are the Main Physical Features of Northern Europe?

**Fjords** are the best known physical feature of Iceland and Norway. These long, deep, narrow, ocean inlets reach far inland. They are like the fingers of the North Atlantic Ocean. Glaciers formed their deep, U-shaped valleys during the last ice age.

The fjords are usually deepest farther inland. There, at the head of the fjord, the glaciers were the thickest and had more force. Steep cliffs rise on both sides of a fjord. Beautiful waterfalls drop from these cliffs to the sea. The fjord waters are usually calm. They help protect the Scandinavian fishing fleets from the stormy waters of the North Atlantic Ocean.

Islands are a second feature of northern Europe. In fact, volcanoes near Iceland are still forming islands. One of the newest is Surtsey. Volcanoes formed this island in 1963. More than 150,000 islands dot the Norwegian coast. No one lives on most of these islands. However, Stockholm, Sweden's capital, is built on 14 islands. Denmark has over 400 islands.

**Fjords like this one are common in Iceland and Norway.**

Mountains are a third important feature. Iceland sits on top of the Mid-Atlantic Range, an underwater mountain chain. Norway has Europe's second highest mountains. They are the Jotunheimen, or "Land of the Giants." Only the Alps in western Europe are higher than Norway's mountains.

**Geysers** are a fourth important land feature. They are common in Iceland. A geyser is a hot spring that throws out jets of water and steam. Hot volcanic rocks deep inside Earth heat the water. When the underground pressure becomes too great, the hot water and steam **erupt,** or burst out of the ground. The people of Iceland make good use of this geothermal energy source. Most Icelandic homes and businesses use geothermal heating and hot-water systems.

## What Are Northern Europe's Main Bodies of Water?

Thousands of years ago, glaciers covered all of northern Europe. As they melted, they left behind thousands of lakes. Many are so small they have no name. Finland has over 50,000 lakes. Sweden and Norway have even more. They also have large areas of marshy bogs, especially in Finland. Lake Vanern in Sweden is northern Europe's largest lake. Scandinavia has many small rivers.

## What Is the Climate of Northern Europe Like?

Many tourists think that the climate of northern Europe is always cold because of the Arctic Circle. However, the Gulf Stream brings warmth to these countries. Norway's coastal areas have a marine west coast climate. Southern and central Sweden, where most of the people live, also has a moderate climate, as does much of southern Finland. No town in Denmark sits more than 50 miles from the sea. As you know, water has a moderating effect on the climate. The mountain areas of northern Europe, of course, have highland climates.

Some people call northern Europe "the land of the midnight sun." During some months, the sun does not set at all. The amount of daylight and night differs from place to place on Earth. At the equator, days and nights are equal in length. However, the farther a person travels north or south, the greater the difference between night and day.

The countries of northern Europe lie far north, so they have great differences in daylight and night. Areas above the Arctic Circle have long summer days. The **summer solstice** is the longest day of the year. On this day in the Arctic Circle, the sun never sets. During the winter, however, the people may not see the sun for weeks.

# Average Annual Rainfall in Europe

This map shows the average annual rainfall for most of Europe. What city has the highest average annual rainfall? In what areas does most of the rain usually fall?

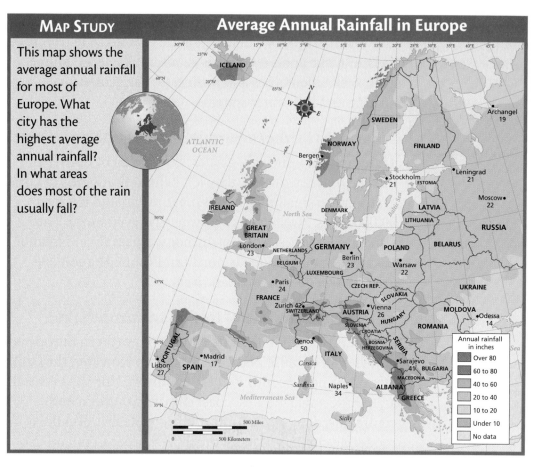

**Section 2 Review** On a separate sheet of paper, write answers to these questions.

1) What is a fjord?

2) Which country in northern Europe has the highest mountains?

3) What is a geyser?

4) Why is Scandinavia's climate so mild despite its far northern location?

5) Why do people call parts of northern Europe "the land of the midnight sun"?

**What do YOU think?** Why are most people in the United States not able to use geothermal energy sources?

**Homogenous**
*Belonging to the same group; alike in many ways*

**Minority**
*A small group within a larger group*

**Nomad**
*A person who moves from place to place*

**Refugee**
*A person who has left home and gone to another country because of war or political danger*

## What Cultures Does Northern Europe Have?

The cultures of Scandinavia are alike. They have shared a similar history for the last 1,000 years. Finland was part of Sweden for nearly 600 years; Iceland was part of Denmark. It became independent in 1944.

The population of the five countries of northern Europe is **homogenous.** This means that nearly everyone is descended from one group of people. Most Scandinavians are descended from Germanic tribes that settled in northern Europe hundreds of years ago.

Since the 1970s, Scandinavia has welcomed **refugees.** These people have left their native countries because of war or political danger. Today, people from the former Yugoslavia and from Turkey, Vietnam, and the Middle East live in the big cities of Scandinavia.

About 30,000 Sami live in Norway, Sweden, and Finland. They are the largest **minority** group in these three countries. A minority is a small group of people within a larger group. The Sami lived in northern Europe long before the Germanic tribes arrived there. Because they are originally from Asia, the Sami are darker and shorter than most Scandinavians.

About two-thirds of the 30,000 Sami live in Norway. In the past, the Sami were **nomads.** They moved from place to place, following the herds of reindeer. Many modern Sami have given up being nomads. They live in villages all year; they work at many jobs besides reindeer herding.

**The Sami are the largest minority group in Norway, Sweden, and Finland.**

## What Religion Do Northern Europeans Practice?

The five countries of northern Europe share a common religion. Most Scandinavians are Christians. Until the 1500s, they were Roman Catholics. Then the king of Sweden became a Protestant. Since then, the Lutheran Church has been the official church of northern Europe. However, the five Scandinavian countries give complete religious freedom to their citizens.

## What Languages Do Northern Europeans Speak?

Icelandic, Norwegian, Swedish, and Danish are Germanic languages in northern Europe. In fact, a person who reads one of these languages can easily read a book written in another of these languages. English is also a Germanic language. These four northern European languages share many words with English. For example, the Swedes say *god morgan* for "good morning" and *god natt* for "good night."

The Finnish language is not like the four other languages of northern Europe. It is related to Estonian and Hungarian. Probably thousands of years ago, people from northern Asia settled Finland. Today, all Finns learn Swedish, which is Finland's second official language.

All the school children in Scandinavia study English. They often speak it without an **accent.** That is, they pronounce English in the same way that native speakers do. Tourists from the United States are often surprised to hear how well young people in northern Europe speak English.

## Where Do the People of Northern Europe Live?

Northern Europe has a low population density. Many big cities around the world have more people than any one of the Scandinavian countries. Most people live in urban areas. About one-third of the Swedish people live in the metropolitan areas of Stockholm, Göteborg, and Malmö. One out of every five Finns lives in the capital of Helsinki. One-fourth of all Danes live in Copenhagen. It is Scandinavia's biggest city.

## What Problems Do the People Face?

Northern Europe has a slow growth in population. One reason for this is its low birthrate. The other reason is that, until recently, few people immigrated to northern Europe from other places. Most families have only one child. Nearly half the people in northern Europe live alone or in homes with just one other person.

A second problem is high taxes. Many Scandinavian workers pay more than 50 percent of what they earn in taxes. The governments of northern Europe use this tax money to pay for their **welfare** systems. Welfare is money or help that a government gives to people who are in need.

The welfare systems in northern Europe provide for people out of work, for older people, and for health care for everyone. People say that this welfare system provides care from "cradle to grave." This system allows all people to share their nation's wealth. Few people are wealthy, but few are poor.

The population of northern Europe is aging. Because of this, people are paying higher taxes so that the governments can take care of their older people. If the economy slows down, the governments will have less money to pay for welfare services. The governments of northern Europe continue to increase taxes to pay for welfare. Because of this, the economy may suffer.

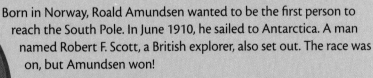

| Biography | ROALD AMUNDSEN: 1872–1928 |
| --- | --- |

Born in Norway, Roald Amundsen wanted to be the first person to reach the South Pole. In June 1910, he sailed to Antarctica. A man named Robert F. Scott, a British explorer, also set out. The race was on, but Amundsen won!

On October 19, 1911, Amundsen and his crew left Antarctica's coast with sleds, 52 Eskimo dogs, and skis. They reached the South Pole on December 14 and left a Norwegian flag there. Later, Amundsen became the first explorer to sail around the world by the Northwest and Northeast passages. He was also the first to fly over the North Pole in an airship.

**Section 3 Review** Choose the letter of the answer that correctly completes each sentence. Write your answers on a separate sheet of paper.

1) Almost all the people of northern Europe are descended from _____ tribes.

    a. Germanic          c. Estonian

    b. Russian           d. Central Asian

2) The _____ are the largest minority group in Norway, Sweden, and Finland.

    a. Russians          c. Hungarians

    b. Turks             d. Sami

3) Most Scandinavians belong to the _____ Church.

    a. Roman Catholic    c. Lutheran

    b. Eastern Orthodox  d. Presbyterian

4) _____ is the only Scandinavian language that is not Germanic.

    a. Swedish           c. Icelandic

    b. Norwegian         d. Finnish

5) Most Scandinavians pay about _____ percent of what they earn in taxes.

    a. 30                c. 50

    b. 40                d. 60

---

**What do YOU think?** Would you be willing to pay high taxes to provide care from "cradle to grave" for everyone? Explain your answer.

Socialism
*An economic system in which a government controls many of a country's biggest industries*

## What Is Northern Europe's Economy Like?

The people of northern Europe enjoy a high standard of living. All five countries have highly developed industries. People describe their economies as "the middle way" because they mix a free market with **socialism.** Socialism is an economic system in which the government controls many of the biggest industries. However, in northern Europe, about 85 percent of the industries are privately owned.

## What Natural Resources Does Northern Europe Have?

Northern Europe is rich in natural resources. Norway's most important resource is oil. In 1969, large oil and natural gas deposits were found in the Norwegian section of the North Sea. Today, Norway is Europe's largest oil producer. Norway exports both oil and natural gas. Most of these go to other European countries.

Iron, copper, lead, and zinc have been found in northern Europe. Many of these minerals are in the far north. These minerals are hard to get to, so mining has not been developed fully.

Forests and water are two other important resources in Scandinavia. Forests cover nearly three-fourths of Finland and half of Sweden. Both countries use their forests in large paper and pulp-making industries. Sweden is the world's third largest producer of paper products and pulp. Workers sometimes float logs down the many rivers of northern Europe. The rivers provide a highway from the forests to the sawmills. These fast-moving rivers also provide hydroelectric power.

## What Are Some of Northern Europe's Main Industries?

As in all industrialized countries, most people in northern Europe work in service industries, such as banking, tourism, and trade. More than half of all Scandinavian workers work in service jobs.

**Fishing is a major industry in northern Europe, especially in Norway.**

However, manufacturing is also important to the Scandinavian countries. Sweden manufactures the most products. Sweden manufactures many cars and trucks that are sold worldwide. It is also a big producer of telephones. Many Swedish industries manufacture chemicals, electronics, plastics, medicines, and paints.

Norway produces and exports chemical products. It is also the world's second largest exporter of metal products. Only Canada, which you read about in Chapter 2, exports more metal products.

Nearly one-fourth of all the people in Denmark work in manufacturing. Food processing, chemical products, electronics, and furniture making are the most important. Finland produces forest products, electronic goods, and motors.

Northern Europe's closeness to the sea explains why shipping is a key industry. Norway is one of the world's four biggest shipping countries. Fishing is also a big industry in Norway, just as it is in Iceland and Denmark. Many people in Iceland fish for a living. Fish processing provides them with many jobs. Norway is one of the world's top fishing countries. **Aquaculture,** or fish farming, has become an important industry there. Norwegian fish farmers raise salmon and trout.

> **Aquaculture**
> *Fish farming*

### What Environmental Problems Does Northern Europe Have?

The environmental problems of northern Europe are the same as those in other industrialized countries. Air and water pollution, destruction of natural areas, wasteful use of energy, and too much garbage are among its biggest problems. However, Scandinavians spend a lot of time outdoors, so they appreciate nature. Because of this, their rate for recycling aluminum, glass, and paper is one of the highest in the world. Environmental issues are important to Scandinavian voters.

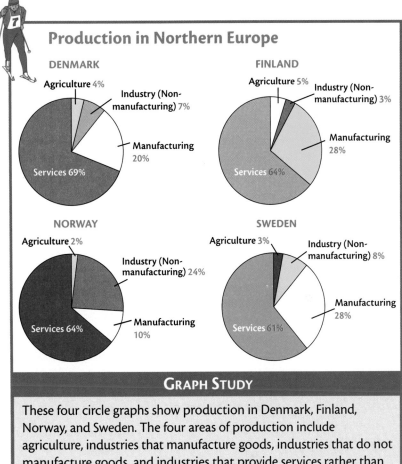

## Production in Northern Europe

**DENMARK**
- Agriculture 4%
- Industry (Non-manufacturing) 7%
- Manufacturing 20%
- Services 69%

**FINLAND**
- Agriculture 5%
- Industry (Non-manufacturing) 3%
- Manufacturing 28%
- Services 64%

**NORWAY**
- Agriculture 2%
- Industry (Non-manufacturing) 24%
- Manufacturing 10%
- Services 64%

**SWEDEN**
- Agriculture 3%
- Industry (Non-manufacturing) 8%
- Manufacturing 28%
- Services 61%

### GRAPH STUDY

These four circle graphs show production in Denmark, Finland, Norway, and Sweden. The four areas of production include agriculture, industries that manufacture goods, industries that do not manufacture goods, and industries that provide services rather than goods. Which country does the most manufacturing? Which country has the highest agriculture production? Which area of production is the highest for all four countries?

**Section 4 Review** On a separate sheet of paper, write *True* if the statement is true or *False* if the statement is not true. Make each false statement true by changing the underlined word.

1) The economies of northern Europe are a mix of free market and <u>socialism.</u>
2) <u>Iceland</u> has large oil and natural gas deposits.
3) <u>Forests</u> cover three-fourths of Finland.
4) Aquaculture is <u>wood</u> farming.
5) Most people in northern Europe work in <u>service</u> industries.

**What do YOU think?**

Would a political party that makes the environment a main issue have much support in the United States? Explain your answer.

# What's in a Name?

This may seem strange, but people have had family names for only the last 1,000 years. Before that, people lived in small villages. All the people knew each other. They rarely left their villages, so they seldom met people who did not know them. Then people began to move from place to place more often. This is when family names became more common.

How did people choose a family name? Many chose a name that was based on the first name of the father. In Scandinavia, many men had the name Carl, Ander, Oli, Erik, or Gunder. The children of these men formed their family name by adding *son* to the father's name. The children of Carl became Carlsons, or Carl's sons; the sons of Erik became Eriksons.

Sometimes people chose a family name from the place where they lived. The Scandinavian word for *shore* is *strand*. People who lived on the shore added *strand* to their first name.

People who lived near hills or mountains added *berg* to their names.

If you were to look at a Swedish telephone book, you would see that many of the names are alike. This makes finding the right person and phone number hard. To help, Swedish telephone books list the job the person has next to the person's name.

## Spotlight Story Wrap-Up

1) When did people first begin to use family names?

2) Why did people not need to use family names before then?

3) What was one of the most common ways for families to choose a family name?

4) What was another way to choose family names?

5) How does a Swedish telephone book help users find the person they are looking for among many people with the same name?

Some Scandinavian family names come from where a person lived. For example, if you were once a Scandinavian living near mountains, your family name may have included *berg*, which is Scandinavian for hills or mountains.

◆ Northern Europe is made up of five countries: Iceland, Norway, Sweden, Denmark, and Finland. They make up Scandinavia. Some parts of these countries are within the Arctic Circle.

◆ Iceland is an island. Norway and Sweden share the Scandinavian Peninsula. Denmark is on the Jutland Peninsula. The Baltic Sea lies between Denmark and Finland.

◆ Most Scandinavians live close to the sea. Long ago, Scandinavian sailors called Vikings took to the sea in long boats. They became great explorers, traders, and warriors.

◆ Volcanoes formed Iceland. Glaciers formed most of the land features of Norway, Sweden, Denmark, and Finland. Mountains cover much of the Scandinavian Peninsula. Denmark is one of the flattest countries in the world.

◆ Iceland has geysers. Like Norway, it also has many fjords, islands, and mountains. The three other northern European countries have many islands, too. Volcanoes in Iceland continue to form new islands. The Scandinavian countries have thousands of lakes and many fast-moving, but not navigable, rivers.

◆ The climate of northern Europe is a marine west coast climate because of the Gulf Stream. The mountainous areas have their own climate.

◆ The cultures of Scandinavia are alike. Most people are descended from Germanic tribes. All but the Finns speak a Germanic language.

◆ The Lutheran Church is the official church of Scandinavia.

◆ Northern Europe has a low population density. Most people live in urban areas.

◆ The economies of northern Europe mix free market with socialism. Most Scandinavians enjoy a high standard of living.

◆ Northern Europe is rich in natural resources. Among these are oil and natural gas in Norway; iron, copper, lead, and zinc; forests; and water.

◆ Manufacturing is important to Scandinavia. Sweden manufactures the most products of northern Europe. Finland has forest products. Fishing is a big industry in Norway, Denmark, and Iceland. Norway is one of the world's four biggest shipping countries. Aquaculture is also important there. Most Scandinavians, however, work in service industries.

◆ Northern Europe faces the environmental problems of industrialization. It faces the social problems of a slow growth in population and high taxes.

## Comprehension: Identifying Facts

On a separate sheet of paper, write the words from the Word Bank to complete each sentence.

**WORD BANK**

Arctic

fjords

Germanic

Scandinavia

socialism

1) _____ is another name for the countries of northern Europe.

2) Much of northern Europe is located in the _____.

3) The long, deep, narrow, ocean inlets that reach far inland in Iceland and Norway are _____.

4) Almost all the people of northern Europe are descended from _____ tribes.

5) People describe the economies of northern Europe as "the middle way" because they mix free-market economies and _____.

## Comprehension: Multiple Choice

On a separate sheet of paper, write the letter of the answer that correctly completes each sentence.

1) Geographers call the imaginary line of latitude that is about 66.5° north of the equator the _____.
   a. Capricorn Circle
   b. Tropic of Capricorn
   c. Tropic of Cancer
   d. Arctic Circle

2) Norway and Iceland have many _____.
   a. fjords
   b. islands
   c. mountains
   d. all of the above

3) _____ caused most of the physical features of northern Europe.
   a. Glaciers
   b. Aquaculture
   c. Rifts
   d. Plate tectonics

4) The population of northern Europe is _____ because most people belong to the same ethnic group.
   a. mixed
   b. homogeneous
   c. Slavic
   d. Sami

**5)** Most people of northern Europe live in _____ areas.

   a. rural          c. forest

   b. urban         d. mountain

## Comprehension: Understanding Main Ideas

On a separate sheet of paper, write the answer to each question. Use complete sentences.

**1)** What are the five countries of northern Europe?

**2)** What are two important problems facing the countries of northern Europe?

**3)** Why are the cultures of Scandinavia so alike?

## Critical Thinking: Write Your Opinion

On a separate sheet of paper, write your opinion to each question. Use complete sentences.

**1)** What do you like best about northern Europe?

**2)** How would northern Europe be different if glaciers had not covered it during the last ice age?

## Applying the Five Themes of Geography

### *Movement*

Why do you think the people of Scandinavia were the first to invent skiing?

**Test-Taking Tip**    When you read test directions, try to restate them in your own words. Tell yourself what you are expected to do. That way, you can make sure your answers will be complete and correct.

# Graphs and Charts

A graph shows relationships between numbers. Bar, line, and circle graphs are used to compare numbers.

Below is a simple circle graph.

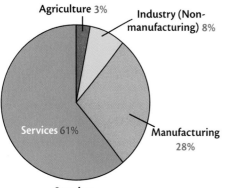

Agriculture 3%

Industry (Non-manufacturing) 8%

Services 61%

Manufacturing 28%

**Sweden**

A chart is a way to put information together so it is clear. The information is in rows that go across or in columns that go up and down. A chart is used to organize information.

The chart below has six columns. The first column names the four countries represented in the chart. The second column tells the number of people who work in each nation. The third column provides the percentage of those not working. The fourth column notes the amount of goods in dollars that each nation exports, or sells, to other countries each year. The fifth column shows the number of goods in dollars that each nation imports, or buys, from other countries each year. The last column shows each country's important industries.

## Economy of Southern Europe

| Country | People in the Workforce | Unemployment Rate | Exports (in billions) | Imports (in billions) | Key Industries |
|---------|------------------------|-------------------|----------------------|----------------------|----------------|
| Spain | 16.2 million | 21% | $94.5 | $118.3 | machinery, tourism, agriculture |
| Portugal | 4.53 million | 7% | $23.8 | $33.9 | textiles, footwear, paper products |
| Italy | 22.8 million | 12.2% | $250 | $190 | tourism, textiles, steel, agriculture |
| Greece | 4.1 million | 10% | $9.8 | $27 | tourism, agriculture |

Study the chart above and answer the following questions:

**1)** Which country has the largest workforce?

**2)** Which country has the lowest unemployment rate?

**3)** Italy exports more than the other three countries combined. How much more?

**4)** What key industries do Italy and Greece have in common?

**5)** Based on this chart, can you guess which nation has the strongest economy?

◆ The British Isles are made up of the two big islands of Great Britain and Ireland and many small islands. Western Europe is made up of seven countries: France, the Netherlands, Belgium, Luxembourg, Austria, Germany, and Switzerland. Southern Europe is made up of four countries: Portugal, Spain, Italy, and Greece. Northern Europe is made up of five countries: Iceland, Norway, Sweden, Denmark, and Finland.

◆ Glaciers once covered much of Europe. When these melted, their water formed the North Sea, the English Channel, and the many lakes and fjords of northern Europe.

◆ Southern Europe has a Mediterranean climate. The climate of the British Isles and western and northern Europe is marine west coast climate because of the Gulf Stream. The mountainous areas have their own climate.

◆ Almost all European countries have their own culture and language. English is the official language of the British Isles. French, Portuguese, Spanish, and Italian are Romance languages. Many languages of western and northern Europe are Germanic.

◆ Most Europeans are Christians. However, immigrants have brought every major religion to Europe.

◆ Both western Europe and Great Britain have a high population density. Northern Europe has a low population density. Most people in Europe live in cities.

◆ The British Isles and western Europe have successful free-market economies. The four countries of southern Europe have different economies. Northern Europe mixes a free-market economy with socialism.

◆ Other than coal, the British Isles and western Europe have few natural resources. Southern Europe has few resources, except for marble in Italy and bauxite in Greece. Northern European is rich in natural resources. Among these are oil and natural gas in Norway; iron, copper, lead, and zinc; forests; and water.

◆ Manufacturing is important in all of Europe. Many people in western and southern Europe farm. However, the largest percentage of workers work in service industries. Trade and tourism are important.

◆ All industrialized countries face the problems of air and water pollution. Southern Europe faces the problems of too little or too much water as well as soil erosion.

"People have passed through a very dark tunnel at the end of which there was a light of freedom. Unexpectedly they passed through the prison gates and found themselves in a square. They are now free and they don't know where to go."

—Václav Havel, president of the Czech Republic, 1990

# Eastern Europe and Russia

In the last unit, you learned about western, southern, and northern Europe. Now you turn eastward to eastern Europe, the Balkans, Russia, and the republics of the former Soviet Union. The nations of this huge region have much in common. Their cultures and languages have common roots. Their histories are also linked. Perhaps most importantly, much of this region was once under Communist rule. Beginning in the late 1980s, communism came to an end in this region. You will find out how this has affected these countries throughout the two chapters of Unit 4.

You will also learn about the varied geography of these lands. The photo on this page shows goat herders in the Altai Mountains in Russia, which is the largest nation in the world. You will learn that Russia's influence over this area has been strong. It remains a powerful nation and a strong influence in this region, but its future is uncertain.

### CHAPTERS IN UNIT 4

**Chapter 10:** Eastern Europe and the
Balkan Countries . . . . . . . . . . . . . . . . . . . . .226

**Chapter 11:** Russia and the
Independent Republics . . . . . . . . . . . . . . .246

# Eastern Europe and the Balkan Countries

Eastern Europe and the Balkans is an area in which great change is taking place. For many years, the former Soviet Union controlled the many small countries in this area. With the fall of communism and the Soviet Union, eastern Europe and the Balkans were left trying to catch up with the rest of Europe. The photo on this page shows farmland in Poland. This flat country is one of the main nations in this region.

## Goals for Learning

▶ To describe where eastern Europe and the Balkan countries are located
▶ To identify their most important physical features and climate
▶ To describe the diverse cultures of eastern Europe and the Balkans
▶ To explain where most people live in eastern Europe and the Balkans
▶ To describe the economy of eastern Europe and the Balkans and the environmental challenges they face

 *Geo-Stats*

### Key Nations of Eastern Europe and the Balkans

 **Nation:** Bosnia and Herzegovina
**Population:** 3,839,000
**Area** (in square miles): 19,741
**Major Cities:** Sarajevo (capital)

 **Nation:** Hungary
**Population:** 10,076,000
**Area** (in square miles): 35,919
**Major Cities:** Budapest (capital), Debrecen, Miskolc, Szeged

**Nation:** Poland
**Population:** 38,674,000
**Area** (in square miles): 120,725
**Major Cities:** Warsaw (capital), Kraków, Wroclaw

 **Nation:** Romania
**Population:** 22,460,000
**Area** (in square miles): 92,699
**Major Cities:** Bucharest (capital), Constantsa, Cluj-Napoca, Timisoara

## Eastern Europe and the Balkans

Study the map and answer the following questions:

**Map Skills**

1) Where is Romania located?

2) What are the main rivers of eastern Europe?

3) What mountain ranges can be found in eastern Europe?

4) What is the capital of Poland? Bosnia and Herzegovina? Hungary?

5) Based on this map, how would you describe the land in the Balkans?

### Where Are the Eastern Europe and the Balkan Countries Located?

Eastern Europe and the Balkan countries are located in the middle latitudes. They lie between 40° and 55° north latitude. Western Europe borders them to the west; Russia borders them on the east. The combined population of all the countries in eastern Europe and the Balkans is about 125 million.

Eastern Europe includes the four countries of Poland, the Czech Republic, Slovak Republic (Slovakia), and Hungary. It also includes the Balkan countries of Romania, Bulgaria, Albania, and the former Yugoslavia (Serbia). In the 1990s, Yugoslavia broke up into the independent states of Bosnia-Herzegovina, Croatia, Macedonia, and Slovenia. All that is left of Yugoslavia are Serbia and Montenegro.

The Balkan countries are located on the Balkan Peninsula. Greece lies to their south. The Adriatic and Ionian Seas border the west side of the peninsula. The Aegean and Black Sea border the east and south. All the other countries of eastern Europe, except for Poland, are landlocked. The Baltic Sea borders Poland on the north.

**Eastern Europe and the Balkans are not as industrialized as the rest of Europe. Some people in towns like this Polish town still use horses to haul things.**

**Balkanization**

*The breaking up of a geographical area or a group of people into smaller political groups; these smaller groups often fight with one another*

## What Four Regions Exist in Eastern Europe?

Eastern Europe has four regions. The North European Plain lies across the northern part of eastern Europe. This plain stretches across western and eastern Europe to the Ural Mountains in Russia. The land has gently rolling hills until they meet the high, Carpathian Mountains on the Poland-Slovakian border. Most of Poland is in this region.

Mountains and rugged hills form the second region. Slovakia and parts of the Czech Republic and Romania are in this region.

The third region, which is another plain, lies between the Carpathian Mountains and the Balkan Peninsula. Much of Hungary, Croatia, and the Danube River Valley of Romania sit on this flat plain. The Balkan Peninsula makes up the fourth region. It is covered with mountains.

## How Did Geography Shape the History of This Region?

Geography has led to problems for the countries of eastern Europe and the Balkans. Poland is one large, flat area with no natural boundaries. Because of this, its more powerful neighbors have invaded Poland many times. Throughout its history, its borders have changed often.

For over 400 years, Turkey controlled the Balkans. Mountains made governing these countries hard. It also made travel difficult. People who lived in this region were also cut off from their neighbors, so different cultures developed. Because of this, people began to mistrust those who were different from them. This led to fighting.

The winners of World War I broke up the old Turkish Empire. Afterward, a new word was added to the English language: **balkanization.** To balkanize is to break a geographical area or a group of people into smaller political groups. These smaller groups often fight with one another.

Writing About Geography

Eastern Europe and the Balkans have experienced great change in recent years. How would you feel if the government system in your country kept changing? Write about how this would affect you and how you would feel about it.

Marie Curie was a Polish-born French chemist. She and her husband, Pierre, studied radioactivity, which is the energy in atoms. Marie received the Nobel Prize in chemistry in 1903 and again in 1911.

The Curies wanted everyone to benefit from their studies. During World War I, Marie helped fit ambulances with x-ray equipment to help wounded soldiers. She even drove ambulances to the front lines. She also taught others how to use the equipment. Her work meant that she was often near radioactive materials. Its dangers were not known at the time. Radiation gave her cancer. In a twist of fate, today we use controlled radiation to treat cancer.

**Section 1 Review** On a separate sheet of paper, write *True* if the statement is true and *False* if the statement is not true. Make each false statement true by changing the underlined word.

1) Russia lies to the <u>west</u> of eastern Europe.

2) The <u>northern</u> part of eastern Europe is a vast plain.

3) <u>Greece</u> lies to the south of the Balkan Peninsula.

4) For over 500 years, <u>France</u> controlled the Balkan countries.

5) To <u>balkanize</u> is to break up a group of people or a geographical area into smaller political groups that are often fighting.

**What do YOU think?** Germany invaded Poland in World Wars I and II. How might the history of Poland be different if it had high mountains on the German-Polish border?

## What Are the Main Physical Features of This Area?

Eastern Europe's main feature is its huge area of plains. They produce most of the grains that the people of eastern Europe use. Farmers grow wheat, rye, corn, potatoes, sugar beets, cabbages, and tobacco on these rich plains.

Mountains are a second feature of eastern Europe. The Sudety Mountains are old mountains. The Carpathian Mountains are much younger and higher. They stretch across eastern Europe like a wide, curved line. Their highest peaks are on the border of Poland and Slovakia. In Romania, these mountains are not as high, but forests cover them.

The Rhodope Mountains are the highest mountains in the Balkan Peninsula. They join the Balkans near the Bulgarian capital of Sofia. The Balkan Mountains, however, give the Balkan Peninsula its name. In fact, *Balkan* is a Turkish word that means mountain. These mountains are located in the center of Bulgaria. Much of the former Yugoslavia has many mountains, too. The Dinaric Alps run down the Balkans along the Adriatic Coast. This region also has many other smaller mountain ranges.

## What Are the Major Bodies of Water in Eastern Europe and the Balkans?

Like other areas of Europe, glaciers helped to shape eastern Europe. Northern Poland has over 9,000 lakes. This is more than any other European country except Finland. However, the largest lake in eastern Europe is Lake Balaton in Hungary.

The glaciers also created many rivers. The most important river of eastern Europe and the Balkans is the Danube. It is 1,777 miles long. The Danube starts high in the Alps of Germany and Austria and flows eastward until it reaches the Black Sea. The Danube has many tributaries. It flows through Slovakia, Croatia, Hungary, Serbia, Romania, and Bulgaria.

The Danube River is an important source of transportation in eastern Europe.

## Mountain Ranges in Eastern Europe and the Balkans

| Mountain Range | Location | Highest Peak |
|---|---|---|
| Alps | France, Italy, Slovenia, Croatia, Bosnia and Herzegovina, Montenegro, Yugoslavia | 15,771 feet (Mont Blanc) |
| Rhodope Mountains | Bulgaria, Greece | 9,596 feet (Mt. Musula) |
| Carpathian Mountains | Slovak Republic, Poland, Romania | 8,711 feet (Mt. Gerlach) |
| Transylvanian Alps | Romania | 8,346 feet (Mt. Moldoveanu) |
| Dinaric Alps | Slovenia, Croatia, Bosnia and Herzegovina, Montenegro | 8,174 feet (Mt. Djeravica) |
| Balkan Mountains | Bulgaria, Yugoslavia | 7,746 feet (Botev Peak) |
| Sudety Mountains | Czech Republic, Poland | 5,256 feet (Snezka) |

### CHART STUDY

Eastern Europe and the Balkans have many mountains. This chart provides some information about the larger mountain ranges. Which mountain range seems to be the largest? Why?

Narrows
*A place where a river becomes narrow; a strait that connects two bodies of water*

The Danube links all the countries of eastern Europe. Each year, people move millions of tons of goods on the river. It is deep enough to allow large ships to travel on it. However, the Danube has a **narrows** that geographers call the Iron Gate. Until workers dug a canal there, larger ships could not travel farther than that point. A narrows is a place where a river becomes narrow or where a strait connects two bodies of water. At the Iron Gate, the Danube flows through a small gap between the steep mountains that line its two sides.

Each country in eastern Europe has important rivers. The Vistula is Poland's longest and most important river. Rivers always flow from high land to low land. This means that all of Poland's rivers flow from south to north because the highest land is in the south. Many of the rivers of the Balkan Peninsula are not navigable. However, they are important because they provide water for drinking and for irrigation.

## What Is the Climate Like?

Eastern Europe and the Balkans have several climates. The western part of this region shares the same marine west coast climate enjoyed by most of western Europe. The eastern part has a more humid continental climate. This is because it is farther away from the ocean. In these eastern lands north of the Danube River, winters are cold and snowy. Many rivers freeze during the winter. Summers may be hot with sudden thunderstorms.

Lands south of the Danube have a humid subtropical climate. Areas along the Adriatic Coast in Albania, Croatia, and the former Yugoslavia have a Mediterranean climate. This mild weather draws tourists to the area, just as it draws them to Mediterranean Europe.

**Section 2 Review** Choose the letter of the answer that correctly completes each sentence. Write your answers on a separate sheet of paper.

1) The large area of plains in eastern Europe is an important _____ area.
   a. industrial          c. urban
   b. farming             d. fishing

2) The _____ Mountains are the highest and largest mountain range of the Balkan Peninsula.
   a. Balkan              c. Rhodope
   b. Sudety              d. Carpathian

3) _____ formed Poland's many lakes.
   a. Flooding            c. Rain
   b. Dikes               d. Glaciers

4) The _____ is the most important river of eastern Europe.
   a. Danube              c. Rhine
   b. Vistula             d. Elbe

5) The eastern part of eastern Europe has a _____ climate.
   a. marine west coast   c. Mediterranean
   b. humid continental   d. tropical

**What do YOU think?**

Why do you think the tourist areas of the Balkans are not as popular as they were twenty years ago? Hint: think of today's newspaper headlines and television news.

Cultural crossroad
*A place where different cultures come into contact with one another*

Cyrillic alphabet
*An alphabet that began in about A.D. 900 and was used to translate the Bible into Slavic languages*

Ethnic group
*A group of people who have a common language, culture, and set of values*

Slavic
*Having to do with people from central Asia who settled in eastern Europe*

## What Cultures Exist in This Region?

The people of eastern Europe and the Balkans have many cultures. In the past, this area was an important **cultural crossroad.** That is, it was a place where different cultures came into contact with one another. People from other places often invaded the area. Each set of invaders left behind some part of its culture.

The Germanic tribes and the Romans invaded from the west. People from central Asia invaded from the east. These **Slavic** tribes lived in some areas of eastern Europe as early as 2000 B.C. They had different cultures and spoke different languages. Some settled in what is today Poland. Others became what today are called Czechs and Slovaks. Bulgarians, Serbs, and Russians are also Slavic people. Magyars from Asia invaded and settled modern Hungary. Turkey greatly influenced the Balkan countries. They left their mark in religion, architecture, and the customs of some of the people.

## What Languages Do the People Speak?

Because of their history, eastern Europe and the Balkans have many different **ethnic groups.** An ethnic group is a group of people who have a common language, culture, and set of values. These ethnic groups have lived in the same area for a long time. However, they often fought each other. Instead of looking at what they have in common, they look at their differences.

One key difference is language. Most of the languages spoken, such as Polish, Czech, Slovakian, Bulgarian, and Serbo-Croatian, are Slavic languages. Even though these languages are related to one another, they are quite different. In the western part of eastern Europe, most people write with Roman, or Latin letters. In the eastern part, they are more likely to use the **Cyrillic alphabet.** This alphabet started to be used in about A.D. 900 to translate the Bible into Slavic languages.

## What Religions Do the People Practice?

Another key difference among the people of eastern Europe and the Balkans is religion. Most people are Christians. The Roman Catholic Church greatly influenced the western part of this area. About two-thirds of the Hungarians are Roman Catholics. About 90 percent of the Polish people are Catholics who attend church regularly. The Eastern Orthodox Church greatly influenced the eastern part.

At one time, Poland had a large Jewish community. However, during World War II, Germany's Nazi Party rounded up most of these Jews. Then they put them in death camps called **concentration camps.** Historians call this the **Holocaust.** The Nazis killed as many as six million Jews in the Holocaust. Many of them came from eastern Europe.

Turkish rule brought a religion called Islam to the Balkans. **Muslims** are the followers of Islam. When the Turks left the Balkans, small pockets of people who followed the Muslim religion stayed behind. Many people in Albania are Muslims. In the 1990s, ethnic and religious fighting broke out in this area. Many people were killed. Many more lost their homes and were forced to move.

The Balkans has been the site of many ethnic wars since the early 1990s. Many people have been forced to leave their homes, as this photo shows.

## Where Do the People of Eastern Europe and the Balkans Live?

Eastern Europe and the Balkans are not as industrialized as the rest of Europe. Many people in this area still farm. For example, one out of every seven Albanians makes a living by farming. Fewer people farm in the other countries of eastern Europe and the Balkans. Still, more people farm than in the rest of Europe. Even in wealthier nations like Poland, the Czech Republic, and Hungary, more than a third of the people live on farms.

The biggest cities of eastern Europe and the Balkans are their capitals: Warsaw, Poland; Prague, Czech Republic; Sofia, Bulgaria; Bucharest, Romania; and Budapest, Hungary. Each of these cities has a population of more than a million people. The capital cities are the business, governmental, and transportation centers of their countries. They are also centers for education and industry.

### What Problems Face the People of Eastern Europe and the Balkans?

The people face three big problems. The first is a low standard of living. Employers do not pay workers very much. Many of the things workers need and want cost a lot of money, too. Many homes do not have heating that runs through the whole house. The electricity does not always work. People in a poor country like Bulgaria earn only about $120 a month. They must spend most of this for food, so they have little left for **consumer goods.** That is, they cannot buy the things they want for themselves and their homes.

The countries with the highest standard of living in eastern Europe are Poland, the Czech Republic, and Hungary. Workers in these countries are better off than workers in other eastern European and Balkan countries. However, they still earn much less than workers in western, southern, and northern Europe.

A second problem is **shortages,** or not having enough of something. Many of the countries have shortages in housing, food, and consumer goods. Many do not have modern machines. Some people still depend on horses for farm work and transportation.

Perhaps the biggest problem in the Balkans is ethnic fighting. Unless the people there can overcome their differences, their economy will not move ahead. Today, thousands of soldiers from the United Nations stay in this area to prevent more wars.

# Ethnic Diversity in Eastern Europe and the Balkans

The words *ethnic diversity* describe people. When many different people live together in one place, there is ethnic diversity. This map shows ethnic diversity in eastern Europe and the Balkans. It shows the percentage of minorities in each country. What percentage of Hungary's people are minorities? Macedonia's? Bosnia and Herzegovina's?

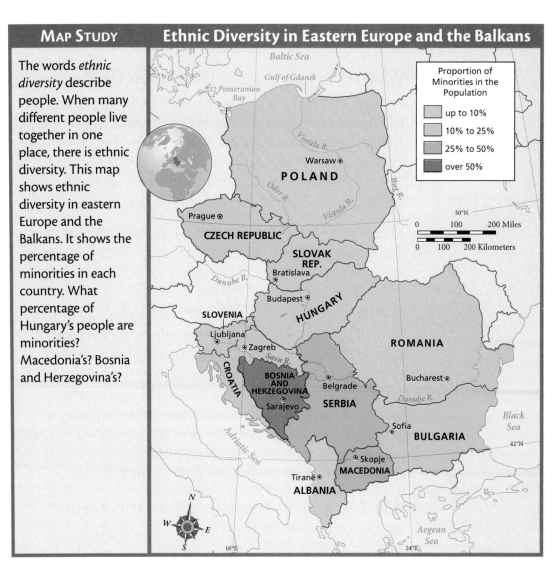

Proportion of Minorities in the Population

- up to 10%
- 10% to 25%
- 25% to 50%
- over 50%

**Section 3 Review** On a separate sheet of paper, write the word from the Word Bank that completes each sentence.

### WORD BANK

- capitals
- cultural crossroad
- ethnic
- Islam
- Slavic

1) A place where different cultures meet is a _____.
2) A(n) _____ group shares many common things.
3) Most eastern Europeans speak a _____ language.
4) Turkish rule brought _____ to the Balkans.
5) The largest cities of eastern Europe and the Balkans are _____.

**What do YOU think?** What might be one way to end the ethnic conflicts in the Balkans?

## What Is the Economy of This Region Like?

For many years, eastern Europe and the Balkan countries had an economy based on communism. In this economic system, people own little private property. The government owns most of the property and produces most of the goods. The government decides what goods the workers should make and how and where they should make them.

In the late 1980s and early 1990s, the countries of eastern Europe and the Balkans refused to accept communism any longer. They began to change their economies. They put more of the economy in the hands of the people. This economic change has been more successful in Poland, the Czech Republic, and Hungary than in the rest of eastern Europe and the Balkans. This is probably because these three countries are more developed than the other countries in this area. Governments still own many factories. The factories are inefficient. However, they do give work to many people. Because these factories provide jobs, the governments keep them running. They fear that closing the factories will cause political problems.

## How Did Russia's Economy Affect This Region?

The economies of eastern Europe and the Balkans have close ties with Russia. Until about 1990, most of their trade was with Russia and each other. Then Russia's economic problems caused problems for the economies of eastern Europe. Because of this, many people are out of work, and the people are suffering from many shortages.

Most of eastern Europe depends on Russia for minerals and energy resources. However, the countries with the best economies are turning to the West. Poland, Hungary, Slovenia, and the Czech Republic now trade more with countries in western Europe. Because of this, they want to join the European Union.

## What Natural Resources Do These Countries Have?

**Developing country**
*A country in which people are poor and earn their living mostly by farming*

The region is not rich in mineral resources. Several countries, such as Poland, Bulgaria, and many of the former Yugoslavian states, do have large coal deposits. Most of the coal is soft, brown coal, or lignite. Other mineral resources common to the area are zinc, lead, tin, copper, and bauxite. The Czech Republic has some iron ore.

Eastern Europe and the Balkans also have some unusual minerals. The mountains on the border of Germany and the Czech Republic have deposits of pitchblende. This ore contains radium. Another unusual mineral is chromium. Some of the best chromium in the world has been found in Albania.

The only country in eastern Europe to have oil and natural gas was Romania. However, most of these deposits have been used up. Many countries of eastern Europe and the Balkans import most of their energy needs.

**Some farmers in developing countries are forced to use traditional farm equipment.**

## What Are the Key Industries?

Most of the countries of this area are **developing countries.** People in developing countries are often poor. Many of them farm; few of them work in manufacturing or service industries. When Communists ruled these countries, the government controlled the economy. Often, what the workers produced was more for the good of Russia than for the local people.

Communist governments thought that heavy industries were important. A heavy industry produces goods that are used to produce other goods. Industries in eastern Europe and the Balkans made cement, steel, ships, machinery, and trucks.

Much of eastern Europe suffers from air pollution. Notice that the sheep in this photo are black from soot. Air pollution has caused this.

Acid rain
*A harmful form of rain that contains acids created when certain materials are released into the air*

As you know, in the late 1980s and early 1990s, the people of eastern Europe and the Balkans threw out the Communists. When that happened, their heavy industries had a hard time keeping up with the global market. They had a hard time selling their goods around the world at a price people could pay. Other countries in the West sold the same goods for less.

The most industrialized countries of this area are Poland, the Czech Republic, and Hungary. They have tried to compete better by importing new machines and technology from the West. Foreign companies have poured money into the new industries of these three countries. Most of these companies are from western Europe, the United States, and Japan. The other countries of eastern Europe and the Balkans have much less industry.

## What Environmental Problems Face Eastern Europe and the Balkans?

In the effort to industrialize, many countries produced more and more goods. While doing this, they paid little attention to the environment. Now they face air pollution and **acid rain.** Because lignite was the cheapest energy source, the people used a lot of it. Lignite contains sulfur. When people burn it, it mixes with rain, snow, or sleet and becomes acid rain. Acid rain is a dangerous form of air pollution. It kills many trees and even eats away at the stone fronts of buildings. It also causes many people to get sick.

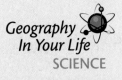

**Geography In Your Life**
SCIENCE

### Global Warming

Global warming is the increase in the average temperature of Earth's surface. Since the Industrial Revolution of the 1800s, Earth's average temperature has increased by 1.1° F. This may not seem like much, but some scientists fear that it will greatly affect Earth. They blame global warming on the burning of oil, natural gas, and coal by industries and automobiles. Gases from these fuels go into the atmosphere. They influence how much sunlight and heat reach Earth. Cutting down trees to raise cattle also changes the atmosphere.

Scientists predict that an increase in temperature will melt the polar ice sheets. Then the sea level will rise. Many coastal cities will flood. Deserts will develop in some areas; warmer weather in others. Some animals will become extinct. People will have to live with more tropical storms. In 1997, over 150 nations agreed to take steps to stop global warming.

Water pollution is a second environmental problem for eastern Europe and the Balkans. Their industries have dumped chemical waste materials into the rivers and lakes. In February 2000, miners in Romania spilled a poison into the Lapas River. The polluted water flowed into the Tisza and Danube Rivers. Tons of dead fish floated to the surface. Many deer, ducks, and other animals drank the poisoned water and died. The spill affects not only Romania, but also other countries in the region. The effects may last many years.

**Section 4 Review** On a separate sheet of paper, write the answers to these questions.

1) What is communism?

2) Which countries in eastern Europe and the Balkans have the closest ties with western Europe?

3) Which kind of coal is common in this region?

4) What are three features of developing countries?

5) What causes acid rain?

**What do YOU think?** Should governments give money to people who get sick because of air and water pollution? Explain your answer.

---

*Chapter 10 Eastern Europe and the Balkan Countries*   **241**

# The Legend of Dracula

Dracula really lived; he was a Romanian prince. His name comes from the Romanian word *Drac*, which means either "devil" or "dragon." His father belonged to a group called the Order of the Dragon. Members of this group wore a special red outfit and a black cape on Sunday.

Dracula lived during the 1400s. At that time, the people of eastern Europe fought with one another all the time. They lived in a feudal system. That is, the king owned all the land. However, he needed loyal nobles to serve him. To win their loyalty, he gave them land. The nobles then gave land to other people to get their loyalty. In a feudal system, people often changed sides because someone offered them more land. Friends then turned into enemies. Nobles killed Dracula's father and brother. More than once, these same nobles took Dracula prisoner. Maybe that is why Dracula became such a mean ruler.

The poor peasant farmers of Romania called Dracula a hero. They say he defended them from their enemies. They remember him for standing up to invaders from Hungary and Turkey. Dracula hated the Turkish invaders. Because of his hatred, Dracula was mean to the Turks. He impaled them on sticks, so people called him "the Impaler." To impale means to drive a stick through a person's body. Some historians think that Dracula may have killed and impaled up to 100,000 people.

Was Dracula a vampire? No! People in the late 1800s liked to talk about vampires. At that time, a British writer wrote a story about Dracula. To make his story interesting, this writer made Dracula a vampire.

**Dracula was an actual person. However, he was not a vampire, as this photo of the popular Hollywood movie shows.**

## Spotlight Story Wrap-Up

1) Who was Dracula?

2) Where did Dracula live?

3) Where did Dracula's famous costume come from?

4) Why did some people think that Dracula was a hero?

5) Who made Dracula a vampire?

◆ Eastern Europe includes Poland, the Czech Republic, Slovakia, Hungary, and the Balkan countries of Romania, Bulgaria, Albania, the former Yugoslavia (Serbia), Bosnia-Herzegovina, Croatia, Macedonia, and Slovenia. The Balkan Peninsula sits between the Adriatic and Ionian Seas on the west and the Aegean and Black Seas on the east and south.

◆ Eastern Europe is divided into the North European Plain; an area of mountains and rugged hills; another plain between the Carpathian Mountains and the Balkan Peninsula; and the Balkan Peninsula.

◆ Because Poland has no natural boundaries, many people have invaded it. The Turks ruled the Balkans for many years. After World War I, the Turkish Empire was divided. This has led to war in the Balkans.

◆ The two main physical features of this area are huge plains and many mountains. Glaciers created many rivers throughout the area. The most important of these is the Danube.

◆ The western part of eastern Europe has a marine west coast climate. The eastern part has a humid continental climate. Land south of the Danube has a humid subtropical climate. Areas along the Adriatic Coast have a Mediterranean climate.

◆ The cultures of eastern Europe and the Balkans differ because this is a cultural crossroad. Germanic tribes, Romans, and Slavs invaded it and settled there. Turkey has greatly influenced the Balkan culture. Most people in this area speak a Slavic language, but these languages differ from one another.

◆ Most of the people are Christians. However, some Muslims live in the Balkans. This has led to ethnic and religious fighting.

◆ Eastern Europe and the Balkans are not as industrialized as the rest of Europe. Many people farm. The biggest cities are the capitals.

◆ For many years, these countries had Communist economies and close ties to Russia. Now they are trying to industrialize. This has been more successful in the developed countries than in the developing countries.

◆ This area's largest natural resource is lignite.

◆ The countries of eastern Europe and the Balkans face the environmental problems of acid rain and water pollution. They face the social problems of a low standard of living, shortages, and ethnic fighting.

# Chapter 10 REVIEW

## Comprehension: Identifying Facts

On a separate sheet of paper, write the words from the Word Bank to complete each sentence.

| WORD BANK |
| --- |
| acid rain |
| balkanize |
| communism |
| cultural crossroad |
| narrows |

1) To break a geographical area or a group of people into smaller political groups is to _____.

2) A _____ is a place where a river flows through a small gap between large mountains.

3) A _____ is a place where different cultures meet.

4) _____ is an economic system in which people own little and the government controls production.

5) _____ is caused by harmful pollutants in the air.

## Comprehension: Multiple Choice

On a separate sheet of paper, write the letter of the answer that correctly completes each sentence.

1) Eastern Europe and the Balkan countries are located in the _____ latitudes.
   a. northern           c. southern
   b. middle             d. low

2) One of the main physical features of eastern Europe is its large area of _____.
   a. rain forests       c. deserts
   b. plains             d. beaches

3) A large number of _____ resulted from the glaciers that once covered eastern Europe.
   a. lakes              c. seaways
   b. fjords             d. valleys

4) _____ greatly influenced the religion, architecture, and customs of the Balkans.
   a. Poland             c. Germany
   b. Greece             d. Turkey

5) _____ are followers of Islam.

   a. Buddhists        c. Muslims

   b. Jews            d. Christians

## Comprehension: Understanding Main Ideas

On a separate sheet of paper, write the answer to each question. Use complete sentences.

1) What are the four main regions of eastern Europe and the Balkans?

2) What are the four main climates found in this area of the world?

3) What are two environmental challenges that the people of eastern Europe and the Balkans face?

## Critical Thinking: Write Your Opinion

On a separate sheet of paper, write your opinion to each question. Use complete sentences.

1) Why are Poland, the Czech Republic, and Hungary more industrialized than the other countries of eastern Europe and the Balkans?

2) Do you think that some of the problems in eastern Europe and the Balkans can be traced back to their years of Communist control? Explain your answer.

## Applying the Five Themes of Geography

### *Movement*

How do the many cultures of eastern Europe and the Balkans reflect the theme of movement?

> **Test-Taking Tip**    Read test directions twice. Sometimes they will give you a hint. For example, the directions may remind you to look for the "best" answer.

# Russia and the Independent Republics

In 1991, a surprising thing happened. The Soviet Union, a country created in 1917, suddenly broke apart. It had been made up of many republics or states. Many of the republics of the old Soviet Union became independent. However, since 1991, Russia and the other independent republics have had problems. The photo on this page shows the Dnieper River in Russia.

## Goals for Learning

▶ To describe where Russia and the independent republics are located

▶ To identify their most important physical features and climates

▶ To describe their diverse cultures

▶ To explain where most people live in Russia and the independent republics

▶ To describe the economy and the environmental challenges Russia and the independent republics face

### Geo-Stats

**Russia and the Key Independent Republics**

 **Nation:** Kazakhstan
**Population:** 15,417,000
**Area** (in square miles): 1,049,039
**Major Cities:** Astana (capital), Qaraghandy, Shymkent, Pavlodar

 **Nation:** Russia
**Population:** 146,519,000
**Area** (in square miles): 6,592,692
**Major Cities:** Moscow (capital), St. Petersburg, Novgorod, Yekaterinburg

 **Nation:** Lithuania
**Population:** 3,700,000
**Area** (in square miles): 25,213
**Major Cities:** Vilnius (capital), Kaunas

 **Nation:** Ukraine
**Population:** 49,910,000
**Area** (in square miles): 233,206
**Major Cities:** Kiev (capital), Kharkov

# Russia and the Independent Republics

*Map Skills*

At one time, all of these countries were republics of the Soviet Union. They formed a huge empire that covered much of Europe and Asia. Now these 15 nations are independent. The main country of this region is Russia. It is the largest country in the world. Several other large countries, such as Ukraine and Kazakhstan, are also important nations. The Baltic States of Latvia, Estonia, and Lithuania lie along the Baltic Sea.

Study the map and answer the following questions:

**1)** Why do you think geographers call Latvia, Estonia, and Lithuania the Baltic States?

**2)** Russia has a region known as Siberia, which you can see on the map. Why do you think this area is so cold?

**3)** What seas totally surrounded by land are pictured on this map?

**4)** What is the capital of Russia? Azerbaijan? Moldova?

**5)** How many former Soviet republics are there?

## Where Is Russia Located?

Russia is the world's biggest country. It is about twice the size of the United States. It is so large that it has eleven time zones! (The continental United States has only four.) When it is 8:00 in the morning in the western part of Russia, it is 6:00 in the evening on its east coast.

The Baltic Sea forms part of Russia's western boundary. The eastern coast of Russia faces the Bering Sea, which separates Russia from Alaska. The Arctic Ocean lies to Russia's north. China and Iran lie to the south. Russia stretches 6,000 miles from west to east and 2,000 miles from north to south.

## Where Are the Independent Republics Located?

When the Soviet Union existed, it was made up of many **republics.** Each had a head of state. Now these republics are independent.

The largest independent republic is Russia. There are 14 other independent republics. Between Russia and eastern Europe sit Moldova, Ukraine, Belarus, Georgia, Armenia, and Azerbaijan. The Baltic Sea borders Estonia, Latvia, and Lithuania. The others are located in central Asia. The largest is Kazakhstan. The others are Uzbekistan, Turkmenistan, Tajikistan and Kyrgyzstan. Russia and each of these independent republics have their own **constitution** and government. A constitution is a nation's written document of rules.

Except for Estonia, Latvia, and Lithuania, all of the independent republics have joined Russia to form the **Commonwealth of Independent States (CIS).** This group is much weaker than the old Soviet Union. The CIS members have close economic ties, but they also have many differences. People wonder if the forces holding the commonwealth together are stronger than the forces pulling it apart.

## What Physical Regions Exist in Russia and the Independent Republics?

This huge area has four main physical regions. The first region is the Russian plain. It extends from the plain that covers much of Europe. Three-fourths of the people live in this region. The three largest cities of Russia and the independent republics are located in this region. These are Moscow and St. Petersburg in Russia and Kiev in the Ukraine. This first region has the most industry, the richest soil, and the most navigable rivers.

The Ural Mountains form the second region. This low mountain range runs about 1,500 miles southward from the Arctic Ocean. The Urals contain huge deposits of minerals. In the past, the Urals were considered the boundary of Europe and Asia. Today, geographers call the two continents Eurasia.

Siberia is the third and largest region. It is nearly one and a half times the size of the United States. Three different landforms make up Siberia. The vast West Siberian Plain lies east of the Ural Mountains. This flat lowland has many rivers, which often flood. As the plain extends eastward, it meets the Central Siberian Plateau. It is rich in undeveloped natural resources. Still farther east lie the high mountains and forests of the East Siberian Uplands.

Central Asia makes up the fourth and final region. Much of this region is a low-lying, desert-like area, which receives little rainfall. This large region also has plains and low plateaus.

**This photo shows the seafront of Yalta. This city is in Crimea, a state in Ukraine by the Black Sea.**

## How Has Geography Influenced the History of This Area?

Geography has often influenced Russian history. In the 1200s, the Mongols, or Tatars, from central Asia invaded the Russian plains. Genghis Khan, one of the world's greatest conquerors, led this army. For nearly 300 years, the Mongols controlled Russia.

The Ural Mountains divide Russia. The western, or European, part of Russia has big cities and much industry. Throughout the ages, it has held almost all the political power. The eastern part of Russia is large, with few people. It has huge, undeveloped resources.

Russia's climate has also influenced its history. For example, the cold freezes many of its ports during the winter. Russia has sometimes gone to war in order to capture ports that it could use year-round.

In the last two centuries, climate and size have kept Russia from being conquered. In 1812, Napoleon tried to capture Russia. He failed because the Russian soldiers kept retreating eastward, deeper and deeper into Russia. Finally, Napoleon ordered his troops home to France. Thousands of French soldiers died from hunger and from the freezing cold.

During the winter of 1941–1942, German troops invaded Russia. Like Napoleon's troops, the German forces faced the cold Russian winter. Because of it, they failed to conquer Russia. Their defeat was a turning point of World War II.

**SECTION 1 REVIEW** On a separate sheet of paper, write answers to these questions.

1) How does Russia compare in size to the U.S.?
2) What is the largest physical region of Russia and the independent republics?
3) Which region is rich in natural resources that the Russians have not developed yet?
4) Which region is a low-lying, desert-like area?
5) How did geography help defeat both Napoleon's army in 1812 and Germany's army in 1941–1942 when they tried to invade Russia?

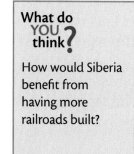

**What do YOU think?**

How would Siberia benefit from having more railroads built?

## What Are the Main Physical Features?

Taiga
*The world's largest forest*

Plains are the most common physical feature of this region. Most of the country's crops are grown here. Farmers grow potatoes, wheat, sugar beets, sunflowers, corn, barley, and other crops.

In Chapter 2, you learned about the tundra and the permafrost of Canada. Russia has these, too. Tundra covers much of the northern part of Russia. The tundra is a flat, treeless plain. The soil is thin and poor; the weather is cold. Mosses and low shrubs are the only plant life. Geographers call its soil permafrost because it is frozen most of the year.

South of the treeless tundra lies the **taiga.** It is the world's largest forest. The taiga contains pine, fir, larch, and other evergreen trees. Trees take a long time to grow in the poor soil of the taiga. Like the tundra, the taiga has few people.

High mountains rise in the eastern part of Russia, especially on its Pacific coast. The Kamchatka Peninsula in eastern Siberia has many active volcanoes. The CIS republics bordering China and Afghanistan have the highest elevation. The Caucasus Mountains lie between the Black Sea and the Caspian Sea. They are the primary feature of the republics of Georgia, Armenia, and Azerbaijan.

## What Are the Major Rivers and Lakes?

Russia has many large bodies of water. The Caspian Sea is part of Russia's southern border. Several rivers, including the huge Volga River (the largest in this region), flow into the Caspian. However, no rivers flow out of it. Other important rivers of western Russia are the Dnieper, Don, Dvina, Neman, and Pechora. Canals link many of these rivers.

Siberia has four huge rivers that flow to the Arctic Ocean: the Angara, Lena, Ob, and Yenisey. They are so wide that someone on one side cannot see someone on the other side. The rivers are frozen much of the year.

**Siberia is a huge, cold region in the northeastern part of Russia. It has a polar or a subarctic climate. This photo shows the camp of Russian nomads called Nenets, who live in Siberia.**

Polar climate
*A climate with long, cold winters and short, warm summers*

All of Russia's rivers are important. They serve as highways because Russia still has few good roads and railroads. Many rivers have been dammed, so they have become an important source of hydroelectric power.

Lake Baykal is the most famous lake in Russia. It is nearly one mile deep, and it holds as much water as all the Great Lakes combined! Its water is so pure that people bottle and sell it. Lake Baykal contains 80 percent of Russia's freshwater supply. While 336 rivers flow into Lake Baykal, only one flows out.

## What Climates Does This Area Have?

Russia and the independent republics cover such a large area that they have many different climates. The far northern part of Russia is above the Arctic Circle. This tundra area has a **polar climate.** Polar climate has long, cold winters and short, warm summers. Little rain falls.

Just south of this belt of polar climate is a large area of subarctic climate. This is like the polar climate except that it receives a little more rain and snow. The subarctic climate supports the huge forests of the taiga.

The climate of Ukraine, Moldova, Belarus, and most of European Russia is the humid continental climate. It has warm summers and cold winters. Rain falls throughout the year. The total amount of snow and rain each year is about 25 inches. This is about the same as in the midwestern part of the United States.

Large areas of southern Ukraine have a steppe climate. It is dry, and its rainfall differs from year to year. Hot, dry winds in the summer may bring drought.

The republics of central Asia have the driest climate of this entire area. Much of this region is desert. Summers are hot; daytime temperatures reach 120° F. Winters are cold, but dry and sunny. Russia even has a small area on the Black Sea with an almost Mediterranean climate.

**SECTION 2 REVIEW** On a separate sheet of paper, write the word from the Word Bank that completes each sentence.

| WORD BANK |
| --- |
| Baykal |
| continental |
| plains |
| taiga |
| Volga |

1) The most common physical feature of Russia is the _____.

2) The _____ is the largest forest in the world.

3) The most important river of Russia is the _____.

4) _____, Russia's most famous lake, contains 80 percent of its freshwater supply.

5) Most people in this area live in a humid _____ climate.

**What do YOU think?** Does climate have a big effect on where the people of Russia and the independent republics live? Explain your answer.

Atheist
*A person who does not believe in God*

## What Cultures Exist in Russia and the Independent Republics?

Like the United States, this region is multicultural. Many ethnic groups, each with a different culture, live in Russia and the independent republics. The Russians are the largest ethnic group. Most of the people of Russia, Ukraine, and Belarus are Slavic people. They are related to the Slavs who settled eastern Europe and the Balkans.

More than 40 other ethnic groups also live in Russia. Among the largest minorities are the Bashkirs, Chechens, Chuvashes, Tatars, and Udmurts. Many people of the republics in central Asia are descendants of the Mongols. These warriors invaded Russia in the 1200s.

## What Languages Do the People Speak?

Russians account for over 80 percent of the population of this area. Because of this, the most widely spoken language is Russian. However, each ethnic group has its own language. Many speak a Slavic language. The Russian and other Slavic languages generally use the Cyrillic alphabet.

The Bashkirs and the Udmurts live in the Ural Mountains and along the Volga River. They speak languages related to Hungarian and Finnish. People of the republics of central Asia speak languages related to Turkish or Persian.

## What Religions Do the People Practice?

In the Revolution of 1917, the Communists made Russia an **atheist** country. They said that the people could not believe in God. The new leaders got rid of religious holidays. They closed churches and other places of worship. However, many Russian people continued to worship at home. In 1991, Communist rule came to an end. Then people began to worship openly again. The main religion of this region is Russian Orthodox. This religion came from the Eastern Orthodox branch of Christianity.

**The Kremlin in Moscow has been the center of Russian government for nearly 900 years. It is the political center of the CIS today.**

The second largest religion in this region is Islam. Most of the people in the republics of central Asia and Azerbaijan are Muslims. At one time, many Jews lived in Russia. However, many people treated them poorly. In the 1970s and 1980s, the Communist government allowed thousands of Jews to leave Russia. They now live in the United States and Israel.

## What Are the Major Cities of This Region?

Russians have said that "Moscow is the heart of Russia, St. Petersburg is its head, but Kiev is its mother." These three cities are the largest and most important cities in the European part of Russia and the independent republics. Kiev, the oldest of the three cities, is the capital of Ukraine. It is a transportation, industrial, and cultural center.

In 1703, Peter the Great, a famous Russian leader, founded St. Petersburg. This beautiful city is Russia's biggest seaport on the Baltic Sea. St. Petersburg is Russia's second largest industrial and cultural center. Today, more than five million people live there.

Moscow, the capital of Russia, is the most important city of the three. It is one of Russia's oldest cities. It played a big role in uniting the country. The city grew up around the Kremlin, an old fort. Even today, the Kremlin is the political center of the CIS. Moscow has over nine million people. It is a large industrial and cultural center. In fact, some people call it the city of museums. The city is also famous for its ballet and opera.

## What Problems Do the People Face?

The people of Russia and the independent republics face many problems. The most important problem is whether the region, with its many minorities, can hold together. Many minorities live in republics where they are the majority. In the past, Moscow, the capital of the old Soviet Union, controlled these republics. Today, many of them want greater control over their own resources. They like their own cultures and their own language.

Some people think that Russia will split into several independent states in the future. Already, the world is seeing that some parts of Russia, like its republic of Chechnya, want to break away. The people of Chechnya have been fighting the Russian army for several years. They want to form an independent country. Russian soldiers have tried to force Chechnya to remain a part of Russia.

A second problem for Russia and the independent republics is ethnic and religious fighting. In the past, the Communist government kept peace among the many ethnic groups in this area. With the fall of the Soviet Union, fighting about religion and ethnic differences began. This has caused war in the independent republics of Armenia, Georgia, and Azerbaijan.

---

| Biography | VLADIMIR PUTIN: 1952– |
| --- | --- |

In March 2000, the people of Russia elected Vladimir Putin to be their new president. For many years, he worked as a spy for the KGB. This Soviet agency gathered information on the countries that were enemies of the Soviet Union. As the Soviet Union was collapsing in 1990, Putin left the KGB and entered politics. In 1999, Boris Yeltsin, the first president of Russia, made Putin prime minister of Russia. As president, Putin says he will strengthen Russia's security forces. This worries some Russians because they think he may turn away from Russia's new democracy.

Chechnya is a republic in Russia. The Chechens are fighting the Russians for independence. This photo shows Chechen refugees leaving Chechnya to escape the fighting.

In the republics of central Asia, two ethnic groups are quarreling. The Uzbeks and the Kyrgyz are fighting one another over land and water rights. So far, the Russian army has been able to keep an uneasy peace. This may not be possible in the future.

A third problem is the breakdown of government. The Russian government seems unable to provide services for its citizens. Many people refuse to pay taxes. The many republics refuse to pay what they owe the central government. They must deal with dishonest government workers and growing crime.

**SECTION 3 REVIEW** On a separate sheet of paper, write *True* if the statement is true or *False* if the statement is not true. Make each false statement true by changing the underlined word.

1) The largest ethnic group in Russia and the independent republics is the <u>Tatars</u>.

2) The most widely spoken language is <u>Russian.</u>

3) The main religion of most people in this region is <u>Islam</u>.

4) <u>Kiev</u> is the capital of Ukraine.

5) The <u>Kremlin</u> is the political center of the CIS.

**What do YOU think?**

How would the breakup of Russia into several more independent republics affect the United States? Explain your answer.

## What Is the Economy of Russia and the Republics Like?

The economy of this region has undergone great change. After communism failed, the republics changed from a **command economy** to a **market economy.** In a command economy, the government makes the key economic decisions. The government decides what to produce, how to produce it, and who will receive what is produced. In a market economy, a business is privately owned. The people who own a business make decisions about it.

The reform effort has had little success. The first problem is that people who run the factories and farms have little experience with privately-owned businesses. They have made many mistakes. The second problem is that many of the big, government-owned businesses are old and inefficient. That is, the machinery in them is old, so the workers waste time and energy producing goods. Because of this, the factories cannot compete with businesses in other countries. Many workers have been fired. They blame their lack of jobs on new economic ideas. A third problem is that foreign governments and companies have limited investment in the republics of the Commonwealth. Without money from overseas, the managers and workers will have a hard time improving the economy.

Because of these three problems, the economic picture for the Commonwealth is bad. Average income is dropping. People earn only about two-thirds of what they made before the Soviet Union split up. Many of the manufactured products are of poor quality. Telephones are expensive, and millions of people have no phone. In some places, there is a food shortage.

## What Natural Resources Exist?

Russia and the independent republics are rich in natural resources. This provides some hope for the future. Russia is the only industrialized country in the world that is almost self-sufficient in the natural resources it needs. The United States, Japan, and Europe must import oil. Russia does not have to do this. It is a world leader in the production of oil, iron ore, manganese, and asbestos. In fact, it has the world's largest supply of natural gas. Russian oil, natural gas, and coal are its chief exports, especially to Europe. These natural resources provide Russia with money to buy the things it cannot produce itself. However, as the price of oil changes around the world, Russia is affected greatly.

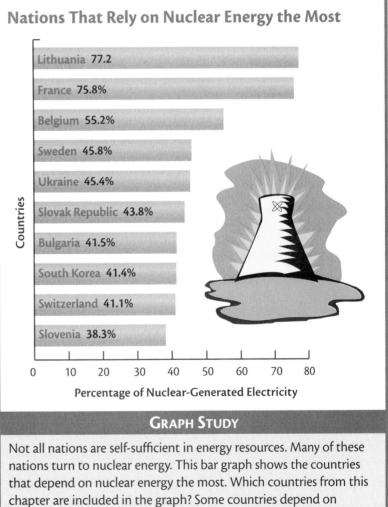

## Nations That Rely on Nuclear Energy the Most

| Countries | Percentage of Nuclear-Generated Electricity |
|---|---|
| Lithuania 77.2 | |
| France 75.8% | |
| Belgium 55.2% | |
| Sweden 45.8% | |
| Ukraine 45.4% | |
| Slovak Republic 43.8% | |
| Bulgaria 41.5% | |
| South Korea 41.4% | |
| Switzerland 41.1% | |
| Slovenia 38.3% | |

### GRAPH STUDY

Not all nations are self-sufficient in energy resources. Many of these nations turn to nuclear energy. This bar graph shows the countries that depend on nuclear energy the most. Which countries from this chapter are included in the graph? Some countries depend on nuclear energy for as much as 77 percent of their energy. Is this dangerous? Why or why not?

**Collective farm**
*A large, state-owned farm worked by the people*

**Privatization**
*Selling state farm land to private owners*

For many years, the resources of some Commonwealth countries have been mined. As a result, they have used up many resources. However, geologists have now discovered rich mineral deposits in Siberia. The problem is that many of these discoveries are in places that are hard to mine. Still, many people think that this region is valuable.

Russia has three other valuable natural resources: forests, furs, and fish. The CIS contains as much as one-fifth of the world's forests, so lumbering is a big industry. Russia is home to many animals, so the fur industry is important. Some hunters trap fur-bearing animals. However, many farmers today raise these animals on fur farms.

The Russian fishing industry is busy all over the world. Many ships in the fishing fleet are so big that people call them "fish factories." Fish is an important part of the Russian diet. However, the fishers catch enough to sell to other countries, too.

## What Are Some Major Industries?

Out of every five workers in Russia, one farms, two work in factories, and two work in service industries. Farmers use about 13 percent of Russia's land for farming. The most productive farmland among the former republics is the steppe region of Russia, Ukraine, and Kazakhstan. The climate in the other republics is too harsh for growing many crops.

However, even good farm areas have problems. The Communists did not believe in private ownership of land. They divided the land into large, state-owned farms, or **collective farms.** The Communists thought that people would work hard for the good of everyone. However, the workers saw no reason to work hard. A person could work a lot or a little and still receive the same pay.

Today, Russian leaders talk about **privatization,** or the selling of farm land to private owners. This is not easy to do. Many farmers do not have the necessary skills, machinery, or money to be successful.

## Why Are Manufacturing Industries in Trouble?

The manufacturing industries have troubles, too. Some heavy industries, like chemicals, steel, and automobiles, are not producing as much as they did under Communist rule. The Communists wanted to make the Soviet Union an industrial power. Because of this, the workers produced goods for the military and for heavy industry.

As a result, few consumer goods were produced. Also, these goods were not of high quality because the factories had no competition. Without competition, the government could produce products of poor quality. The people had no choice but to buy what was available. Today, many industries that used to make military goods now make consumer goods.

## Where Are the Main Industrial Areas?

In Russia and the independent republics, the major industrial areas are in the west. The first industrial area is Moscow. However, many of Moscow's people work in service industries. The second industrial area is St. Petersburg. This important city is located on the Gulf of Finland. Its harbor is open all year around. It is close to the countries of the European Union, which provides a market for St. Petersburg's goods. People look to St. Petersburg for textiles, machinery, and ship-building. The third industrial area is the Volga River valley. Its chief products are cars, chemicals, and food products. The river itself provides hydroelectric power and cheap transportation.

## What Environmental Challenges Exist?

The old Soviet leaders wanted their workers to produce goods. They seemed to care little about the environment. Because of this, they nearly destroyed the Aral Sea. It is located on the border between Kazakhstan and Uzbekistan in central Asia. It was once the fourth largest lake in the world. Then the Soviets decided to raise cotton by the sea. Two rivers flowed into it. The Soviet leaders used the water for irrigation. Now, the soil is becoming salty. Soon, cotton will no longer grow on this salty soil. Since the 1960s, the

Aral Sea has lost over 60 percent of its water. Today, much of the area that the water covered is dry wasteland. This loss of water has wiped out the large fishing industry. Also, harmful chemicals were used in the cotton fields. Now, people who live in the area are being harmed.

The Commonwealth countries also face both air and water pollution. The soft coal they use to create electric power puts harmful gases in the air. Many factories cannot keep these gases from escaping into the air. Cars and trucks give off harmful gases because cars do not have pollution control systems. People living near industrial areas have bad health problems. The people who live in Siberian cities have a high rate of lung cancer and other lung diseases. Poor air quality causes these diseases.

Heavy industry can create a lot of harmful waste. The Soviet leaders used to dump these waste products into the rivers and lakes. Now, harmful chemicals have been washed into the water supply. Even Lake Baykal, which is a big source of water for Russia, shows signs of pollution.

An even bigger problem is **nuclear waste** and nuclear accidents. Atomic power plants produce nuclear waste. This waste used to be put into containers and dumped into the Arctic Ocean. Many people fear that the containers will leak. If this happens, many plants, animals, and people in Russia will die.

**Air pollution from burning coal is a big problem in Russia and the independent republics.**

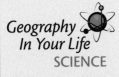

## The Chernobyl Nuclear Power Plant Accident

*Geography In Your Life* SCIENCE

In 1986, the worst nuclear accident in world history took place at the Chernobyl nuclear power plant in northern Ukraine. On April 25, 1986, some engineers there did a test without permission. This set in motion an uncontrolled chain reaction. The next day, an explosion in the nuclear reactor ripped the top off the building. Eight tons of radioactive material shot into the atmosphere. Winds carried it over Europe and it fell on people, animals, soil, water, and plants.

Thirty-one people died immediately from the radioactive material. Hundreds of people became ill. Scientists predict that the accident will lead to 25,000 deaths in the area. Even today, farmers in eastern and northern Europe cannot farm or live on millions of acres of land. So much radioactivity remains in the soil that vegetables and fruits grown in the area would harm people if eaten.

**SECTION 4 REVIEW** Choose the letter of the answer that correctly completes each sentence. Write your answers on a separate sheet of paper.

1) In a _____ economy, the government decides what to produce.

  a. market      c. free enterprise

  b. capitalist      d. command

2) _____ is almost self sufficient in natural resources.

  a. Russia      c. Kazakhstan

  b. Ukraine      d. Lithuania

3) Mineral deposits have been discovered in _____.

  a. Moscow      c. the Aral Sea

  b. Siberia      d. Lake Baykal

4) The destruction of the _____ shows how little the Soviet leaders cared about the environment.

  a. collective farms      c. Aral Sea

  b. Caspian Sea      d. Black Sea

5) In 1986, a nuclear accident occurred in _____.

  a. Moscow      c. Kiev

  b. St. Petersburg      d. Chernobyl

**What do YOU think?**

Why did the leaders of the Soviet Union seem to care so little about the environment?

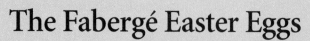

# The Fabergé Easter Eggs

Before 1917, Easter was a special holiday for the Russian people. On that day, they gave gifts to the people they loved. Among these gifts were decorated Easter eggs. These eggs were a symbol of new life.

At that time, powerful rulers called czars controlled Russia. These czars lived in beautiful palaces filled with wonderful treasures. For a czar, the question was what Easter gift to give to a queen who had everything. An ordinary hen's egg would not do!

Each czar had a person who made jewelry for the czar's family. In 1884, Czar Alexander III asked Carl Fabergé, his jewelry maker, to create a special jeweled Easter egg for the queen. He wanted the egg to be beautiful and to contain a surprise inside.

Fabergé was a creative artist. He was also a master goldsmith and a mechanical genius. The first egg he made for the czar had an enameled gold shell. Inside the egg sat a tiny hen with eyes made of rubies. The czar was so pleased that he asked Fabergé to make a special egg for every year after that.

For more than 30 years, Fabergé made these Easter eggs for the czar's family. Each egg was different. In all, Fabergé made 49 special Easter eggs. Today only 44 eggs still exist.

Fabergé made other beautiful jewelry. Still, people think that his Easter eggs are his greatest work. This is because of their unique design and the beautiful way he made them. Once you have seen a Fabergé Easter egg, no Easter egg will ever look the same again!

**Carl Fabergé made 49 eggs for the czar's family. The eggs were made to celebrate Easter.**

## Spotlight Story Wrap-Up

1) Who were the czars?

2) Who was Carl Fabergé?

3) What kind of Easter egg did Fabergé create for the czar's wife?

4) How many Fabergé Easter eggs still exist?

5) Why do some people think that the Fabergé Easter eggs are Fabergé's greatest work?

◆ This region is made up of Russia, the largest country in the world, and many independent republics that used to be part of the Soviet Union.

◆ Their four main regions are the Russian plain, the Ural Mountains, Siberia, and central Asia.

◆ Plains are the main physical feature. The north has tundra and the taiga, the world's largest forest. The Caucasus Mountains are the primary feature of Georgia, Armenia, and Azerbaijan.

◆ The largest river is the Volga. All rivers in this area are important because of the shortage of good roads and railroads. Lake Baykal contains 80 percent of Russia's freshwater supply.

◆ The far northern part of Russia has a polar climate. Below that is a subarctic climate. The climate of Ukraine, Moldova, Belarus, and most of European Russia is a humid continental climate. Large areas of southern Ukraine have a steppe climate. The republics of central Asia have a dry climate. A small area on the Black Sea has an almost Mediterranean climate.

◆ This region is multicultural. The Russians are the largest ethnic group. Russian is the most widely spoken language, but each ethnic group has its own language. Many of these are Slavic languages.

◆ Most people are Russian Orthodox. However, the majority of people in the republics of central Asia are Muslims.

◆ Russia and the republics have changed from a command economy to a market economy. This change has not been very successful. The major cities, all of which are industrialized, are Moscow, St. Petersburg, and Kiev. All major industry is in the western part of the region.

◆ Russia and the independent republics are rich in natural resources. Among Russia's natural resources are oil, natural gas, coal, forests, furs, and fish.

◆ Out of every five workers in Russia, one is a farmer, two work in factories, and two work in service industries.

◆ Russia and the independent republics face the environmental problems of pollution, the destruction of the Aral Sea, and the disposal of atomic waste. Social problems include independence movements, ethnic and religious conflict, and the breakdown of government.

# Chapter 11 REVIEW

## Comprehension: Identifying Facts

On a separate sheet of paper, use the words from the Word Bank to complete each sentence.

| WORD BANK |
| --- |
| Chechnya |
| Cyrillic |
| Slavic |
| taiga |
| tundra |

1) The _____ is a flat, treeless plain that covers much of the northern part of Russia.

2) The _____ is a large forest region covered with pine, fir, larch, and other evergreen trees.

3) Most of the people of Russia, Ukraine, and Belarus are _____ people.

4) Russian and other Slavic languages generally use the _____ alphabet.

5) The people of _____ have been fighting for several years against Russia to try to form an independent country.

## Comprehension: Multiple Choice

On a separate sheet of paper, write the letter of the answer that correctly completes each sentence.

1) The largest country in the world is _____.
   a. the United States
   b. Ukraine
   c. Russia
   d. Kazakhstan

2) Three important cities that lie on the large Russian plain are _____.
   a. Moscow, St. Petersburg, Kiev
   b. Chernobyl, Siberia, Chechnya
   c. Stockholm, Budapest, Helsinki
   d. Rome, Athens, London

3) The most common physical feature of Russia is its ____.
   a. mountains
   b. plains
   c. high plateaus
   d. seas

4) The two main religions are Christianity and _____.
   a. Judaism
   b. Hinduism
   c. Buddhism
   d. Islam

5) The export of _____ provides Russia with money to buy things it cannot produce for itself.

   a. oil and natural gas  c. food products

   b. consumer goods     d. automobiles

## Comprehension: Understanding Main Ideas

On a separate sheet of paper, write the answers to each question. Use complete sentences.

1) What are the four main climates of Russia and the independent republics?

2) Why is this area of the world multicultural?

3) What environmental challenges do Russia and the independent republics face?

## Critical Thinking: Write Your Opinion

On a separate sheet of paper, write your opinion to each question. Use complete sentences.

1) What would you do to solve the problem in Chechnya if you were Russia's president?

2) What would you do to make the new economy of Russia and the independent republics more successful?

## Applying the Five Themes of Geography

### Region

Imagine you are taking a trip across Russia from St. Petersburg in the west to Vladivostok in the east. Describe what landforms you might see and the different climates you might experience.

**Test-Taking Tip**   If you do not know the answer to a test question, put a star beside it and go on. Then when you are finished, go back to any starred questions and try to answer them.

# Understanding Political Maps

You have studied many political maps in this book. What is a political map? It is a map that shows boundaries. A political map may show the boundaries of countries, states, provinces, territories, counties, and cities. Sometimes these maps also show important cities or capital cities. Many of the maps in this book show features of the land, such as rivers and mountains. Political maps are meant to answer questions like the following: Where is it? How big is it? What is close to it?

The map on this page shows the political boundaries of Russia and the independent republics. It tells you that there are 15 former republics. It also shows you capital cities. By looking at this map, you see how geographers divide this area.

Why are political maps important? They show how humans have divided and organized land. Political maps show you where countries begin and end. They show you the size of countries. They show you how far away one country is from another. Political maps also show location, place, and region.

Study the map on this page and answer the following questions.

1) What is the largest country?

2) What four countries lie along the Baltic Sea?

3) Where is Kazakhstan?

4) What country is east of Armenia?

5) What does this political map tell you about the independent republics?

◆ This unit focused on two main regions: eastern Europe and the Balkans; and Russia and the independent republics. Eastern Europe contains many countries, several of which sit on the Balkan Peninsula. East of these countries lie Russia, the largest country in the world, and many independent republics that used to be part of the Soviet Union.

◆ The North European Plain extends from western Europe across eastern Europe into Russia. Eastern Europe also has mountains and rugged hills; another large plain; and the Balkan Peninsula. The four main physical regions of the land beyond eastern Europe are the North European Plain, the Ural Mountains, Siberia, and central Asia.

◆ Plains and mountains are the main physical features of eastern Europe. Plains are the main feature of Russia. Northern Russia has tundra and the taiga. The Caucasus Mountains are the primary feature of Georgia, Armenia, and Azerbaijan.

◆ These regions have many climates. These range from the polar and subarctic in northern Russia, to humid continental climate, to humid subtropical south of the Danube River in eastern Europe, and steppe in the Ukraine. Some southerly parts of both regions have a Mediterranean climate.

◆ Both regions are multicultural with many ethnic groups. Most people speak a Slavic language. These languages differ from one another. Russian is the most widely spoken language in Russia and the independent republics.

◆ Most people in both regions are Christians. However, some Muslims live in the Balkans. The majority of people in the republics of central Asia are Muslims.

◆ Eastern Europe and the Balkans are not as industrialized as the rest of Europe, partly because they used to have a Communist government. Most industry in Russia and the independent republics is in the west. Russia and the independent republics are turning from a command economy to a market economy.

◆ Eastern Europe's largest natural resource is lignite. Russia and the independent republics are rich in natural resources, such as oil, natural gas, forests, furs, and fish.

◆ Both regions face air and water pollution. Eastern Europe has a problem with acid rain. Russia has a problem with the disposal of atomic waste. They both face the social problems of ethnic and religious fighting.

"All that you have given me Africa
Makes me walk
With a step that is like no other."

—Anoma Kanié, African poet, from
"All That You Have Given Me Africa," 1978

# Africa and the Middle East

In Units 3 and 4, you studied Europe. Now you turn southward to two huge regions, Africa and the Middle East. Africa is a large continent south of the Mediterranean Sea and east of the Atlantic Ocean. It is a land of many nations, cultures, and huge open spaces. The Serengeti, a national park in Tanzania, is pictured to the left. This is just one example of what visitors to Africa can see. Africa is also home to the longest river in the world, the Nile, and the largest desert in the world, the Sahara.

The Middle East is east of the Mediterranean Sea and northeast of Africa. Sometimes this region is called Southwest Asia, because it is the southwest part of the Asian continent. The Middle East has much in common with parts of North Africa, as you will see in Chapter 15. This unit will show you how Africa and the Middle East are two regions that are slowly developing in the modern world.

### CHAPTERS IN UNIT 5

**Chapter 12:** West Africa . . . . . . . . . . . . . . . . . . . . . . . . . . . .272
**Chapter 13:** Southern Africa . . . . . . . . . . . . . . . . . . . . . . .292
**Chapter 14:** Central and East Africa . . . . . . . . . . . . . .312
**Chapter 15:** North Africa and the Middle East . . . . .332

# West Africa

Some West African countries are large and have many people. Others are small with few people. Rain forests cover some areas; deserts cover others. In the past, West Africa had great empires. From the 1500s to the 1800s, West Africa supplied millions of slaves for the Caribbean, South America, and the United States. In the 1800s, the European powers divided West Africa among themselves. Today, this area is one of the poorest in the world. The photo on this page shows mangroves, tropical trees that you will learn about in this chapter.

## Goals for Learning

▶ To describe where West Africa is located
▶ To identify its most important physical features and climate
▶ To identify the cultures of West Africa
▶ To explain where and how most people live in West Africa
▶ To describe its economy and the environmental challenges it faces

 *Geo-Stats*

### Key Nations of West Africa

 **Nation:** Ghana
**Population:** 19,678,000
**Area** (in square miles): 92,100
**Major Cities:** Accra (capital), Kumasi, Tamale, Tema

**Nation:** Niger
**Population:** 9,962,000
**Area** (in square miles): 489,191
**Major Cities:** Niamey (capital), Zinder, Maradi, Tahoua

 **Nation:** Mali
**Population:** 10,960,000
**Area** (in square miles): 478,841
**Major Cities:** Bamako (capital), Ségou, Mopti, Sikasso, Kayes

**Nation:** Nigeria
**Population:** 113,829,000
**Area** (in square miles): 356,669
**Major Cities:** Abuja (capital), Lagos, Ibadan, Ogbomosho

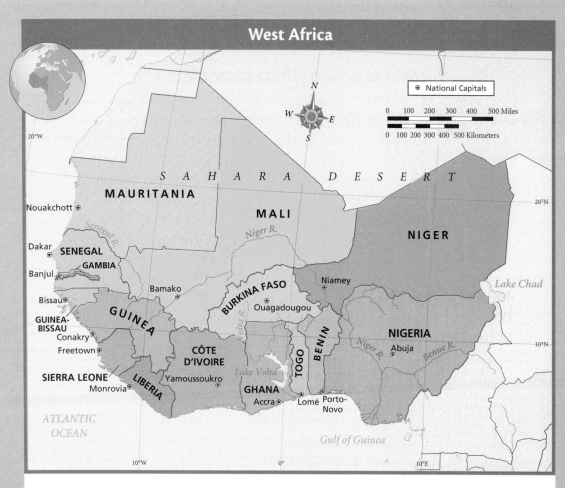

# West Africa

National Capitals

| 0 | 100 | 200 | 300 | 400 | 500 Miles |

| 0 | 100 | 200 | 300 | 400 | 500 Kilometers |

20°W

S A H A R A   D E S E R T

**MAURITANIA**

Nouakchott ⊛

20°N

**MALI**

*Senegal R.*

Dakar

**SENEGAL**

*Niger R.*

**NIGER**

**GAMBIA**

Banjul ⊛

Bamako ⊛

**BURKINA FASO**

Niamey ⊛

*Lake Chad*

Bissau ⊛

**GUINEA-
BISSAU**

**GUINEA**

Ouagadougou

**NIGERIA**

Conakry ⊛

*Volta R.*

*Niger R.*

Abuja ⊛

*Benué R.*

10°N

Freetown ⊛

**CÔTE
D'IVOIRE**

**TOGO**

**BENIN**

**SIERRA LEONE**

**LIBERIA**

Yamoussoukro ⊛

*Lake Volta*

**GHANA**

Monrovia ⊛

Accra ⊛

Lomé

Porto-
Novo

**ATLANTIC
OCEAN**

*Gulf of Guinea*

10°W

0°

10°E

Map Skills

Africa is the second largest continent in the world. It also has the second highest population. The Sahara Desert lies to the north of West Africa. It is the largest desert in the world. The Atlantic Ocean touches the western and southern shores of West Africa.

Study the map and answer the following questions:

**1)** What country is smallest?

**2)** Which gulf do many of the countries of West Africa touch?

**3)** Which country is farthest west? farthest east?

**4)** What is the capital of Nigeria? Guinea? Mali?

**5)** What appears to be the most important river in this region? Why?

Mangrove
*A tropical tree that grows on swampy, coastal ground*

## Where Is West Africa Located?

West Africa is a huge region. It covers an area of over 2.3 million square miles. This is roughly the size of the United States without Alaska. Most of West Africa sits in the low latitudes, between the equator and 20° north latitude. It includes 16 countries: Benin, Burkina Faso, Cape Verde, Côte d'Ivoire (Ivory Coast), The Gambia, Ghana, Guinea, Guinea-Bissau, Liberia, Mali, Mauritania, Niger, Nigeria, Senegal, Sierra Leone, and Togo. All of these countries, except for Cape Verde, are located on the western part of the African mainland. Cape Verde is an island nation. The Atlantic Ocean and the Gulf of Guinea border many of these countries. However, land completely surrounds several of them.

## What Physical Regions Exist in West Africa?

West Africa has four physical regions. The first is the delta of the Niger River. Actually, this river has two deltas: the inland delta in Mali and the coastal delta in Nigeria. The inland delta is one of Africa's largest wetland areas. **Mangroves,** tropical trees that grow in swampy, coastal ground, cover much of the coastal delta.

*Geography In Your Life* HEALTH

### Insects in West Africa

If you have ever had a mosquito bite or a bee sting, you know that some insects can be harmful. Some West African insects are even deadly. The savanna is home to the tsetse fly and the black fly. The tsetse sucks blood from humans and animals. As it does this, it can give them sleeping sickness. This disease damages the heart, changes a person's personality, causes headaches, and makes talking and walking difficult. Finally, the person goes into a long coma, or sleep, and dies.

Swarms of West African black flies, each only 1/8 inch long, can cover a farm animal's body and bite it to death! This fly also bites humans and leaves behind small roundworms. The worms then blind the humans. The only way to control tsetse and black flies is to burn the grasses in which they live.

Desertification
*The change from land that produces crops to desert land*

Sahel
*A belt of semiarid land that stretches across Africa from Senegal on the west coast to the highlands of Ethiopia in the east*

Savanna
*A flat, grassy plain in the Tropics with few trees*

The second region is the wide coastal plain. At one time, tropical rain forests completely covered this area. West Africans use the wood from these forests for fuel. In rural areas, wood is often the only energy source available. West Africa also export lots of timber from these forests. For these reasons, many rain forests have been cut down.

The third region is the **savanna.** It is a flat, grassy plain in the Tropics. With few trees and rich soil, a savanna is good for farming. However, the tsetse fly and the black fly live there. The tsetse kills cattle and causes sleeping sickness in people. The black fly can blind people. It is most common along rivers, so people tend to avoid these areas, even though the land is best for farming.

The fourth region is the **Sahel.** This Arabic word means "shore." In this case, the "shore" is that of the Sahara Desert. The Sahel is a belt of semiarid land. It stretches across Africa from Senegal on the west coast to the highlands of Ethiopia in the east. Rainfall in this region varies each year. In the 1950s and 1960s, enough rain fell to raise crops. However, in the 1970s, almost no rain fell. Because of lack of rain, a way of life ended. Many nomads raised cattle, sheep, and goats, but the drought killed their animals. It also destroyed crops. Then farmers had no seed to start again when the rains returned. Many nomads and farmers migrated to cities. The desert gradually took over the deserted farmland. Geographers call this **desertification.** This change from land that produces crops to land that is only desert is a major problem in West Africa.

**Section 1 Review** On a separate sheet of paper, write *True* if the statement is true or *False* if the statement is not true. Make each false statement true by changing the underlined word.

1) <u>Cape Verde</u> is the only West African island nation.

2) <u>Deserts</u> cover the coastal delta of Nigeria.

3) The <u>Sahel</u> is experiencing desertification.

4) The <u>savanna</u> is the home of the tsetse fly.

5) Tropical rain forests once covered the <u>inland delta</u>.

**What do YOU think?**

Should the governments of the Sahel region dig wells for the people there? Explain your answer.

Dredge
*To clear away the sand and mud from the bottom of a waterway*

Escarpment
*A line of cliffs or slopes from a plateau to the plains below*

Lagoon
*A shallow body of water separated from the sea*

Sandbar
*A ridge of sand built up by ocean waves*

## What Are the Main Physical Features?

West Africa has a long coastline, but few harbors. The harbors have many **sandbars,** or ridges of sand built up by ocean waves. They also have **lagoons,** or shallow bodies of water separated from the sea. The only natural deepwater harbor is in Freetown, Sierra Leone. The two other important West African ports are Lagos in Nigeria and Abidjan in Côte d'Ivoire. Ships reach the Lagos harbor through a lagoon that must be **dredged** regularly. Sand and mud must be cleared from the bottom of the harbor. To open up the Abidjan harbor, a canal through a large sandbar had to be dug.

West Africa is mostly made up of plains and basins. The coastal areas are flat. Gradually, these plains change to basins. Higher land surrounds these level lowlands. However, West Africa has few upland areas. Guinea has the Fouta Djallon plateau. Nigeria has two plateaus, the Jos and Mambila. These plateaus are separated on all sides by cliffs. This is called an **escarpment.** When rivers flow over an escarpment, they become beautiful waterfalls.

Mountains rise on the edge of the plateaus. The highest mountains in West Africa stand on the Freetown peninsula in Sierra Leone. The first Europeans who saw these mountains thought they looked like a sleeping lion, so they called them "Serra Lyoa." This Portuguese term means "lion mountains" and became the name for the country. The highest mountain peaks are Bintuman in Sierra Leone and Dimlang on the border of Nigeria and Cameroon.

## What Are the Major West African Rivers and Lakes?

The Niger is the most important West African river. Its 2,597 miles make it the third longest river in Africa. The Niger begins in the Fouta Djallon plateau of Guinea in the west. It then flows northward through Mali. Next, it bends sharply south through Niger and into Nigeria. Finally, it

Harmattan
*The dry, dusty wind on the Atlantic coast of West Africa*

empties into the Gulf of Guinea. The Benue River is the Niger's biggest tributary. Other important rivers in West Africa are the Senegal, the Volta, and the Gambia. They provide hydroelectric power and water for irrigation.

Lake Chad is the largest lake in West Africa. It is about the same size as Lake Erie in the United States. Lake Chad is between Nigeria and Niger. Lake Volta, a smaller lake, was created in 1966 when the Volta River was dammed.

## What Is the Climate Like in West Africa?

Most of West Africa has a tropical or a subtropical climate. Temperatures are high throughout the year. As a general rule, the climate is wettest on the coast. It becomes drier inland. Some of the upland areas, however, have more rain and lower temperatures than the surrounding lowlands.

Areas in the lower latitudes have only two seasons: dry and rainy. Along the coast, the rainy season lasts from May to October. Each year, about 135 inches of rain fall on the rain forest areas like Sierra Leone. The rainy season inland is shorter. The city of Timbuktu in Mali receives only 7.8 inches.

West Africa falls into several climate regions. Near the equator lies the belt of tropical rain forest climate. Just north is a region with tropical savanna climate. Farther north, in the savanna, the climate becomes much drier. The Sahel region has a steppe climate.

West African climate also has the **harmattan.** This dry, dusty wind affects the northern part and the Atlantic coast of West Africa the most. The dust is sometimes so thick that cars must use their lights even in the middle of the day. Between December and March, the harmattan brings cool air from the Sahara desert.

Some of the earliest African kingdoms formed in West Africa. This drawing shows Timbuktu, which was a great center of learning and travel in the 1300s. The city still exists today.

# Physical Features of Africa

This map shows the main physical features of the African continent. What does this map tell you about Africa as a whole? What does this map tell you about the climate of West Africa? How does West Africa differ from the rest of Africa as shown on this map?

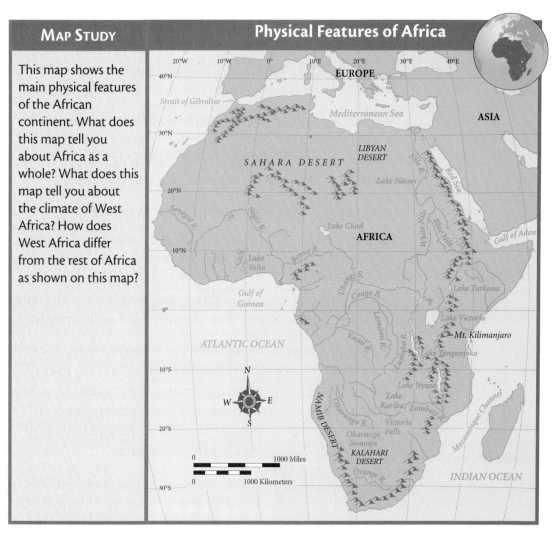

| WORD BANK |
| --- |
| Chad |
| escarpment |
| harmattan |
| lagoon |
| Niger |

**Section 2 Review** On a separate sheet of paper, write the word from the Word Bank that completes each sentence.

1) A(n) _____ is a body of water separated from the sea.

2) A(n) _____ is a line of cliffs.

3) The _____ is the most important West African river.

4) Lake _____ is the largest West African lake.

5) The _____ is a dry wind.

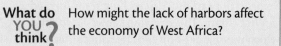

**What do YOU think?** How might the lack of harbors affect the economy of West Africa?

**Cultivator**
*A farmer who grows crops to sell and to support the family*

**Missionary**
*A member of a church who travels to spread religious beliefs*

**Pastoralist**
*A person who looks after animals*

## What Are the Cultures of West Africa?

Many people think that all Africans are alike. In fact, West Africa has a great deal of diversity. Unlike many other countries, most West African countries have many ethnic groups. In fact, Nigeria alone has more than 200 different ethnic groups! The ethnic groups of West Africa can be divided into two groups.

**Cultivators** make up the first cultural group. Cultivators are farmers. They grow crops to sell and to support themselves and their families. The largest group of cultivators are the Mandinka in Senegal and Gambia, the Yoruba in Nigeria, the Mende in Sierra Leone, and the Ashanti in Ghana.

**Pastoralists** make up a second large cultural group. Pastoralists look after animals. Sometimes they are nomads. They move long distances to search for water and grassy fields where their animals can eat. The Fulani live in the savanna region. The Tuareg live further north in the Sahel region. Other ethnic groups fish. These include the Ewe, Togo, and the Fanti of Ghana.

## What Languages Do West Africans Speak?

More languages are spoken in West Africa than anywhere else in the world. European countries controlled this area for a long time. Because of this, French, English, and Portuguese are the official languages. However, each ethnic group has a language of its own. Many people, especially in the Sahel and savanna regions, speak Arabic.

## What Are the Major West African Religions?

West Africa is a region of great religious diversity. In the past, Europeans called **missionaries** came to the West African coast. They spread Christian beliefs, so many West Africans became Christians. Muslim Arabs came to the dry northern region of West Africa, so many people there became Muslims and practice Islam.

**Many West Africans are Muslims. Muslims use mosques like this one in which to worship.**

Ancestor worship
*Worshiping members of one's family who lived long ago*

Animist
*A person who believes that things in nature contain a spirit and who worships ancestors*

Shantytown
*A slum that surrounds a city and that has shelters made from weak materials*

People in many rural communities hold on to their native beliefs. Many are **animists.** They believe that things in nature like trees, rivers, and the sky contain a spirit. They also practice **ancestor worship.** That is, they worship members of their family who lived long ago. An African chief once described his people as a "vast family, of which many are dead, few are living, and many more are not yet born."

## Where Do Most West Africans Live?

Most West Africans, especially those in the savanna region, live in rural villages and are subsistence farmers. That is, they eat most of what they grow and have little to sell. These farmers build their homes with sunbaked mud bricks. They group these homes into family units. The Muslim religion allows men to have as many as four wives. Muslim families are sometimes very large, as women bear many children. In some villages all the people are members of the same family.

Of course, many people live in cities, too. Lagos, Nigeria, has more than 8 million people. It is the largest city of West Africa. With its high-rise buildings, Lagos looks like any big city in Europe or North America. Cars crowd its streets.

Many farmers have migrated to the West African cities. They live in the **shantytowns** that surround these cities. In these slums, poor people find shelter in cardboard boxes and other unfit materials. Dirt roads run through these shantytowns. The city does not remove the garbage or provide sewers, water, or transportation. The people have no indoor plumbing. Often the people must drink unclean water.

## What Are the Population Trends in West Africa?

Population growth in West Africa is among the highest in the world for two reasons. First, the countries have a high birthrate. Families need many children to work in the fields or to herd the animals. Second, the death rate is falling. In the past, many children died as babies. Now, modern medicine has changed that. People live longer in West Africa than they used to.

Many countries have a growth rate of between 2 and 4 percent. A growth rate of 2.9 percent will double the population in just 23 years! Children under the age of 15 make up more than half the population of many West African countries. This creates a huge burden on the governments of these countries. They have no money to pay for education, medical care, and important services.

## What Problems Do West Africans Face?

Poverty is West Africa's biggest problem. Four out of the five poorest countries in the world are in West Africa. Niger is the poorest. Many people earn less than $200 a year. Another problem in West Africa is **life expectancy,** or the average number of years a person is expected to live. Life expectancy is lower in West Africa than anywhere else in the world. In Sierra Leone, it is only 40 years.

| Biography | ABD AL-RAHMAN IBRAHIMA: 1762–1829 |

Ibrahima was a prince of the powerful Fula people in Guinea. He studied in Timbuktu. There he learned to speak and to write Arabic. When he returned home, he led his people in battle.

In 1787, Ibrahima was captured in battle and sold to white slave traders. They shipped him and hundreds of other Africans to the United States. There, he became a slave. Although he escaped once, this African prince spent 42 years in slavery. In 1829, an antislavery group won Ibrahima's freedom. He returned to Africa. However, he died before he could get home to his people.

The growth rate in West Africa has created a large population. The government has trouble providing services such as education.

West Africa has other problems that result from poverty. For example, Burkina Faso has only one doctor for every 57,000 people. Also, the production of food cannot keep up with the growing number of people. This has caused widespread hunger. Most countries in the region depend on food aid from countries like the United States.

Many of West Africa's problems go back to when European countries took over Africa. Europeans drew the borders, but they did not think about human geography. They sometimes divided an ethnic group among several countries. They also put people who had been enemies into the same country. This has led to ethnic and religious warfare.

**Coup**
*A sudden overthrow of a government*

The governments of most West African countries have kept the people from solving all these problems. Many countries have a tradition of one-person rule. This often leads to dishonesty. The leader and those in high positions often become rich while most of the people stay poor. For example, the leader of Nigeria died suddenly in 1998. The next day, government officials stopped his wife as she tried to leave the country. She was carrying 38 suitcases stuffed with money. The dead ruler may have stolen more than $4 billion in less than five years!

Many countries have had five or more **coups** since becoming independent in the 1950s and 1960s. A coup is a sudden overthrow of the government. In some countries, an army official has taken over the government. The countries of West Africa may have to start solving their many problems by looking at their political ones first.

## African Refugees

| Major Sources of African Refugees | Number of Refugees |
|---|---|
| Sierra Leone | 480,000 |
| Somalia | 421,000 |
| Sudan | 352,000 |
| Eritrea | 323,000 |
| Liberia | 310,000 |
| Angola | 302,000 |
| Congo | 136,000 |
| Burundi | 125,000 |
| Western Sahara | 105,000 |

Total Refugees From Africa: 2,922,000
Total Refugees in the World: 13,469,000

### CHART STUDY

Many Africans have become refugees. That is, war, political problems, poverty, or lack of food have forced them out of their homeland. This chart shows where many African refugees come from each year. How many refugees come from Sierra Leone? Liberia? How many of the world's refugees come from Africa?

**Section 3 Review** On a separate sheet of paper, write answers to these questions.

1) What is the difference between a cultivator and a pastoralist?

2) Why are European languages the official languages of some West African nations?

3) What three major religions do West Africans practice?

4) What are shantytowns?

5) What is one reason for the ethnic and religious wars in West Africa?

**What do YOU think?** What might happen if leaders redrew the boundaries of West African countries?

### What Is the West African Economy Like?

Most West Africans farm. Nearly 70 percent of the people earn their living by working the land. Subsistence farmers grow many different crops to feed their families. What they grow depends on the soil, rainfall, and temperature.

Most farmers grow **staple crops.** These foods are the ones the family usually eats. For example, in Europe and the United States, families often eat a potato product or one made of wheat. In Asia, people often eat rice. In the drier areas of West Africa, the staple crops include root crops like cassava and yams, a kind of sweet potato. In areas that receive more rain, subsistence farmers grow corn, millet, and sorghum. In the areas that receive the most rain, farmers grow tropical fruits like mangoes, bananas, papaws, and papayas.

**Intercropping** is another kind of subsistence farming in West Africa. Farmers plant different crops in the same field. People in the United States are used to seeing large fields of wheat or corn, so West African fields look disorganized. However, experts think intercropping is a good way to use

**Intercropping**
*Planting different crops in the same field*

**Staple crop**
*A food that people eat most often*

Some West Africans make a living as pastoralists. They raise animals by herding them from place to place. However, most West African farmers grow crops. They are called cultivators.

West African soil. This system of farming provides families with many different types of foods. The larger plants shade the smaller plants that might not do well in the hot sun. Also, the thick crop cover protects the soil from erosion during heavy storms.

Some farmers in the savanna and forest areas move from place to place every few years. To clear a plot of land, they cut and burn the trees and grasses. The ash from the fire makes the soil better for growing crops at first. However, in a year or two, the heavy rains wash away all the valuable minerals in the soil. Some of the minerals are pushed too deep in the ground for plant roots to reach. Farmers need fertile land to grow crops, but without minerals, land becomes infertile. No crops will grow. The farmers then move to another place and start all over again. This type of farming is called **shifting agriculture.** Gradually, a more settled form of farming is replacing shifting agriculture. Farmers grow crops on the same piece of land every year. This is because West Africa has less land to farm and more and more people.

West Africa also produces cash crops, such as cacao, coffee, peanuts, and cotton. Farmers grow these crops to sell. Cash crops usually bring in more money than other crops. However, sometimes prices change quickly. This depends on world demands. Côte d'Ivoire is the world's largest producer of cacao. It is also an important coffee producer. Farmers in Nigeria and Senegal grow peanuts. Farmers raise cotton in Mali, Nigeria, and Côte d'Ivoire.

## How Does Trade Affect West Africa's Economy?

Most West African countries trade mainly with the European countries that at one time ruled them. For example, about a third of Senegal's exports go to France. France also provides Senegal with about a third of its imports. Ghana, once a British colony, sends about 16 percent of its exports to England. Ghana receives 12 percent of its imports from England. The main exports are farm products and **raw materials,** from which other countries make things to sell.

West Africa's exports bring in some money, but the imports cost more than the exports. This has led to a **trade imbalance.** That is, West Africa pays for more than it sells, so it owes money to other countries. To make up the difference, West African countries must borrow money. Now these countries need to figure out how to pay the huge debt they owe to other countries.

## What Natural Resources Does West Africa Have?

West Africa is rich in natural resources. Nigeria has large deposits of oil, tin, and coal. It has about half of the world's supply of columbite. This metal hardens stainless steel. Guinea is the world's second largest producer of bauxite. Niger is the second largest producer of uranium. Ghana produces more manganese than any other country. This mineral is necessary for the production of steel, an important raw material.

At one time, West Africa was an important producer of gold. In fact, people once called Ghana the Gold Coast. Workers there still mine gold, but production has dropped. This is also true of diamonds. The West African country with the most diamonds is Sierra Leone.

The hardwood trees of the rain forests are another important West African resource. However, workers cut down these trees faster than they replace them. Since the 1940s, nearly 85 percent of the rain forests have been destroyed in Côte d'Ivoire.

## What Environmental Problems Face West Africa?

West Africa's growing population has been hard on the environment. The main environmental problems are water shortages, pollution, deforestation, soil erosion, and desertification. These problems affect one another. For example, the loss of forests can cause soil erosion. Trees hold soil in place, but rain can wash away treeless soil. Wind blows it away. This turns an area into desert.

**Writing About Geography**

Imagine that you are a political leader in West Africa. Look back over this chapter. Then list one problem African nations face. Write a three-point action plan for how you would solve this problem. Give details for how you will make the plan work.

In urban areas, the biggest environmental problems are a result of overcrowding. Housing is often poorly built. In the large shantytowns, people sometimes have to drink unclean water that causes disease.

**Section 4 Review** Choose the letter of the answer that correctly completes each sentence. Write your answers on a separate sheet of paper.

1) Most of the West African economy is based on _____.
   a. natural resources    c. fishing
   b. mining               d. farming

2) _____ are the foods that people most often eat.
   a. Meats                c. Junk food
   b. Staple crops         d. Carbohydrates

3) _____ is the planting of different crops in the same field.
   a. Intercropping        c. Commercial farming
   b. Shifting agriculture d. Organic farming

4) The biggest trade partner of most West African countries is _____.
   a. South America        c. Southeast Asia
   b. North America        d. Europe

5) The West African country of _____ has large deposits of oil, tin, coal, and columbite.
   a. Mali                 c. Ghana
   b. Nigeria              d. Niger

 **What do YOU think?** What might the trading partners of West Africa do to help these African countries solve their problem of high foreign debt?

# Songhai: The Last Great Empire of West Africa

Beginning around A.D. 400, many great empires developed in West Africa. Ghana was the first empire. It was an important center of trade from the Sudan to North Africa. Its empire lasted for hundreds of years. Then, in A.D. 1000, North African soldiers invaded Ghana. The empire lost its power.

Next, Mali became a great empire. Like Ghana before it, Mali controlled all the main trade routes. Its empire lasted for several hundred years, too. However, in time, invaders also attacked Mali. By the mid-1500s, this empire had split into several independent states.

The last and largest empire of West Africa was the kingdom of Songhai. Like Ghana and Mali, Songhai grew powerful by controlling the gold and salt trade. Strong rulers led this empire. During the late 1400s, one ruler, Sonni Ali, expanded it to include most of the West African savanna. His empire stretched from the Atlantic Ocean eastward nearly 1,800 miles.

Askia Muhammad, Sonni Ali's son, made Songhai the largest empire West Africa ever had. These two leaders ruled well. They devoted themselves to Islam, the religion of all Muslims. They appointed Muslim judges to make sure that their people obeyed Islamic laws.

Other countries wanted Songhai's riches and attacked it. At first, Songhai's army easily defeated its attackers. Then, in 1590, the Moroccan ruler in North Africa sent an army to attack Songhai. His soldiers had a powerful new weapon, the gun. Songhai soldiers had only spears, swords, bows, and arrows. In 1596, Songhai fell. The empire broke apart, and West Africa was never united again.

**Sonni Ali was a powerful African ruler. He ruled Songhai from 1464 to 1492.**

## Spotlight Story Wrap-Up

1) What were the three great West African empires?

2) How did all three empires become so powerful?

3) Who was Sonni Ali?

4) What religion did Sonni Ali and his son follow?

5) How were the Songhai soldiers defeated?

◆ Africa is the second largest continent. West Africa, with 16 countries, covers an area of over 2.3 million square miles.

◆ West Africa has four physical regions: the Niger River delta, the wide coastal plain, the savanna, and the Sahel. Most of West Africa is plains and basins with a few uplands. It has a long coastline, but few harbors.

◆ West Africa's most important river is the Niger. The largest lake is Lake Chad.

◆ Most of West Africa has a tropical or a subtropical climate with two seasons: dry and rainy. The dry, dusty harmattan wind affects the northern parts of West Africa.

◆ Several hundred ethnic groups live in West Africa. They form two cultural groups: cultivators and pastoralists. Cultivators farm; pastoralists raise animals.

◆ In the past, European countries controlled West Africa. Because of this, French, English, and Portuguese are official languages. However, each ethnic group has its own language. Many people also speak Arabic.

◆ Many coastal West Africans are Christian. Northern people in West Africa are Muslims. Many people are animists who believe that spirits live in nature.

◆ Most West Africans live in rural villages on the savanna and are subsistence farmers. Because of drought, many have moved to overcrowded cities.

◆ Population growth in West Africa is among the highest in the world. West African governments have little money to provide education, medical care, clean water, sewage, and other services.

◆ Most West Africans farm. Many are only subsistence farmers of staple crops; others raise cash crops, such as cacao, coffee, peanuts, and cotton.

◆ West Africa trades mainly with Europe. A trade imbalance has developed, so West Africa is in great debt.

◆ West Africa is rich in natural resources, but diamond and gold production has dropped, and the rain forests are being destroyed.

◆ West Africa's main environmental problems are water shortages, pollution, deforestation, soil erosion, and desertification.

◆ West Africa has low life expectancy, ethnic and religious wars, and poor political leadership. Poverty is its biggest problem. Four out of the five poorest countries in the world are in West Africa. Niger is the poorest.

## Comprehension: Identifying Facts

On a separate sheet of paper, use the words from the Word Bank to complete each sentence.

**WORD BANK**

animists
farming
harmattan
pastoralists
Sahel

1) The region of West Africa that is experiencing desertification is the _____.

2) The dry, dusty wind that creates dust storms is the _____.

3) _____ make their living by looking after animals.

4) _____ believe that things in nature contain a spirit.

5) Most of the West African economy is based on _____.

## Comprehension: Multiple Choice

On a separate sheet of paper, write the letter of the answer that correctly completes each sentence.

1) Most of West Africa consists of _____ and basins.
   a. highlands
   b. plains
   c. lowlands
   d. lakes

2) The _____ is the largest and most important river of West Africa.
   a. Nile
   b. Gambia
   c. Volta
   d. Niger

3) _____ are areas of unfit shelters that surround the big cities of West Africa.
   a. Harmattans
   b. Intercrops
   c. Shantytowns
   d. Suburbs

4) Cassavas and yams are _____ crops, because most West Africans eat them.
   a. harmattan
   b. pastoral
   c. share
   d. staple

5) West Africa's growing _____ has been hard on the environment.

   a. rain forests     c. population

   b. intercropping     d. life expectancy

## Comprehension: Understanding Main Ideas

On a separate sheet of paper, write the answer to each question. Use complete sentences.

1) What is the climate of West Africa like?

2) What are the two main ethnic groups in West Africa?

3) What are five environmental problems of West Africa?

## Critical Thinking: Write Your Opinion

On a separate sheet of paper, write your opinion to each question. Use complete sentences.

1) In the past, slave ships carried millions of slaves away from West Africa to the United States. Should the U.S. pay the West African countries money to make up for what they lost? Explain your answer.

2) Should West African countries encourage more farmers to grow cash crops? Why or why not?

## Applying the Five Themes of Geography

### *Interaction*

How has poor management of the environment added to West Africa's problems?

**Test-Taking Tip**    Read test questions carefully to identify those questions that require more than one answer. Read your answers to make sure that you answered all the questions.

*13*

# Southern Africa

The photo to the left shows the Okavango delta in Botswana, a nation located in southern Africa. For nearly 300 years, European countries ruled most of southern Africa. A small white population controlled the much larger black population. In 1994, the Republic of South Africa was the last country to give up its whites-only government. This and many other changes are affecting southern Africa.

## Goals for Learning

▶ To describe where southern Africa is located

▶ To identify its most important physical features and climate

▶ To describe the diverse cultures of southern Africa

▶ To explain how and where most people live in southern Africa

▶ To describe its economy and the environmental challenges it faces

## *Geo-Stats*

### Key Nations of Southern Africa

**Nation:** Angola
**Population:** 12,479,000
**Area** (in square miles): 481,354
**Major Cities:** Luanda (capital), Huambo, Lobito, Benguela

**Nation:** Mozambique
**Population:** 19,124,000
**Area** (in square miles): 308,642
**Major Cities:** Maputo (capital), Beira, Nampula, Pemba

**Nation:** South Africa
**Population:** 42,579,000
**Area** (in square miles): 471,445
**Major Cities:** Pretoria, Cape Town (capitals), Durban, Johannesburg, Port Elizabeth

**Nation:** Zimbabwe
**Population:** 11,163,000
**Area** (in square miles): 150,804
**Major Cities:** Harare (capital), Bulawayo, Chitungwiza, Gweru

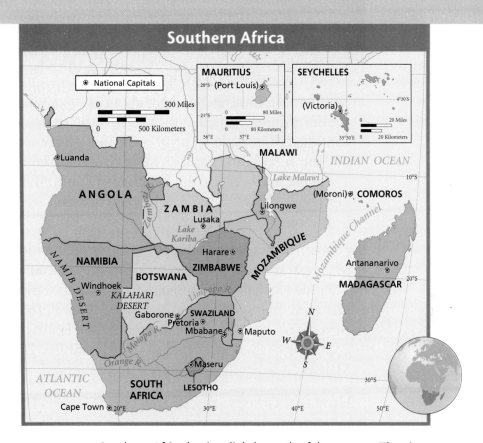

# Southern Africa

National Capitals

**MAURITIUS**
(Port Louis)

**SEYCHELLES**
(Victoria)

0        500 Miles

0        500 Kilometers

Luanda

MALAWI

*INDIAN OCEAN*

**ANGOLA**

**Z A M B I A**

Lusaka

Lake Kariba

Lake Malawi

(Moroni) **COMOROS**

Lilongwe

*Mozambique Channel*

**N A M I B   D E S E R T**

**NAMIBIA**

Windhoek

*KALAHARI DESERT*

**BOTSWANA**

Gaborone

Harare

**ZIMBABWE**

**MOZAMBIQUE**

*Limpopo R.*

*Molopo R.*

Pretoria

**SWAZILAND**

Mbabane

Maputo

Antananarivo

**MADAGASCAR**

*Orange R.*

Maseru

N
W        E
S

**ATLANTIC OCEAN**

**SOUTH AFRICA**

**LESOTHO**

Cape Town

*Map Skills*

Southern Africa begins slightly south of the equator. Then it stretches south to the southernmost tip of Africa. Important countries in this large area include the Republic of South Africa, Zimbabwe, and Mozambique. Southern Africa also includes the large island nation of Madagascar. It is located to the east of Mozambique across the Mozambique Channel. Southern Africa contains the Kalahari desert and several large lakes and rivers.

Study the map and answer the following questions:

**1)** Which two oceans surround southern Africa?

**2)** Where is the Kalahari desert located?

**3)** Which rivers flow through southern Africa?

**4)** Where is the Namib desert located?

**5)** Most of the rainfall in southern Africa is to the north and east. Why do you think this is true?

## Where Is Southern Africa Located?

Southern Africa stretches from about 10° to about 35° south latitude. Located at the southern tip of the African continent, it is made up of 14 countries. The most northern of these are Angola, Zambia, Malawi, and Mozambique. The most southern are the Republic of South Africa, Lesotho, and Swaziland. Sandwiched between are Namibia, Botswana, and Zimbabwe.

Southern Africa also includes the four island nations of Madagascar, the Seychelles, the Comoros, and Mauritius. They are located in the Indian Ocean, which washes the eastern shore of Mozambique and the Republic of South Africa. The Atlantic Ocean borders Namibia, Angola, and South Africa's western side. Lesotho, Botswana, Zimbabwe, Malawi, Swaziland, and Zambia are landlocked.

## How Did Geography Shape This Region's History?

In the 1400s, Europeans began to look for a sea route to Asia. They did this because the country that controlled the trade route to Asia would become rich and powerful. A sea route would be cheaper than a land route. As explorers sailed down the west coast of Africa, the Portuguese found its southern tip. They called it the Cape of Good Hope. In 1652, the Dutch built a small settlement on Africa's tip. They called it Cape Town. Later, German, French, and British settlers joined the Dutch. Southern Africa offered them rich farmland and a mild climate. The settlement grew. Soon the European holdings also grew. The white settlers fought more and more with the native blacks.

In 1886, gold-bearing rocks were found on a farm in South Africa. News of this spread quickly. Soon thousands of people rushed there, searching for gold. A small town grew up near the gold site. It became Johannesburg, South Africa. Today, it is the economic center of the Republic of South Africa.

**Writing About Geography**

Gold has been important to Africa. What do you think is the most important thing that comes from the earth? Explain your answer in one or two paragraphs.

The Kalahari Desert is more than 100,000 square miles. It stretches across Botswana, Namibia, and South Africa.

## What Regions Exist?

Southern Africa has four main regions. In the southern part, the Little Karroo and the Great Karroo plateaus and the Drakensberg Mountains make up a highland region. Mountains also rise in Malawi. Some call it the "Switzerland of Africa" because of its mountain scenery.

A second region is the **veld.** This grassy plain stretches across central South Africa to the west of Lesotho. The veld is like the steppes of Russia, the pampas of Argentina, and the American prairie. The only difference is the type of grass that grows on the land. All these grasslands have rich soil for growing grain.

The third region is a desert region. A large desert stretches across the western part of southern Africa. The Namib covers much of Namibia. The Kalahari, the largest desert in southern Africa, covers two-thirds of Botswana and stretches into Namibia and South Africa.

Forests cover the low-lying plain of the northern part of southern Africa. This fourth region receives the most rainfall. Woodlands cover the northern parts of Zambia, Malawi, and Mozambique. A low coastal plain is located to the east. In southern Mozambique, this coastal plain broadens. Heavy rains sometimes cause its many rivers to flood.

**Veld**
*A grassy plain in southern Africa*

**Section 1 Review** On a separate sheet of paper, write *True* if the statement is true or *False* if it is not true. Make each false statement true by changing the underlined word.

1) <u>Cape Town</u> is the economic center of the Republic of South Africa.

2) The <u>veld</u> is like the American prairie.

3) The Kalahari is a <u>lake</u> in southern Africa.

4) <u>Malawi</u> is sometimes called the "Switzerland of Africa."

5) Southern Africa is made up of <u>14</u> countries.

**What do YOU think?**

Think about what you learned in Chapter 12. Why did Europeans prefer to settle in southern Africa rather than in West Africa?

### What Are the Main Physical Features?

The shape of southern Africa's land is like an upside-down plate. Much of the land is a large plateau. Along the coast, the plateau drops sharply to a coastal plain. Escarpments form the edges of the plateau. One escarpment is the Drakensberg Mountains in eastern South Africa.

The Kalahari is also part of the plateau area. Most people think of deserts as having few plants. However, grass and shrubs cover the Kalahari. Underground water near the surface supports the plants, since the area only gets about 16 inches of rain per year. The Namib runs along the entire west coast of Namibia. This desert is much drier than the Kalahari. Because of this, huge sand dunes with few plants cover most of the Namib.

## Major Deserts of the World

| Desert | Location | Area in Square Miles |
|---|---|---|
| Sahara | North Africa | 3,500,000 |
| Gobi | Mongolia/Northeastern China | 500,000 |
| Patagonian | Argentina | 260,000 |
| Rub' al Khali | Southern Arabian Peninsula | 250,000 |
| Chihuahuan | Mexico/Southwestern United States | 140,000 |
| Taklimakan | Northern China | 140,000 |
| Great Sandy | Northwestern Australia | 130,000 |
| Great Victoria | Southwestern Australia | 130,000 |
| Kalahari | Southwestern Africa | 100,000 |
| Kyzyl-Kum | Uzbekistan | 100,000 |

### CHART STUDY

The world has many large deserts. Two of the ten largest are in Africa. The largest is the Sahara in North Africa. The Kalahari in southern Africa is the ninth largest. How large is the Sahara? What deserts are located in Asia?

## What Are the Major Rivers and Lakes?

The eastern part of southern Africa has many rivers and lakes. Some 50 rivers flow eastward through Mozambique alone! However, many rivers in the western part of southern Africa are dry during much of the year.

The two most important rivers are the Zambezi and the Orange. The Zambezi is southern Africa's longest river. It begins in northwest Zambia and flows between Zambia and Zimbabwe. At their border stands Victoria Falls. This waterfall is more than one mile across! People miles away can hear the thunder of the Zambezi as it drops 354 feet over the falls. The Zambezi flows into Mozambique and then empties into the Indian Ocean. The Orange is the largest river located entirely within southern Africa. It begins in the highlands of Lesotho and travels through the Republic of South Africa. There, it empties into the Atlantic Ocean.

Southern Africa's two largest lakes are human-made. They were formed by damming the Zambezi River. Lake Kariba is on the Zambia-Zimbabwe border. Lake Cabora Bassa is in Mozambique. The dams provide hydroelectric power. The hydroelectric plant at Cabora Bassa is one of the largest in the world. Fish have been added to the lake to improve the diet of people in poorer parts of Mozambique.

Southern Africa also has salt lakes. Some people call them "pans." The largest ones are in Botswana. They are more than 93 miles across, but they are not deep. Thousands of years ago, these shallow lakes were part of a large lake. Today, they are dry for much of the year.

**Victoria Falls is named after England's Queen Victoria. It is located on the border of Zambia and Zimbabwe.**

## What Is Southern Africa's Climate Like?

Southern Africa has four climate types. The southernmost tip has a Mediterranean climate. Winter is mild. The most rain falls during the winter months from May to August.

**Prevailing winds** affect the slopes of the Drakensburg Mountains. These are winds that usually blow from the same direction. Differences in air pressure cause wind. Areas with warm temperatures like the Tropics have low air pressure. Areas with cooler temperatures like the polar regions have high air pressure. Air always flows from places of high air pressure to places where the air pressure is lower. This is the way heat is spread around the globe. The prevailing winds affect the ocean currents. The ocean currents carry warm water toward the poles and cold water toward the equator. This circular flow of water and air is very important to maintaining life on the planet Earth.

Ocean currents affect southern Africa greatly. The western shore of Namibia is very dry, even along the coast. This is because the prevailing winds flow in a southeast direction away from the land. Maritime climates like those of the eastern coast of South Africa are the result of the prevailing winds blowing from the Indian Ocean toward the land. This moist air is forced to rise as it hits the windward slopes of the Drakensburg Mountains. As it rises, it cools. Its ability to hold moist air lessens and it rains.

Much of the inner part of southern Africa is far from the ocean. The prevailing winds have dropped most of their precipitation as they crossed the mountains. The result is a steppe or desert climate. Winters are dry, with clear skies and high temperatures. The little bit of rain comes mostly in the summer.

The eastern coastal area of southern Africa has a humid subtropical climate. Summers are hot and humid; winters are mild. Rain falls throughout the year, but is heaviest in the summer months.

**WORD BANK**

escarpment

Kalahari

Namib

prevailing

Zambezi

**Section 2 Review** On a separate sheet of paper, write the words from the Word Bank to complete each sentence.

1) The Drakensberg Mountains are a(n) _____.

2) Grass and shrubs cover the _____ desert.

3) Large sand dunes cover the _____ desert.

4) The _____ is southern Africa's longest river.

5) _____ winds often blow in the same direction.

**What do YOU think?** Why might a person want to travel to southern Africa?

## What Cultures Exist in Southern Africa?

For many years, only a few people lived in southern Africa. Most of them had migrated there from somewhere else. This long history of people migrating to southern Africa has created diversity. Today, the main population groups include African peoples, Europeans, Asians, and a growing number of people of mixed race.

Outsiders usually divide the people of southern Africa simply into black people and white people. However, both are made up of many different ethnic groups. For example, 75 percent of the population of the Republic of South Africa are blacks. However, this group includes many different ethnic groups. A small number of people trace their roots back to the earliest settlers, the San or "Bushmen." One large ethnic group is the Nguni. They include the Zulu, Swazi, Ndebele, Pondo, Temba, and Xhosa people. Two other large groups are the Sotho and the Tswana.

The white people in the Republic of South Africa also differ. Most of them are descendents of Dutch, German, French, and British colonists. The ancestors of the largest group, the Afrikaners, came from the Netherlands.

## Why Do People Still Migrate in Southern Africa?

People migrate from rural villages to towns and cities to find more safety and better jobs. Many men from neighboring countries come to the Republic of South Africa to work in mines, on farms, and in factories. Over one-third of the adult male population of Lesotho live and work in South Africa. War also causes people to leave their homeland. During a long civil war in Mozambique, over 1.5 million people fled the country. Many of them lived in refugee camps in Malawi and Zimbabwe. Since the end of the fighting in 1992, many have returned to their homeland.

## What Religions Do Southern Africans Practice?

The European colonists introduced Christianity to Africa. Because of this, many people in Mozambique are Roman Catholic. In the Republic of South Africa and Namibia, many people are Protestant. They belong to the Dutch Reformed Church. Many people in the northern coastal areas of Mozambique practice Islam. A large minority group in the Republic of South Africa migrated there from India. They practice Hinduism, a religion they brought from their native country.

Many people in southern Africa practice their traditional African religions like animism. Africans sometimes add parts of European religions to their own beliefs. They may pray in church on Sunday. Then, during the week, they ask the spirits of their ancestors to help them with problems.

## What Languages Do Southern Africans Speak?

The many ethnic groups of southern Africa speak different languages. Many black Africans speak one of the Niger, or Bantu, languages. Another language family, spoken by the San people, is Khoisan. This language uses different clicking sounds made by the tongue and the roof of the mouth.

The official languages of many countries in southern Africa go back to the colonial period. People from Angola and Mozambique speak Portuguese. Some people in Namibia still speak German. English is widely spoken in the Republic of South Africa and Zimbabwe. The most commonly spoken language among whites is Afrikaans. This language is a mixture of Dutch and African languages. People in South Africa, Namibia, and Zimbabwe speak Afrikaans.

## What Are the Population Trends in Southern Africa?

The population of southern Africa is growing fast. The number of young people is high. In fact, nearly 50 percent of the people are below the age of 15. (In the United States, only 20 percent of the population is below the age of 15.) As they grow up and have children, the growth rate is likely to increase even more.

## What Problems Do Southern Africans Face?

Population growth is one of the biggest problems. In the past, most countries in southern Africa raised enough food to feed all their people. Then, as the population grew, many countries began to spend lots of money to import food. Countries then had little money left to provide some services to the people. To improve daily life, the government must find a way to slow population growth.

**Civil unrest** is another problem. It occurs when people rebel because they are unhappy with the conditons in their country. Many people are unhappy because a small, white population holds all the power. This is especially true in the Republic of South Africa. In 1948, the whites there introduced **apartheid,** or "apartness." This system set blacks and other nonwhite South Africans apart from whites. Apartheid laws defined whom blacks could marry and where they could travel, eat, or go to school. Whites did not allow nonwhites to vote. Whites decided where nonwhites could live. Apartheid no longer exists, but black political groups and whites still fight. Crime has increased. Law and order has broken down.

Another problem in southern Africa is that whites control much of the land. For example, whites number less than one percent in Zimbabwe. Yet whites there own 70 percent of the land. In the Republic of South Africa, blacks make up 75 percent of the population, but they live on less than 15 percent of the land. Blacks make up 95 percent of Namibia, yet whites own 44 percent of the land.

**Apartheid**

*A system that set blacks and other nonwhite South Africans apart from whites*

**Civil unrest**

*A situation in which people rebel because they are unhappy with the conditions in their country*

**Blacks in South Africa have more rights today, such as the right to vote. This photo shows South Africans waiting in line to vote.**

**Biography** | **NELSON MANDELA: 1918–**

Nelson Mandela, the son of a Tembu chief, was the first black president of South Africa. When apartheid began in 1948, Mandela practiced peaceful protest. Then, in 1960, the government killed some unarmed Africans at Sharpeville. When Mandela protested, the government arrested him. He spent the next 28 years in prison. During that time, he became a symbol for his people. In 1990, the white government freed Mandela. He began to work to end apartheid. This happened in 1992, followed by free elections in April 1994. Mandela became president and developed a new democratic constitution. He served as president until 1999. He received the Nobel Peace Prize, the highest honor in the world.

The black-controlled governments want to buy back the land from the whites. Then the governments would give the land to their black citizens. However, these governments have no money to buy the land. Also, the governments know that most blacks have no training in large-scale farming, so they might not manage the land well. If the governments took over the white-owned farms, many black workers would lose their jobs.

**Section 3 Review** On a separate sheet of paper, write the answers to these question.

1) Why is it incorrect to divide the population of southern Africa simply into a white group and a black group?

2) What are three reasons why people migrate?

3) What religions besides Christianity do the people of southern Africa practice?

4) What is the Afrikaans language and where is it spoken?

5) What was apartheid?

---

**What do YOU think?** Whites own much of the land in southern Africa. Would you change this situation? Explain your answer.

---

## What Is Southern Africa's Economy Like?

The Republic of South Africa and Zimbabwe have large manufacturing industries. In fact, manufacturing is the second largest employer in South Africa. However, most southern African people are subsistence farmers. Some families have animals to help with the work, but most people do their farm work by hand.

Crops are different in each country. The main crop in Botswana is sorghum, a type of grain. In Mozambique, it is cassava, which is like a sweet potato. In Lesotho and Zimbabwe, the main crop is corn.

Many people must work two jobs to make enough money to live. For example, in Botswana, 85 percent of the people live in rural areas and farm. However, farming accounts for less than 35 percent of their income. Their land is not fertile and sometimes there is little water. One or more family members, usually men, must work in the cities or in the mines to support the family.

Some people in southern Africa earn their living by farming on large plantations. Workers use machinery to plow, plant, and harvest. The plantation owners make money by exporting much of what the workers grow. The plantation crops are also different in each country. In Mozambique, farmers grow cotton on irrigated lands. The Cape region of the Republic of South Africa produces fruit and wine. Sugarcane accounts for about one-third of Swaziland's export dollars. In

Southern Africa has many manufacturing industries. However, some southern Africans still rely on subsistence farming. The San (Bushmen) of the Kalahari still live off the land. This photo shows a San man making a fire in front of his hut.

**Southern Africa has many important minerals. Mining is a major industry there.**

Zimbabwe, tobacco is an important export.

Botswana and Namibia are too dry for farming, so people raise cattle. Almost 60 percent of the land is used to raise cattle. In fact, twice as many cattle as people live in Botswana. Families own most of the cattle. The cows supply them with milk and meat. The people also hitch the cattle to a plow for work or use them to pull a cart for transportation.

### What Natural Resources Exist?

Mining is important in southern Africa. Minerals are the chief exports of Botswana, Zimbabwe, Zambia, and Namibia. The Republic of South Africa exports gold. Many people work in mines. Their working conditions are difficult and dangerous. However, the miners earn more than they could in their rural villages.

Southern Africa contains some of the world's richest deposits of minerals. Iron, copper, and gold have been mined there for hundreds of years. This mineral wealth created some of the great African kingdoms of the past.

Minerals are still important to the economy of today's southern African countries. In 1886, gold was discovered near Johannesburg in the Republic of South Africa. Gold is still mined there today. In fact, South Africa produces about one-third of all the gold in the world. Many other important minerals exist. South Africa ranks third in the world in the production of diamonds and uranium. It also has the largest coal deposits in Africa.

Botswana is another country rich in minerals. Most of its export money comes from the sale of diamonds, copper, and nickel. Zambia depends on its large copper deposits for about half of its income. Angola has large oil deposits and exports 60 percent of its oil to the United States. Angola also produces diamonds.

The landscape and wildlife of southern Africa are also important natural resources. In rural areas, the animals are an important source of meat. In addition, southern Africa's national parks attract tourists from all over the world.

## What Are Some Important Industries?

The Republic of South Africa is the richest and most industrial of all the countries in southern Africa. It produces many of the cars and buses that people in other parts of Africa use. South Africa also has other important manufacturing industries, such as iron, steel, textiles, clothing, engineering, metalworking, chemicals, food, tobacco, televisions, and computers.

*Geography In Your Life*
**CAREERS**

### Tourism

Would you like working with people in a fun industry? You might be interested in a job in tourism. In Africa and other parts of the world, people work in service jobs in tourism. They work in hotels, restaurants, transportation industries, or recreation industries. Anything related to travel is part of the tourism business.

Ecotourism has created a new type of tourist job. Ecotourism workers say "take nothing but photographs and leave behind nothing but footprints." These workers help people enjoy nature without destroying it. One of the first countries to ask workers to be part of ecotourism was Kenya in East Africa. It collected fees from tourists who were going into the national parks to look at wild animals. Kenya used this money to take care of the park and the animals. Kenya has shown that ecotourism brings more money to the native people than farming does. Workers in this new service industry want to keep parks, rain forests, wildlife, and beautiful land alive and well. Their job is to encourage people to respect nature.

**Ecotourists view animals and enjoy Africa's natural beauty. This photo shows ecotourists in Kenya, one of the first countries to practice ecotourism.**

**Ecotourism** is another important industry in southern Africa. In this type of tourism, people come to a country because of its wildlife and the beauty of its land. The money that tourists bring into southern Africa is becoming an important source of its income. Tourism creates jobs because tourists need a place to stay and to eat. New hotels and restaurants need to be built. Because of tourism, many people in southern Africa work in service jobs.

## What Environmental Problems Exist?

Southern Africa's biggest problem is that it has too many people and too little farmland. Few of the countries can produce enough food to feed all their people. Southern Africa has another big problem. How can it balance the needs of poor people with the needs of wildlife? The high population growth rate in many countries puts pressure on the environment. For example, thousands of poor villagers need wood for firewood, so they chop down woodlands. Already they have cut down many of the forest areas where wild animals live.

Tourism is both good and bad for southern Africa. Often, people from other countries own the hotels and restaurants there. Because of this, the money tourists bring into a country soon leaves the country. Also, some of these owners build hotels and other tourist spots without taking care of the environment. Large numbers of tourists threaten the animals the tourists come to see. The cars, buses, and vans the tourists use add to air pollution.

Mining can be harmful, too. Hills of yellow waste materials from gold mines surround Johannesburg. **Runoff** from the mines pollutes rivers. Runoff is material mixed with water that washes into rivers and lakes after it rains. The coal-burning power stations also produce air pollution.

**Section 4 Review** Choose the letter of the answer that correctly completes each sentence. Write your answers on a separate sheet of paper.

1) _____ is the main work of most people in southern Africa.

   a. Gold mining      c. Manufacturing

   b. Subsistence      d. Diamond mining
      farming

2) One of the plantation crops grown in southern Africa is _____.

   a. wheat      c. cork

   b. strawberries      d. cotton

3) _____ is the southern African country richest in gold.

   a. Namibia      c. Mozambique

   b. the Republic of      d. Botswana
      South Africa

4) _____ is the southern African country with the most industry.

   a. Zimbabwe      c. Namibia

   b. Zambia      d. the Republic of South Africa

5) Southern Africa's biggest problem is _____.

   a. too many people and too little farmland

   b. hotel owners from other countries

   c. too much wildlife

   d. tourism

---

**What do YOU think?** Is tourism helpful or harmful to the countries of southern Africa? Explain your answer.

# Diamonds:
# Southern Africa's Best Friend

Southern Africa is the largest producer of diamonds in the world. In 1867, a fifteen-year-old boy discovered the first diamond in this area. Erasmus Jacobs found it on his father's farm on the south branch of the Orange River in the Republic of South Africa.

The discovery set off a diamond rush. Many British fortune-seekers came to southern Africa. They bought land and made a claim to the diamonds. Soon, two of these English immigrants bought out all the claims. Cecil Rhodes brought together the holdings of the two men. In 1889, he founded the De Beers company. Today, his company sells almost all the diamonds in the world.

High temperatures and pressure deep within the earth form diamonds. The action of volcanoes brings these diamonds to the surface of the earth. Diamonds lie in volcanic pipes called kimberlite.

Skilled workers cut and polish the diamonds to bring out their color and brilliance. The best diamonds become gems used in diamond rings and other jewelry. The poorer diamonds are not as pretty, but they are still important. Industries use them to grind, smooth, or polish other materials.

**Many diamond mines exist in southern Africa.**

Seven countries control 80 percent of the world's diamond production. Four of these countries are in southern Africa. They are Botswana, Zaire, Angola, and the Republic of South Africa. However, today diamonds can be manufactured rather than mined. Manufactured diamonds are competing for sales with mined diamonds.

## Spotlight Story Wrap-Up

1) When and where were the first diamonds in southern Africa discovered?

2) Who was Cecil Rhodes and what was his connection to the diamond industry?

3) What is kimberlite?

4) What is the difference between gem diamonds and industry diamonds?

5) What four southern African countries produce the most diamonds in this area?

◆ Southern Africa, with 14 countries, covers the southern tip of Africa.

◆ Southern Africa has four main regions: the southern highlands, the veld, the western deserts, and the northern low-lying plain covered with forests.

◆ Much of southern Africa is a large plateau with escarpments, such as the Drakensberg Mountains.

◆ The most important deserts are the Kalahari and the Namib.

◆ The eastern part of southern Africa has many rivers. The two most important are the Zambezi and the Orange.

◆ The southernmost tip of southern Africa has a Mediterranean climate. The slopes of the Drakensberg Mountains have a maritime climate. Much of the inner part of southern Africa has a steppe climate. The eastern coastal area's climate is humid subtropical.

◆ Many ethnic groups live in southern Africa. People from the Netherlands, Germany, France, England, and India have migrated to southern Africa. Migrations still occur because people want safety from war and better jobs.

◆ The many ethnic groups of southern Africa speak different languages, such as Bantu. Some people speak Portuguese, German, or English. The most common language among whites is Afrikaans, which is a mixture of Dutch and native languages.

◆ Among the religions people in southern Africa practice are Christianity, Islam, Hinduism, and animism.

◆ Most southern Africans are subsistence farmers or they raise cattle. To support their families, many men work in cities or mines. Some people work on plantations where they raise cotton, fruit, sugarcane, and tobacco for export.

◆ Southern Africa is rich in minerals, such as iron, copper, diamonds, and gold. The Republic of South Africa is the richest and most industrial of the countries of southern Africa.

◆ Ecotourism is becoming an important source of money as tourists come to southern Africa to see the wildlife.

◆ Southern Africa's main environmental problem is that it has too many people and too little farmland. It must also balance the needs of the poor with the needs of wildlife.

◆ Southern Africa faces a growing population, civil unrest, and white control of the land.

## Comprehension: Identifying Facts

On a separate sheet of paper, use the words from the Word Bank to complete each sentence.

apartheid

Good Hope

Kalahari

prevailing

Zambezi

1) The Cape of _____ is located at the southern tip of Africa.

2) The largest desert in southern Africa is the _____.

3) The longest river of southern Africa is the _____ River.

4) _____ winds refer to winds that usually blow from the same direction.

5) _____ was the policy put in place in the Republic of South Africa to keep blacks apart from whites.

## Comprehension: Multiple Choice

On a separate sheet of paper, write the letter of the answer that correctly completes each sentence.

1) The economic center of the Republic of South Africa is _____.

   a. Durban          c. Harare

   b. Johannesburg    d. Gaborone

2) The _____ is the grassy plain of central South Africa.

   a. steppe          c. pampas

   b. veld            d. prairie

3) _____ are the white descendents of the original European settlers of the Republic of South Africa.

   a. Afrikaners      c. Mesoafricans

   b. Bushmen         d. Sons of Europe

4) In the dry areas of Botswana and Namibia where conditions for farming are poor, many people _____.

   a. fish            c. conduct tours

   b. raise cattle    d. join the army

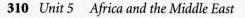

**5)** The richest and most industrialized country of southern Africa is _____.

    a. Botswana          c. Mozambique

    b. Zimbabwe        d. the Republic of South Africa

## Comprehension: Understanding Main Ideas

On a separate sheet of paper, write the answer to each question. Use complete sentences.

**1)** Where is southern Africa located?

**2)** What are southern Africa's main kinds of physical features?

**3)** What are two environmental problems that the countries of southern Africa face?

## Critical Thinking: Write Your Opinion

On a separate sheet of paper, write your opinion to each question. Use complete sentences.

**1)** Why do you think a small white minority in the Republic of South Africa adopted a policy of apartheid?

**2)** Should the United States and other rich countries do more to help the struggling countries of southern Africa? Explain your answer.

## Applying the Five Themes of Geography

*Movement*

How does the history of southern Africa reflect the theme of movement?

Test-Taking Tip    After you have completed a test, reread each question and answer. Ask yourself, "Have I answered the question that was asked? Have I answered all parts of the question?"

# Central and East Africa

Central and East Africa is a place of big differences. Its languages and cultures are diverse. Some countries, like the Republic of São Tomé and Príncipe, are little. It is only a little bigger than New York City! Other countries, like Sudan, are big. It is the largest country on the continent of Africa. Rain forests cover some parts of Central Africa. Much of this area receives over 400 inches of rain a year! Other parts are dry. The photo on this page shows the Congo, the most important river in Central Africa.

## Goals for Learning

▶ To describe where Central and East Africa is located

▶ To identify its important physical features and climate

▶ To describe its cultural diversity

▶ To identify some of the problems the people of Central and East Africa face

▶ To describe the economy and environmental challenges of Central and East Africa

 *Geo-Stats*

**Key Nations of Central and East Africa**

 **Nation:** Ethiopia
**Population:** 59,680,000
**Area** (in square miles): 424,934
**Major Cities:** Addis Ababa (capital), Diredawa, Harar, Nazret, Gondar

 **Nation:** Sudan
**Population:** 28,883,000
**Area** (in square miles): 963,600
**Major Cities:** Khartoum (capital), Nyala, Port Sudan, Kassala

 **Nation:** Kenya
**Population:** 28,809,000
**Area** (in square miles): 228,861
**Major Cities:** Nairobi (capital), Mombasa, Kisumu, Nakuru

 **Nation:** Tanzania
**Population:** 31,271,000
**Area** (in square miles): 364,900
**Major Cities:** Dar es Salaam (capital), Mwanza, Tabora, Mbeya, Tanga

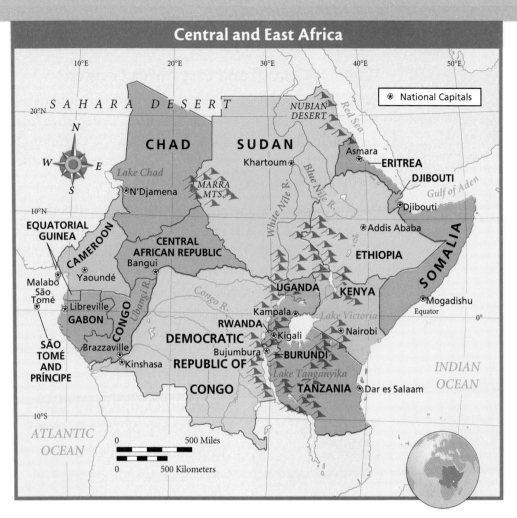

## Central and East Africa

**Central and East Africa**

10°E    20°E    30°E    40°E    50°E

⊛ National Capitals

S A H A R A   D E S E R T

20°N

NUBIAN DESERT

Red Sea

CHAD     SUDAN

Lake Chad

Khartoum ⊛

Asmara

ERITREA

⊛N'Djamena

MARRA MTS.

DJIBOUTI

Gulf of Aden

10°N

White Nile R.

Blue Nile R.

⊛Djibouti

EQUATORIAL GUINEA

CAMEROON

CENTRAL AFRICAN REPUBLIC

Bangui

⊛Addis Ababa

ETHIOPIA

SOMALIA

Malabo
São Tomé

⊛Yaoundé

Ubangi R.

Congo R.

UGANDA    KENYA

⊛Libreville

GABON

CONGO

Kampala ⊛

Lake Victoria

⊛Mogadishu

Equator

0°

⊛Nairobi

SÃO TOMÉ AND PRÍNCIPE

⊛Brazzaville

DEMOCRATIC REPUBLIC OF

RWANDA

⊛Kigali

Bujumbura ⊛

BURUNDI

⊛Kinshasa

Lake Tanganyika

INDIAN OCEAN

10°S

CONGO

TANZANIA ⊛Dar es Salaam

ATLANTIC OCEAN

0     500 Miles

0     500 Kilometers

*Map Skills*

Central and East Africa is the largest single region of Africa. It also has the most mountains in Africa. This region also has some of the largest lakes in the world, such as Lake Victoria.

Study the map and answer the following questions:

**1)** What African nations on this map border the Red Sea?

**2)** Which ocean touches Africa to the east?

**3)** Where is the Nubian desert?

**4)** What is the capital of Somalia? Sudan? Kenya?

**5)** In which part of this region do you think most of the people live?

## Where Is Central and East Africa Located?

Horn of Africa
*The four countries of Djibouti, Eritrea, Ethiopia, and Somalia, which stick out like a rhinoceros horn on the eastern coast of Africa*

Central and East Africa is located in a wide belt between about 20° north and 10° south latitude. It stretches from the Indian Ocean on the east to the Atlantic Ocean on the west. The Sahara desert and the Sahel are located to the north. Southern Africa is to the south.

Central Africa is made up of eight countries: Chad, Cameroon, Gabon, Congo, the Democratic Republic of Congo, Equatorial Guinea, the Central African Republic, and the island nation of São Tomé and Príncipe. East Africa has ten countries: Eritrea, Ethiopia, Somalia, Sudan, Djibouti, Kenya, Uganda, Rwanda, Burundi, and Tanzania. Djibouti, Eritrea, Ethiopia, and Somalia together are shaped like the horn of a rhinoceros. People call this area the **Horn of Africa** because of its shape.

**Nairobi, Kenya, has over two million people. The city looks much like any modern city.**

## How Did Geography Shape the History of This Region?

Geography has played a big role in the history of Central and East Africa. People have lived there for millions of years. In its highland areas, the climate is not too hot, and the land is good for farming. Because of this, Europeans have settled there. They took control of much of the land that the Kikuyu people owned. To encourage the Europeans to settle, the British government built a railroad from the coast in Kenya. The railroad workers had to climb mountains, overcome the heat, build many bridges, and deal with the tsetse fly. Nairobi, the largest city in this region, grew along the rail line.

**Strategic**
*Important for military reasons*

Geography has also kept people out of Central and East Africa. The Serengeti Plain, a huge open grassland, is located in Tanzania. Much wildlife lives on this plain, but so does the tsetse fly. In the past, this fly had kept most people out of the Serengeti. Because of the tsetse, life there has stayed pretty much as it had been for thousands of years. Today, however, people have found new ways to control the tsetse fly. Now many tourists visit the Serengeti National Park. It is one of the world's greatest parks.

Geography also kept people from settling in the Congo River Basin in Central Africa. Thick tropical rain forests cover it. They made travel hard, so most people chose to live in the nearby grasslands. Many believed that evil spirits lived in the forests, so they did not want to go there.

East Africa has a **strategic** location. That is, its location is important for military reasons. The countries on the Horn of Africa guard the way into the Red Sea. Oil-producing countries in the Middle East sell much of the world's oil. They ship it through the Gulf of Aden and the Red Sea. For this reason, the United States, which buys some of the oil, wants to keep this area free of conflict.

**Section 1 Review** On a separate sheet of paper, write *True* if the statement is true or *False* if the statement is not true. Make each false statement true by changing the underlined word.

1) Central and East Africa stretch from the Indian Ocean to the <u>Pacific</u> Ocean.
2) The tsetse fly lives on the <u>Serengeti</u> Plain.
3) Europeans settled in the <u>lowland</u> areas of Central and East Africa.
4) <u>Nairobi,</u> the largest city of Central and East Africa, grew along the railroad lines that the British built.
5) East Africa is important to the United States because it guards the sea through which countries ship <u>oil.</u>

**What do YOU think?**

Ethiopia is a landlocked country. Do you think this may cause wars with neighboring countries in the future? Explain your answer.

## What Are the Main Physical Features?

Geological fault
*A break in the
earth's crust*

Great Rift Valley
*A long valley in
Africa that is a
geological fault*

The **Great Rift Valley** is the main physical feature of this region. The valley, which is over 4,000 miles long, is a large **geological fault.** A fault is a break in the earth's crust, or outer layer. Solid rock on one side of the fault may move up, down, or sideways from the rock on the other side. Sometimes, the movement is slow. No one notices it. At other times, the movement is quick and causes earthquakes.

Along this fault line stand many beautiful mountains, valleys, and lakes. The Great Rift Valley, which includes the Red Sea, cuts through the highlands of Ethiopia. Around Lake Victoria, the rift splits into two parts. On the western side are many long, thin lakes. The largest are Lake Tanganyika and Lake Malawi. The other side of the Great Rift Valley is located on the eastern side of Lake Victoria.

Central Africa is part of the large plateau that covers most of Africa. Many countries are high and flat. Several highland areas rise in this area, especially in East Africa. The highlands on both sides of the Great Rift Valley contain the best farmland in Kenya.

Africa's highest mountain peaks are in East Africa. Kilimanjaro, Africa's highest mountain, stands 19,340 feet tall. It rises from the plains on the border of Kenya and Tanzania. Even though Kilimanjaro is near the equator, snow covers its peak. People can see it from hundreds of miles away.

Africa's highest mountain, pictured here in the background, is Mt. Kilimanjaro.

## Major Lakes of the World

| Lake | Location | Area in Square Miles |
|------|----------|----------------------|
| Caspian Sea | Azerbaijan, Russia, Kazakhstan, Turkmenistan, Iran | 143,239 |
| Superior | United States, Canada | 31,688 |
| Victoria | Tanzania, Kenya, Uganda | 26,820 |
| Aral Sea | Kazakhstan, Uzbekistan | 24,903 |
| Huron | United States, Canada | 22,991 |
| Michigan | United States | 22,400 |
| Tanganyika | Tanzania, Democratic Republic of Congo, Zambia, Burundi | 12,695 |
| Baykal | Russia | 12,162 |
| Great Bear | Canada | 12,091 |
| Malawi | Malawi, Tanzania, Mozambique | 11,146 |

### CHART STUDY

This chart lists information about the ten largest lakes in the world. Three of them, Victoria, Tanganyika, and Malawi, are in Africa. What is the largest lake in the world? How large is Lake Victoria? In which countries is Lake Tanganyika located?

**Evaporate**
*The changing of liquid water into water vapor*

Mount Kenya in Kenya and Mount Elgon in western Uganda are two other high mountains. Tropical forests cover the Ruwenzori Mountains of Uganda. These forests contain some plants and animals that live nowhere else in the world.

## What Are the Main Bodies of Water?

Lake Victoria is Africa's largest lake. It borders Tanzania, Kenya, and Uganda. Lake Tanganyika is located in the Great Rift Valley. It separates Tanzania from the Democratic Republic of Congo and is the world's longest freshwater lake.

Central and East Africa have many other lakes. They are located in areas with high average temperatures. This causes water to **evaporate.** That is, the water turns into water vapor. When the lake water evaporates, it leaves behind salt. The water is then too salty for most animals. However, the flamingo likes salty lakes. Millions of these pink birds with long necks and legs live in Central and East Africa. They especially like Lake Nakuru in Kenya.

Many of Africa's rivers begin in the highlands of East Africa. The Blue Nile (called the Abbai in Ethiopia) begins in the Ethiopian highlands, flows through Lake Tana, and then follows a curving route westward. It joins the White Nile at Khartoum, Sudan. The Blue and White Nile combine to form the Nile River. It is the longest river in the world. The Nile flows northward and empties into the Mediterranean Sea.

Many African rivers are not navigable. However, the Congo River (also called the Zaire) is navigable for over 1,000 miles. It is the most important river of Central Africa. It drains the huge Congo Basin and then flows into the Atlantic Ocean. The Congo is an important highway to the middle of Africa. It is also an important source of food for people who live near it. It has several large tributaries. Among them are the Ubangi and the Kasai Rivers.

## What Is the Climate Like?

Much of Central Africa has either a tropical rain forest or a tropical savanna climate. Temperatures are high throughout the year because much of the area is near the equator. However, these two climates differ in rainfall. In the tropical rain forest climate, rain falls throughout the year. However, the tropical savanna climate has a dry season and a rainy one. The northern edges of Central Africa are quite dry. Much of Chad and northern Cameroon have desert or steppe climates.

The climate of East Africa is different in different places. The coastal strip and the low valley areas are warm all year. Sudan has some of the driest deserts in Africa. Djibouti, Somalia, and Eritrea are also mostly desert. Their northernmost parts have temperatures close to 100° F for much of the year. Ethiopia's lowlands are hot and dry. The Ethiopian highlands enjoy cooler and wetter weather than the savanna areas that surround them.

Life in East Africa depends on the rains. The amount that falls can mean life or death. Long dry periods, or droughts, bring death. Lack of water means crops and animals die, causing a lack of food. During the East African droughts in the 1980s and early 1990s, many people and animals died.

**Volcano Expert**

Volcanologists study volcanoes. They know that these explosive mountains helped to create Earth's atmosphere and to balance the chemicals in Earth's crust. However, when volcanoes erupt, or blow up, they kill people and destroy property. For example, a volcano killed 1,700 people in Cameroon in 1986. Volcanologists study volcanoes to predict when they will erupt. In that way, people can prepare for the eruption.

Volcanologists use machines called seismographs to measure and record earthquake tremors. These trembling movements happen several months before a volcano erupts. The tremors help the scientists predict volcanic eruptions. Experts also use tiltmeters and laser beams to predict eruptions. These tools detect a change in the angle of a volcano.

Some volcanologists work in stations on the rim of active volcanoes, such as Kilauea in Hawaii. From these stations they observe what is taking place in the volcanoes. They study them to help people and to learn about the formation of Earth.

Population
distribution
*Where people live*

## How Does Geography Affect the People?

The physical environment affects how people live in Central and East Africa. First, it affects **population distribution,** or where people live. Most people live in areas with mild climates. Fewer people live in areas with very hot climates or in areas with forests and mountains. Second, the physical environment makes building roads and railroads hard, so travel is difficult. Third, the physical environment affects how people live and work. Many people farm. They depend on nature and the land. People in these African countries cannot afford many things, so they have little control over their lives. They also cannot control disease among people and cattle.

**What do
YOU
think?**

Should humans try to control their physical environment by changing it or should they just learn to live with it? Explain your answer.

**Section 2 Review** On a separate sheet of paper, write answers to the following questions.

1) What is the main physical feature of this region?

2) What makes Mount Kilimanjaro different from many other mountains in Africa?

3) What is Africa's largest lake?

4) What is the climate of Central Africa like?

5) What are three ways the physical environment of Central and East Africa affects the people?

Bantu
*An African cultural group that mostly farms for a living*

Nilotic
*An African cultural group that mostly herds animals for a living*

## What Cultures Exist in Central and East Africa?

Central and East Africa is home to many different ethnic groups. Kenya alone has over 70 different groups. Each group has its own language. Each lives its own way. The countries along the eastern coast have a culture that is different from the countries in the middle of Africa. This coastal belt has had trade ties with Arabs, Asians, and the Portuguese. As time passed, many Europeans, Arabs, and people from India settled in East Africa. People from the British Isles settled in the fertile farmland of Kenya.

Africa can be divided into two groups of people: the **Bantu** and the **Nilotic** people. The Bantu mostly farm. In the beginning, many of them lived in western Africa. Among the Bantu people are the Kikuyu in Kenya, the Sukumu in Tanzania, and the Ganda in Uganda.

The Nilotic people herd animals. They include the Lango in Uganda and the Luo in Kenya. One of the largest groups of Nilotic people is the Masai. They live in southern Kenya and northern Tanzania. Another large group is the Somali. They live in Somalia, Ethiopia, Kenya, and Djibouti. The Hutu and the Tutsi are the two major ethnic groups in Rwanda and Burundi. They have been at war for many years.

## What Languages Do the People Speak?

There are almost as many languages in this region as there are ethnic groups. Visitors to the big cities and capitals of Central and East Africa may hear European languages like French and English. Many people speak several languages.

The people in the Horn of Africa speak Cushite languages. Ethiopia has two large ethnic groups that make up about 45 percent of the population. Thousands of years ago, the two groups spoke Ge'ez. Over time, three different languages developed out of Ge'ez. Now the people use Ge'ez only in religious services.

Mosque
*An Islamic house of worship*

Swahili
*An African language that combines African languages with Arabic, Portuguese, Malay, and Persian words and that first developed for the purpose of trade*

Most people in Central Africa and the southern part of East Africa speak one of the Niger-Congo languages. However, communication remains a big problem. Tanzania alone has over 100 different languages! Most people speak **Swahili.** This language began to make trading with other countries easier. It contains words from African languages, Arabic, Portuguese, Malay, and Persian. Swahili is the official language of Kenya and Tanzania.

## What Religions Do the People Practice?

Each African ethnic group has its own native religion. However, the main religion in much of Africa is Islam. Many years ago, Muslim traders crossed the Indian Ocean. They brought Islam to East Africa. This religion is strongest in Somalia, Tanzania (especially its island of Zanzibar), parts of Ethiopia, and the northern parts of Central Africa. The large cities of these countries have **mosques,** or Islamic houses of worship.

People from India brought Hinduism to Africa, so some cities have Hindu temples. Over two thousand years ago, a small group of Jews settled in Ethiopia. They practiced their religion for centuries without anyone harming them. However because of recent wars, many of these "Falashas" or "Black Jews" had to resettle in Israel, which was created in 1948.

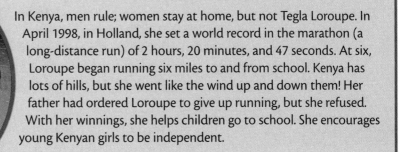

**Biography**   **TEGLA LOROUPE: 1973–**

In Kenya, men rule; women stay at home, but not Tegla Loroupe. In April 1998, in Holland, she set a world record in the marathon (a long-distance run) of 2 hours, 20 minutes, and 47 seconds. At six, Loroupe began running six miles to and from school. Kenya has lots of hills, but she went like the wind up and down them! Her father had ordered Loroupe to give up running, but she refused. With her winnings, she helps children go to school. She encourages young Kenyan girls to be independent.

**Droughts and the growing population have led to starvation in East Africa.**

People have practiced Christianity in East Africa for thousands of years. Some Africans combine their native religions with Christianity. Countries with a large European population usually have the most Christians.

## What Are the Population Trends?

Parts of Central Africa and all of East Africa have one of the fastest growing populations in the world. Uganda's population may grow by 216 percent by 2050! Ethiopia, the Congo, and Ghana may double their population in about 25 years. In all of these countries, nearly half of the people are under age 18. They need food, homes, education, and jobs. However, many Central and East African countries have trouble providing these.

## What Problems Do the People Face?

The first problem is ethnic war. As in West Africa, Europeans drew the borders of Central and East African countries during the colonial period. These Europeans sometimes divided an ethnic group among several countries. They also put people who had been enemies into the same country. Because of this, people often feel more loyal to their ethnic group than to the nation they live in. This has led to war. In these wars, hundreds of thousands of people have become refugees.

The second problem is health care. People in Central and East Africa suffer from diseases like malaria, tuberculosis, cholera, and meningitis. The tsetse fly causes sleeping sickness, which can lead to death. East Africa has one of the highest rates of HIV infection. HIV usually leads to AIDS. With money, the people of Central and East Africa could cure all these diseases, except for AIDS. However, most countries in this area cannot afford to do this. Countries in

Starvation
*Suffering or dying from lack of food*

other parts of the world have cut back on the aid they are sending. Because of all this, the life expectancy of millions of Africans is dropping.

A third problem is **starvation,** or suffering and dying from lack of food. In the 1980s the rains failed in East Africa. Drought brought death to hundreds of thousands of people. For the past few years, little rain has fallen in Ethiopia, Eritrea, Sudan, Djibouti, Kenya, and Uganda. Millions of people in these countries face starvation.

A fourth problem is urbanization. Because of drought, many people have moved to the cities. Shantytowns have developed. The rainy season floods these shantytowns. People then lose their homes and the few things they own. Often, they become sick because of the diseases the flooding waters bring with them.

**Section 3 Review** Choose the letter of the answer that correctly completes each sentence. Write your answers on a separate sheet of paper.

1) _____ greatly influenced the culture of East Africa.
   a. Pirates        c. Traders
   b. Sailors        d. Soldiers

2) The Bantu people are mostly _____.
   a. fishermen     c. herders
   b. farmers       d. teachers

3) Most people in Tanzania speak _____.
   a. Swahili       c. Ge'ez
   b. French        d. Arabic

4) Parts of Central Africa and all of East Africa have _____.
   a. few ethnic groups   c. only one religion
   b. few languages      d. a growing population

5) _____ drew the borders for many African countries.
   a. Arabs         c. Asians
   b. North Americans   d. Europeans

**What do YOU think?**

Should the United States and the United Nations send soldiers to Africa to stop the killing of innocent people in the ethnic wars there? Explain your answer.

Dictator
*A person who makes all the laws for a country and rules by force*

Horticulture
*The growing of flowers, fruits, and vegetables for sale*

Safari
*An African hunting trip*

## What Is the Economy Like?

Farming is the main activity in East Africa. More than 80 percent of the population farms. Many people are subsistence farmers. They grow chilies, tomatoes, beans, corn, millet, sorghum, cassava, and matoke, a banana-like fruit.

Some landowners produce cash crops. Kenya and Uganda produce coffee and tea. Zanzibar is the world's biggest producer of cloves, a spice used in cooking. Other cash crops include cashew nuts and tobacco. Large plantations in Tanzania and Kenya grow sugar, wheat, and rice. The Central African Republic grows cotton. The Congo produces sugarcane.

Fishing is important to the people living around Lake Victoria and other freshwater lakes. The most common fish is the tilapia and the small omena. In the 1950s, the British introduced a large fish called the Nile perch. Today, many of these are exported to Europe.

A new industry is **horticulture.** This is the growing of flowers, fruits, and vegetables for sale. Products include roses, lilies, mangoes, melons, green beans, and avocados. Africans export over 80 percent of these products to European countries.

Tourism provides many service jobs and is important to the economy. The tourist industry is most developed in Kenya. Tourists come there because of its climate, natural beauty, and parks. Many tourists go on **safaris** in these parks. In the past, safaris were hunting trips with guns. Today, tourists generally photograph animals. Tanzania also has huge wildlife parks. In fact, the Selous Game Reserve is larger than the whole country of Switzerland!

Several Central and East African countries have struggling economies. **Dictators** have ruled these countries for many years and have left them poor. They make all the laws for a country and rule by force. Often, their laws make money for only a small group of people who help the dictators keep their power. These dictators often take land from the poor and give it to the rich.

Many farmers cannot get their goods to market because of lack of roads. For example, the Democratic Republic of the Congo is the largest country in Central Africa. Yet it has only about 12,000 miles of paved roads!

## What Natural Resources Are Important to the Economy?

When compared to southern and West Africa, Central and East Africa have few mineral resources. The Atlantic coast of Cameroon, Gabon, and the Congo has oil. Gabon also has diamonds, gold, iron, and manganese. The Democratic Republic of the Congo is rich in mineral resources, but the resources have not been managed well. The country's economy is weak.

Congo produces over 60 percent of the world's cobalt. It also has large deposits of copper, zinc, tin, gold, silver, iron, coal, and industrial diamonds. Kenya has some gold; Tanzania has tin and gold; Uganda's most important mineral is copper. The Central African Republic, Somalia, and Ethiopia have uranium.

The greatest natural resources in Central and East Africa are its wildlife and its forests. The tropical rain forests of Central Africa include hardwood trees that are important exports. However, the countries are cutting down much of the forests for cattle ranching and farming. Many rural areas have no electricity, so people cut down trees for firewood. These countries do little replanting.

Tourists come to this area to see the wildlife: lions, elephants, giraffes, wildebeest, zebras, gazelles, water buffaloes, hippopotami, topi, warthogs, leopards, and hyenas. These animals live on the grassy savannas of the Serengeti. Birds number in the millions!

## What Are Some Major Industries?

There is not much industry in Central and East Africa. Mombasa in Kenya refines some oil. Both Uganda and Kenya have some metal-**processing** and car plants. Processing prepares raw materials for sale. Mining and the processing of raw materials are important in the Congo. One growing industry is the processing of products such as coffee, tea, vegetables, and fruit. This is important because exporting processed goods brings in more money than exporting raw materials.

## Who Are Central and East Africa's Trade Partners?

Central and East Africa have close ties with the countries that used to rule them. Because of that, their chief trading partners are often European countries, such as Great Britain, France, Germany, and Spain. East Africa also does a lot of business with Japan and India.

## What Environmental Challenges Exist?

Many native people say that their government puts the needs of animals above the needs of people. The countries value the animals because many tourists come to see them in national parks. However, many poor Africans live around these parks. They say that wild animals damage their crops. Also, many Africans depend on wild animals for food.

**Poaching,** illegal hunting in the parks, is common. Loggers are destroying forests in which some **endangered** animals, like the Ugandan mountain gorillas, live. Endangered animals are ones that may become extinct. If they become extinct, tourists may no longer come to Central and East Africa.

Every day, thousands of acres of rain forest are cut down for farming, ranching, logging, and mining. Many farmers think that rain forests grow on fertile land. However, that is not true. They are able to farm on the rain-forest land for only a few years. Then they must move away and clear more land. This eats up the forests. Better planning and increased education would likely solve these problems.

**Herders in Central and East Africa are called Nilotic people. Farming and raising animals are important to this region's economy.**

**Section 4 Review** On a separate sheet of paper, write the word from the Word Bank that completes each sentence.

<table>
<tr><td>WORD BANK</td></tr>
<tr><td>cash crops</td></tr>
<tr><td>European</td></tr>
<tr><td>horticulture</td></tr>
<tr><td>farming</td></tr>
<tr><td>trees</td></tr>
</table>

1) The main economic activity in East Africa is

_____.

2) Coffee, tea, cloves, cashew nuts, sugarcane, and tobacco are _____ grown in Central and East Africa.

3) _____ is the growing of flowers, fruits, and vegetables for sale.

4) Wood from hardwood _____ is an important export of Central Africa.

5) The chief trading partners of Central and East African countries are often _____ countries.

**What do YOU think?** What can the countries of the world do to protect the endangered rain forests and wildlife of Africa and at the same time help the people who live nearby?

# Africa:
# The First Home of Humans?

Many scientists believe that present-day humans came from Africa. The earliest known members of the human family may have appeared in Africa about four million years ago. The human family probably had many branches. Only one, *Homo sapiens,* still exists today. Scientists believe that *Homo sapiens* evolved, or changed over time, at least 100,000 years ago. A number of years ago, an archaeologist found a jawbone near Lake Turkana in northern Kenya. This jawbone belonged to a distant relative of humans. It may be over four million years old!

Scientists use biological studies to show the links between people all over the world. Their studies suggest that human life began in East Africa. From there, people migrated to the Middle East and then to Europe. Members of the human family also migrated to East Asia from Africa.

Archaeologists are scientists who find and study things people left behind. They have not yet found a complete skeleton of an ancient human. However, they have found many human fragments, or pieces, such as the jawbone. They have also found tools, such as hand axes and spear points, that our human ancestors made and used.

Scientists believe that language has made modern humans different from those who lived long ago. The development of language allowed humans to work together to obtain food and water. With language, they could exchange and share ideas. Most importantly, they could pass down what they had learned from one generation to the next.

**Archaeologists find and study things people have left behind in the past. They study these objects to learn more about people who lived long ago.**

## Spotlight Story Wrap-Up

1) When did the earliest members of the human family first appear?

2) What branch of the human family has lived on to the present?

3) Why do scientists think that humans around the world are related?

4) What have archaeologists found that makes them think humans lived in Africa?

5) Why was the development of language important?

◆ Eighteen countries make up Central and East Africa. People live in the highland areas where farming is good. The Serengeti Plain in Tanzania has few people because of the tsetse fly.

◆ The most important physical feature of Central and East Africa is the Great Rift Valley.

◆ Mount Kilimanjaro is the highest peak in Africa. Lake Victoria is Africa's largest lake.

◆ Many of Africa's rivers begin in the highlands of East Africa. The Nile is the longest river in the world. The Congo, which is navigable, is Central Africa's most important river.

◆ Much of Central Africa has either a tropical rain forest or a tropic savanna climate. Life in East Africa depends on rains. Droughts killed many people there in the 1980s and 1990s.

◆ Many ethnic groups live in Central and East Africa. Most are members of the Bantu and the Nilotic. Arabs, Europeans, and Indians have also settled there.

◆ These ethnic groups speak different languages, such as Swahili, which began as a language of trade.

◆ Among the religions people in Central and East Africa practice are Islam, Hinduism, Judaism, Christianity, and native religions.

◆ Most Central and East Africans are subsistence farmers. Some farmers produce the cash crops of coffee, tea, cloves, cashew nuts, tobacco, sugar, wheat, rice, and cotton for export. Fishing, horticulture, and tourism are all important to the economy.

◆ Central and East Africa have fewer minerals than southern and West Africa. Wildlife and tropical rain forests are important natural resources. Wildlife attracts tourists. Tropical forests have hardwood for exporting. The area has little industry; however, the processing of products is growing.

◆ Central and East Africa's main problem is balancing the needs of people with the needs of wildlife. The region faces a fast growing population, ethnic wars, health problems like AIDS, drought, starvation, and urbanization that has led to shantytowns.

## Comprehension: Identifying Facts

On a separate sheet of paper, use the words from the Word Bank to complete each sentence.

**WORD BANK**

geological fault

strategic

Swahili

starvation

tsetse fly

1) The _____ is one of the reasons why many people never settled on the Serengeti Plain.

2) East Africa occupies a _____ location because it guards the sea through which ships transport much of the world's oil.

3) A _____ is a break in the earth's crust along which solid rock may move up, down, or sideways.

4) Many people in Kenya and Tanzania speak _____, which began as a trade language.

5) Because of drought, many people in East Africa have died of _____.

## Comprehension: Multiple Choice

On a separate sheet of paper, write the letter of the answer that correctly completes each sentence.

1) The East African countries of Eritrea, Djibouti, Ethiopia, and Somalia make up the _____.
   a. poorest countries    c. Horn of Africa
   b. Sahel                d. largest rain forest

2) Most African people are members of the Bantu and _____ people.
   a. Nilotic              c. Indian
   b. Arab                 d. Asian

3) The main physical feature of East Africa is the _____.
   a. Serengeti Plain      c. Ruwenzori Mountains
   b. Great Rift Valley    d. the Red Sea

4) The biggest difference in the climates of Central Africa is the _____.
   a. amount of rain       c. temperature range
   b. prevailing winds     d. length of winter

**5)** The main religion in much of Africa is _____.

   a. Christianity       c. Judaism

   b. Hinduism        d. Islam

## Comprehension: Understanding Main Ideas

On a separate sheet of paper, write the answer to each question. Use complete sentences.

**1)** What are the most important physical features of Central and East Africa?

**2)** What cultures exist in this region?

**3)** What are the chief natural resources of Central and East Africa?

## Critical Thinking: Write Your Opinion

On a separate sheet of paper, write your opinion to each question. Use complete sentences.

**1)** Some people describe the countries of Central and East Africa as "failing nations." Do you agree with this? Explain your answer.

**2)** What do you consider to be the biggest problem for Central and East Africa and how would you solve it?

## Applying the Five Themes of Geography

### *Movement*

How do the many religions practiced in this region reflect the theme of movement and migration?

**Test-Taking Tip** When you read over your written answer, imagine that you are someone reading the answer for the first time. Ask yourself if the ideas and information make sense. Revise and rewrite to make the answer as clear as you can.

# North Africa and the Middle East

This region is the birthplace of three great religions. For thousands of years, people and ideas from Europe, Africa, and Asia came together here. The region is also very dry. The photo on this page shows nomads in the Sahara Desert, the main physical feature of North Africa. Today, North Africa and the Middle East supply the world with much of its oil.

## Goals for Learning

▶ To describe where North Africa and the Middle East are located

▶ To identify their most important physical features and climate

▶ To identify the cultures of North Africa and the Middle East

▶ To explain where and how most North African and Middle Eastern people live

▶ To describe their economy and the environmental challenges they face

 *Geo-Stats*

### Key Nations of North Africa and the Middle East

**Nation:** Algeria
**Population:** 30,774,000
**Area** (in square miles): 919,595
**Capital:** Algiers

**Nation:** Egypt
**Population:** 66,924,000
**Area** (in square miles): 386,662
**Capital:** Cairo

**Nation:** Iran
**Population:** 66,208,000
**Area** (in square miles): 636,296
**Capital:** Tehran

**Nation:** Iraq
**Population:** 22,450,000
**Area** (in square miles): 169,235
**Capital:** Baghdad

**Nation:** Israel
**Population:** 6,135,000
**Area** (in square miles): 8,019
**Capital:** Jerusalem

**Nation:** Saudi Arabia
**Population:** 20,899,000
**Area** (in square miles): 830,000
**Capital:** Riyadh

# North Africa and the Middle East

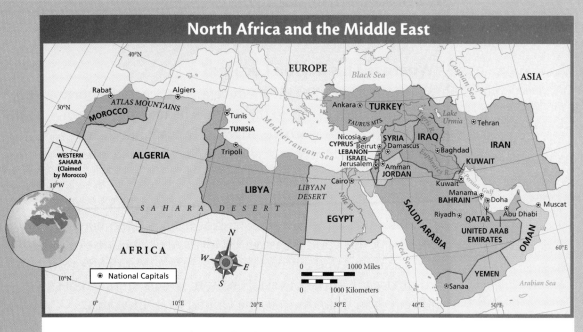

The map shows national capitals across North Africa and the Middle East, including labels such as EUROPE, ASIA, AFRICA, Black Sea, Caspian Sea, Mediterranean Sea, Red Sea, Arabian Sea, Persian Gulf, Sahara Desert, Libyan Desert, Atlas Mountains, Taurus Mts., and countries Morocco, Western Sahara (Claimed by Morocco), Algeria, Tunisia, Libya, Egypt, Turkey, Cyprus, Syria, Lebanon, Israel, Jordan, Iraq, Iran, Kuwait, Saudi Arabia, Bahrain, Qatar, United Arab Emirates, Oman, Yemen with capitals Rabat, Algiers, Tunis, Tripoli, Ankara, Nicosia, Beirut, Damascus, Jerusalem, Amman, Cairo, Baghdad, Tehran, Kuwait, Manama, Doha, Abu Dhabi, Muscat, Riyadh, Sanaa.

**Map Skills**

The North African nations are located in the northern part of Africa. The Middle East is part of Asia. The Middle Eastern nations begin at the eastern shore of the Mediterranean Sea and the Red Sea. They stretch eastward as far as the nation of Iran.

Study the map and answer the following questions:

**1)** What are the countries of North Africa?

**2)** What seas do the nations of North Africa touch?

**3)** What is the largest nation in the Middle East?

**4)** Which gulf separates Saudi Arabia from Iran?

**5)** Why do you think this area is a region, even though it contains nations from two continents?

**Fertile Crescent**
*The land between the Tigris and Euphrates Rivers in Iraq and the Jordan River in Israel and Jordan*

**Levant**
*The coastal farming region of Syria, Lebanon, and Israel*

**Maghreb nations**
*Morocco, Tunisia, and Algeria, which are farthest west in North Africa*

## Where Is This Region Located?

North Africa borders the Mediterranean Sea to the north and the Sahara Desert to the south. The five countries of North Africa are Morocco, Algeria, Tunisia, Libya, and Egypt. The first three are called the **Maghreb nations.** In Arabic, this means "land farthest west."

The Red Sea divides North Africa from the Middle East. The Middle East is part of Asia. However, geographers often link the Middle East with North Africa because of their religious and cultural ties. The fifteen Middle Eastern countries are Turkey, Syria, Lebanon, Israel, Saudi Arabia, Jordan, Iran, Iraq, Kuwait, the United Arab Emirates, Bahrain, Qatar, Oman, and Yemen. Geographers often group Cyprus with the Middle East. This is an island nation in the Mediterranean Sea.

## What Subregions Exist?

North Africa and the Middle East have six subregions. The first one is a narrow coastal plain in Morocco and Algeria. It includes the most fertile land. Another subregion is the Plateau of Anatolia. It includes most of Turkey and the mountainous areas of Iran and Afghanistan. It has many earthquakes. Another subregion is called the **Levant.** It is the coastal farming region of Syria, Lebanon, and Israel, and borders the Mediterranean Sea. The Nile River Basin is another subregion. Without the Nile, Egypt would be only a desert. The Nile gives Egypt fertile farmland. Because of this, people call Egypt the "gift of the Nile."

Another area of rich farmland lies between the Tigris and Euphrates Rivers in Iraq and the Jordan River in Israel and Jordan. This subregion is shaped liked a crescent, or quarter, moon, so it is called the **Fertile Crescent.** It was the home of many early civilizations. The last main subregion is the desert. The Sahara covers 3.5 million square miles. Almost all of Europe could fit inside it! It

### Writing About Geography

Look for a newspaper article about North Africa or the Middle East. Read the article. Use your own words to summarize what it says. Finally, write your opinion about the main idea of the article.

Ancient Egyptians built huge pyramids like this as tombs for their rulers, who were called "pharaohs."

stretches 4,500 miles across North Africa and the Arabian Peninsula. The Rub' al Khali is the huge desert on the large interior plateau of the Arabian Peninsula.

## How Did Geography Shape This Region's History?

One of the world's first great civilizations developed along the Nile in Egypt. The river provided the Egyptians with well-watered farmland. The deserts on either side of the Nile separated them from their neighbors. This helped the Egyptians develop their own culture. The Nile also linked the Mediterranean Sea to the heart of Africa. For thousands of years, this crossroads was the center of important trade routes.

The Phoenicians lived in present-day Lebanon. They traded cloth, glass, wood, and beautiful metal objects with people in other lands. They sailed to England to search for tin and copper. They traveled to parts of Africa for ivory. They founded colonies in France, Spain, and present-day Tunisia. The Phoenicians and other traders sold goods for their neighbors in North Africa, Arabia, and the Fertile Crescent. Over thousands of years, many different people fought over this area near the Mediterranean Sea. As a result, it has a diverse culture.

**SECTION 1 REVIEW** On a separate sheet of paper, write the word from the Word Bank that completes each sentence.

| WORD BANK |
| --- |
| Anatolia |
| Egypt |
| Levant |
| Maghreb |
| Phoenicians |

1) Geographers sometimes call Morocco, Tunisia, and Algeria the _____ nations.

2) The _____ is the coastal farming region of Syria, Lebanon, and Israel.

3) Many people call _____ the "gift of the Nile."

4) The _____ traded goods from North Africa, Arabia, and the Fertile Crescent.

5) The Plateau of _____ in Turkey and the mountain areas of Iran and Afghanistan have many earthquakes.

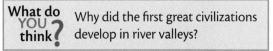

**What do YOU think?** Why did the first great civilizations develop in river valleys?

## What Are the Main Physical Features?

The main physical feature of this region is the large area of desert. Many people think that sand covers deserts. However, only about one-seventh of the Sahara has sand dunes. The rest of it is rocky plateaus and infertile plains.

The large belt of desert lies between 15° and 30° north latitude. Most large deserts of the world are also located in this latitude. The air patterns create these subtropical deserts. Hot, wet air near the equator rises and cools. It drops its precipitation as heavy, tropical rains. The resulting cooler, drier air moves away from the equator. As the air reaches the subtropics, it drops down and warms. As a result, few clouds and little rain form.

A second feature of this region is its highlands and high plateaus. Saudi Arabia's Hejaz Mountains rise along the Red Sea. Mountains border the high plateaus of Turkey and Iran. In northernTurkey are the Pontic Mountains. The Taurus Mountains rise in the south. Iran has the Elburz Mountains in the north and the Zagros to the west. The Atlas Mountains stretch across Morocco, Algeria, and Tunisia. The Atlas Mountains are important, because they stand between the Mediterranean Sea and the Sahara Desert. In winter, they catch the rain-bearing winds. Because of this, most people live north of the mountains. Enough rain falls there to support farming.

Three large tectonic plates come together in Turkey and Iran. When the plates collided with each other, the edge of one plate slid up over another and formed mountains. This created all the mountains in the region. Today, the plates still shift, causing deadly earthquakes.

Millions of years ago, Arabia was part of Africa. Then this peninsula began to break away from Africa along the fault called the Great Rift Valley. As the two landmasses pulled apart, the ocean flooded the northern Great Rift Valley to form the Red Sea.

**The Red Sea is an important waterway between Saudi Arabia and East Africa. Oil tankers such as this are used to ship oil across the Red Sea.**

## What Are the Major Bodies of Water?

Life depends on water. Most people live where they can get water. Large parts of North Africa and the Middle East are almost empty because there is so little water.

An **oasis** is a desert area with enough freshwater to grow crops or sustain life. Life depends on these oases. Underground water sources called **aquifers** supply the water. In some places, a natural spring brings the water to the surface. In other places, people have dug wells. Some of these are hundreds of years old.

The Nile is the most important river in this region. It travels northward for over 4,000 miles and is the world's longest river. In most places, the Nile creates a narrow green belt through the desert. This belt is between two and five miles wide. Where it meets the sea, the Nile forms a huge delta. The delta is about 100 miles long and 125 miles wide. Today, the Nile River Valley and this delta support almost 60 million Egyptians.

The Tigris and the Euphrates are two other important rivers in this region. They flow through southeastern Turkey, Syria, and Iraq and empty into the Persian Gulf. In ancient times, these rivers, as well as the Nile, flooded every spring. The floods carried much-needed water and **silt.** This is fertile soil and small rocky pieces. The floods left this silt behind in the river valleys. It helped form deltas and fertile farmland.

**Aquifer**
*An underground water source*

**Oasis**
*An area in the desert with enough freshwater to grow crops or sustain life*

**Silt**
*The fertile soil and small rocky pieces carried along by running water*

The Nile River flows northward through Egypt and is the longest river in the world. Several huge Egyptian civilizations started in the Nile River Valley long ago. The Nile is still important to Egyptians today.

Fertilizer
*A material that makes crops grow*

Sirocco
*A hot, dusty summer wind that sweeps northward from the Sahara*

In 1964, the Egyptian government built the Aswan Dam about 425 miles upstream from Cairo. The government wanted to control the flooding that took place every year. The dam created Lake Nasser. It is one of the largest human-made lakes in the world. Nasser provides irrigation water. Because of the Aswan Dam, the Nile no longer floods. Farmers can now plant three crops a year instead of just one. The dam is also used for hydroelectric power. However, without flooding and silt, the land is less fertile. Farmers now have to use costly **fertilizers,** or materials that make their crops grow.

Humans also made the Suez Canal, which opened in 1869. It allows large oceangoing ships to sail from the Mediterranean Sea to the Indian Ocean by way of the Red Sea. Because of this, ships do not have to take the long trip around the southern tip of Africa.

## What Is the Climate Like?

This region has several climates. Most of it has a desert climate: hot days, cold nights, and little rainfall. In the summer, **siroccos** sweep northward from the Sahara. These hot, dusty winds sometimes cross the Mediterranean Sea and travel as far as southern Europe. Their fine dust covers everything.

The northern highlands of Turkey and Iran have a steppe climate. They are much wetter than the rest of the region, except for the coast. This is partly because they are located farther north. Also, mountains force wet air to rise. As it does, it cools. The result is rain or snow.

The coastal areas around the Mediterranean Sea have a Mediterranean climate. Summers are hot; winters are mild with lots of rain. Spring is pleasant and cool.

**SECTION 2 REVIEW** Choose the letter of the answer that correctly completes each sentence. Write your answers on a separate sheet of paper.

1) _____ create the subtropical deserts located between 15° and 30° north latitude.

   a. Air patterns     c. Mountains
   b. Oceans     d. Rivers

2) _____ formed the mountains and high plateaus of this region.

   a. Rivers     c. Colliding tectonic plates
   b. Earthquakes     d. Floods

3) The Nile River no longer floods because of the _____.

   a. Suez Canal     c. Great Rift Valley
   b. Aswan Dam     d. none of the above

4) The most important river of this region is the _____.

   a. Tigris     c. Amazon
   b. Euphrates     d. Nile

5) A _____ is a hot, dusty summer wind that sweeps north from the Sahara.

   a. steppe     c. oasis
   b. sirocco     b. aquifer

**What do YOU think?** Do you think it was a mistake for Egypt to build the Aswan Dam? Explain your answer.

**Scholar**
*An expert in at least one subject*

## What Cultures Exist In This Region?

North Africa and the Middle East have much cultural diversity. More than half of the people are Arabs who share three things: they speak the same language, 90 percent are Muslims, and they are proud of their culture.

At one time, the Arab world was the center of learning in the world. Arabs made important contributions in science, mathematics, literature, art, and medicine. In fact, Al-Razi, an Arab doctor, wrote a set of 25 books about medicine hundreds of years ago. There were many Arab **scholars** who were experts in at least one subject, such as science, geography, or math.

Arab scientists were the first to study light. They learned that curving a lens causes things to appear larger. They were the first to figure out that the world was round. They correctly guessed that it was about 25,000 miles around. Al-Idrisi was an early geographer and map-maker.

Poetry is important to Arab culture. Omar Khayyám is a well-known Arab poet. Arabs are famous for creating beautiful designs for rugs, leather goods, and swords. Muslims decorate their mosques, or places of worship, with beautiful designs and letters.

*Geography In Your Life*
MATH

### The Ancient Islamic World's Influence on Math

After A.D. 750, the Islamic Empire produced many famous scholars in mathematics. They invented algebra. In this type of mathematics, letters and symbols represent unknown numbers. One Arab mathematician worked on trigonometry.

Arab scholars also expanded on what they learned from other people. They kept alive the important mathematical works of the Greeks. From India, they borrowed the nine numbers that we still use today. We call these "Arabic numbers" even though they came from India. From the Hindus, the Arab mathematicians borrowed the decimal system. They based this new system on the number 10. It includes the idea of 0. This system has served us well for hundreds of years. Before that time, many people used the Babylonian system. It was based on the number 60.

Four groups of people in this region are not Arabs. Many North Africans are descended from Berbers. These light-skinned people probably came from Europe or Asia. After Arabs conquered the Berber lands, some Berbers and Arabs married one another. Most Berbers have become Muslims and speak Arabic. However, in some places the people have kept their Berber culture.

The Turkish people originally came from Central Asia. They conquered and ruled a large area. At one time, their empire included much of the Middle East and North Africa. It stretched as far west as southeastern Europe. This empire lasted more than 600 years.

Iran was once called Persia. Its history goes back more than 2,500 years. Greeks, Arabs, Mongols, and Turks invaded this land. The culture reflects all of these invaders, yet it remains different. Even today, Iranians still memorize parts of an **epic,** which is a long poem about ancient heroes. The Persian poet, Firdawsi, wrote the poem around the year 1000.

About six million people of the Middle East are Israelis, most of whom are Jews. They live in the country of Israel. Many migrated there after 1948 when modern-day Israel was founded. These immigrants came from Europe, the Middle East, North Africa, Asia, and the Americas.

The Kurds are a large ethnic group with no country of their own. About 25 million Kurds live in Turkey, Iraq, and Syria. They have kept their own culture even though other groups have controlled them for centuries. The Kurds call the whole area where they live Kurdistan. Many Kurds have fought for years to make this area an independent country.

## What Religions Exist?

The Middle East is the birthplace of three major religions. The oldest of these is Judaism. This religion is over 3,000 years old. Abraham, a Jewish leader long ago, encouraged them to believe in only one god. This idea is called **monotheism.** The ancient Jews lived near present-day Lebanon and Israel.

Muslims pray five times each day, as instructed by the Koran, the holy book of Islam.

The second religion to come out of the Middle East was Christianity. Christians follow the teachings of Jesus. They believe that he is the Son of God. Jesus, a Jew, was born in Palestine. At that time, the Romans ruled this land along the eastern shore of the Mediterranean. The Jews believed that some day a leader called a **messiah** would free them from Roman rule. Some people believed Jesus was this messiah. The Romans put him to death by nailing him to a cross.

**Alms**
*Charity to the poor*

**Hajj**
*The pilgrimage to Mecca that is a religious duty of all Muslims, if they can afford it*

**Islam**
*The religion that began in Saudi Arabia and that follows the Islamic holy book, the Koran; Muslims are those who follow Islam*

**Messiah**
*A leader who saves others*

**Ramadan**
*The ninth month of the Muslim calendar; the month is holy to followers of Islam*

**Islam** is the third religion to develop in the Middle East. Its followers are called Muslims. This religion began in the 600s in what is now Saudi Arabia. An Arab named Muhammad believed that he was meant to teach the word of God, or Allah. Today's Muslims follow Muhammad's teachings as given in the Koran. This holy book is as important to Muslims as the Bible is to Christians and Jews.

The Five Pillars of Faith in the Koran list a Muslim's duties. First, a person must say the following: "There is no God but Allah, and Muhammad is his prophet." Second, a Muslim must pray five times a day at certain times. Third, Muslims must give **alms,** or charity to the poor. Fourth, Muslims must not eat or drink from sunrise to sunset during the holy month of **Ramadan.** This is the ninth month of the Muslim calendar. Fifth, Muslims must make the **Hajj,** a trip to Mecca in Saudi Arabia at least once, if they can afford it.

## What Languages Do the People Speak?

Most people of North Africa and the Middle East speak Arabic. This language is closely tied to Islam. Most Muslims want to read the Koran, which is written in Arabic. Written Arabic is the same for all Arabic speakers across the region. The spoken language, however, differs from country to country. In countries that are far from one another, the differences in the spoken language can be great.

All large minority groups speak their own language. The Turks speak Turkish. The Kurds speak Kurdish. The Iranians speak Farsi, an Indo-European language related to English.

Since France ruled much of North Africa during the colonial period, many people there read and write French. Some read newspapers published in French, and many people use French for business. Many of the more educated people speak English.

The people of Israel have come from many countries. On the streets of its big cities, a person might hear Russian, German, or Arabic. Most Israelis speak both Hebrew and English.

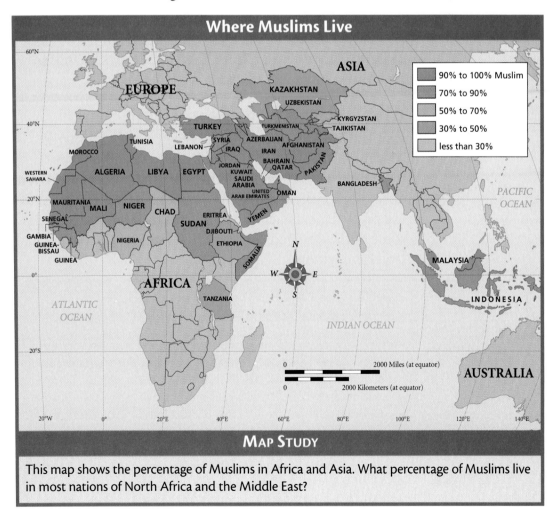

## Where Muslims Live

| | |
|---|---|
| | 90% to 100% Muslim |
| | 70% to 90% |
| | 50% to 70% |
| | 30% to 50% |
| | less than 30% |

## MAP STUDY

This map shows the percentage of Muslims in Africa and Asia. What percentage of Muslims live in most nations of North Africa and the Middle East?

## What Are the Population Trends?

This region has one of the highest birthrates in the world. Islamic countries expect everyone to marry and have many children. Some families have eight or more. Most of the population is less than 15 years old. The population of the region has doubled in the last 40 years. Scientists expect it to double again in less than 30 years.

As in many other places, people in North Africa and the Middle East are moving from rural areas to towns and cities. Many people migrate to cities because the land can no longer support them. Some cities are doubling in size in just 15 years.

Over seven million people live in Istanbul, Turkey. It is the largest city in this region. Cairo, Egypt, has nearly the same population. Other large cities with a population over three million include Tehran, Iran; Baghdad, Iraq; Alexandria, Egypt; and Ankara, Turkey.

## What Problems Do the People Face?

People of different cultures and religions often disagree. This may cause war. Israel and its Arab neighbors have fought five wars since 1948, the year Israel became a nation. Israel's Arab neighbors do not think Israelis have a right to live on the land. Israel won each of its five wars. Nevertheless, some of the defeated Arab countries still refuse to recognize Israel as a nation.

---

**Biography**  **PRINCESS BASMA BINT ALI: 1970–**

Princess Basma is a member of the royal family of Jordan and a major in the Jordanian army. In the 1990s, she became the first Jordanian woman to qualify as a navy diver. However, she is famous worldwide because she works to protect the undersea world in the Gulf of Aqaba. It is part of Jordan's coastline along the Red Sea. No other place matches the Red Sea for coral life, so many scuba divers come there. Princess Basma is president of the Jordan Royal Ecological Diving Society. She works to conserve this beautiful part of the world. She is also active in politics for Jordan.

---

**Iraqi forces were defeated in the Persian Gulf War in 1991.**

A group of people called the Palestinians are Arabs who were forced out or chose to leave Israel in 1948. Today, they demand their own homeland. Some Palestinians formed the **Palestinian Liberation Organization (PLO).** Some PLO members believe that the only way they will ever gain a homeland is by using force. The United States has tried to get Israel and its neighbors to settle their differences. Israel has signed peace treaties with Egypt and Jordan. However, Israel has not reached an agreement with the Palestinians or with Syria.

Iran and Iraq also have a long history of disagreement. In late 1980, Iraqi forces invaded Iran and fought an eight-year war, killing more than a million people. The war left Iraq with a weakened economy and large debts. Iraq then took over Kuwait and its rich oil fields to solve its money problems. The United Nations told Iraq to leave Kuwait. Iraq refused. This led to the Persian Gulf War in 1991. Forces from many countries, including the United States, defeated the Iraqis.

Unemployment is also a problem in this region. Many people who come to the cities cannot find jobs. The region also has **underemployment.** This is when a person who is trained for one job must accept another job that often pays less and requires less skills.

Palestinian Liberation Organization (PLO)
*An organization of Arabs in Palestine who want their own homeland*

Underemployment
*When a person trained for one job must accept another job that often pays less and requires less skills*

**SECTION 3 REVIEW** On a separate sheet of paper, write answers to these questions.

1) Which Arabs made contributions in poetry, medicine, and geography?
2) What three religions developed in the Middle East?
3) What is the holy book of Islam?
4) What one language do most people of North Africa and the Middle East speak?
5) What is the largest city in this region?

**What do YOU think?**

What do you think was the most important contribution Arabs made to world civilization?

## What Is the Economy Like?

Organization of
Petroleum
Exporting
Countries (OPEC)
*A group of oil
producing countries
that tries to control
the supply of oil by
setting production
limits*

Phosphates
*Materials used to
make fertilizer*

In this region, many people earn a living much as their ancestors did hundreds of years ago. Some are nomads who move from place to place, though the number of nomads is decreasing. Many tend herds of camels, sheep, or goats.

Even though the region has many deserts, nearly half of the people are farmers. They live in small villages. Many are subsistence farmers who have few machines. In most places, they irrigate their land to grow crops. Along the Mediterranean coast, farmers grow grains like wheat and barley. Other crops include olives, grapes, oranges, and cork. In the Nile River Delta, farmers grow rice, cotton, sugar, barley, and wheat.

## What Natural Resources Are Important?

North Africa and the Middle East have the world's largest known deposits of oil. Saudi Arabia has one-fourth of these. The United Arab Emirates, Qatar, Bahrain, Kuwait, Iraq, and Iran also have large oil fields. In North Africa, Algeria and Libya have huge oil deposits.

Industry throughout the world greatly depends on oil as its chief energy source. Because of this, the countries of North Africa and the Middle East have a lot of economic power. In 1960, the world's main oil producing countries formed the **Organization of Petroleum Exporting Countries (OPEC).** This group tries to control the supply of oil by setting production limits. The sale of oil pays for the building of roads, housing, and schools. With oil money, the governments of these countries can develop other parts of their economy, such as manufacturing and tourism.

This region also has other mineral resources. Morocco is one of the world's largest producer of **phosphates.** They are used to make fertilizers. The Sahara and the Nile Delta have large natural gas fields.

## World Oil Trade

| Major Oil Trading Partners | Millions of Tons of Oil Traded Per Year |
|---|---|
| Middle East to Asia (not Japan) | 294.4 |
| Middle East to Japan | 218.1 |
| Middle East to Western Europe | 187.9 |
| South and Central America to the United States | 132.1 |
| North Africa to Western Europe | 97.9 |
| Commonwealth of Independent States to Western Europe | 90.8 |
| Middle East to the United States | 86.9 |
| Canada to the United States | 72.7 |
| West Africa to the United States | 68.3 |
| Mexico to the United States | 68.0 |
| **Total World Oil Trade in Millions of Tons: 1,978.9** | |

### CHART STUDY

This chart shows the main oil trading partners of the world. Who is the Middle East's largest oil customer? From which regions and countries does the United States get its oil?

## What Environmental Problems Exist?

The building of the Aswan Dam helped Egypt in many ways. However, it has also created environmental problems. Before the dam was built, the Nile flushed out things that polluted the water. Now, the Nile flows more slowly, so the level of pollution is rising. The Nile also used to wash harmful water snails out to sea. Now snails are working their way upstream. They spread a disease that affects workers in irrigated lands. Irrigation has also become a problem. It builds up salt in the soil. If this continues, the land will be useless for farming.

**SECTION 4 REVIEW** On a separate sheet of paper, write *True* if the statement is true or *False* if the statement is not true. Make each false statement true by changing the underlined word.

1) Many people in this region are <u>nomads</u>.

2) The world's largest known deposits of oil are in <u>Europe.</u>

3) OPEC tries to control the <u>supply</u> of oil.

4) <u>Algeria</u> produces a large amount of phosphates.

5) The <u>Sahara</u> Dam has caused environmental problems.

**What do YOU think?**

Should OPEC have the power to set production limits on oil? Explain your answer.

# Graffiti Is Nothing New

**Egyptians were among the first people to write and draw pictures on walls. This photo shows Egyptian wall art.**

Graffiti is writing or drawing on a public surface, such as a wall. Most people think that graffiti is new. In fact, even thousands of years ago, people put their marks onto public places. Long ago, someone carved the names of powerful priests into the sandstone sides of Egyptian monuments. This was nearly 3,000 years ago, yet this graffiti was not even close to being the first!

Even 50,000 years ago, people left reminders that they had been there. In caves where people lived, people today can see cave art. The people who lived in these caves carved their handprints on the walls. This is not unlike the modern "taggers" who want to leave their mark.

Archaeologists have found graffiti on royal Egyptian buildings that are at least 3,400 years old. They have found even older graffiti on rocks and in caves along desert roads. Egyptian traders traveled these roads 5,000 years ago. The graffiti tells archaeologists about these long-ago times. They think that priests created the graffiti, as priests were among the few people who knew how to read and write.

Archaeologists have also found Greek graffiti on ancient Egyptian temples. This tells them about the long period of time when the Greeks influenced Egypt. Scholars believe that the Greeks who wrote the graffiti were still using the Egyptian temples. The reason they think this is because the writing is near the bottom of the walls. If the buildings were not being used, sand would have covered the lower parts. Because of the sand, the Greeks would have had to write their graffiti higher on the walls. In these ways, the ancient graffiti helps archaeologists learn new things about old cultures.

## Spotlight Story Wrap-Up

1) What is graffiti?
2) What is the earliest form of graffiti?
3) Where have archaeologists found the oldest Egyptian graffiti?
4) How do scholars know only a few people in Egyptian society could have done this graffiti?
5) What does the graffiti in Greek tell us about the history of Egypt?

◆ North Africa has five countries. The Red Sea divides North Africa from the Middle East, which is made up of fifteen countries.

◆ This region has many subregions. Morocco and Algeria have a narrow, but fertile, coastal plain. The Plateau of Anatolia includes most of Turkey and the mountainous areas of Iran and Afghanistan. Another region is the Levant coastal farming area of Syria, Lebanon, and Israel. A fourth subregion is the Nile River Basin. A fifth is the Fertile Crescent between the Tigris and Euphrates Rivers and the Jordan River. The sixth subregion is the desert.

◆ The most important physical feature of North Africa and the Middle East is the large area of desert. A second feature is its rugged highlands and high plateaus.

◆ The Aswan Dam and the Suez Canal are two important human-made waterways.

◆ Much of North Africa and the Middle East have a desert climate. The northern highlands of Turkey and Iran have a steppe climate. The coastal areas around the Mediterranean have a Mediterranean climate.

◆ More than half of the people of North Africa and the Middle East are Arabs. Other groups include Berbers, Turks, Iranians (Persians), Israelis, and Kurds.

◆ This region has one of the highest birthrates in the world.

◆ The Middle East is the birthplace of three important religions: Judaism, Christianity, and Islam.

◆ Most people of North Africa and the Middle East speak Arabic. However, the minority groups speak their own language.

◆ Many people in North Africa and the Middle East are nomads who tend herds of animals. Others are subsistence farmers. Among the crops are wheat, barley, olives, grapes, oranges, cork, rice, cotton, and sugar.

◆ North Africa and the Middle East contain the world's largest known oil deposits.

◆ The main problems in this region are war between people of different cultures and religions, unemployment, and underemployment.

◆ The Aswan Dam has helped Egypt, but it has also produced some environmental problems that threaten the land and its people.

## Comprehension: Identifying Facts

On a separate sheet of paper, use the words from the Word Bank to complete each sentence.

1) The _____ is north of North Africa.

2) The _____ divides North Africa from the Middle East.

3) _____ is often called the "gift of the Nile."

4) More than half of the people of North Africa and the Middle East are _____.

5) The Middle East is the birthplace of Judaism, Christianity, and _____.

## Comprehension: Multiple Choice

On a separate sheet of paper, write the letter of the answer that correctly completes each sentence.

1) The three countries in North Africa that are located farthest west are Algeria, Tunisia, and _____.
   a. Turkey
   b. Egypt
   c. Morocco
   d. Iran

2) _____ cover most of the Sahara.
   a. Rocky plateaus and infertile plains
   b. Savanna-like grasses
   c. Sand dunes
   d. Palm trees and oases

3) One-fourth of the world's oil deposits are in _____.
   a. Saudi Arabia
   b. Iran
   c. Libya
   d. Kuwait

4) The forces of many countries, including the United States, defeated _____ in the Persian Gulf War.
   a. Iran
   b. Kuwait
   c. Israel
   d. Iraq

**5)** North Africa and the Middle East have the largest known deposits of \_\_\_\_\_.

   a. natural gas       c. gold

   b. diamonds        d. oil

## Comprehension: Understanding Main Ideas

On a separate sheet of paper, write the answer to each question. Use complete sentences.

**1)** What kind of climate does most of North Africa and the Middle East have?

**2)** What are the three main rivers of this region?

**3)** What are the six main cultural groups that live in this region?

## Critical Thinking: Write Your Opinion

On a separate sheet of paper, write your opinion to each question. Use complete sentences.

**1)** A big problem in North Africa and the Middle East is the gap between the rich and the poor. How would you go about making things more equal?

**2)** What steps should other nations take to get the Arabs and the Israelis to settle their differences?

## Applying the Five Themes of Geography

### Interaction

How does the Aswan Dam show both the good and the bad that can happen when people interact with their environment?

**Test-Taking Tip**   After you have taken a test, go back and reread the questions and your answers. Make sure that you have spelled the words correctly. Check to see that you have used proper grammar and punctuation in your sentences.

# Understanding Physical Maps

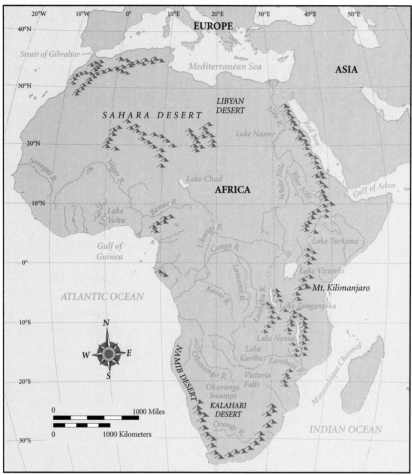

There are many kinds of physical maps. These maps show what the land looks like and what is on it. A physical map might show rivers, lakes, and mountains. It might also show relief, or elevation, of the land. Elevation is how high the land is above or below sea level. The maps in this book usually show physical features. They also show political boundaries and cities.

The map on this page is a physical map of Africa. It does not show elevation. It does show the names of rivers, lakes, and mountains.

Study the map on this page and answer the following questions.

1) What areas of Africa have mountains?

2) What areas of Africa are probably flat?

3) What makes this a physical map?

4) What other things can appear on physical maps?

5) Why do you think physical maps are important?

◆ Africa is the second largest continent. It is made up of West Africa, southern Africa, Central and East Africa, and North Africa. The Red Sea divides North Africa from the Middle East. The Middle East is part of Asia.

◆ Africa and the Middle East have many regions with deltas, coastal plains, deserts, basins, mountains, plateaus, and valleys. Some of the more well-known physical features are the Niger River and Nile River deltas; the Sahara, Kalahari, and Namib deserts; the Drakensberg and Taurus mountains; the Plateau of Anatolia; and the Great Rift Valley.

◆ Africa and the Middle East have many climates that range from subtropical to steppe to Mediterranean to desert.

◆ Several hundred ethnic groups live in West Africa. Many ethnic groups as well as descendants of European settlers live in southern Africa. Most ethnic groups in Central and East Africa are members of the Bantu and the Nilotic. More than half of the people of North Africa and the Middle East are Arabs.

◆ These ethnic groups speak many different languages, such as Bantu, Cushite, Swahili, Arabic, and a number of European languages.

◆ Among the religions people practice are Christianity, Islam, and Judaism. The Middle East is the birthplace of these three religions. Many African people practice their own native religions. Some people practice Hinduism.

◆ Most people in Africa and the Middle East farm. Many are subsistence farmers. Others raise cash crops.

◆ Central and East Africa have fewer minerals than the rest of Africa. North Africa and the Middle East contain the world's largest know oil deposits. Ecotourism is becoming an important source of money in southern Africa as tourists come to see the wildlife.

◆ Population growth is high throughout this region. Also, different ethnic groups throughout Africa are fighting.

◆ West Africa's biggest problem is poverty.

◆ Southern, Central, and East Africa must balance the needs of the poor with the needs of wildlife.

◆ In North Africa and the Middle East, people of different cultures and religions are fighting.

"Nothing and no one can destroy the Chinese people. They are relentless survivors. They are the oldest civilized people on Earth. Their civilization passes through phases, but its basic characteristics remain the same. They yield, they bend to the wind, but they never break."

—Pearl S. Buck, American author,
from *China: Past and Present*, 1972

# Central and East Asia

In Unit 5, you learned about Africa and the Middle East. Now you head east to Central and East Asia. There you will discover China, the Koreas, and Japan. Did you know that this region has much of the world's population? You will encounter this large region's geography, history, and culture. You will learn about flooding rivers, terrace farming (Chinese terraces are pictured to the left), and yak herding. You will also learn about the region's many languages, its important cities like Beijing and Tokyo, and the highest peak in the world—Mount Everest.

**CHAPTERS IN UNIT 6**

**Chapter 16:** China . . . . . . . . . . . . . . . . . . . . . . . . . . . . . . .356
**Chapter 17:** Japan and the Koreas . . . . . . . . . . . . . . . .376

# China

People have lived in China for thousands of years. In fact, farming began there more than 8,000 years ago. Before the 1980s, the Communist government owned and controlled everything in this large country. Over the last ten years, many changes have taken place. China's economy is now one of the fastest growing economies in the world. However, China is still among the world's poorest countries. The photo on this page shows China's Gobi Desert. You will learn about it and other features of China in this chapter.

## Goals for Learning

▶ To describe where China is located
▶ To identify the most important physical features and climates of China
▶ To describe the many cultures of China
▶ To explain where most people in China live
▶ To describe the economy and the environmental challenges China faces

 *Geo-Stats*

 **China**
**Population:** 1,254,062,000
**Area** (in square miles): 3,705,829
**Length of Roads** (in miles): 718,497
**Longest River:** Yangtze (3,915 miles)
**Highest Mountain:** Everest (29,028 feet)

**Major Cities:** Beijing (capital), Shanghai, Tianjin, Shenyang, Guangzhou
**Major Religions:** Buddhism, Islam
**Major Languages:** Mandarin-Chinese, other local languages
**Workforce:** 623.9 million
**Number of Daily Newspapers:** over 70
**Number of Television Sets:** 75 million

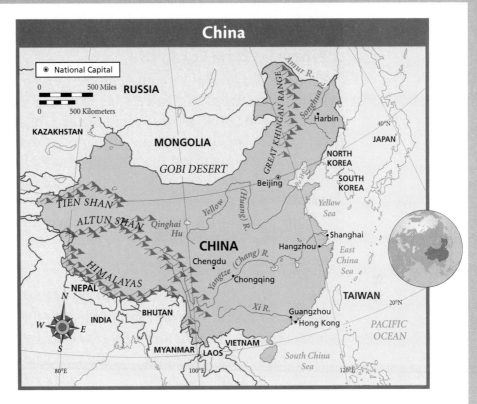

# China

National Capital

0 ——— 500 Miles
0 ——— 500 Kilometers

RUSSIA

KAZAKHSTAN

MONGOLIA

GOBI DESERT

TIEN SHAN

ALTUN SHAN    Qinghai
Hu

HIMALAYAS

NEPAL

INDIA    BHUTAN

MYANMAR  LAOS

VIETNAM

Amur R.

GREAT KHINGAN RANGE

Songhua R.

Harbin    40°N

JAPAN

NORTH
KOREA

Beijing    SOUTH
KOREA

Bo Hai

Yellow
Sea

CHINA

Chengdu

Yellow
(Huang) R.

Yangtze (Chang) R.

Chongqing

Xi R.

Guangzhou

Hong Kong

Shanghai

Hangzhou    East
China
Sea

TAIWAN    20°N

PACIFIC
OCEAN

South China
Sea

80°E    100°E    120°E

*Map Skills*

China is the third largest country in area in the world. It is located south of Mongolia and Russia and north of the Indian subcontinent and Southeast Asia. The Pacific Ocean and several seas touch its shores to the east. China has a population of almost 1.3 billion people. This means that one out of every five people in the world is Chinese.

Study the map and answer the following questions:

**1)** What is China's capital city?

**2)** Which rivers can be found in China?

**3)** Which desert is located in northern China and southern Mongolia?

**4)** What are some mountain ranges in China?

**5)** Where do you think the first civilizations started in China? Explain your answer.

## Where Is China Located?

China is located almost entirely in the middle latitudes, between the Tropic of Cancer and 50° north latitude. This is roughly the same as the United States. Only Russia and Canada are larger than China. It shares borders with Russia and Mongolia to the north; Vietnam, Laos, Myanmar, India, Bhutan, and Nepal to the south; and India, Pakistan, Kazakhstan, Kyrgyzstan, Tajikistan, and Afghanistan to the west. North Korea, South Korea, the Yellow Sea, the East China Sea, and the South China Sea are located to the east of China.

## How Did Geography Shape China's History?

Geography has played a big role in China's history. Civilization first developed there in the valley of the Huang He (Yellow) River. Huang means "yellow" in Chinese. The river got its name from the fine silt it carries. The Huang He runs through plains of fertile loess soil deposited by the wind. The Huang He region had everything necessary for civilization to develop nearby, especially rich farmland and a good water supply. People could also use the river for transportation.

China's natural borders include high mountains, huge deserts, jungles, and seas. These natural barriers isolated and protected China from foreign invaders. The Chinese also built a barrier of their own to keep out invaders, a huge wall that today is called the Great Wall. Its main part is over 2,000 miles long and 25 feet high.

## What Regions Exist in China?

Few nations are as geographically diverse as China. It has four regions. The North China Plain is northeast of China's capital city, Beijing. Mountains surround this plain on three sides. Loess covers the western part of the plain. Poor farmers make up most of the plain's population. They often face floods and droughts. Even so, nearly one out of every five Chinese lives on the plain. Plains farmers raise much of

**The Great Wall of China is about 2,200 years old.**

the food for the millions of people who live in China's great cities.

China's second region is the Manchurian Plain. It is north of the North China Plain. The Manchurian Plain is the leading industrial area of China. It has rich coal and iron deposits. Most of its people live in the valley of the Liao River.

Highlands and high plateaus make up China's third region. Mountains cover one-third of China. The highest ones stand in the west. The Qinghai-Tibet Plateau is the largest highland region in the world. People call it "the roof of the world." Few people live in this isolated part of China because of its harsh climate and geography. Highland areas covered with forests are located in the eastern part of China, though they are not as high as those in the west.

Deserts and steppes make up China's fourth region. The Taklimakan is one of the world's largest and driest deserts. It is north of the Kunlun Mountains. The Gobi Desert shares China's border with Mongolia. Both deserts are rich in mineral resources, but they are just beginning to be developed. Steppes are south and east of the deserts. Nomadic Mongols and Tibetans have raised sheep and goats there for many years. Lack of rainfall makes farming hard.

**Section 1 Review** On a separate sheet of paper, write the word from the Word Bank that completes each sentence.

1) _____ is the third largest country in the world.

2) Most Chinese people live on the _____.

3) The _____ River is yellow because of its silt.

4) People call the _____ "the roof of the world."

5) The _____ is one of the driest deserts in the world.

**WORD BANK**

China

Huang He

North China Plain

Qinghai-Tibet Plateau

Taklimakan

**What do YOU think?** Do you think that all Chinese people live in the same type of houses and eat the same foods? Explain your answer.

### What Are China's Main Physical Features?

Terrace
*A broad, level step dug into a hillside for the growing of crops*

Mountains are China's main physical feature. Western China has some of the highest mountain ranges in the world. Nine of the world's highest peaks stand in China. Mount Everest in the Himalayas is the highest point on Earth. It rises 29,028 feet, or about 5½ miles, above sea level! Two large tectonic plates smashed together to create these mountains. The crash forced the earth's crust thousands of feet upward. The two plates are still pushing against one another, so the mountains grow a few inches higher each year.

The high plateau of Tibet is located in southwestern China. Most of the plateau is over 14,000 feet high. High mountains separate it from the rest of China. This plateau is the bed of a huge lake that covered central Asia more than 50 million years ago.

Plains cover much of eastern China. About 95 percent of the Chinese people live on these fertile plains. Farmers have built **terraces** into the hillsides to create new farming areas. Terraces are broad, level steps dug into a hillside for the growing of crops. They are common throughout Asia.

**Biography** | **DALAI LAMA: 1935–**

The title Dalai Lama means "teacher whose wisdom is great as the ocean." A Dalai Lama has led the Tibetan Buddhists since 1391. Today, the 14th Dalai Lama, Tenzin Gyatso, leads his people from India. This is a result of China invading Tibet in 1950. In 1959, the Tibetan people rebelled. The Chinese threatened to kill the Tibetan god-king, or Dalai Lama. In March 1959, he fled Tibet, crossed the world's highest mountains, and set up his government in India. In 1989 he won the Nobel Peace Prize because of his nonviolent efforts to free Tibet from Communist China.

**Floodplain**
*A level area of land built up by flood deposits*

## What Are China's Main Rivers?

China has many rivers. Most of them begin in the high western mountains. The Huang He is the longest northern river. People call it "China's Sorrow" because it has flooded so often. In 1931, the Huang He flooded and killed over 3.7 million people.

Over millions of years, flooding rivers leave behind deposits of silt. This builds up an area of level land. Geographers call this a **floodplain.** The huge floodplain of the Huang He became the North China Plain.

The Yangtze (Chang), is the longest river in central China. It divides northern from southern China. From its source in the western mountains, the river flows nearly 4,000 miles to the China Sea. It has 700 tributaries, some of which are themselves important rivers. The wide, fertile plain of the lower Yangtze is one of China's best agricultural areas.

The Xi Jiang is the third most important Chinese river. The area around it produces rice, tea, and cotton. All three rivers are important highways into the middle of China. They also provide drinking and irrigation water.

## What Is China's Climate Like?

China has many different climates. The mountainous areas of western China have highland climates. People call the Qinghai-Tibet Plateau the "Land of Snows" because some snow remains on the ground all year around. On any given day, temperatures on the plateau may reach 100° F in the afternoon and fall below freezing at night. China's great deserts also have these temperature extremes. Summers are hot; winters are cold. The deserts are far from the sea and high mountains block wet winds. For these reasons, the deserts receive little rain or snow.

Large areas of northern China, including much of the North China Plain, have a steppe climate. They often border deserts. However, they receive a little more rain than the deserts do. Dust storms and droughts are common. The parts of northern China closer to the sea have a humid continental climate with four seasons.

Most of southern China has a humid subtropical climate. The growing season is long, so farmers often raise two crops a year. The summers are long, hot, and wet. The winters are short.

## How Does China's Physical Environment Affect the People?

Many Chinese people eat rice, but many do not. This is because geography affects what they eat and how they live. The people who live in the western mountain regions live in **adobe** houses. Adobe is sun-dried bricks. Adobe houses protect people from the harsh climate. People eat wheat noodles, wheat bread, and lamb meat. People of the North China Plain live in mud-based houses. They eat wheat products and potatoes and steam their food.

South of the Yangtze River, the climate is milder. People call the valley between the Yangtze and the Xi Rivers "China's Rice Bowl." Farmers grow about half of China's grain in this area. Houses are built on the sloped land, leaving the flatter land for food production. People eat rice and more vegetables than the people in other parts of China because the climate is good for growing vegetables. People living near the sea eat fish at nearly every meal.

**Section 2 Review** On a separate sheet of paper, write answers to these questions.

1) What is the main physical feature of China?
2) What is the highest peak in the world?
3) What are the three most important rivers of China?
4) What part of China has a humid subtropical climate?
5) What are two ways that China's physical environment affects its people?

**What do YOU think?** Why do you think Chinese farmers build terraces?

## What Cultures Exist in China?

About 92 percent of Chinese people are Han Chinese. This cultural group began in the valley of the Huang He about 5,000 years ago. The remaining people, more than 100 million, belong to many different minority groups.

Filial piety
*Respect for one's parents and ancestors*

Yak
*A large, longhaired ox*

The largest minority is the Zhuang. They live mostly in south-central China. Another large group is the Uygurs. They live in the mountainous, desert areas of western China. Mongol people live in the northern part of China. Some Mongols are nomads who tend sheep, goats, horses, and **yaks.** A yak is a large, longhaired ox. There are also over three million Tibetans. In 1950, Chinese soldiers invaded Tibet, which was an independent country. Since that time, Tibetans have been part of China. About 200,000 Chinese troops remain in Tibet. However, the Tibetans refuse to give up their culture.

## What Religions Do the Chinese Practice?

The Communists who rule China allow religious freedom, but they keep a close watch on all religions. The government thinks religions mislead people. Still, many Chinese people follow their ancient beliefs. **Filial piety,** or respect for one's parents and ancestors, is part of their religion. The Chinese believe that prayers and sacrifices to these ancestors join the worlds of the living and the dead.

The teachings of Confucius have influenced Chinese beliefs. Confucius did not think of his teachings as a religion. He wanted to help people organize society. He thought that each person had a place in society. People owed respect to those above them, such as a ruler or a father. In turn, the ruler or father should set a good example.

The Chinese have had other influences. Traders brought Islam from the Middle East to China. Many Uygurs became Muslims. Beginning in the 1500s, Christian missionaries tried to bring Christianity to China. Many Chinese saw it as a foreign religion. They linked it to western efforts to

Buddhism
*A religion based on the teachings of Buddha and practiced mainly in central and eastern Asia*

Ideogram
*A picture, symbol, or mark that stands for a thing or an idea in the Chinese language; a character*

change China. Because of this, only a small number of Chinese became Christians.

Most Tibetans practice **Buddhism.** They follow the teachings of a wise man named Siddhartha Gautama who lived from 563 to 483 B.C. His followers called him Buddha, which means the "Enlightened One." Buddhism has several branches. Tibetan Buddhists try to understand the suffering of others. They believe that greed, hatred, and ignorance cause all human suffering.

## What Languages Do the Chinese Speak?

More people in the world speak Chinese than English. The written Chinese language has no alphabet with letters that stand for sounds. The Chinese make up sentences from thousands of characters, or **ideograms.** These pictures, symbols, or marks stand for a thing or an idea. Ideograms must be memorized. A 12-year-old knows about 3,000 characters. A highly educated adult might learn 10,000 characters. Chinese people everywhere can read these ideograms. This is not true of spoken Chinese, since there are dozens of dialects. About two-thirds of the Chinese people speak the Mandarin dialect. Most large minority groups in China speak their own languages.

### Languages of the World

| Language | Speakers in Millions | Areas Where Spoken |
|---|---|---|
| Han Chinese (Mandarin) | 874 | China, Taiwan, Singapore |
| Hindi | 366 | northern India |
| Spanish | 358 | Spain, Latin America, southwestern United States |
| English | 341 | British Isles, Anglo-America, Australia, New Zealand, South Africa, former British colonies in tropical Asia and Africa, Philippines |
| Bengali | 207 | Bangladesh, eastern India |
| Arabic | 206 | Middle East, North Africa |
| Portuguese | 176 | Portugal, Brazil, southern Africa |
| Russian | 167 | Russia, Kazakhstan, parts of Ukraine, other former Soviet Republics |
| Japanese | 125 | Japan |
| German | 100 | Germany, Austria, Switzerland, Luxembourg, eastern France, northern Italy |

#### CHART STUDY

This chart lists the world's top ten languages and the number of speakers per language. What is the most commonly spoken language? How many people speak Spanish? English?

## Where Do the Chinese Live?

China has a larger population than any other country. About 90 percent of its people live on about 17 percent of the land area. Most of them live in the eastern and southeastern regions and work the land. The rest live in more than 3,500 towns and cities. China has almost 40 cities with more than a million people each.

Shanghai is China's largest city. More than 14 million people live in this port city and its suburbs. Beijing, China's second largest city, is its capital. Other large cities include Hong Kong, Tianjin, Shenyang, and Wuhan. All of these cities are larger than Chicago, the third largest city in the United States.

## What Are China's Population Trends?

Between 1950 and 1990, China's population doubled. The government wanted to develop the country. However, to do this, it had to control the population growth. In 1980, the government made a "one child" rule. If a couple had one child, the government gave the parents money. If a couple had more than one child, they had to pay the government money. In cities, the government refused to give the second child free medical care or schooling. In rural areas, the government had a hard time enforcing this rule. Farm families needed more children to help work the land.

## What Problems Do the Chinese People Face?

Population growth is a big problem in China. About 20 million Chinese are born each year. Every 17 years, the population growth alone equals the total U.S. population. The growing population will need more food, housing, schools, and medical care. In fact, they will need more of everything. This growth is already affecting the quality of life for every Chinese person.

The lack of city housing is also a problem. Young, single people usually live together in small apartments. They sign up for an apartment and have to wait seven or eight years to get one. Most families are crowded into apartments with only two rooms. Several families may share the bathroom or the kitchen. In Shanghai, many families live in apartments with no indoor plumbing.

China's people are migrating from rural areas to cities, so its cities are growing. Over 3 million migrants have come to Beijing. Most live in poor housing on the edge of the city. They have no plumbing and few schools. Many people can find only part-time work at low-paying jobs.

A political problem is China's relationship with Taiwan. In 1949, a long civil war ended in China. The Communists won the war. The non-Communists fled to the nearby island of Taiwan. There, they established the Republic of China. The government of China considers Taiwan part of China. It does not accept Taiwan as an independent state. From time to time, China threatens to take over Taiwan by force. If this happens, war will probably break out.

**Section 3 Review** On a separate sheet of paper, write *True* if the statement is true or *False* if the statement is not true. Make each false statement true by changing the underlined word.

1) About 92 percent of the Chinese people are known as Han Chinese.

2) The Uygurs follow the Buddhist religion.

3) The teachings of Confucius have influenced Chinese beliefs.

4) Almost 50 percent of China's people live on 17 percent of the land.

5) To help slow down population growth, the Chinese government introduced the "two child" rule.

> **What do YOU think?** Is life in China easier in the cities or in the country? Explain your answer.

## What Is China's Economy Like?

Reform

*A change in how something is done to make things better*

In 1949, the Communists took over China. The government tried to control every part of Chinese life. It told the Chinese people what to grow, where to live, where to work, and what books to read. The leaders wanted to make China an industrial power without any help from other countries.

In 1976, Chinese leader Deng Xiaoping introduced a new plan for economic **reform,** or change. Once again, he let people own businesses and property. He invited foreign countries to invest in China. Since that time, China's economy has changed. It had been a centralized, controlled economy. The government made all the decisions. Now it is moving toward becoming a free-market economy. People decide for themselves what to buy and sell.

Today, the Chinese government allows farmers to grow what they like. Farmers can sell their crops at a price they set. Many people have opened businesses. Incomes are rising. For the first time, many people are able to buy things that they want, such as televisions, radios, fans, watches, washing machines, and refrigerators.

China's economy is one of the fastest growing in the world. Since 1976, it has grown four times larger. Many foreign companies are investing in China. They see China's huge population as a market for their products. One of China's biggest customers is the United States.

## What Natural Resources Does China Have?

China was the first country to mine coal and use it as an energy source. Today, China is still the world's third largest producer of coal. Coal provides over 70 percent of China's energy needs.

The open lands of China's northwest have huge, undeveloped deposits of oil. Getting the oil out of the ground costs a lot of money. Bringing it to places where it can be processed is expensive, too. The Chinese government now allows foreign oil companies to develop new offshore oil fields. Today, China produces all the coal and oil it needs for itself.

China has large deposits of bauxite, uranium, tungsten, and low-grade iron ore. Most of these resources are under-developed because they are located far from the important centers of industry. Until China develops a better transportation system to get these resources to industry, the economy will not benefit from these resources. Waterpower is another underdeveloped resource. China's many fast-moving rivers could make this Asian country the world's largest producer of hydroelectric power.

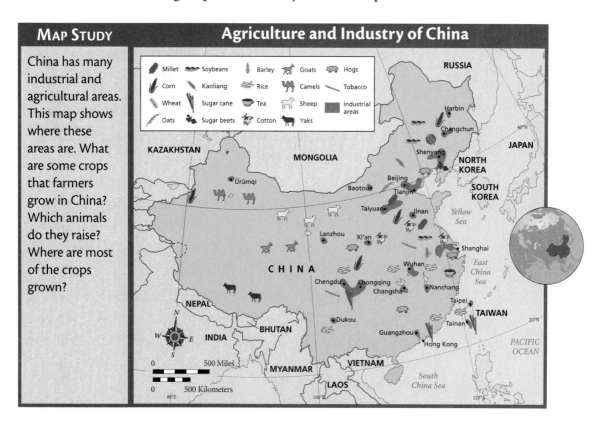

**MAP STUDY**

China has many industrial and agricultural areas. This map shows where these areas are. What are some crops that farmers grow in China? Which animals do they raise? Where are most of the crops grown?

**Agriculture and Industry of China**

Millet · Soybeans · Barley · Goats · Hogs
Corn · Kaoliang · Rice · Camels · Tobacco
Wheat · Sugar cane · Tea · Sheep · Industrial areas
Oats · Sugar beets · Cotton · Yaks

## What Are Some Important Chinese Industries?

Most Chinese people still farm for a living. Their farms are small. The staple crop north of the Yangtze River is wheat. Farmers also grow other grain crops, such as sorghum, corn, millet, and soybeans. They make vegetable oil for cooking from rapeseed and peanuts. South of the Yangtze, the climate is more subtropical. There, rice is the main crop. Other crops include tea, tobacco, silk, rubber, and fruits. Farmers grow vegetables, such as cabbage, onions, and beans, all over China. Because most farmers have little machinery, they do most of their work by hand.

Only about 20 percent of China's workers work in industry. However, more and more industrial jobs are being created. One of Deng's reforms was to shift the economy from heavy industry to **light industry**. Light industry is the making of everyday products that people use. For example, light industries produce clothing, appliances, and bicycles.

Most of China's industrial growth has taken place in the southeast. In the late 1970s, the Chinese government created four areas called Special Economic Zones (SEZs). The government gave these zones **tax breaks,** which means they had to pay less money to the government for taxes. Because of this, foreign companies invested in China. These four zones have been successful. Huge fields that once grew rice are now industrial areas with factories, apartments, schools, and traffic jams.

Today, China's economy produces many goods. It is the world's leading producer of textiles, or cloth. China produces 25 percent of the world's cotton cloth and 70 percent of the world's silk. It is an important producer of iron and steel. Its large industries make machines, chemical fertilizers, cement, weapons, automobiles, toys, and consumer electronics.

**Many Chinese people work on small farms.**

## What Environmental Problems Exist?

China's economic growth has come at a high price to the environment. The burning of coal has caused bad air pollution. Beijing, China, in Asia and Mexico City, Mexico, in North America have the worst air quality in the world. Chongqing is an industrial city on the Yangtze River. Lampposts in that city had to be replaced because acid rain had eaten them away.

Chinese cities are like Mexico City in another way. They are growing so fast that the government cannot provide all of the services the people need. For example, many people do not have safe water to drink. Human and industrial waste flow into the sea without being treated.

Deforestation is another problem. Some farmers cut down trees on steep hillsides to provide more farmland for their families. This often causes soil erosion. Some experts believe that China has lost 20 percent of its **arable land** since 1949. Arable land is land on which farmers can raise crops. Many industrialized countries, including the United States, have lost arable land because of economic development. This has happened in China. Homes, factories, and businesses now cover farmland. However, poor management is the main reason for the loss of good farmland in China.

Another environmental problem is finding enough water. Some experts believe that as many as 300 Chinese cities face serious water shortages. The **water table** is dropping. A water table is the level at which underground water can be reached. For example, in 1950, workers in Beijing had to drill only 16 feet into the ground to reach water. Now, they must drill 165 feet. The problem is most serious in western China.

As in most countries, China is trying to take care of its environment while developing its economy. This is not easy to do. For example, the government is building a huge series of dams on the Yangtze River. This Three Gorges Dam Project will control flooding and generate hydroelectric power. However, some people think that the project could harm the environment.

**The Building of the Three Gorges Dam in China**

In 1994, China began to build the Three Gorges Dam at Sandouping. When completed, the dam will be the world's largest. It will create a 385-mile-long and 575-feet-deep reservoir, or lake, behind it. The dam will control flooding along the Yangtze River. It will also provide hydroelectricity that will reduce air pollution from burning coal. Finally, the dam will make the Yangtze navigable for 1,400 miles.

The dam's reservoir will flood 570,00 acres of fertile land. It will cover nearly 2,000 villages, towns, and cities. Over one million people will lose their homes. Environmentalists say that the Chinese alligator, the finless porpoise, the river dolphin, and the white crane will become extinct. Some scientists think that the reservoir's weight will cause an earthquake that will destroy the dam. Because of all this, many engineers believe that a series of smaller dams along the Yangtze would be better.

**Section 4 Review** Choose the letter of the answer that correctly completes each sentence. Write your answers on a separate sheet of paper.

1) China used to have a _____ economy that the government controlled.
   a. free-market     c. capitalist
   b. staple     d. centralized

2) The Chinese economy is now moving toward becoming a _____ economy.
   a. free-market     c. socialist
   b. staple     d. Communist

3) _____ provides over 70 percent of China's energy needs.
   a. Oil     c. Hydroelectric power
   b. Coal     d. Atomic energy

4) China is the world's leading producer of _____.
   a. cars     c. textiles
   b. computers     d. steel

5) As many as 300 Chinese cities face serious _____.
   a. water shortages     c. global warming
   b. deforestation     d. desertification

**What do**
**YOU think?**

Why do you think China's economy is doing so well?

# The Secret of Silk

People sometimes call silk "the queen of fibers." A thread of silk is stronger than the same size thread of steel. Silk is light, smooth, and soft. Manufacturers can make it in a way that keeps us warm. They can also make it in a way that keeps us cool.

No one knows for sure who discovered silk or when. According to a Chinese legend, the first emperor's wife did. She was sipping a hot drink under a mulberry tree. A silkworm's cocoon accidentally fell into the hot water. As she tried to remove the cocoon, it started to fall apart. She reeled it out and discovered that one fine thread was unwinding itself from the cocoon. She had discovered silk!

This may be only a story, but historians do know that China was the first country to use silk. For about 3,000 years, the Chinese were the only people to know its secret. Their silk became famous throughout the world.

Chinese merchants sold silk to traders from ancient Persia, which is now Iran. These traders carried silk to the Middle East. At this important crossroads, the people of Europe first learned about silk. Merchants called the route from China to the shores of the Mediterranean Sea the Silk Road.

The Chinese traded other things besides silk. They sold spices to Europeans. China also sold the furs of animals unknown in Europe. Europeans learned about such fruits as peaches, apricots, and rhubarb from the Chinese. China and Europe also exchanged ideas. Traders introduced the religions of Islam and Buddhism into China.

**This woman is taking care of silkworms by feeding them their favorite food, mulberry leaves. Silk production is a major industry in China.**

## Spotlight Story Wrap-Up

1) Which is stronger, a thread of silk or a thread of steel?

2) According to legend, how was silk discovered?

3) Where was silk first used?

4) For how long were the Chinese able to keep the secret of silk?

5) What was the Silk Road?

◆ China is the third largest country in the world. High mountains, huge deserts, jungles, and seas isolated China for centuries.

◆ China has four geographic regions: the North China Plain, the Manchurian Plain, highlands and plateaus, and deserts and steppes.

◆ Mountains are the most important physical feature of China. At 29,028 feet, Mount Everest in the Himalayas is the highest point on Earth.

◆ The three most important Chinese rivers are the Huang, the Yangtze, and the Xi. All three rivers are important highways to the middle of China.

◆ About 92 percent of Chinese people are Han Chinese. Those remaining belong to minority groups, such as the Zhuang, the Uygurs, Mongols, and the Tibetans.

◆ The Communists who rule China say that religion misleads people. However, many Chinese people still follow their ancient beliefs. Confucius greatly influenced them. The Uygurs are Muslims. Most Tibetans practice Buddhism. A small number of Chinese are Christians.

◆ More people in the world speak Chinese than speak English. There are dozens of different dialects. About two-thirds of the Chinese people speak the Mandarin dialect. Most of the large minority groups speak their own language.

◆ China has more people than any other country. About 90 percent of these people live on about 17 percent of the land area. Most Chinese work the land. The others live in more than 3,500 cities and towns.

◆ China has enough coal and oil for itself. It has many minerals.

◆ Most Chinese people farm for a living. About 20 percent of the people work in industry. Under its new economic plan, China is developing light industry.

◆ China's main problems are population growth, lack of city housing, its relationship with Taiwan, air pollution, deforestation, soil erosion, and water shortages.

## Comprehension: Identifying Facts

On a separate sheet of paper, write the words from the Word Bank to complete each sentence.

| WORD BANK |
| --- |
| floodplain |
| ideograms |
| isolate |
| light industry |
| terraces |

1) China's geography helped to _____ it, or keep it away from other people.

2) Chinese farmers create new areas to farm by building _____ in the hillsides.

3) A _____ is an area of level land that a flooding river creates over hundreds of years.

4) The written Chinese language is made up of thousands of _____.

5) A _____ makes everyday products that people use.

## Comprehension: Multiple Choice

On a separate sheet of paper, write the letter of the answer that correctly completes each sentence.

1) China is located almost completely in the _____ latitudes.
   a. low
   b. high
   c. middle
   d. arctic

2) The highest point on Earth is _____.
   a. the North China Plain
   b. the Manchurian Plain
   c. Mount Everest
   d. the Kunlun Mountains

3) The _____ River is called "China's Sorrow" because it floods so often.
   a. Yangtze
   b. Xi
   c. Huang He
   d. Liao

4) The _____ Plateau, called "the roof of the world," is the largest highland region in the world.
   a. Qinghai-Tibet
   b. Xi
   c. Himalayan
   d. North China

**5)** The largest city in China is _____.

   a. Beijing        c. Wuhan

   b. Hong Kong     d. Shanghai

## Comprehension: Understanding Main Ideas

On a separate sheet of paper, write the answers to each question. Use complete sentences.

**1)** What is China's most important physical feature?

**2)** What cultures are there in China?

**3)** What are China's most serious environmental problems?

## Critical Thinking: Write Your Opinion

On a separate sheet of paper, write your opinion to each question. Use complete sentences.

**1)** Why are businesses all over the world interested in investing in China?

**2)** Why have Deng's economic reforms worked in China?

## Applying the Five Themes of Geography

### *Place and Movement*

Why is there a housing shortage in most Chinese cities?

Test-Taking Tip     When taking a matching test, match all the items that you know go together for sure. Cross these items out. Then try to match the items that are left.

*17*

# Japan and the Koreas

The ancient cultures of Japan and the Koreas have much in common. They are lands of great contrasts. They have great modern cities with high-rise buildings. They also have beautiful mountain areas with few people. The photo on this page shows Japan's coast. Japan and the Koreas are both surrounded by water. War has separated Korea into two parts: North and South. Japan and South Korea have strong economies and are technologically advanced. However, North Korea is one of the most isolated countries in the world. Its economy is poorly developed and it suffers from food shortages.

## Goals for Learning

▶ To describe where Japan and the Koreas are located

▶ To identify their most important features and climate

▶ To describe the culture of Japan and the Koreas

▶ To explain how and where most Japanese and Korean people live

▶ To describe their economy and the environmental challenges they face

### *Geo-Stats*

**Japan**
**Population:** 126,745,000
**Area** (in square miles): 145,875
**Major Cities:** Tokyo (capital), Yokohama, Osaka, Nagoya, Sapporo
**Major Religions:** Shintoism, Buddhism, Christianity
**Major Language:** Japanese
**Number of Daily Newspapers:** 121
**Number of Television Sets:** 100 million

**North and South Korea**
**Population:** 68,290,909
**Area** (in square miles): 84,500
**Major Cities:** Pyongyang (capital of North Korea), Seoul (capital of South Korea), Hamhung, Pusan, Inchon
**Major Religions:** Buddhism, Confucianism, Christianity
**Major Languages:** Korean, English
**Number of Daily Newspapers:** over 70
**Number of Television Sets:** 9.7 million

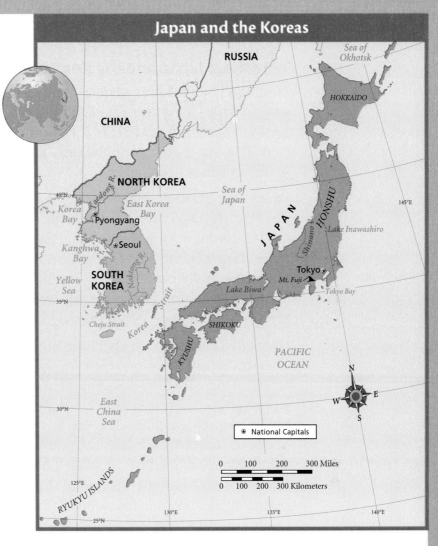

*Map Skills*

Japan is made up of many small islands and four large ones off of the eastern coast of Asia. Across the Sea of Japan to the west is a large peninsula. This peninsula contains two other countries: North Korea and South Korea.

Study the map and answer the following questions:

**1)** Which four large islands make up Japan?

**2)** What is the capital of North Korea? of South Korea?

**3)** What important bays does this map show?

**4)** What mountain is located in Honshu, Japan?

**5)** How might the geography of this region affect the way the people live?

## Where Are Japan and the Koreas Located?

North and South Korea share a peninsula on the eastern edge of Asia. China and a small part of Russia border North Korea to the north. The Yellow Sea borders Korea to the west. The Sea of Japan is to the east. The Korea Strait separates Korea from Japan.

Japan is an island nation. The Japanese archipelago is made up of nearly 4,000 islands. This string of islands gently curves around northeast Asia's mainland for about 1,800 miles. Together, the islands are about as large as the state of California in the United States. The Japanese call Japan "source of the sun," because at one time they thought that they were the first people to see the sun each day.

Four main islands make up 95 percent of Japan's land area. The northernmost island is Hokkaido. About 5 percent of Japan's people live there. South of Hokkaido is Honshu, Japan's largest island. About half of Japan's roughly 130 million people live there. The Pacific coastline of Honshu is one of the most densely populated areas in the world. Tokyo, Japan's capital city, is located on Honshu. South of Honshu is Shikoku, the smallest of the four large islands. Between Honshu and Shikoku is the Inland Sea. The southernmost island is Kyushu.

Many of Japan's smaller islands are part of the Ryukyu Islands. These islands are southwest of Japan's four larger islands.

## How Did Geography Shape This Region's History?

Japan's nearest neighbors are Korea and China. Less than 150 miles of water separates Korea and Japan. Roughly 450 miles of water separates Japan from China. In the past, sailing the seas was difficult, so these distances were great barriers. Water isolated Japan geographically. This allowed Japan to borrow from other cultures without being taken over by them.

**Samurai warriors like this one fought battles for the Japanese shoguns.**

Japanese culture has much in common with China and Korea. One written form of the Japanese language uses a writing system that came from China. Buddhism came to Japan from China through Korea. Early rulers of Japan stressed Confucian values of orderly society that obeys those in power.

Throughout much of its history, civil war divided Japan. For hundreds of years, powerful military leaders called **shoguns** fought each other for control of the land. In 1600, Tokugawa Ieyasu won an important battle. He united all of Japan. The Tokugawa family ruled Japan until 1867. They believed that dealing with foreigners was bad for their country. In 1637, the ruling family made all foreigners leave Japan. The rulers did not let Japanese people travel to other lands. Japan remained closed to outsiders for more than 200 years.

**Shogun**
*A powerful Japanese military leader*

**SECTION 1 REVIEW** On a separate sheet of paper, write *True* if the statement is true or *False* if the statement is not true. Make each false statement true by changing the underlined word.

1) North and South Korea are located on a <u>peninsula</u> on the eastern edge of Asia.

2) The Korea Strait, a narrow passageway less than 150 miles wide, separates Korea from <u>China.</u>

3) Nearly <u>1,000</u> islands make up the Japanese archipelago.

4) <u>Honshu</u> is the largest Japanese island and the one on which more than half of the Japanese people live.

5) Geography shaped <u>Japan's</u> history because water isolated it from the rest of the world.

**What do
YOU
think?**

What effects do you think the long period of isolation had on Japanese culture?

## What Are the Physical Features of This Region?

Tsunami
*A huge ocean wave produced by underwater Earth movement or volcanic eruption*

Mountains cover nearly 80 percent of Japan. Korea is also made up mostly of mountains and hills. Japan and Korea are located where several tectonic plates meet. Millions of years ago, these plates smashed together and formed the mountains. The pressure from the tectonic crash created heat. The temperature melted rocks. Volcanoes erupted, sending lava, or the melted rock, to the surface. Even today, the tectonic plates continue to rub against each other. This causes earthquakes and **tsunamis,** which are huge ocean waves. Japan has about 1,500 earthquakes every year. Underwater earthquakes or offshore volcanoes often cause the tsunamis.

Mt. Fuji in Honshu is 12,388 feet tall. It is a volcano, but it has not erupted for almost 300 years.

The Japanese Alps is Japan's longest and highest mountain range. It runs like a backbone down the length of Honshu. Mt. Fuji stands on the Pacific coast of Honshu. It is Japan's most famous landmark. This volcano, which has not erupted since 1707, has an almost perfectly shaped cone.

Japan's other main landform is a narrow coastal plain. Almost all of the Japanese people live on it. The largest area of flat land is the Kanto Plain of east-central Honshu. It is an important center of population, farming, and industry. Tokyo, the capital of Japan, and Yokohama, an important seaport, are both located on the Kanto Plain. Kinki Plain stretches across southern

Honshu. The cities of Osaka, Kyoto, and Kobe are located on this coastal plain.

Mountains cover more than 70 percent of Korea. The highest mountains are to the east and north.

The largest and highest are the Nangnim and T'aebaek ranges. The most famous mountains are Mt. Sorak in South Korea and Mt. Kumgag in North Korea.

## What Are the Main Bodies of Water?

The rivers of Japan and Korea are short, swift streams. In the past, they were important for travel. Today, trains and trucks have replaced the slow riverboats. However, the rivers are still important. The people use them to irrigate their crops and to create hydroelectric power.

Many of Japan's and Korea's lakes are located in the mountains. Some, such as the Five Fuji lakes in Japan, form when volcanic material dams a river. Others form when rain fills the bowl-shaped opening at the mouth of a volcano. This is called a **crater.** The largest of Japan's many lakes is Lake Biwa on Honshu.

The seas surrounding Japan and Korea provide fish and seaweed. The Japanese dry the seaweed. Then they use it to add flavor and protein to their food. The age-old Japanese meal consists of fish and rice. Not surprisingly, Japan is one of the world's leading fishing nations.

## What Is the Climate Like in Japan and the Koreas?

Imagine that you could place the four main islands of Japan on a map of the East Coast of the United States. You would see that Hokkaido lines up with Maine. Kyushu, Japan's southernmost island, would be roughly the same latitude as Georgia and Alabama. This means that Japan has several climates like those on the East Coast of the United States.

Northern Japan has the long, harsh winters of the humid continental climate. Icy winds blow from Siberia. As these winds cross the Sea of Japan, they pick up **moisture,** or wetness. When the winds reach the Japanese Alps, the

mountains force the winds to rise. Then they drop their moisture in the form of snow. The northwestern coastal regions of Honshu receive as much as five or six feet of snow per year.

Southern Japan includes the southern half of Honshu and the islands of Kyushu and Shikoku. This area has a humid subtropical climate. Winters are usually mild and sunny. The Japan Current is much like the Gulf Stream that warms the northeastern United States and western Europe. This warm water current helps keep temperatures mild along the coastal plain.

Korea also has several climates. In the north, the climate is humid continental. Parts of the south have an almost subtropical climate. Over half of Korea's rain falls during the summer months of June, July, and August.

During late summer and fall, **typhoons** sometimes cause flooding in Japan and Korea. These tropical windstorms form over the ocean. Most often, typhoons follow the warm ocean currents. They bring strong winds and heavy rains and sometimes damage homes and crops. (In the Americas, typhoons are called hurricanes.)

**Typhoons occur in Japan and the Koreas in the summer and late fall. They bring heavy rain and strong winds.**

Typhoon
*A tropical windstorm that forms over the ocean*

### How Does the Environment Affect the People?

Almost all of Japan is green with lots of woods. This is because plenty of rain falls and mountains cover much of the land. The Japanese people feel a special relationship with nature. Maybe that is because no part of Japan is more than 70 miles from the sea. Also, the Japanese people can see mountains from almost everywhere in their country.

Bonsai
*A small plant or tree*

Harmony
*The ability to work together and to blend in*

Individuality
*The condition in which people act and think for themselves*

Uninhabitable
*Not suited for human activity*

Because of so many mountains, nearly 80 percent of the land is **uninhabitable,** or not suited for human activity. This has forced people to live close to each other and to become dependent on each other. In America, we often stress our **individuality.** We often act and think in a way that is best for ourselves. The Japanese people think of themselves as members of a group. The group can be the family, school, community, company, or even the country. The Japanese do what is best for the group. **Harmony,** or the ability to work together and to blend in, is important to the Japanese.

The Japanese have found ways to create more space and smaller things. To create space, they store things on top of one another. They also fold things and roll them up. An example of creating smaller things is **bonsai,** which are small plants and trees.

**SECTION 2 REVIEW** On a separate sheet of paper, write the word from the Word Bank that completes each sentence.

1) The main physical feature of both Japan and Korea is _____.

2) Underwater earthquakes or offshore volcanoes can cause a _____, or huge ocean wave.

3) Both northern Japan and northern Korea have a humid _____ climate.

4) A _____ is a tropical windstorm that forms over the ocean and sometimes causes flooding and damage to homes and crops.

5) Working together and blending in, or _____, is important to the Japanese.

**WORD BANK**

continental

harmony

mountains

tsunami

typhoon

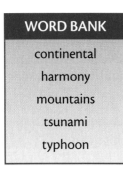

Writing About Geography

Write a poem about harmony, as defined in this section. In the poem, explain what you think harmony means and why it might be important to some people.

What do YOU think? Why are none of Japan's main cities located in the mountains?

## What Cultures Exist in This Region?

Japan has little cultural diversity. The Japanese people see themselves as a single people, living in a united country. Japan is one of the most homogeneous societies in the world. That is, the people are pretty much the same. However, Japan does have three minority groups: the **Ainu,** the Koreans, and foreign workers.

The Ainu are the original people of Japan. At one time, they lived on all or most of the Japanese islands. Starting in the 700s, invaders forced the Ainu out of most of Japan, except Hokkaido. Today, there are only about 15,000 Ainu. They have their own culture. However, the Japanese government does not recognize them as a separate ethnic group.

Koreans are the largest non-Japanese group living in Japan. Between 1910 and 1945, Japan ruled Korea. During that time, the Japanese forced many Koreans to work in Japanese factories. The descendants of these Korean workers now speak only Japanese. However, the Japanese government does not recognize them as citizens. They cannot vote in elections.

In recent years, foreign workers from neighboring countries have entered Japan. Many entered illegally. They do **manual labor,** or physical work that requires little skill. Often, they do the work that well-educated Japanese do not want to do. Most foreign workers are poor. They fear that the Japanese government will arrest them and send them back to their own countries.

Like Japan, Korea is a homogeneous society. Mountains and seas have protected it from invasion. For over 250 years, Korea was cut off from all outside contacts. Its culture developed in isolation.

## What Languages Do the People Speak?

Nearly everyone living in Japan speaks Japanese. This language developed over thousands of years. Most westerners think Japanese is a hard language to learn

**Ainu**
*The original people of Japan*

**Manual labor**
*Physical work that requires little skill*

because of the way it sounds. However, what makes it hard is really its speech "levels." Each level uses different forms of verbs, adjectives, and nouns. For example, teenagers use one level of speech when talking to their teachers. They use another level with their friends. They may use a third level with their family.

Japanese writing goes from top to bottom instead of from left to right. A written page begins in the upper right-hand corner. Japanese books begin at what westerners would call the "back" and read through to the "front." Newspapers, however, go from top to bottom and left to right.

The Korean language is unlike any other language. It is related to Turkish, Hungarian, and Finnish. It uses some Chinese characters and has the same sentence structure as Japanese. Traveling around a mountainous peninsula is hard, so many regional differences developed in Korea. People in different areas speak different dialects and eat different foods. They dress differently and even have different types of homes.

## Geography In Your Life
### FINE ARTS
### The Arts in Japan

Japan has three traditional, or centuries-old, forms of plays. The Noh play presents history and legend with music, dance, and a chorus. Everything in the Noh play follows a traditional rule. The puppet play uses puppets that stand up to four feet high. A kabuki play uses colorful costumes and makeup. The actors exaggerate their movements. That is, they make movements with more energy than normal.

Noh and kabuki plays are popular art forms in Japan.

After World War II, many artists turned away from Japan's traditional art forms. The government began to pick artists who had the courage to practice them. Japan calls these artists "Living National Treasures." These "living treasures" may dye the kimonos that women wear; weave bamboo baskets; perform with puppets; make swords; shape pottery; fold paper to make birds, flowers, and fish in the origami style; or act in Noh plays. Each artist keeps alive the treasured art forms of Japan's past.

## What Religions Do the People Practice?

The main religions in Japan are **Shintoism** and Buddhism. Not many Japanese go to a place of worship or pray regularly. However, many Japanese follow both Buddhist and Shinto customs in their everyday life.

*Shinto* means "way of the gods." This religion began thousands of years ago in Japan. The early Japanese believed that gods or spirits existed all around them in nature. Mountains, trees, rocks, and rivers were gods. By worshipping these spirits, they tried to live in harmony with nature. Nearly every Japanese town and city has a Shinto shrine. People visit the shrine to celebrate the New Year and to ask the gods for help in hard times.

Japanese Buddhists believe that humans must purify, or make clean, their hearts and minds. Arranging flowers and participating in a tea ceremony help them purify themselves. Japanese Buddhists also want to get rid of desire. They believe that judo, archery, and swordsmanship help them do this.

Buddhists believe in **reincarnation.** This is the belief that when people die, their souls are reborn into another living form. Buddhists do not think that death is the end of everything. Because of this, most Japanese pray to Buddha as they get older. Most funerals are Buddhist, and Buddhist priests lead the funerals. They say prayers for the person who died. Most Japanese see no problem in believing in more than one religion.

Like the Japanese, many Koreans combine the beliefs of several religions. However, most identify themselves as Buddhists. With regard to religion, Korea is different from Japan in one big way. More Koreans are Christians. Only about 1 percent of the Japanese people are Christians. However, nearly 25 percent of all Koreans are Christians. Most belong to Protestant churches, although there are over two million Roman Catholics. South Korea has more Christians than any other country in Asia, except for the Philippines.

## What Problems Do the People Face?

One of Japan's biggest problems is the change in population balance. People are having fewer children, so the birthrate is dropping. In 1930, the average number of children per family was 4.7. Now it is less than 1.5. This means the number of younger people is falling. However, the number of older people is rising. The Japanese have the longest life expectancy of any ethnic group. Both males and females born today in Japan may live more than 80 years. (In the United States, life expectancy is 76 for men and 77 for women.) The number of people in the workforce is getting smaller. This is happening because there are fewer young people to fill the jobs. At the same time, more older people are retiring.

Urbanization is a second problem for Japan. Eleven of Japan's cities have more than a million people. Some are so close to each other that they form a megalopolis. The Tokyo-Yokohama megalopolis is the largest in the world. More than 28 million people live in it. Its population density is 37,000 people per square mile. To understand how crowded this is, think of 64 people making their homes on a football field. Osaka, Kyoto, and Kobe make up another large urban area.

Urbanization is a problem for South Korea, too. One quarter of its people live in the capital city of Seoul. However, the biggest problem facing Korea is a political one. Since 1945, Korea has been a divided country. North Korea, or the Democratic People's Republic of Korea, is Communist. Its economy is based on farming and it is becoming more isolated. On the other hand, the people of South Korea, or the Republic of Korea, are much freer. They live in an industrial nation and seek closer ties with other countries.

Most Koreans hope that one day the two Korean republics will be united again. In June 2000, leaders of North and South Korea met and promised to work toward reuniting Korea. The Koreans still have to work out how to do this. However, this meeting was an important first step.

The world has many cities with large populations. This chart shows the 15 most populated cities. How many cities on this list are in Asia? What is the population of Seoul, South Korea? Osaka, Japan? How many of these 15 cities are in the United States? What is the U.S. city with the highest population? How many people live there?

### Most Populated Cities in the World

| City | Population |
| --- | --- |
| Tokyo, Japan | 28,836,000 |
| São Paulo, Brazil | 16,417,000 |
| New York, United States | 16,329,000 |
| Shanghai, China | 15,082,000 |
| Mexico City, Mexico | 15,048,000 |
| Bombay, India | 12,572,000 |
| Los Angeles, United States | 12,410,000 |
| Beijing, China | 12,362,000 |
| Seoul, South Korea | 11,641,000 |
| Jakarta, Indonesia | 11,500,000 |
| Buenos Aires, Argentina | 11,256,000 |
| Calcutta, India | 10,916,000 |
| Tianjin, China | 10,687,000 |
| Osaka, Japan | 10,601,000 |
| Lagos, Nigeria | 10,287,000 |

**SECTION 3 REVIEW** On a separate sheet of paper, write answers to these questions.

1) What are the original people of Japan called?

2) What makes spoken Japanese so difficult for most westerners?

3) What religion is common to both Japan and Korea?

4) What is reincarnation?

5) Why is the change in population balance a problem for Japan?

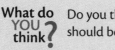

**What do YOU think?** Do you think that North and South Korea should be reunited? Explain your answer.

## What Is the Economy Like?

Japan's economy is the second strongest in the world. Only the economy of the United States is stronger. Until recently, South Korea's economy had been growing quickly.

Japan and South Korea each have a strong economy for many reasons. The workforce is large, hardworking, and skilled. The governments offer money and technology to help industry develop. The governments also encourage the export of Japanese and South Korean products and limit foreign imports. Companies apply new ideas, such as **robotics.** This technology uses machines to do factory work. More than half of the industrial robots in the world are in Japan. The United States has also helped Japan and South Korea. The U.S. has invested and loaned millions of dollars to the two countries.

**Export economy**
*A type of economy in which a country depends on exports for growth*

**Robotics**
*The technology of using machines to do factory work*

The economies of both Japan and South Korea are **export economies.** In this type of economy, a country depends on exports for growth. Trade with other countries is very important. One example is the automobile industry. Japan makes 25 percent of all the cars sold in the United States.

Japan has huge investments in other countries. Labor and other costs are high in Japan. Japanese companies have built factories in countries where costs are lower, such as Taiwan, Vietnam, and Malaysia. South Korea is now following Japan's example and is building factories in other countries.

## What Natural Resources Exist?

Japan has few natural resources. It imports raw materials like oil, coal, iron ore, copper, aluminum, and wood. Japan spends more money on oil than any other imported product. To reduce its need for imported oil, Japan has developed nuclear power. However, nuclear power produces dangerous waste and risks nuclear accidents.

The automobile industry is a major part of Japan's export economy. This photo shows cars being assembled at a Japanese auto plant.

**Consumer electronics**
*Electronic products that people use in their homes*

Japan must import nearly all the raw materials it uses in manufacturing. Japan must ensure the flow of these materials. To do this, Japan has invested millions of dollars in resource-rich countries, such as Russia, Indonesia, and Australia.

Korea has a little more natural resources. Pyongyang, the capital of North Korea, is located near large deposits of coal and iron ore. Like Japan, South Korea must depend on imported raw materials and on nuclear power.

## What Are Some Important Industries?

Japan is a world leader in technology. It has created industries around many different kinds of electronics. However, cars are Japan's biggest industry and most important export. Japan also manufactures steel, ships, machinery, electrical equipment, and chemicals. Nearly 25 percent of Japanese workers are in manufacturing jobs. Almost 60 percent have jobs in the service industries.

South Korea manufactures **consumer electronics.** These are products like microwave ovens, toasters, televisions, stereo equipment, and computers. It has large steel mills. It also makes textiles and clothing.

## What Environmental Problems Exist?

The growth of industry after World War II has led to serious air and water pollution in Japan. One cause of air pollution is too many automobiles. Another cause is the use of too much oil that contains sulfur. Japan's mountains also block the winds that might blow the pollution away. Since the 1970s, the Japanese government has spent billions of dollars to cut down pollution.

A second problem is too much garbage. Every person in Japan throws away over 2.2 pounds of garbage a day. Factories and construction add to the waste. The Japanese have few places to bury their garbage, so they burn it. This adds to air pollution. Japan is now creating new land with the garbage. This is done by closing off areas of the sea and draining the water. Then the dry area is filled with garbage and covered with soil.

| Biography | AKIO MORITA: 1921–1999 |

In Japan, the group, not the individual, is important. However, Akio Morita is one Japanese businessman who was an important individual. He founded a global electronics company. With his partner, Masaru Ibuka, Morita introduced Japan's first transistor radio in 1955. In 1960, his company introduced the world's first transistor television. In 1979 came the hand-held tape player with headphones that a person could wear while walking. Morita changed the way the world thought of Japanese products. Now, many people think of him as the most important Asian man of the twentieth century.

**SECTION 4 REVIEW** Choose the letter of the answer that correctly completes each sentence. Write your answers on a separate sheet of paper.

1) The Japanese and South Korean governments help their economy by limiting _____.

   a. exports          c. investment

   b. imports         d. robotics

2) Using machines to do factory work is called _____.

   a. consumer electronics  c. robotics

   b. nuclear power      d. free market

3) _____ are Japan's most important export.

   a. Electronics       c. Chemicals

   b. Machinery       d. Cars

4) Nearly 60 percent of Japanese workers work in _____ industries.

   a. fishing          c. manufacturing

   b. service         d. construction

5) Japan has invested money in resource-rich countries such as _____.

   a. North Korea     c. France

   b. Russia         d. all of the above

**What do YOU think?** What do you think would happen to Japan's economy if the country were to become isolated like it was in the past?

# Sumo—An Ancient Tradition

Sumo wrestling is Japan's national sport. It is more than 1,500 years old. In the past, Japan held matches at local Shinto shrines. They did this during rice planting and harvesting as a way to please the gods. Today, sumo combines sport and ritual. Every year, Japan holds six major tournaments.

Sumo wrestlers are all men. Most weigh over 300 pounds. Some weigh nearly 500 pounds. Wrestlers wear a cloth around their hips. They style their hair in a topknot. The wrestling ring is a circle that is 15 feet across. Its surface is made of hand-packed clay covered with a thin layer of sand.

**Sumo wrestling is a mixture of sport and ritual. Wrestlers are very large, but they need to have great strength, speed, and balance.**

When the two men enter the ring, they go through several steps. First, they clap their hands together twice. Then they show their palms to prove that they are not carrying any weapons. Next, they raise their feet high and stamp several times. This drives away the evil spirits. Then they toss salt into the air. By doing this, they purify themselves and the ring.

To win, the sumo wrestler must force his opponent out of the ring or throw him to the ground. As soon as this happens, the match is over. Matches usually last less than a minute. People who do not understand this Japanese sport think that the wrestlers are just pushing and shoving. However, sumo requires great strength, balance, speed, and a long training period.

## Spotlight Story Wrap-Up

1) What is Japan's national sport?

2) When and where were sumo matches held in the past?

3) What is the purpose of throwing salt into the air?

4) Why do the wrestlers stamp their feet down several times before the match?

5) What determines who wins the match?

◆ Japan is an East Asian country made up of many small islands and four large ones.

◆ Across the Sea of Japan is the large peninsula of Korea, made up of the nations of North Korea and South Korea.

◆ Water and rulers isolated Japan for hundreds of years. Mountains and seas isolated Korea. This isolation shaped both cultures.

◆ Mountains are the most important physical feature of Japan and Korea. Japan's other main landform is a coastal plain.

◆ The rivers of Japan and Korea are short, swift streams. They provide water for irrigation and hydroelectric power. The seas provide fish, which is a staple of the Japanese diet.

◆ Northern Japan has a humid continental climate. Southern Japan has a humid subtropical climate. The northern part of Korea has a humid continental climate. Parts of the south have an almost subtropical climate.

◆ Because of mountains, nearly 80 percent of Japan is uninhabitable. This has forced the Japanese to become dependent on one another and to value the group and harmony.

◆ Both Japan and Korea are homogeneous societies. Only three minorities live in Japan: the Ainu, the Koreans, and foreign workers.

◆ Buddhism and Shintoism are the main religions. Most Koreans identify themselves as Buddhists. However, nearly 25 percent are Christians.

◆ Nearly everyone living in Japan speaks Japanese. The Korean language is unlike any other.

◆ Both Japan and South Korea have export economies. Japan's economy is the second strongest in the world. Cars are its biggest industry and most important export. Consumer electronics is a big industry in South Korea.

◆ Both South Korea and Japan depend on imported raw materials. North Korea has coal and iron ore.

◆ Japan's main problems are the change in population balance between young and old, air and water pollution, and too much garbage.

◆ Korea's biggest problem is reuniting the two republics.

◆ Both Japan and Korea face the problems of urbanization.

## Comprehension: Identifying Facts

On a separate sheet of paper, use the words from the Word Bank to complete each sentence.

| WORD BANK |
| --- |
| exports |
| group |
| Mt. Fuji |
| peninsula |
| robotics |

1) Korea is on a _____ on the eastern edge of Asia.

2) The Japanese think of themselves as members of a _____ and not as individuals as westerners do.

3) Japan's most famous landmark and highest peak is _____.

4) The technology that uses machines for factory work is _____.

5) The economies of Japan and South Korea depend heavily on _____.

## Comprehension: Multiple Choice

On a separate sheet of paper, write the letter of the answer that correctly completes each sentence.

1) Japan is located in _____.
   a. eastern Asia        c. southern Asia
   b. western Asia        d. northern Asia

2) The most common physical feature of Japan and Korea is _____.
   a. mountains        c. plains
   b. deserts        d. many islands

3) The two main religions of Japan are Buddhism and _____.
   a. Christianity        c. Islam
   b. Shintoism        d. Hinduism

4) Japan's culture is _____ because almost all of the people belong to the same ethnic group.
   a. dominant        c. homogeneous
   b. mainstream        d. diverse

**5)** The cities of Tokyo and Yokohama form a _____.

   a. peninsula        c. megalopolis

   b. mountain        d. industry

## Comprehension: Understanding Main Ideas

On a separate sheet of paper, write the answers to each question. Use complete sentences.

**1)** What are three environmental and two social problems that Japan faces?

**2)** What is the climate like in Japan and Korea?

## Critical Thinking: Write Your Opinion

On a separate sheet of paper, write your opinion to each question. Use complete sentences.

**1)** What was most important in shaping the unique cultures of Japan and Korea? Explain your answer.

**2)** Why do you think South Korea's economy is so much more developed than North Korea's?

**3)** The United States stresses individuality, or the ability to think for oneself. Why do you think this is not as important to the Japanese people?

## Applying the Five Themes of Geography

### *Interaction*

Japan is the world's leading producer of pearls. Oysters produce natural pearls. Only a few oysters, however, produce pearls. A Japanese man named Kokichi Mikimoto invented a process to create almost perfect pearls from every oyster. How does this show the theme of interaction?

**Test-Taking Tip**    When taking a multiple-choice test, read every choice before you answer a question. Put a line through choices you know are wrong. Then choose the best answer from the remaining choices.

# Understanding Special-Purpose Maps

H ave you ever drawn a map for someone? If so, that map was probably a special-purpose map. A special-purpose map shows information beyond what a physical or political map shows. It shows special information such as roads, climates, vegetation, population, resources, time zones, or ethnic groups.

Special-purpose maps use symbols. These objects represent things on a map. Special-purpose maps also have a key, or legend. It shows what the symbols stand for. On some maps, the symbols are letters or colors. On other maps, they may be pictures or shapes.

The map on this page is a resource map of North Korea and South Korea. It has two special purposes. It shows where you can find natural resources in these two nations. It also shows where you can find agricultural products in them.

Study the map on this page and answer the following questions.

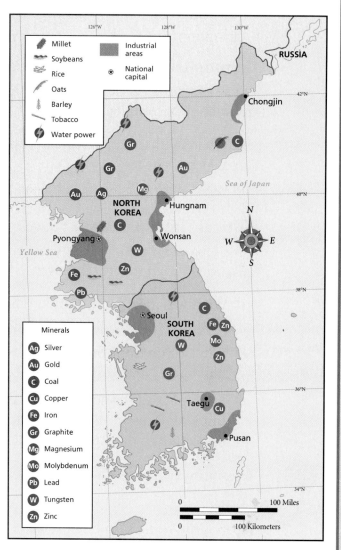

1) What minerals can be found in North and South Korea?

2) What crops can be found in North and South Korea?

3) What is the special purpose of this map?

4) What other kinds of special-purpose maps are there?

5) How can you tell whether a map is a special-purpose map?

◆ China is the third largest country in the world. Japan is made up of many small islands and four large ones. Korea occupies a peninsula across the Sea of Japan.

◆ Mountains are the most important physical feature of China, Japan, and Korea. For centuries, these mountains and the sea isolated these nations. This isolation shaped their cultures.

◆ The three most important Chinese rivers are the Huang He, the Yangtze, and the Xi. They are highways into the middle of China. Japanese and Korean rivers are short, swift streams that provide water for irrigation and hydroelectric power.

◆ About 92 percent of Chinese people are Han Chinese. The remaining people belong to several minority groups. Both Japan and Korea are homogeneous societies.

◆ The Chinese Communists mistrust religion. However, many Chinese people still follow their ancient beliefs, which Confucius influenced. Several Chinese minorities practice Islam. The main religions in Japan are Shintoism and Buddhism. Most Koreans are Buddhists, but nearly 25 percent are Christians.

◆ More people in the world speak Chinese than speak English. Most of China's large minority groups speak their own language. Nearly everyone living in Japan speaks Japanese. The Korean language is unlike any other.

◆ China has more people than any other country. About 90 percent of them live on about 17 percent of the land area. Most Chinese people work the land. Because of mountains, people inhabit only about 20 percent of Japan. About half of them live on Honshu.

◆ Japan's economy is the second strongest in the world. Cars are its biggest industry and most important export. Consumer electronics is a big industry in South Korea. Both South Korea and Japan depend on imported raw materials. China has enough coal and oil for itself. Most Chinese people farm for a living. Both Japan and South Korea have export economies.

◆ Japan's main problems are the change in population balance, air and water population, and too much garbage. Korea's biggest problem is reuniting the two republics. Among China's problems are population growth, its relationship with Taiwan, deforestation, and water shortages.

"A nation's culture resides in the hearts and in the soul of its people."

—Mohandas Gandhi, political leader of India during the 1930s and 1940s

# South Asia, Southeast Asia, and the Pacific

In Unit 6, you studied China, Japan, and Korea. Now, you travel to the subcontinent of South Asia. Perhaps you will wear hiking boots to cross the Khyber Pass from Afghanistan into India. Invaders have slipped through this pass for thousands of years. When you leave India, you will cross the seas to Southeast Asia. There, you will hear over 1,000 different languages. Finally, you will sail into the Pacific World of Australia and New Zealand. The photo on this page shows Uluru, also known as Ayers Rock, in Australia. You will learn about this and many other features in this unit.

### CHAPTERS IN UNIT 7

**Chapter 18:** South Asia . . . . . . . . . . . . . . . . . . . . . . . . . . . .400

**Chapter 19:** Southeast Asia . . . . . . . . . . . . . . . . . . . . . . .420

**Chapter 20:** The Pacific World . . . . . . . . . . . . . . . . . . . .440

*18*

# South Asia

Afghanistan, Pakistan, India, Sri Lanka, Nepal, Bhutan, and Bangladesh make up South Asia. India is its largest country and has more than a billion people. It has an ancient civilization and is the birthplace of two of the world's great religions: Buddhism and Hinduism. South Asia is a region of great economic, political, cultural, and geographical differences. The photo to the left shows the Ganges, one of the most important rivers on the Indian subcontinent.

## Goals for Learning

▶ To describe the location of the Indian subcontinent
▶ To identify its most important physical features and its climates
▶ To describe its diverse cultures
▶ To explain where and how most people live in South Asia
▶ To describe the economy and the environmental challenges it faces

 *Geo-Stats*

### Key Nations of South Asia

**Nation:** Bangladesh
**Population:** 125,721,000
**Area** (in square miles): 55,598
**Major Cities:** Dhaka (capital), Chittagong, Khulna, Rajshashi, Rangpur

 **Nation:** India
**Population:** 1,000,848,550
**Area** (in square miles): 1,269,346
**Major Cities:** New Delhi (capital), Bombay, Delhi, Calcutta

 **Nation:** Pakistan
**Population:** 146,488,000
**Area** (in square miles): 307,374
**Major Cities:** Islamabad (capital), Karachi, Lahore, Faisalabad

 **Nation:** Sri Lanka
**Population:** 19,003,000
**Area** (in square miles): 25,332
**Major Cities:** Colombo (capital), Dehiwala-Mount Lavinia, Moratuwa, Jaffna

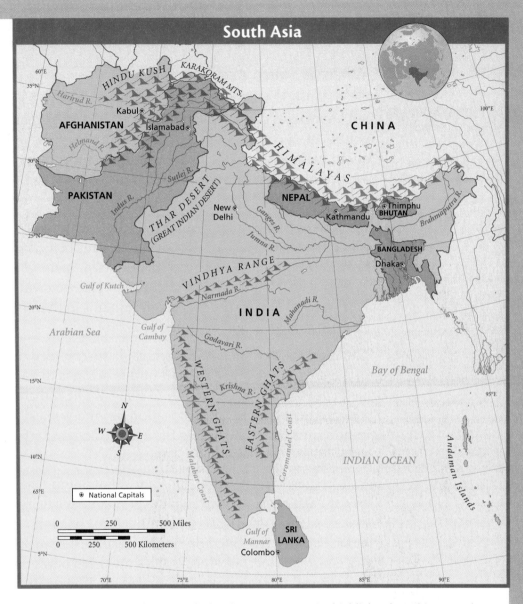

## South Asia

*Map Skills*

South Asia includes the seven countries highlighted on this map. The northern part of this region is mountainous. The mighty Himalayas there contain some of the highest peaks in the world. Two rivers, the Indus and the Ganges, are also important to this region.

Study the map and answer the following questions:

1) Which two mountain ranges are located on the western and eastern coasts of India?

2) Which desert is located in northwestern India?

3) Which island nation is located southeast of India?

4) Which bodies of water surround India?

5) How do you think the geography of this region affects the people?

## Where Is South Asia Located?

The peninsula of South Asia is sometimes called a **subcontinent,** or a large landmass that is smaller than a continent. It covers about 1.5 million square miles, which is about half the size of the U.S. Most of the subcontinent is located in the low latitudes between the equator and the Tropic of Cancer.

Millions of years ago, the Indian subcontinent was a huge island floating on a large tectonic plate. This plate drifted northward until it crashed into the Eurasian plate. The Indian plate pushed under the Eurasian plate to create the Himalayas. They are the highest mountains in the world. They separate South Asia from the rest of Asia.

The Indian subcontinent is a peninsula surrounded by the Indian Ocean. The western part of this ocean is the Arabian Sea. The eastern part is the Bay of Bengal. The Indian subcontinent has a strategic location. It is between several important regions, including the Middle East and Africa to the west and Southeast Asia to the east.

India shares borders with China and all of South Asia, except Afghanistan and Sri Lanka. Sri Lanka is a tear-shaped island located 22 miles off the coast of southern India. Pakistan is located on India's northwest border. Afghanistan is located on Pakistan's northern border. India's neighbor to the east is Bangladesh. The small kingdoms of Nepal and Bhutan are located among the Himalayas.

## How Did Geography Shape This Region's History?

Much of the time, mountains have protected South Asia from invaders. However, many armies have marched into South Asia. They reached India through mountain passes like the Khyber Pass. Armies have tried to take control of Afghanistan because it controls this pass.

The people who came through the mountain passes changed the history of the subcontinent. Each group brought new ideas. The newcomers sometimes married the people who had come before. The cultures of the region today reflect the many different groups that came through the passes.

Rivers play an important part in the history of South Asia. One of the first great civilizations developed in the Indus River Valley. Around 2500 B.C., people there grew wheat and rice and herded cattle. Harappa and Mohenjo-Daro, their two great cities, had wide, straight streets and houses made of clay bricks.

## What Regions Exist in South Asia?

South Asia can be divided into four geographical regions. Mountains are the first region. The Himalayas, the Hindu Kush, and other mountains stretch for more than 1,500 miles across the northern part of South Asia. Few people can live on the steep slopes of the mountains.

The Indo-Gangetic Plain is a second region. Most of India's people live on this plain. It begins at the Indus River in Pakistan. It continues west to the delta of the Ganges River. The Ganges deposits fertile **alluvial** soil on the floodplain. Flooding rivers leave behind alluvial soil.

The third region is the peninsula. Its largest part is the Deccan Plateau south of the Indo-Gangetic Plain. Much of India's mineral wealth is in the northeastern part of the peninsula.

The Thar, or Great Indian Desert, is the fourth region. This western desert covers nearly 100,000 square miles and separates India from Pakistan.

**Section 1 Review** On a separate sheet of paper, write *True* if the statement is true or *False* if the statement is not true. Make each false statement true by changing the underlined word.

1) The Indian subcontinent is a huge island.

2) The bay east of India is the Bay of Bengal.

3) Nepal and Bhutan are located among the Himalayas.

4) Armies marched into India through the Khyber Pass.

5) Much of India's mineral wealth is in the Thar Desert.

**What do YOU think?**

In what ways do you think geography has helped or hurt the people of South Asia?

### What Are the Main Physical Features of South Asia?

The Himalayas form the natural boundary between India and China. These mountains are the main physical feature of South Asia. The Himalayas are actually made up of some smaller ranges, including the Karakoram and the Hindu Kush.

The Karakoram forms the border of Pakistan and China. The Hindu Kush is located mostly in Afghanistan. These young mountains continue to shift, grow, and move. The world's highest mountain peak is Mt. Everest. It is located near the border between Nepal and Tibet. *Himalaya* means "home of the snows" in Nepali, the official language of Nepal. Glaciers and snow cover the mountains of India year round.

The Deccan Plateau is another interesting landform. Part of it is 600 million years old! The plateau covers most of the Indian subcontinent. Most of this flat land stands about 3,200 feet high. The highlands of the Eastern and Western Ghats border the plateau. Some parts of the plateau have rich volcanic soil. However, much of it is dry. Enough rain falls in the northeast to support farming. The western and southern parts have little rain, so farming is difficult.

### What Are the Major Rivers?

The Ganges River begins in the Himalayas and flows to the heartland of India, the Indo-Gangetic Plain. One third of India's people live on this plain. The Ganges joins the Brahmaputra River in the easternmost part of the plain. The low floodplain and delta of the two rivers make up most of Bangladesh. This low-lying delta is one of the most densely populated places in the world. Each year, the rivers flood much of the floodplain and destroy the crops. Fields often lie under water.

The third important river of South Asia is the Indus. It flows from the Himalayan and Karakoram ranges south to the Arabian Sea. The river forms a large floodplain that is the richest farm region of Pakistan. The Pakistani province of Punjab is in the northern part of this region. *Punjab* means "the five waters." The people call the area Punjab because five important tributaries of the Indus flow through it. Most of Pakistan's people live in Punjab.

## What Is the Climate Like in South Asia?

The Indian subcontinent has many climates. The **monsoon** winds influence the Indian climate. These winds change direction according to the time of year. Two monsoon winds blow over India. In summer, southwest winds blow toward the huge low pressure area over Central Asia. They bring heavy rains. In winter, the winds blow from Central Asia to the ocean. Little rain falls during this time. In autumn, the monsoon changes to the northeast. This wind is weaker than the summer monsoon, but farmers in east India still depend on it. The northeast monsoon can draw **cyclones** off the Bay of Bengal. Cyclones are storms with strong winds that spin in a circular motion. They damage low-lying coastal areas. In 1990, cyclones killed many people in India and Bangladesh and caused millions of dollars in damage.

Monsoons bring heavy rainfall that can cause flooding in South Asia, as this photo shows.

Most of India, Sri Lanka, and Bangladesh have either tropical monsoon or tropical savanna climates. Temperatures are hot year around because these areas are close to the equator. The coastal areas of India that receive high seasonal rainfall have monsoon forests. The savannas are located farther north. Their natural vegetation is grasses with a few trees. Most of the Deccan Plateau has a tropical savanna climate.

Northern Pakistan and the foothill area south of the Himalayas in northern India have a humid subtropical climate. This climate differs from the tropical climates in that there is a cooler season. Rain falls all year around, although most of it falls in the summer.

**The Richter Scale**

Seismologists are scientists who study earthquakes. One tool they use is the Richter scale. It records ground movements caused by earthquakes. Charles Richter, himself a seismologist, developed this tool in 1935. Its scale is a series of numbers. Each number represents a tenfold increase in the distance the ground moves. Imagine that an earthquake records 7 on the scale. That would mean that the ground moved 10 times more than it moved for a recording of 6.

While moving the ground, an earthquake releases energy. Each number on the Richter scale represents a release of about 30 times the amount of energy represented by the number below it. An earthquake that records 7 would release 30 times the energy of a 6 recording.

Few earthquakes that record 5 or less cause much damage. However, an earthquake that records around 7 or higher can kill many people and cause great damage. For example, an earthquake of 6.9 on the Richter scale killed over 4,700 people in Afghanistan in 1998.

The Indus River Valley of Pakistan and much of Afghanistan have a steppe climate. It is dry and hot much of the year. Farming depends on irrigation. The Indus Valley is one of the world's largest irrigated regions in the world. Western Pakistan has a desert climate. It receives less than five inches of rain a year. Summers are hot, but winter temperatures may reach freezing. Nepal and Bhutan have a highland climate. Temperatures are cooler the higher a person travels in these mountain kingdoms. Most people are subsistence farmers or they herd animals. Snow covers the ground much of the year.

**Section 2 Review** On a separate sheet of paper, write the words from the Word Bank that complete each sentence.

**WORD BANK**

Deccan

Indus

Himalaya

monsoon

humid subtropical

1) The Nepali word _____ means "home of the snows."

2) The _____ Plateau is 600 million years old.

3) The three major rivers of South Asia are the Ganges, Brahmaputra, and _____.

4) A _____ is a wind that changes direction according to the time of year.

5) Northern Pakistan has a _____ climate.

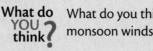

**What do YOU think?** What do you think happens if the monsoon winds fail?

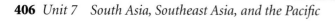

## What Cultures Exist in South Asia?

South Asia has many cultures with great diversity in religion, languages, and education. The culture of the people who live in villages differs from those who live in cities. People from the east and south are usually shorter and darker skinned than people in the north. People in different areas eat different food and dress in different ways. Technology, education, and contact with other cultures are changing this region.

## What Languages Do the People Speak?

Many languages are spoken on the subcontinent. Hindi is the national language of India. However, only one-third of the people, mainly in the north, speak it. From 1750–1947, India was a colony of Great Britain, so English is the language of government and larger businesses. India has more than a thousand other languages. The many languages cause communication problems.

Many people in Pakistan and Bangladesh also speak English. However, the national language of Pakistan is Urdu. Many people also speak Punjabi. In Bangladesh, most people speak Bengali. Many people in the southern part of the subcontinent speak Dravidian languages. Among these is Tamil. It is one of the two languages spoken in Sri Lanka. The other language is Sinhalese. Most of the people living in Nepal and about a quarter of those living in Bhutan speak Nepali. Bhutan's official language is called Dzongkha.

## What Is Hinduism?

Many people in this region practice **Hinduism.** This religion began about 5,000 years ago. Most Indians are Hindu. Hindus worship many gods, but they worship three main ones: **Brahma, Vishnu,** and **Shiva.** Brahma is the creative face, Vishnu is the preserving face, and Shiva is the destroying face of God.

Brahma
*A Hindu god; the creative face of God*

Hinduism
*A religion in which followers worship many gods*

Shiva
*A Hindu god; the destroying face of God*

Vishnu
*A Hindu god; the preserving face of God*

Many Hindu temples such as this one exist in India.

Hindus believe in reincarnation. This is the belief that when a person dies, the person's soul is reborn into another living form. Many Hindus think of life as a play in which each person plays a part. This is their **dharma,** or duty. The way people perform their dharma determines their future, or their **karma.** If they follow their dharma well and have good karma, they may be reborn to a higher level in the next life. The goal of Hinduism is to break this cycle of reincarnation. Then a person becomes one with the eternal spirit. This perfect state of mind is **nirvana.**

Caste
*A Hindu social group*

Dharma
*One's duty*

Jati
*A small group within a larger caste*

Karma
*One's future*

Nirvana
*A perfect state of mind*

Untouchable
*A Hindu who belongs to no caste and works with death, blood, leather, and dirt*

Hinduism is both a religion and a way of life. Hindus believe that hurting people and animals is wrong, so many do not eat meat. They also believe that a person is born into a **caste,** or social group. The priests and their families belong to the highest caste. People cannot change the caste they are born into in this life. However, if they fulfill their dharma, they may return in a higher caste in the next life.

Each of the four main caste groups is divided into smaller groups called **jatis.** Members of different jatis do not mix with members of other jatis. People marry within their own jati. Each jati has its own rules about what foods to eat and other social practices. Each jati is linked to one type of job.

One group of people, the **untouchables,** does not belong to any caste. Other Hindus look down upon the untouchables because they do the dirtiest jobs. They work with death, blood, leather, and dirt.

### What Other Religions Do the People Practice?

Islam is also a common religion in South Asia. Almost all of the people of Afghanistan, Pakistan, and Bangladesh are Muslims.

**Jainism**
*A religion that began as a protest against the caste system*

**Poverty**
*The condition in which people lack one or more of the basic things needed to live*

**Sikhism**
*A religion that combines parts of the Muslim religion with Hinduism*

A large number of Buddhists live in Bhutan and Sri Lanka. Millions of Sikhs live in northern India. **Sikhism** was founded in the 1500s. It combines the Muslim belief in one god with the Hindu belief in reincarnation. However, it has no caste system. Sikhism and **Jainism** began as protests against the caste system. Jainists respect all life. They do not even kill insects. They refuse to farm because they might harm living things. Because of this, many Jains have become successful in business. About 20 million Christians also live in India. Most Christians live in the south. Many untouchables have converted to Christianity.

## What Problems Do the People Face?

The biggest problem in South Asia is **poverty**. Poverty means that people lack one or more of the basic things needed to live. They may not have enough food, housing, health care, or educational services.

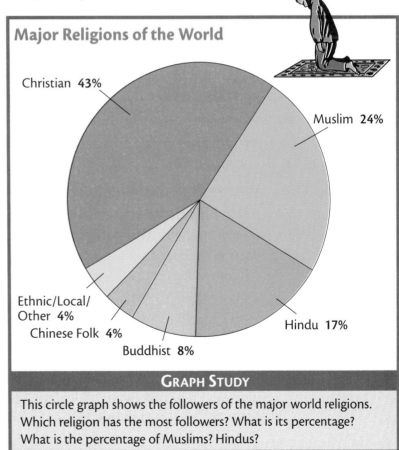

**Major Religions of the World**

Christian 43%
Muslim 24%
Hindu 17%
Buddhist 8%
Chinese Folk 4%
Ethnic/Local/Other 4%

**GRAPH STUDY**

This circle graph shows the followers of the major world religions. Which religion has the most followers? What is its percentage? What is the percentage of Muslims? Hindus?

Per capita income is one way to compare countries. It is the average amount of wealth for everyone in a country. To determine this income, divide the total wealth a country produces in one year by the number of people. Using 1997 figures, the per capita income in the U.S. is nearly $29,000. The per capita income in India is $390!

The caste system is another problem. The Indian government has tried to end this system and give people in the lower castes more opportunities. The caste system, however, is an old tradition. Change is hard. Most Hindus think that the caste is an important part of their religion.

Another problem is population growth. In 2000, the population of India went over a billion. The birthrate is dropping, but the death rate is dropping faster because of better health and cleaner living conditions. The birthrate is dropping because of better family planning, improved education for girls and women, changes in ideas about family size, and changes in the age of marriage.

Another big problem is urbanization and migration. Most people still live in the countryside, but towns and cities are growing. People are leaving rural areas and moving into urban areas where there are more opportunities for work. Many end up living in shantytowns. Usually, these lack running water and trash collection.

## Why Is Civil and Religious Unrest a Problem?

In 1947, India became independent of Great Britain. However, the British **partitioned,** or split, India into two parts. This partition caused many problems because of religious differences. Indians were mainly Hindu. However, there were many Muslims in eastern and western India. Eastern India became East Pakistan. Western India became West Pakistan. The partition left millions of people homeless. Refugees crossed the new borders in both directions. Many feared death if they did not move. In fact, many people were killed while fleeing. In 1971, East Pakistan became the independent country of Bangladesh.

## MOTHER TERESA: 1910–1997

Everywhere, people called Mother Teresa "the saint of the gutters." An Albanian, she became a nun and went to India to teach in 1928. In 1948, she left her convent to work among the poor. Soon, other women joined her. They became the Missionaries of Charity. Mother Teresa's nuns care for the dying, the sick, the abandoned children, and the elderly in many cities in India. She also started missions in other parts of South Asia, Europe, Africa, Australia, Latin America, the Middle East, and the United States. For her work, Mother Teresa was awarded the Nobel Peace Prize in 1979.

Today, religious conflicts still exist. One example is Kashmir, a state in northern India. Most of the people of Kashmir are Muslims, but India claims that Kashmir is part of its country. Thousands of Indian troops stay in the area to prevent violence.

There are other examples of religious and civil unrest. Some Sikhs want a state of their own. In Sri Lanka, the two major ethnic groups are fighting. There was also a civil war in Afghanistan through most of the 1980s. The war has ended, but fighting between different religious and political groups continues.

**Section 3 Review** On a separate sheet of paper, write answers to these questions.

1) Why are the many languages spoken in India a problem?
2) What is the caste system of the Hindu religion?
3) Why is the birthrate falling on the Indian subcontinent?
4) Who is Brahma?
5) What two religions began as a protest against the caste system of Hinduism?

**What do YOU think?** Why do you think people continue to move to cities even though many have to live in shantytowns?

## What Is the South Asian Economy Like?

More than half of the population of South Asia farms. The only exception is Sri Lanka. In Nepal and Bhutan, more than 90 percent of the population farms. Most are subsistence farmers. They use simple tools and little machinery on their small farms. Some Afghan farmers raise opium poppies as a cash crop. People make illegal drugs like heroin from the flowers of this plant.

More than half of the land in India is farmed. In Bangladesh, even more land is farmed. Many farmers depend on monsoon rains to grow crops. Farmers grow rice, wheat, corn, potatoes, beans, spices, sugarcane, and fruit. In areas that receive much rain, the main crop is rice. Little rain falls in Pakistan, so irrigation is used.

Location and religion influence what people eat. People who live along the coasts eat a lot of fish. In southern India, people eat a lot of rice. In the north, people usually eat bread with their meal. Hindus never eat meat. Muslims do not eat pork. Many people cannot afford to eat a healthy diet.

Commercial farming is also common. Crops are raised to sell and export. India's main exports are cotton, tea, rice, cashew nuts, and spices. It also produces sugarcane, coffee, leather, and jute. (Rope and bags are made from jute.) Pakistan exports cotton, rice, fish, and leather.

The other nations of the Indian subcontinent also export crops. Sri Lanka is the world's biggest exporter of tea. Bhutan is one of the world's biggest exporters of cardamom. People use this spice for baking and cooking. Bangladesh's most important export is jute.

## What Natural Resources Does South Asia Have?

South Asia is rich in natural resources. For example, the fast-flowing rivers of South Asia create cheap hydroelectric power. However, many other resources are not evenly distributed among all of the countries.

Cottage industry
*The making of a product at home*

India has huge deposits of coal and iron ore. India supplies one-third of its oil needs from its own wells. Offshore wells in the Arabian Sea may provide even greater oil production some day. New iron ore fields are being developed, so iron ore is likely to become an important export.

Pakistan produces enough oil for its needs and for export. Pakistanis also mine chromite (used to make metals), limestone, and rock salt. Sri Lanka exports many gemstones. Bangladesh has few natural resources other than natural gas. Bhutan may have mineral wealth, but very little development has taken place there.

## What Are the Main South Asian Industries?

India has many industries. It has all the raw materials needed for a modern steel industry. Its supply of iron ore is enough to last 160 years! It has enough coal to last 100 years! India also has limestone and manganese in large amounts. However, many of India's steel mills are old and inefficient.

Like China, India turned away from heavy industry in the 1980s. Many new industries now produce consumer products for sale to people in India and for export. The computer industry is growing. Some multinational corporations are now investing in India. The result has been a steady improvement in the standard of living. A middle class is growing. Many people now have bicycles, cars, televisions, and radios.

Even though they are small, **cottage industries** are an important part of the subcontinent's economy. Cottage industries are ones in which people make products in their homes. One generation after another hands down the skills needed to make these products. Among the products of cottage industries are needlework, tie-dye, papier-mâché, basket weaving, jewelry, and carpet making. Whole families often work together to make carpets. Some carpets take a year to make. The family may receive only a few hundred dollars for their work. However, people may pay $50,000 for such a carpet when sold in New York or London.

### Writing About Geography

In this book, you have learned about many sources of energy. What do you think will be the main energy source in the future? Write your opinion. Include at least three details or facts to support your opinion.

The making of a product at home is called a cottage industry. This photo shows a cottage industry in India.

## What Environmental Problems Exist?

Air pollution is a big problem in South Asia. Traffic and industry cause this pollution, which can lead to death. India's air pollution may cause as many as 40,000 deaths per year. The Indian cities of Calcutta and Mumbai (Bombay) have high levels of poisonous gases in the air. These levels are above what the World Health Organization considers safe. In December 1984, a cloud of poisonous gas escaped from a chemical plant in Bhopal, India. The gas killed over 2,000 people and injured many thousands more in nearby shantytowns. Many of the injured later died.

Water pollution is also a problem. Few towns throughout the subcontinent have systems to remove human waste. Businesses often dump untreated animal waste and factory runoff into the nearest river. Human waste usually ends up in the river, too. Because of this, many rivers are badly polluted. About 25 percent of the Ganges River is so badly polluted that it has become a health hazard.

Other environmental problems are deforestation and soil erosion. Forests have been cut down to build power and irrigation dams and to develop new mines. In some places, people cut trees for firewood. When forests disappear, nothing is left to hold the soil in place during the rainy season. This leads to soil erosion. The Indian government and environmental groups in India want to save India's remaining forests. The government wants to plant millions of new trees, but it does not have the resources to do this.

**Section 4 Review** Choose the letter of the answer that correctly completes each sentence. Write your answers on a separate sheet of paper.

1) About _____ of all the land in India is farmed.
    a. one quarter      c. one third
    b. half      d. one eighth

2) The countries of South Asia export _____.
    a. jute      c. tea
    b. spices      d. all of the above

3) India has all the materials it needs for a modern _____ industry.
    a. ship      c. diamond
    b. space      d. steel

4) People make products in their homes in a _____ industry.
    a. subsistence      c. heavy
    b. cottage      d. consumer

5) _____ causes water pollution in South Asia.
    a. The monsoon      c. Dumping untreated waste in the rivers
    b. A melting glacier      d. None of the above

**What do YOU think?** What does the growth of high-tech businesses tell you about the level of education in India?

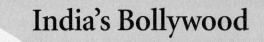
# India's Bollywood

**Many films have been made in India's Bollywood. This movie poster shows common themes of Indian movies—bright costumes and beautiful landscapes.**

Unless you are of Indian descent, you probably have never heard of Bollywood. Bollywood is the nickname for India's film industry. India has been making films for more than 100 years. Last year India produced more than 600 films.

The filmmaking industry is centered in Mumbai (Bombay). The filmmakers create their films in 17 different Indian languages. The films and the actors who appear in them are popular. Rural communities sometimes build temples to actors who play the roles of gods in the films.

Few of the Indian films are original. Many are fairy tales based on religious stories. The films contain music and dance. The actors appear in brightly-colored costumes. Beautiful green landscapes are often the setting. These films offer the poor people of India a brief escape from poverty.

Many of these films are popular with Indians who have migrated to other countries. Indian audiences in the United States, Great Britain, the Persian Gulf countries, and some countries in Africa enjoy these films. They remind them of the India they left behind. Some films make more money overseas than they do in India.

## Spotlight Story Wrap-Up

1) What is Bollywood?

2) Where is Bollywood?

3) Why are these films so popular in India?

4) Why are the films popular with Indians who now live overseas?

5) What are some places with large Indian communities?

◆ India, Pakistan, Afghanistan, Bangladesh, Nepal, Bhutan, and Sri Lanka make up South Asia. India is the largest of these with more than a billion people.

◆ The subcontinent of South Asia is a peninsula that is surrounded by the Indian Ocean.

◆ South Asia has four geographical regions: the Himalayas to the north, the Indo-Gangetic Plain that stretches across South Asia, the peninsula with its large Deccan Plateau, and the Thar (Great Indian) Desert.

◆ The main physical feature of South Asia is the Himalayas. The major rivers are the Ganges, Brahmaputra, and Indus.

◆ The monsoon winds influence the many climates of South Asia. Most of India, Sri Lanka, and Bangladesh have either a tropical monsoon or a tropical savanna climate. Northern Pakistan has a humid subtropical climate. Nepal and Bhutan have a highland climate.

◆ South Asia has many cultures. Britain ruled India from 1750–1947, so English is the language of government and big business. However, India's national language is Hindi. India has more than a thousand other languages. All of these languages cause communication problems.

◆ India is the birthplace of Hinduism with its caste system. Islam, Sikhism, and Jainism also have a large following. About 20 million Christians also live in India.

◆ More than half of the people of South Asia farm. They depend on the monsoon rains. Most are subsistence farmers, but some sell and export their crops of cotton, tea, rice, cashew nuts, spices, sugarcane, and coffee.

◆ South Asia is rich in natural resources. Both India and Pakistan have big oil deposits. The fast-flowing rivers supply cheap hydroelectric power. India has all the raw materials it needs to develop a modern steel industry.

◆ Cottage industries are an important part of the subcontinent's economy.

◆ South Asia's main environmental problems are air and water pollution, deforestation, and soil erosion.

◆ South Asia's biggest social problem is poverty and population growth. Other problems are urbanization, migration, civil unrest, and religious conflict.

## Comprehension: Identifying Facts

On a separate sheet of paper, use the words from the Word Bank to complete each sentence.

WORD BANK

Ganges

monsoon

Muslims

passes

peninsula

1) The Indian subcontinent is a huge _____.

2) _____ in the mountains have enabled invaders to reach India.

3) The _____ begins in the Himalayas and flows to the heartland of India.

4) The _____ winds change direction according to the time of year and bring rain to farmers.

5) Most of the people of Pakistan and Bangladesh are _____.

## Comprehension: Multiple Choice

On a separate sheet of paper, write the letter of the answer that correctly completes each sentence.

1) The island off the southern coast of India is _____.

a. Australia

b. Bangladesh

c. Pakistan

d. Sri Lanka

2) Most of India's people live on the _____.

a. Himalayas

b. Peninsula

c. Indo-Gangetic Plain

d. Great Indian Desert

3) India's national language is _____.

a. English

b. Hindi

c. Punjabi

d. Bengali

4) The caste system is a feature of _____.

a. Buddhism

b. Sikhism

c. Islam

d. Hinduism

5) A big industrial accident that resulted in a cloud of poisonous gas escaping into the air occurred in _____.

   a. Bhopal, India      c. Calcutta, India

   b. Karachi, Pakistan    d. Dhaka, Bangladesh

## Comprehension: Understanding Main Ideas

On a separate sheet of paper, write the answers to each question. Use complete sentences.

1) Where is the Indian subcontinent located?

2) What are the three most important rivers of the subcontinent?

3) What are the major environmental problems the region faces?

## Critical Thinking: Write Your Opinion

On a separate sheet of paper, write your opinion to each question. Use complete sentences.

1) Do you think that making English the national language of India would benefit the people there? Explain your answer.

2) Do you think religion plays too big of a role in life on the Indian subcontinent? Explain your answer.

## Applying the Five Themes of Geography

### Movement

Give an example of the theme of movement as it applies to India.

*Test-Taking Tip* When taking a true-false test, read each statement carefully. Write *true* only when the statement is totally true. Write *false* if part or all of the statement is false. After each item, ask yourself "Is this entire item true?" If not, mark it false.

*19*

# Southeast Asia

Southeast Asia is home to nearly 500 million people. The countries of Southeast Asia differ from one another in many ways. They have different forms of government. Some are large; others are small. Some have many natural resources; others have few. Many have developing economies; others have some of the fastest growing economies in the world. Cities are modern with tall buildings, but some people live much as their ancestors did hundreds of years ago. Southeast Asia also has many rain forests, as the photo on this page shows.

## Goals for Learning

▶ To describe where Southeast Asia is located
▶ To identify its most important physical features and climate
▶ To describe its diverse cultures
▶ To explain how and where most Southeast Asians live
▶ To describe Southeast Asia's economy and environmental challenges

 *Geo-Stats*

### Key Nations of Southeast Asia

 **Nation:** Indonesia
**Population:** 212,941,810
**Area** (in square miles): 741,101
**Major Cities:** Jakarta (capital), Surabaya, Bandung, Medan

 **Nation:** Malaysia
**Population:** 22,710,000
**Area** (in square miles): 127,317
**Major Cities:** Kuala Lumpur (capital), Ipoh, Johor Baharu

 **Nation:** Thailand
**Population:** 61,818,000
**Area** (in square miles): 198,457
**Major Cities:** Bangkok (capital), Nakhon Ratchasima, Songkhla, Nonthaburi

 **Nation:** Vietnam
**Population:** 79,490,000
**Area** (in square miles): 127,242
**Major Cities:** Hanoi (capital), Ho Chi Minh City, Haiphong, Da Nang

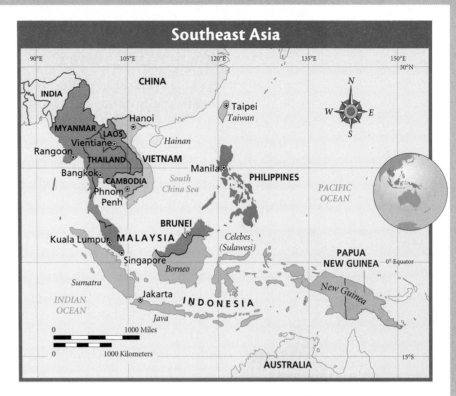

## Southeast Asia

*Map Skills*

The large peninsula of Southeast Asia is east of the Indian subcontinent and south of China. Southeast Asia also includes many island nations in the Indian Ocean and the South Pacific Ocean. This map shows the main countries of this region.

Study the map and answer the following questions:

**1)** In which part of Southeast Asia is Vietnam?

**2)** Where are the Philippines?

**3)** What is the capital of Thailand? Cambodia?

**4)** Which three larger countries surround Southeast Asia?

**5)** Island nations like those in Southeast Asia face special problems. What do you think these problems are?

## Where Is Southeast Asia Located?

Southeast Asia is located in the Tropics. It extends from about 25° north latitude to about 10° south. It is made up of peninsulas and islands. Geographers call the largest peninsula the Indo-Chinese Peninsula. It extends southeast off of the mainland of Asia and borders both India and China. Vietnam, Laos, and Cambodia are located on this peninsula. Most of Myanmar and Thailand are also located there.

Bangkok, Thailand, is one of the largest Southeast Asian cities. This photo shows the Chao Phraya River, which flows through Thailand.

Stretching southward from this peninsula is the long, narrow Malay Peninsula. The rest of Thailand and Myanmar are located in the northern part of this peninsula. Malaysia occupies the southern part. The small island country of Singapore is located off the southern tip of the Malay Peninsula.

All of the other countries of Southeast Asia are islands in the Pacific Ocean. These countries include Indonesia, the Philippines, Brunei, and Papua New Guinea. Indonesia is the largest of these countries. It extends over 3,000 miles from east to west. Altogether, its thousands of islands make up a land area three times the size of Texas. The Philippines are another archipelago of more than 7,000 islands.

## How Did Geography Shape the Region's History?

Southeast Asia's geographic location makes it an important region. It is located between the Indian and the Pacific Oceans. In the past, this was the main water route between China and India. Even today, Southeast Asia is located on one of the world's most important shipping routes. Much of the world's trade passes through its busy seaports.

Europeans arrived in Southeast Asia in the sixteenth century. They discovered that Southeast Asia was rich in mineral and agricultural resources. The riches of the Spice Islands of eastern Indonesia (now called the Moluccas) attracted the Europeans. At that time, spices like pepper, cloves, and nutmeg were far more valuable than they are today. People had no refrigerators, so food spoiled quickly. Spices kept food from spoiling and made it taste better. Europe could not produce these spices.

Soon all the countries of Southeast Asia, except for Thailand, became European colonies. Portugal, the Netherlands, Great Britain, Spain, and France controlled most of Southeast Asia. The United States took over the Philippines in 1898, but they became independent in 1946.

Geography also helps to explain the many diverse cultures of Southeast Asia. Because of its location, it attracted people from many different lands. The Malays were the first large wave of migrating peoples. They came from China. Other groups followed. The different groups brought their customs, cultures, and lifestyles. Traders from India introduced the Hindu and Buddhist religions. Muslim traders brought Islam to Malaysia and Indonesia. Europeans introduced western ideas while in control of the region, including Christianity.

**Section 1 Review** On a separate sheet of paper, write the word from the Word Bank that completes each sentence.

**WORD BANK**

Hindu
Islam
peninsulas
spices
Tropics

1) Southeast Asia is located in the _____.

2) The mainland nations are all located on _____.

3) Europeans were first attracted to the region because it grew _____.

4) Traders from India introduced the _____ and Buddhist religions to Southeast Asia.

5) Muslim traders brought _____ to Malaysia and Indonesia.

**What do YOU think?** The people of Indonesia and the Philippines are spread over many islands. How might this affect the unity of these countries?

### What Are Southeast Asia's Main Physical Features?

The physical features of "mainland" and "island" Southeast Asia differ. The mainland countries of Cambodia, Laos, Myanmar, and Thailand have high mountains in the north. These mountains separate them from the neighboring countries of India and China. Several mountain ranges extend southward through the Indo-Chinese Peninsula. They stretch all the way to the sea and make east-west travel and communication hard. Thick, tropical forests cover many mountains.

Thousands of volcanic islands also make up Southeast Asia. Much of the region is located along an important geological fault. Shifting along the fault can produce earthquakes and volcanoes. Indonesia alone has more than 100 active volcanoes. In 1883, the largest volcanic explosion ever recorded occurred on the Indonesian island of Krakatau. It killed more than 36,000 people.

### What Are Southeast Asia's Main Bodies of Water?

Between the mountain ranges of the Indo-Chinese Peninsula are the valleys of several rivers. The most important are the Irrawaddy, the Chao Phraya, the Mekong, and the Red. Each year, these rivers flood, leaving silt behind. It forms fertile, flat, fan-shaped deltas. Farmers grow rice on them. Over hundreds of years, farmers have terraced the hillsides to create more flat land for rice farming.

Many parts of Southeast Asia have few good roads or railroads. Because of this, people and goods travel up and down the rivers. In drier areas, farmers irrigate with river water. The rivers could provide hydroelectric power, but so far, Southeast Asia has built only a few dams and power plants.

Most of the people of mainland Southeast Asia live in cities in river valleys and deltas. Among them are Rangoon in Myanmar; Bangkok in Thailand; and Ho Chi Minh City and Hanoi in Vietnam.

Mainland Southeast Asia has only one large lake. Tonle Sap, or Great Lake, is located in the lowland of Cambodia. It is an important source of fish. The largest lake on the islands of Southeast Asia is Lake Toba in Indonesia.

The ocean is also important to Southeast Asia. All of the countries, except for landlocked Laos, have a long coastline. Many people depend on fishing for a living. The ocean provides fish for eating and tropical fish. People sell tropical fish to collectors around the world.

## What Is the Climate Like?

Most of Southeast Asia is close to the equator, so much of the region has a tropical climate that receives the sun's direct rays all year around. Temperatures are high throughout the year. Only highland areas have cooler weather.

Rainfall, not temperature, divides the seasons. A lot of rain falls on some places; other places receive much less. The northern and southern edges of Southeast Asia have a dry season that may last six months. Places near the equator have no dry season.

Monsoons cause the seasons. The rainy season on the Indo-Chinese Peninsula usually lasts from May to October. It rains almost every day. Warm, wet winds that blow inland from the Indian Ocean bring the rains. In late October, the winds shift direction and come mainly from the northeast. As they blow across the Pacific Ocean, they pick up moisture. They drop this moisture on the windward side of the coastal mountains. By the time the winds cross the mountains, they have become drier and warmer. Because of this, they soak up moisture from the land.

Island nations like Indonesia, Brunei, Papua New Guinea, and the southern part of the Philippines have a tropical rain forest climate. Rain falls almost daily. It is always hot and humid. Typhoons destroy homes and crops and kill hundreds of people. Sometimes these typhoons cause floods and **landslides.** A landslide occurs when a mass of earth, rocks, or mud falls quickly down a slope.

If the islands were flat, the temperature and rainfall would be similar on each island. However, some of them have mountains. The windward sides of these mountains receive more rain. Temperatures are cooler in mountain areas. Snow covers some mountain peaks all year.

**Many people in Southeast Asia live in houses built on stilts.**

## How Does the Environment Affect the People?

In many parts of Southeast Asia, people live in houses built on stilts. Floods do not wash away houses on stilts. Stilts also provide protection from wild animals or burglars. They also shelter a family's work animals, usually water buffalo.

**Remote**
*Far away; isolated*

The climate, the lack of transportation, and the thick jungles have slowed development in Southeast Asia. Because of this, many people live much as their ancestors did hundreds of years ago. These tribal people live in **remote,** or far away, mountain villages and on islands.

**Section 2 Review** On a separate sheet of paper, write *True* if the statement is true or *False* if the statement is not true. Make each false statement true by changing the underlined word.

1) <u>Islands</u> are the main physical feature of mainland Southeast Asia.

2) Most of the people of <u>mainland</u> Southeast Asia live in cities in river valleys and deltas.

3) The most important rivers of <u>island</u> Southeast Asia are the Irrawaddy, the Chao Phraya, the Mekong, and the Red.

4) The only Southeast Asian country without a coastline is <u>Laos</u>.

5) <u>Temperature</u> divides the seasons of Southeast Asia.

**What do YOU think?** What do you think a typical meal in Southeast Asia would be? Explain your answer.

## What Cultures Exist in Southeast Asia?

**Majority**
*More than half of a group of people or things*

Southeast Asia is located at an important crossroads, so many cultures exist there. Almost all of the countries have many different ethnic groups. For example, the Myanmans are the largest group in Myanmar, but the country also has four large minority groups. Members of these groups have fought against the government since the country got its independence in 1948.

In Malaysia, the population is almost equally divided between the Malays and the Malaysian Chinese. The Thais are Thailand's largest group, but large groups of Malay, Miao (or Hmong), Vietnamese, and Lao peoples also live in Thailand.

Like Africa, colonial powers drew the borders of Southeast Asia. These borders separated people with strong cultural links to one another. For example, Myanmar's Shan minority is more closely related to the Thai of Thailand than to the Myanmar **majority**. A majority is more than half of a group of people or things.

---

### Biography | AUNG SAN SUU KYI: 1945–

Since 1988, Aung San Suu Kyi has led the fight for democracy in Myanmar (Burma). Leadership is a family trait. Her father, Aung San, is called the father of independent Burma.

In 1988, Myanmans protested against military rule. As a result, troops shot or arrested thousands. Aung San spoke out for human rights. She helped the National League for Democracy win 80 percent of the seats in the legislature. The rulers ignored the results and kept her under house arrest for six years. In 1991, she won the Nobel Peace Prize. The generals still limit her freedom to speak and travel, however.

---

## What Languages Do Southeast Asians Speak?

Southeast Asia's diverse peoples speak many different languages. The main languages of island Southeast Asia are closely related. All of them are of Malay origin. However, the people cannot easily understand each other. To understand this, think about the English language. English, French, Spanish, and Italian are related languages. However, many people in the United States can understand only English.

There are 583 dialects or languages spoken in Indonesia alone. There are 9 native languages spoken in the different parts of the Philippines and 3 official languages. Papua New Guinea has about 700 ethnic groups, each with its own language.

## What Religions Do Southeast Asians Practice?

Indian traders brought Hinduism to Southeast Asia. Today, it is a popular religion only on the Indonesian islands of Bali and Lombok. About 90 percent of the people of Indonesia follow Islam, which is also the main religion of Brunei. Arab traders from the Middle East brought Islam there. Large groups of Muslims also live in Malaysia and the southern Philippines.

Most people in Myanmar, Thailand, Laos, Cambodia, and Vietnam are Buddhists. Traders from India and Sri Lanka helped spread Buddhism to these countries. Just as the beliefs of Catholic Christians differ from Protestant Christians, Buddhists also differ in their beliefs. For example, Chinese Buddhism influenced Vietnamese Buddhism, so it differs from Buddhism in other parts of Southeast Asia.

Christianity is another religion found in Southeast Asia. Catholic and Protestant missionaries from Europe and the United States brought it there. Missionaries were most successful in spreading Christianity in the Philippines, where 90 percent of the population is Christian.

Southeast Asian ceremonies and festivals include colorful costumes and dancing.

## Where Do Most Southeast Asians Live?

The population of Southeast Asia is not evenly distributed. Indonesia has the fourth largest population in the world. About 60 percent of Indonesians live on Java. This island covers only 6 percent of Indonesia's land area. The part of Indonesia that shares a large island with Papua New Guinea is Irian Jaya. It is three times the size of Java, but has less than two million people.

Most of Southeast Asia's people live in small rural villages and farm for a living. Their homes are made of wood or bamboo. Often the villages are located along rivers, canals, or roads. Gardens, fields, and pastures surround the village.

The cities of Southeast Asia are growing rapidly. Each year, thousands of people migrate to the cities. Some work in these urban areas for only part of the year and then return to their rural villages. Many others stay in towns and cities. All are searching for a better life.

The largest of Southeast Asia's cities are Jakarta, the capital of Indonesia, and Bangkok, the capital of Thailand. Manila is the largest city and capital of the Philippines. Vietnam has two large urban centers: Ho Chi Minh City and Hanoi. The country of Singapore is made up entirely of cities and suburbs. Yangon (Rangoon) is the capital and largest city of Myanmar. Almost all the biggest cities are the center of government and business. They are also important seaports.

## What Are the Population Trends?

The population of Southeast Asia is growing. Better health care, food, and living conditions have helped bring this about. Fewer babies now become sick and die; adults live longer. The birthrate is over 3 percent. This means that in less than 25 years, the population of Southeast Asia will double. Because of this, most of its countries have introduced family planning to limit population growth.

## What Problems Do the People Face?

The biggest problem of Southeast Asia is poverty. Most of its countries are poor. Two out of three people farm for a living, but farms are often too small to support each farmer's family. Farmers still use simple hand tools. Water buffalo or oxen pull their plows. Sometimes rats, grasshoppers, or other pests damage the crops. Most farmers cannot afford fertilizers. In many parts of Southeast Asia, the farmers do not own the land they farm. Landowners often charge them high rent.

Ethnic and religious differences threaten to break up some countries. A strong military rule held Indonesia together for over 30 years. Then, in 1998, the dictator was forced to leave office. The country had no strong government to hold it together. Because of this, people in East Timor and the province of Aceh pushed for independence. Fighting has also occurred in Irian Jaya and the Moluccas.

In the Philippines, Muslims on the island of Mindanao have pushed for greater independence. In Malaysia, the Malays have many government posts, but the Chinese control most of the economy.

### Writing About Geography

Poverty is a worldwide problem. Write five things related to geography that can cause poverty. Choose the one that you think is most responsible. Then write three ways to prevent this from being a cause.

**Section 3 Review** Choose the letter of the answer that correctly completes each sentence. Write your answers on a separate sheet of paper.

1) Southeast Asia is a mix of many cultures because it is a _____.

    a. peninsula        c. crossroads

    b. continent        d. island

2) Most of the languages of island Southeast Asia belong to the _____ language group.

    a. Malay        c. Vietnamese

    b. Chinese        d. English

3) Arab traders brought _____ to Brunei.

    a. Hinduism        c. Buddhism

    b. Christianity        d. Islam

4) Most Southeast Asians live in _____ areas.

    a. urban        c. hurricane

    b. rural        d. desert

5) The biggest problem facing Southeast Asians is _____.

    a. ethnic fighting        c. poverty

    b. a low birthrate        d. none of the above

**What do YOU think?** What would happen if Indonesia or the Philippines broke up into several smaller countries?

**Capitalism**
*An economic system in which people own their own businesses that the government does not control*

**Leach**
*To wash out minerals from soil*

## What Is Southeast Asia's Economy Like?

The economic geography of Southeast Asian countries varies. Vietnam, Cambodia, Laos, and Myanmar are experimenting with communism. The other countries of Southeast Asia practice **capitalism.** In this economic system, people own their own businesses and encourage foreign investment. The government does not run these businesses.

Most Southeast Asian countries have poorly developed economies. Two out of three people farm. This is surprising because the land is not suited for farming. Swamps and thick forests cover much of the region. The heavy rains **leach,** or wash out, the minerals in the soil. The environment encourages the spread of disease, so some areas are not healthy places to live. On the other hand, the weather is always warm and rain is plentiful. The river deltas are fertile. The volcanic soil on the islands of Southeast Asia is also rich.

Most of the farmers are subsistence farmers. Poor farmers often clear the land by cutting down the forest and burning it. Because this damages the soil, the farmers must move to a new field in a few years. The farmers of Southeast Asia grow cassavas, yams, beans, corn, peanuts, and some fruit.

The climate of Southeast Asia is wonderful for growing rice. Because of this, rice has become the staple crop in this region. Farmers use over half of their farmland to grow rice. They sometimes grow three crops of rice per year. Indonesia, the Philippines, and Thailand are able to grow enough rice to sell to other countries.

**Rice is a staple crop in Southeast Asia. It is grown on paddies that look like the one in this photo.**

Rice requires a lot of water, so farmers usually grow it in river valleys and coastal lowlands. **Paddies,** or water-covered fields, cover much of the land. Southeast Asia has little flat land. Because of this, people have built terraces on the mountain slopes.

During the many years of colonial rule, Europeans introduced large plantation farming. The plantation owners exported most of their crops. Today, some big plantations still exist, but many have been divided into smaller plantations. The native people own them. Plantations still export rubber, coffee, sugarcane, oil palms, rice, spices, and coconuts.

Some countries are developing their economies rapidly. Singapore is Southeast Asia's wealthiest country. It owes its wealth to its location. It is on the important sea route linking Europe and the Middle East with East Asia. This has made Singapore one of the world's busiest seaports. Singapore is also an important manufacturing center. Shipbuilding, food processing, machinery making, and technology products are leading industries. This island country is Southeast Asia's banking center and oil refiner. Thailand, Malaysia, and Indonesia have also grown industrially.

---

*Geography In Your Life*
ECONOMICS

### Rice

Rice is a staple in the diet of more than half of the people in the world. Farmers in more than 100 countries grow this grain. However, Asian farmers grow nearly 90 percent of it because rice needs a warm, wet climate. The Southeast Asian countries of Thailand, Vietnam, and Indonesia are among the top producers of rice.

Farmers in Southeast Asia flood their fields before planting. This gives moisture to the plants and kills weeds and bugs. The farmers drain their rice fields about three weeks before the harvest. They do most work in the rice fields by hand. However, some farmers use oxen or water buffaloes to pull their plows.

The people of Southeast Asia eat most of the rice they grow. Less than 5 percent of the rice crop in the world is traded internationally. However, Thailand is one of the chief exporters of rice. This helps its economy.

## What Natural Resources Are Important?

Most countries of Southeast Asia have many important natural resources, such as the huge tropical forests. Wood is exported to Japan and Europe. There, the wood is made into products such as furniture. The most valuable Southeast Asian woods are mahogany, ebony, and teak.

Southeast Asia also has valuable mineral resources. Malaysia, Thailand, and Indonesia produce more than half of the world's tin. Indonesia, Malaysia, and Brunei are important exporters of oil and natural gas, especially to Japan. Indonesia and Malaysia export bauxite. Once again, Japan is the biggest buyer. The Philippines are a leading producer of chromium, nickel, copper, and gold.

## What Environmental Problems Exist?

Southeast Asia has hundreds of different types of trees and thousands of types of plants. It also has some animals found only in that part of the world. However, many Southeast Asian countries are too poor to protect the environment.

Deforestation is a problem in nearly every Southeast Asian country. Each year, an area of rain forest the size of New Jersey is cut down. Indonesia loses more than 3.2 million acres of forest per year, more than any other country except Brazil. Tribal peoples who live in the forests can no longer live in their traditional ways.

Air pollution, soil erosion, and water pollution are problems, too. Cars and factories pollute the air. Traffic pollution in Bangkok is greater than in Los Angeles.

Farming on steep slopes has caused soil erosion. **Sediment** has filled rivers and killed fish. Sediment is rocks, sand, and dirt carried to a place by water, wind, and glaciers. The Chao Phraya River south of Bangkok is so polluted that nothing can grow or live in it.

Fossil fuels include oil, coal, and natural gas. When we burn these fuels, they produce carbon dioxide. This gas is harmful to the environment. This circle graph shows the percentage of carbon dioxide released by different areas of the world. Which area creates the most carbon dioxide? What is its percentage?

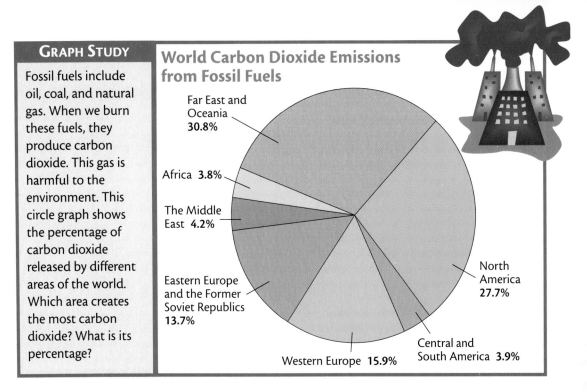

**World Carbon Dioxide Emissions from Fossil Fuels**

Far East and Oceania **30.8%**

Africa **3.8%**

The Middle East **4.2%**

Eastern Europe and the Former Soviet Republics **13.7%**

Western Europe **15.9%**

Central and South America **3.9%**

North America **27.7%**

Another problem for Southeast Asia is the fast growth of its cities. There is not enough housing. Many people live in slums with no running water. Bangkok is one of the fastest growing cities in the world. It cannot provide water treatment services for whole areas of the city. To provide drinking water, many wells have been built. They are pumping so much water out of the ground that Bangkok is sinking three inches a year. This causes lots of flooding during the rainy season.

**Section 4 Review** On a separate sheet of paper, write answers to the following questions. Use complete sentences.

1) How do most Southeast Asians earn their living?

2) What is the staple crop of the Southeast Asian diet?

3) What are some of the natural and mineral resources of Southeast Asia?

4) Which Asian country is an important market for Southeast Asia's natural resources?

5) Of all the environmental problems in Southeast Asia, which one most affects tribal peoples?

**What do YOU think?**

Why might a person not want to live in Bangkok?

# The War in Vietnam

Vietnam was once part of France's colonial empire. During World War II, Japanese forces took control. When the war ended, France tried to regain control. However, some Vietnamese did not want France to rule them any longer. They declared Vietnam independent.

In 1954, a treaty granted independence to Laos and Cambodia. This same treaty divided Vietnam into North and South Vietnam. Communist forces controlled North Vietnam; non-Communist forces governed South Vietnam. The United States supported the government of South Vietnam because it was noncommunistic. The U.S. government was afraid that North Vietnam and its Communist supporters in the South would make all of Southeast Asia Communist.

In 1964, the United States began sending thousands of soldiers to help South Vietnam. By 1968, more than 500,000 Americans were fighting there. The fighting lasted nine years. The U.S. and the Communists dropped thousands of bombs on both parts of Vietnam. About two million Vietnamese were killed, four million wounded, and six million made homeless. The U.S. lost nearly 58,000 soldiers.

During the war, the United States greatly damaged Vietnam's environment. U.S. planes dropped a chemical called Agent Orange on the thick vegetation of the jungles. This chemical killed about one fifth of Vietnam's forests. Agent Orange also poisoned the water and the soil. It destroyed the crops. People and animals who were accidentally sprayed often got sick.

**About 58,000 American soldiers died in the Vietnam War.**

Vietnam is slowly recovering from the war. However, it is a poor country with limited resources. Visitors to Vietnam today still see many reminders of a terrible war that ended more than 25 years ago.

## Spotlight Story Wrap-Up

1) What country controlled Vietnam before World War II?

2) Why did the U.S. support the government of South Vietnam?

3) How many Vietnamese people and how many U.S. soldiers died in the war?

4) What was Agent Orange?

5) Why has Vietnam not yet recovered from a war that took place more than 25 years ago?

◆ Southeast Asia is a large peninsula south of China and east of the Indian subcontinent. It also includes many island countries in the Indian and South Pacific Oceans.

◆ Geography shaped Southeast Asia's history because it is located on the water route between China and India. In the sixteenth century, Europeans began to colonize the region because of the valuable spices there.

◆ The main physical feature of mainland Southeast Asia is mountains. Volcanic islands are the main island feature.

◆ The most important rivers are the Irrawaddy, the Chao Phraya, the Mekong, and the Red.

◆ Most of Southeast Asia is close to the equator, so it has tropical climates. Rainfall, not temperature, divides the seasons. Monsoons cause these seasons.

◆ Southeast Asia has many diverse cultures. The people speak many different languages. The main languages of island Southeast Asia are of Malay origin.

◆ Among the religions of Southeast Asia are Hinduism, Islam, Buddhism, and Christianity.

◆ Most of the people of mainland Southeast Asia live in cities in river valleys and deltas. Cities are growing rapidly as people migrate to them.

◆ Two out of three people of Southeast Asia farm. Most are subsistence farmers.

◆ Over half of Southeast Asia's farmland is used to grow rice, which is a staple crop. Some plantations export rubber, coffee, sugarcane, oil palms, rice, spices, and coconuts.

◆ Some countries of Southeast Asia are experimenting with communism. Others are becoming capitalist.

◆ Most Southeast Asian countries have poorly developed economies. The climate, lack of transportation, and thick jungles have slowed development in Southeast Asia.

◆ Southeast Asia is rich in natural and mineral resources and exports wood products from its many tropical rain forests.

◆ Southeast Asia's main environmental problems are deforestation, air and water pollution, and rapidly growing cities that cannot provide services.

◆ Southeast Asia's biggest social problem is poverty. It also has civil unrest and religious conflict.

## Comprehension: Identifying Facts

On a separate sheet of paper, use the words from the Word Bank to complete each sentence.

**WORD BANK**

Tropics

farming

Malay

monsoons

teak

1) Southeast Asia is located in the _____.

2) _____ cause the seasons in Southeast Asia.

3) The main languages of the island nations of Southeast Asia are of _____ origin.

4) Two out of three Southeast Asians earn their living by _____.

5) Wood cut from the forests of Southeast Asia include mahogany, ebony, and _____.

## Comprehension: Multiple Choice

On a separate sheet of paper, write the letter of the answer that correctly completes each sentence.

1) _____ frequently occur on the islands of Southeast Asia.

   a. Forest fires      c. Volcanic eruptions
   b. Tornadoes         d. Killer bees

2) To create more flat land for farming, Southeast Asian farmers have _____.

   a. built hillside terraces   c. bulldozed hilly areas
   b. drained swamps            d. filled coastal bays with landfill

3) Much of Southeast Asia has a _____ climate.

   a. continental      c. highland
   b. arctic           d. tropical

4) The richest and most highly developed economy of Southeast Asia is in _____.

   a. Indonesia        c. Singapore
   b. the Philippines  d. Vietnam

**5)** Most Southeast Asian countries have a _____ economy in which people own their own businesses.

   a. Communist       c. subsistence

   b. capitalist        d. cash crop

## Comprehension: Understanding Main Ideas

On a separate sheet of paper, write the answer to each question. Use complete sentences.

**1)** What makes Southeast Asia's location so important?

**2)** Why does Southeast Asia have so many cultures?

**3)** What environmental challenges does Southeast Asia face?

## Critical Thinking: Write Your Opinion

On a separate sheet of paper, write your opinion to each question. Use complete sentences.

**1)** Imagine that a U.S. company hires you to give advice about expanding overseas. Would you recommend investing in Southeast Asia? Explain your answer.

**2)** Indonesia's national motto is "Unity in Diversity." Do you think this would be a good motto for the United States, too? Explain your answer.

## Applying the Five Themes of Geography

Which theme explains why the economy of Southeast Asia is growing?

**Test-Taking Tip** When you read true-false questions, the statement must be absolutely correct. Words like *always* and *never* tell you that the question is probably false.

# 20

# The Pacific World

The Pacific World is a huge area that includes much of the South Pacific Ocean. It includes two large island nations: Australia and New Zealand. It also includes many smaller ones. Australia is the world's largest island. It is four-fifths the size of the United States. Both Australia and New Zealand have much in common. Both were colonies of Great Britain and most of their people speak English. Europe has strongly influenced their culture. However, their future is closely linked with Japan, Southeast Asia, and other nations near the Pacific Ocean. The photo on this page shows Sydney, Australia.

## Goals for Learning

▶ To describe where the Pacific World is located

▶ To identify its important physical features and climates

▶ To describe its cultural diversity

▶ To explain how and where most of its people live

▶ To describe its economy and its environmental challenges

## Geo-Stats

### Key Nations of the Pacific World

**Nation:** Australia
**Population:** 18,981,000
**Area** (in square miles): 2,966,153
**Major Cities:** Canberra (capital), Sydney, Melbourne, Brisbane, Perth

**Nation:** Federated States of Micronesia
**Population:** 117,000
**Area** (in square miles): 271
**Major Cities:** Palikir (capital)

**Nation:** Fiji Islands
**Population:** 794,000
**Area** (in square miles): 7,056
**Major Cities:** Suva (capital), Lautoka, Nadi, Ba

**Nation:** New Zealand
**Population:** 3,817,000
**Area** (in square miles): 103,883
**Major Cities:** Wellington (capital), Auckland, Christchurch, Hamilton

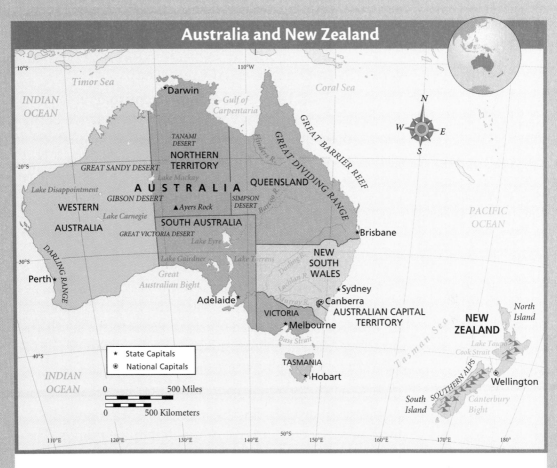

*Map Skills*

Australia and New Zealand are the two largest countries in the Pacific World. In fact, Australia is the sixth largest country in the world. The island continent of Australia has many large deserts and mountain ranges. New Zealand is made up of two large islands and many smaller ones.

Study the map and answer the following questions:

**1)** How many states and territories does Australia have?

**2)** What are the names of New Zealand's two large islands?

**3)** What are the national capitals of Australia and New Zealand?

**4)** What are Australia's major deserts?

**5)** How would you describe the land of Australia based on what you see on this map?

## Where Is the Pacific World Located?

Hemisphere
*One half of Earth*

Meridian
*An imaginary line that circles Earth and runs through the North and South Poles*

The Pacific World is in the Southern **Hemisphere.** A hemisphere is one half of Earth. Geographers divide Earth into northern and southern hemispheres at the equator. They also divide it into the eastern and western halves at a **meridian.** A meridian is an imaginary line that circles Earth and runs through the North and South Poles. The Southern Hemisphere is the half of Earth that is south of the equator.

Australia is the largest part of the Pacific World. This continent extends both north and south of the Tropic of Capricorn. The Pacific Ocean is to the east, the Arafura Sea and the Timor Sea are to the north, the Indian Ocean is to the west and south, and the Tasman Sea is to the south and east. New Zealand is about 1,000 miles southeast of Australia in the South Pacific Ocean.

The Pacific Islands have three subregions. Melanesia is northeast of Australia and New Zealand. Micronesia is north of Melanesia and east of the Philippine Islands. The water area of Micronesia is as large as the U.S. However, its land area is smaller than Rhode Island. Polynesia covers an even larger area east of Micronesia and Melanesia.

### States and Territories of Australia

| State/Territory | Area in in Square Miles | Population |
|---|---|---|
| New South Wales | 309,500 | 6,274,400 |
| Victoria | 87,900 | 4,605,100 |
| Queensland | 666,990 | 3,401,200 |
| Western Australia | 975,100 | 1,798,100 |
| South Australia | 379,900 | 1,479,800 |
| Tasmania | 26,200 | 473,500 |
| Australian Capital Territory | 900 | 309,800 |
| Northern Territory | 519,800 | 187,100 |

**CHART STUDY**

Australia has many states and territories. This chart lists each one, its size, and its population. How large is Western Australia? How many people live in New South Wales?

Australia's largest city is Sydney, located on the east coast of New South Wales.

## What Are the Countries of the Pacific World?

Australia and New Zealand are the biggest countries of the Pacific World. The islands in this area include many small countries. Fiji, the Solomon Islands, Vanuatu, and New Caledonia are all in Melanesia. Of those, New Caledonia is the only one that is not an independent country. Micronesia has five independent countries: the Republic of Palau, the Federated States of Micronesia, the Republic of the Marshall Islands, Nauru, and Kiribati. The independent countries of Polynesia are Tuvalu, Western Samoa, and the Kingdom of Tonga. Foreign countries still govern many Polynesians.

## How Did Geography Shape This Region's History?

Geography helps to explain why so few people live in the Pacific World. The region is far from the world's main population centers. Sydney is Australia's largest city. From Sydney to Tokyo, Japan, is 5,000 miles; from Sydney to Singapore is 3,900 miles; and from Sydney to Honolulu, Hawaii, is 5,100 miles. The distance to Europe and the United States is even farther. In the past, few settlers wanted to make the long and hard trip to this region. The population is also small because of the harsh climate. Deserts cover much of Australia. Most European settlers wanted to move to lands like those they left behind.

**SECTION 1 REVIEW** On a separate sheet of paper, write *True* if the statement is true or *False* if the statement is not true. Make each false statement true by changing the underlined word.

1) The Pacific World is in the <u>Northern</u> Hemisphere.
2) New Zealand is 1,000 miles <u>northwest</u> of Australia.
3) The water area of <u>Micronesia</u> is as large as the U.S.
4) Foreign countries still govern many <u>Polynesians.</u>
5) <u>Few</u> people live in the Pacific World.

**What do YOU think?**

How might Australia's history be different if it were located in the South Atlantic instead of the South Pacific?

## What Are the Main Physical Features?

Magma
*Hot liquid rock*

Reef
*A string of rock, sand, or coral close to the surface of a body of water*

Australia occupies one of Earth's oldest landmasses. The flat Central Plateau covers more than 75 percent of the land area. The Great Dividing Range stands on the eastern edge of the plateau. This low mountain range runs parallel to Australia's east coast. The Australian Alps rise at the south end of the range. Australia's highest point is Mt. Kosciusko, which is 7,310 feet tall.

Uluru, or Ayers Rock, is located deep in the heart of Australia. This huge sandstone rock formation contains iron oxide, which gives the rock an orange-red color. The rock rises over 1,000 feet above the desert plain.

Coral islands make up the Great Barrier **Reef.** A reef is a string of rock, sand, or coral close to the surface of a body of water. The Great Barrier Reef follows the northeastern coastline of Australia for about 1,250 miles. More than 1,000 different types of fish live among the coral of the Great Barrier Reef. Many tourists come to see it.

**Great Barrier Reef extends for about 1,250 miles off of the northeastern coast of Australia.**

New Zealand has a very different geography. It is made up of two main islands: North Island and South Island. They are located along the border of the Australian and Pacific tectonic plates. Because of this, New Zealand has many earthquakes and volcanoes. However, most of these volcanoes no longer erupt. Beneath the surface of these volcanoes, hot liquid rock called **magma** heats underground water. Geysers, or natural springs, shoot hot water and steam into the air. Pools of boiling mud, geysers, and hot-water springs are found south of Lake Taupo on North Island.

Outback
*The hot, dry land in the middle of Australia*

Mountains cover much of New Zealand. The Southern Alps run down the entire length of South Island. Mt. Cook is New Zealand's highest mountain. It is over 12,000 feet high. Glaciers wore down New Zealand's mountains and carved out valleys and fjords. Tasman Glacier is the largest glacier at 18 miles long.

The Pacific Islands were formed in two ways. Some are the tops of huge underground volcanoes that rise from the ocean floor. Others are atolls. These low coral islands surround a sunken volcanic peak. They are often circle-shaped with a shallow lagoon in the center.

## What Are the Main Bodies of Water?

The middle area of Australia is called the **outback.** It is hot and dry with few rivers and lakes. Most of Australia's rivers flow eastward from the Great Dividing Range. Australia's biggest cities are located on the east coast along these rivers. Sydney is located on the Parramatta River. Melbourne grew up near the Yarra River. The Murray River is the longest river in Australia. The Darling and Murrumbigee Rivers are its two most important tributaries. The Murray-Darling system captures the rainfall off the western slopes of the Great Dividing Range and carries it inland. These waters provide irrigation.

New Zealand has many short, fast-moving rivers that provide hydroelectric power. The longest river is the Waikato on North Island. New Zealand also has many small lakes. A huge volcanic explosion created Lake Taupo. It is the largest in New Zealand.

## What Is the Climate of the Pacific World Like?

The Pacific World is in the Southern Hemisphere. Because of this, its seasons are opposite those of the Northern Hemisphere. This happens because the two hemispheres have opposite positions to the sun. The hottest summer months in the Southern Hemisphere are December, January, and February. Winter occurs in June, July, and August.

Australia has several climates. Northern Australia has a tropical savanna climate with high temperatures all year long. The summer months from November to April receive the most rain. Tropical cyclones may occur. The dry season is from May to October. Two-thirds of Australia has a desert climate with hot days and cool nights. The southeastern corner of Australia has a Mediterranean climate with mild, wet winters and warm, dry summers. The eastern coastal areas have a humid subtropical climate that is much like that of the southeastern United States.

High mountains and its closeness to the sea affect New Zealand's weather. The southwest coast of South Island is one of the wettest areas in the world. This is because western winds bring wet air from the sea. As the air rises, it cools and releases its moisture as rain. The east side of the mountains receives much less rain. Most of New Zealand has a marine west coast climate with mild temperatures.

## How Does the Environment Affect the People?

Most people like mild climates. Because of this, few people have settled in the hot desert climate of Australia's outback. The outback is also too far from the coasts to attract many people. About 90 percent of Australians live along the southeastern and eastern coasts, within 100 miles of the ocean. These areas have dependable rainfall and the mildest temperatures.

In New Zealand, most people also live in areas with the mildest climate. About 75 percent of the population live on North Island. About 80 percent of the people live in cities. Auckland, a city of over a million people, is the largest city. It is located on the east coast of North Island.

The Pacific World is very far from Europe. Because of this, most European immigrants made the shorter trip to settle in North America. It offered an environment that was similar to the lands they left behind. As a result, the population of the Pacific World is much lower than all the other continents you have studied, except for Antarctica.

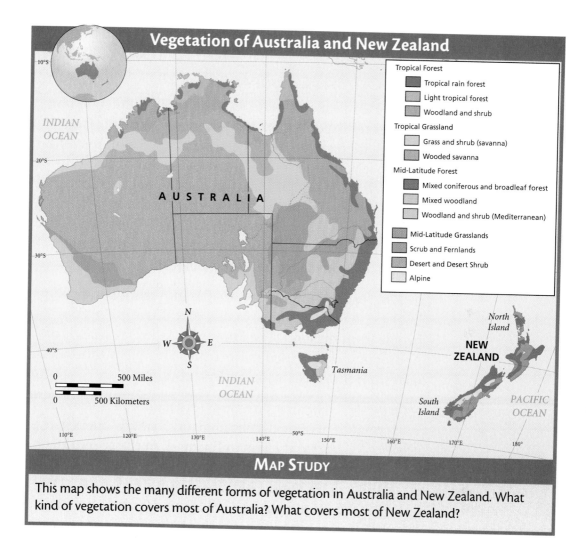

## Vegetation of Australia and New Zealand

**Tropical Forest**
- Tropical rain forest
- Light tropical forest
- Woodland and shrub

**Tropical Grassland**
- Grass and shrub (savanna)
- Wooded savanna

**Mid-Latitude Forest**
- Mixed coniferous and broadleaf forest
- Mixed woodland
- Woodland and shrub (Mediterranean)

- Mid-Latitude Grasslands
- Scrub and Fernlands
- Desert and Desert Shrub
- Alpine

INDIAN OCEAN

AUSTRALIA

INDIAN OCEAN

Tasmania

North Island

**NEW ZEALAND**

South Island

PACIFIC OCEAN

10°S
20°S
30°S
40°S
50°S

110°E 120°E 130°E 140°E 150°E 160°E 170°E 180°

0   500 Miles
0   500 Kilometers

N W E S

## MAP STUDY

This map shows the many different forms of vegetation in Australia and New Zealand. What kind of vegetation covers most of Australia? What covers most of New Zealand?

**SECTION 2 REVIEW** On a separate sheet of paper, write answers to the following questions.

1) How much of Australia does the Central Plateau cover?

2) In what country of the Pacific World would a tourist find many geysers and pools of boiling mud?

3) Why are Australia's biggest cities located on its east coast?

4) What are the two types of smaller islands found in the Pacific World?

5) Why are the seasons of the Southern Hemisphere the opposite of those in the Northern Hemisphere?

**What do YOU think?**

Why is the Great Barrier Reef important to the Pacific World?

## What Cultures Exist in Australia?

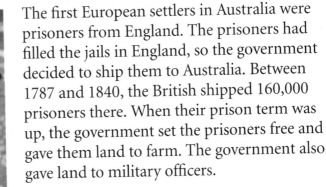

Aborigine
*One of the original people of Australia*

Boomerang
*A wooden weapon curved so that it returns to the person throwing it*

Before Europeans arrived, between 300,000 and a million **Aborigines** lived in Australia. Aborigines, or Kooris, as they call themselves, were the original people of Australia. These Melanesian people hunted and gathered plants to eat. Their main weapon was the wooden **boomerang.** It is curved so that it returns to the person throwing it. The Aborigines lived in groups scattered across Australia. They spoke many languages, but had no writing. They passed along their knowledge by word of mouth.

In 1787, the first Europeans arrived in Australia from England. As in the United States, they drove the native people from the land. The Europeans killed thousands of Aborigines who refused to leave the land. Many thousands died from the diseases the settlers brought.

**Aborigines such as this man were the original people of Australia.**

The first European settlers in Australia were prisoners from England. The prisoners had filled the jails in England, so the government decided to ship them to Australia. Between 1787 and 1840, the British shipped 160,000 prisoners there. When their prison term was up, the government set the prisoners free and gave them land to farm. The government also gave land to military officers.

By 1850, Australia's European population was close to a million. Even today, many of the white people have European ancestors. Many still have relatives living in England or Ireland. After World War II, large numbers of immigrants came to Australia from Greece and Italy.

In recent years, immigrants have come to Australia from Malaysia, Hong Kong, Singapore, Vietnam, Laos, and Cambodia. Today, Australia has one of the highest

## Writing About Geography

The Pacific World is a mix of old cultures and new ways of life. Write about how this mix can strengthen a society.

percentages of immigrants in the world. Over 22 percent of its people were born in another country.

## What Cultures Exist in New Zealand?

The **Maori** are New Zealand's native people. Historians believe that they are a Polynesian people who migrated around A.D. 1350. They fished, hunted, and grew vegetables. They created beautiful carvings with stone tools. As in Australia, the Europeans who came to New Zealand introduced new diseases, alcohol, and guns.

The first Europeans hunted whales and seals near New Zealand. These people mistreated the Maori and the missionaries there. In 1840, the Maori and the British government signed a treaty. It made New Zealand a British colony. It promised the Maori the right to their land.

Today, Maori make up about 9 percent of New Zealand's population. Most of the white population is European. As in Australia, most came from the British Isles. Later immigrants came from Germany, France, Scandinavia, southern Europe, and even Australia.

New Zealand has been more willing than most other countries to accept refugees. After World War II, a number of Jews, Poles, and Hungarians came to New Zealand. After the Vietnam War, about 7,000 refugees resettled in the country. Since the 1980s, other Asian immigrants have come from Hong Kong, China, Taiwan, and South Korea.

## What Religions Do the People Practice?

Most Australians and New Zealanders are Christians. However, because of Asian immigration, other religions, such as Buddhism and Islam, are growing fast.

The Aborigines practice a religion built around an idea called **dreamtime.** The idea is that the past, present, and future are all part of now. Aborigines believe that nature has powerful spirits. They also believe that the spirits of their ancestors live in nature. Some Aborigines are Christians, but many still follow their ancient religion.

## What Languages Do the People Speak?

English is the official language of Australia and New Zealand. Many of the first European settlers came from the poorest areas of England, and this is reflected in Australian English. Some Aboriginal words have become part of the language, as have some American-English words. Other immigrants have brought their own languages with them. The big cities have newspapers in Italian, Greek, Arabic, Chinese, and English.

## What Are the Population Trends?

The Pacific World has an aging population. Compared to Africa, Southeast Asia, and the Middle East, the Pacific World has a low percentage of people under the age of 15. The region also has a growing population. Since World War II, the birthrate has risen, and the death rate fallen. This is one reason for an increasing population. Another is the large number of immigrants. The immigrants from Asia and the Middle East tend to have larger families. Australia's population has grown from about 6 million in 1930 to nearly 20 million in 2000.

Another trend is the movement to big cities. Most Australians and New Zealanders live in large cities. The Auckland area is home to nearly one-third of all New Zealanders. More than 80 percent of Australia's people live in towns and cities. About two-thirds live in the biggest cities of Sydney, Melbourne, Brisbane, Adelaide, and Perth.

| Biography | CATHY FREEMAN: 1973– |

In 1997, Cathy Freeman, an Aborigine sprinter, won the world championship for the 400 meter event. Afterward, many people cheered and clapped, but others booed as she ran around the track carrying two flags. One flag represented her Australian citizenship; the other flag represented her Aborigine background.

Freeman is the leading track star of Australia. In 1990, at 16, she won the gold medal at the Commonwealth Games. That same year she was named Young Australian of the Year. Then, in 1996, she won a silver medal at the Olympic Games in Atlanta. In 2000, she won a gold medal at the Olympic Games in Sydney, Australia.

## What Problems Do the People Face?

Australia and New Zealand are members of the British **Commonwealth of Nations**. This group of nations was once part of the British Empire. Now the countries are independent but choose to work together. Both Australia and New Zealand must decide whether to remain in the Commonwealth.

A second problem facing Australia and New Zealand is their treatment of the native peoples. In the past, European settlers mistreated these peoples. They gave them little education, medical care, and housing. Both nations have passed laws promising rights to the native peoples. For example, the Australian government gave the Aborigines special rights to Uluru because it is sacred to them.

**SECTION 3 REVIEW** Choose the letter of the answer that correctly completes each sentence. Write your answers on a separate sheet of paper.

1) The original people of Australia are called _____.

   a. Indians          c. Aborigines
   b. Maori            d. Ainu

2) The first European settlers in Australia were _____.

   a. farmers          c. whalers
   b. prisoners        d. missionaries

3) Australia and New Zealand have many immigrants from _____.

   a. the United States   c. South America
   b. California          d. Asia

4) The official language of Australia is _____.

   a. English          c. French
   b. Polynesian       d. Japanese

5) Most Australians and New Zealanders live in _____.

   a. rural areas      c. large cities
   b. small towns      d. the outback

**What do YOU think?**

How do you think the small number of children who live in the Australian outback and remote places in New Zealand get their schooling?

## What Is the Economy Like?

Mutton
*The meat of full-grown sheep*

Australia and New Zealand have well-developed economies. Their people enjoy a high standard of living. Originally, they based their economy on agriculture. However, farming is less important today. As in the United States, agriculture in Australia now accounts for only 3 percent of its economic activity. In New Zealand, it is 9 percent.

New Zealand is slowly making the change from farming to industry. Manufacturing makes up about 20 percent of its economy. In Australia, manufacturing makes up 14 percent. Most manufacturing companies are small. They are located around cities on the east coast.

The largest number of people in both Australia and New Zealand work in service industries, the fastest growing part of the economy. Service industries include construction, trade, banking, communications, education, business services, and tourism. Tourism is the fastest growing and largest part of the service industry.

The economy of most of the Pacific Islands is based on tourism. Tourists come because of the mild climate and the beautiful scenery. Tourism provides many jobs. Many people work in hotels and restaurants. Local artists earn a living by selling their work to tourists.

## How Does Trade Affect the Economy?

Both Australia and New Zealand have large export markets. Because their populations are small, trade with other countries is important. New Zealand is the world's largest exporter of lamb and **mutton,** the meat of full-grown sheep. It is the third largest exporter of wool. It also is an important fruit producer. It ships apples and its native kiwi fruit around the world. Fish and shrimp are also important exports.

**Lamb and sheep farming is a major industry in New Zealand.**

Australia exports resources and minerals. Of Australia's top 25 exports, 21 are raw materials. Its main exports are coal, gold, meat, wool, bauxite, and machinery. Australia is the world's fourth largest exporter of wheat and the sixth largest exporter of beef. Its other farm exports include fruit and wine. It also exports seafood. In the past, Australia traded mainly with Europe and the United States. Today, Japan is Australia's main trade partner.

## What Natural Resources Exist?

Australia has many natural resources, including coal, bauxite, iron ore, natural gas, and oil. It also has rich deposits of lead, zinc, copper, nickel, and silver. Australia produces gemstones, such as diamonds, sapphires, and pearls. From its mines come 60 percent of the world's natural opals.

New Zealand's mineral resources include natural gas, iron ore, and coal. However, other natural resources are more important. Its coastal waters provide seafood. Its fast-flowing rivers provide two-thirds of New Zealand's electricity.

Only a few of the Pacific Islands have any mineral resources, some of which are mined. However, trade is limited because of the great distance between these islands and foreign markets.

## What Are Some Major Industries?

Both Australia and New Zealand raise many sheep for food and wool. However, modern fibers have forced down the price of wool, so it is now of less importance to the economy. Australians raise cattle on the hot, dry grasslands of the outback. Food processing and wood and paper products are the leading manufacturing industries of New Zealand. Tourism is growing in New Zealand.

Australia has a wide range of industries. Its biggest manufacturing industries are chemicals, electronics, food processing, clothing, and wine. Construction of cars and ships, oil refining, paper products, and steel products are other industries. Tourists come to see Australia's many beaches and golf courses. They enjoy its sunny weather.

## What Environmental Problems Exist?

Australia has many plants and animals that do not exist anywhere else. Kangaroos, koalas, wombats, and wallabies are **marsupials.** These animals carry their young in a pouch. In some areas, people think of kangaroos as pests because there are so many of them. Some Australians want the government to let them hunt kangaroos to control the population. Others think this is wrong. Koalas live in the forests of eastern Australia and eat only the leaves of a special tree. As forests are cut down to make room for housing or roads, the future of the koalas is threatened.

Another problem is animals that Europeans brought to Australia. Before these settlers came, Australia had no cats, rabbits, or foxes. After Europeans brought these animals to Australia, cats and foxes hunted and killed the native marsupials and birds. Some areas of Australia now have few marsupials left. Rabbits are a problem because they multiply quickly. They eat anything that grows and destroy pasture land and native plants. With few plants to hold the soil down, soil erosion occurs.

**Koalas live in Australia's forest land. Life for the koalas is threatened as forests are cut down.**

Poor land management has caused **overgrazing.** This means that the land cannot support all the animals that graze on it. When the animals eat the plants down to the roots, the plants die. Then the land becomes a desert. Brushfires are a natural environmental hazard. Fires occur often in many parts of the country during dry periods. Lightning causes most of the fires, but careless people cause some of them.

The Great Barrier Reef is one of Australia's biggest tourist attractions. However, tourists sometimes break off pieces of corals. Their powerboats cause pollution that kills the coral. The development of hotels near the reef also threaten its future.

**Park Ranger**

Australia has about 500 national parks that cover over 100,000 square miles. Two of the most famous are Great Barrier Reef Marine Park and Kakadu National Park. Kakadu contains prehistoric cave paintings. These provide evidence of human life in Australia some 30,000 years ago.

Park rangers must protect these parks. Rangers also protect people. They may rescue a lost camper or help a rock climber get back to solid ground. They may chase away a wild animal that comes too close to campers. Rangers must know first aid to help injured campers. They must also work to prevent forest fires.

Park rangers are skilled campers themselves. They help campers understand the relationship between plants, animals, and the environment. They teach people to respect this environment. High school students who want to be park rangers study earth science, social studies, and speech. College students study park management, forestry, and other related subjects.

Oceans cut off New Zealand from the rest of the world, so only animals that could fly were able to reach it. Some of its birds, however, cannot fly. They live only in New Zealand. One is the kiwi, the symbol of New Zealand. Many of these birds are now extinct. Because New Zealand gets plenty of rain, it does not have Australia's problems of overgrazing and brush fires.

**SECTION 4 REVIEW** On a separate sheet of paper, write the word from the Word Bank that completes each sentence.

**WORD BANK**

European

Japan

mutton

opals

service

1) The largest number of people in both Australia and New Zealand work in _____ industries.

2) New Zealand is the world's largest exporter of lamb and _____.

3) Australia's biggest trade partner is _____.

4) Australia produces gemstones such as _____.

5) _____ settlers introduced animals to Australia that killed the native animals and caused environmental problems.

**What do YOU think?** What is good and what is bad about tourism in the Pacific World?

# The 2000 Olympics

The Olympic Games began in ancient Greece. At that time, they were part of a religious feast in honor of Zeus, the main god of the Greeks. The first modern Olympics were held in 1896, in Athens, Greece. Pierre baron de Coubertin of France had the idea of starting the games again. For these new games, 34 countries sent athletes to the Olympics.

The Olympic torch is the symbol of the Olympic Games. The torch for the 2000 Olympics was shaped like a boomerang, as shown in this photo. The torch for the 2000 Olympics was even carried underwater!

The symbol of the games is the Olympic torch. A runner lights the flame in Olympia, Greece. That is where the ancient games were held over 2,750 years ago. Runners then carry the flame to the place where the new Olympic Games are being held. A final runner lights the flame that begins the new games.

The 2000 Olympic Games were held in Sydney, Australia. The Sydney torch was a turquoise, white, and silver boomerang. Runners carried the flame through 13 Pacific Island countries including New Zealand, Fiji, and Tonga before arriving in Australia at Uluru on June 8, 2000. The torch then made a 100-day round-Australia journey before being used to open the games on September 15, 2000.

The Olympic Games have been held only two times in the Southern Hemisphere: once in Melbourne and once in Sydney. More than 15,000 athletes from over 200 countries came to Sydney for the Olympics in 2000. They took part in 28 sports.

## Spotlight Story Wrap-Up

1) In what country did the Olympic Games first begin?

2) When were the first modern Olympic Games held?

3) What form did the Sydney torch have?

4) Through what countries was the Olympic torch carried before reaching Uluru in Australia?

5) How many countries and athletes participated in the 2000 games?

◆ The Pacific World is located in the Southern Hemisphere. The island continent of Australia makes up its largest part. The second largest country is New Zealand, with its two large islands and many small ones. The subregions of Melanesia, Micronesia, and Polynesia are also located in the Pacific World.

◆ The three most important physical features of Australia are its Central Plateau, Uluru, and the Great Barrier Reef.

◆ Earthquakes, geysers, and mountains are important features of New Zealand.

◆ The smaller islands of the Pacific are coral atolls or the tops of huge underground volcanoes.

◆ Most of Australia's rivers flow eastward, so its biggest cities are on the east coast. New Zealand's fast-moving rivers provide hydroelectric power.

◆ Australia has several climates: tropical savanna in the north, desert in the outback, Mediterranean in the southeast, and humid subtropical in the eastern coastal areas.

◆ New Zealand's southwest coast is one of the wettest areas in the world.

◆ The original people of Australia are the Aborigines. The original people of New Zealand are the Maori.

◆ The main language of Australia and New Zealand is English. The native peoples have their own languages.

◆ Most Australians and New Zealanders are Christians. Asian migration has also brought Buddhism and Islam to these two countries. The native people practice their own religion.

◆ Fewer people are farming in both Australia and New Zealand than in the past. The largest number of people work in service industries.

◆ Australia's main environmental problems are deforestation, overgrazing, soil erosion, and destruction of the Great Barrier Reef.

◆ The social problems of Australia and New Zealand include the mistreatment of native people and whether to continue to belong to the British Commonwealth.

## Chapter 20 REVIEW

### Comprehension: Identifying Facts

On a separate sheet of paper, use the words from the Word Bank to complete each sentence.

**WORD BANK**

boomerangs

desert

flat

geysers

marsupials

1) The _____ climate is one of the reasons few people live in Australia's outback.

2) _____ are wooden weapons used by the Aborigines.

3) New Zealand is mountainous while Australia is _____.

4) _____ are mammals that carry their young in a pouch.

5) _____ are natural hot springs that shoot columns of hot water and steam into the air.

### Comprehension: Multiple Choice

On a separate sheet of paper, write the letter of the answer that correctly completes each sentence.

1) The Pacific World is located in the _____ Hemisphere.
   a. Northern
   b. Southern
   c. Western
   d. Arctic

2) A large _____ covers more than 75 percent of Australia.
   a. forest
   b. rock
   c. plateau
   d. glacier

3) Sydney and Melbourne are among the largest cities of _____.
   a. Australia
   b. Hawaii
   c. New Zealand
   d. Fiji

4) The Aborigines and the Maori are the _____ of Australia and New Zealand.
   a. immigrants
   b. prisoners
   c. original native people
   d. physical features

5) Both Australia and New Zealand have large _____ markets.

   a. import

   b. export

   c. zoo

   d. none of the above

## Comprehension: Understanding Main Ideas

On a separate sheet of paper, write the answer to each question. Use complete sentences.

1) What are the main physical features of Australia?

2) What country had the greatest influence on the culture of Australia and New Zealand?

3) What are the chief natural resources of Australia and New Zealand?

## Critical Thinking: Write Your Opinion

On a separate sheet of paper, write your opinion to each question. Use complete sentences.

1) Are Australians similar to or different from people living in the United States? Explain your answer.

2) Why are Australia and New Zealand more dependent on foreign trade than countries like the United States, China, and India?

## Applying the Five Themes of Geography

### Location

How has the location of the Pacific World affected its history and development?

Test-Taking Tip

If you are asked to compare and contrast things, be sure to tell how they are alike (compare) and how they are different (contrast).

# Analyzing Aerial Photographs

Have you ever looked down on Earth from an airplane? Have you ever seen pictures of the land taken from high above? If so, you probably gained a better understanding of the area's geography after seeing things from so high up. Geographers use photos from airplanes or outer space to study an area's physical geography. They call these aerial photographs. These photographs tell many things about the land, the people, and patterns around the world.

Just what can be seen from above? Geographers can study such things as vegetation, population, land use, weather, and other important details. Colors can show how land is divided. An aerial photograph taken at night can show population patterns by pointing out where human-made lights appear. Two aerial photographs of the same place taken years apart can show how land has changed over time. Aerial photographs are taken from high up. Because of this, geographers can study many things that would not have been clear from on land.

The aerial photo on this page shows Australia. The land looks different in this photo from how you would see it if you stood on land. This way of looking at Earth can answer many questions about the geography of our planet.

Study the photo on this page and answer the following questions.

1) What does the aerial photograph on this page tell you about Australia?
2) How might this aerial photograph help geographers?
3) Why are aerial photographs helpful?
4) What things can geographers discover from aerial photographs?
5) What would you want to learn about Earth from an aerial photograph?

◆ India, Pakistan, Afghanistan, Bangladesh, Nepal, Bhutan, and Sri Lanka make up South Asia.

◆ Southeast Asia is a large peninsula south of China and east of the Indian subcontinent. It also includes many island countries in the Indian and South Pacific Oceans.

◆ The Pacific World is located in the Southern Hemisphere. Australia and New Zealand are its two largest countries.

◆ The main physical feature of South Asia are the Himalayas. Southeast Asia and New Zealand also have mountains.

◆ The monsoon winds influence the many climates of South Asia. Monsoons cause the seasons in Southeast Asia.

◆ South Asia and Southeast Asia have many diverse cultures.

◆ The original people of Australia are the Aborigines. The original people of New Zealand are the Maori.

◆ English is the main language of Australia and New Zealand. It is the business language of India. The people of Southeast Asia speak many different languages.

◆ Most Australians and New Zealanders are Christians. The native people practice their own religion. India is the birthplace of Hinduism. Among its other religions are Sikhism, Jainism, Islam, and Christianity. Among the religions of Southeast Asia are Hinduism, Islam, Buddhism, and Christianity.

◆ More than two-thirds of the people of Southeast Asia and half of the people of South Asia farm. Fewer people are farming in both Australia and New Zealand where industry is growing.

◆ South Asia, Southeast Asia, Australia, and New Zealand are rich in natural resources. India and Pakistan have large oil deposits.

◆ Both South Asia and Southeast Asia have the problems of air and water pollution and deforestation. Australia's main environmental problems are deforestation, overgrazing, soil erosion, and destruction of the Great Barrier Reef. The main social problem of South Asia and Southeast Asia is poverty. Both areas also have civil unrest and religious conflict. Australia and New Zealand have the problem of treating native people fairly.

# Geography and Today's World

Today, the countries of the world are more closely linked than ever before. People and goods move freely from nearly all parts of the globe. New technology and new ways to communicate bring the people of Earth closer together. Space technology, as the picture on this page shows, is an example of this. At the same time, ethnic, religious, and political differences cause war. Economic development is uneven.

## Goals for Learning

▶ To describe how the world is a global village

▶ To explain how technology is affecting communication and transportation

▶ To identify the environmental issues that will affect the future of the world

▶ To explain how humans are affecting the environment and being affected by it

▶ To identify the ways society may change in the future

▶ To describe the state of the global economy

 *Geo-Stats*

### The World Today

**Population:** over 6 billion

**Estimated World Population by 2050:** 9.3 billion

**Most Populated Country:** China (1.25 billion)

**Most Populated Continent:** Asia (3.6 billion)

**Largest Country:** Russia (6,592,692 square miles)

**Highest Average Annual Rainfall:** Hong Kong, China (87.2 inches)

**Highest Gross Domestic Product:** United States ($8.08 trillion)

**Highest Gross Domestic Product Per Capita:** Luxembourg ($33,700)

**Average World Life Expectancy:** 64 (males), 68 (females)

**Highest Divorce Rate:** United States (4.6 per thousand people)

**Highest Use of Cellular Phones:** United States (69.8 million)

**People Using the Internet:** about 332.7 million

**Number of Languages:** 3,000–6,000

# Urban Population of the World

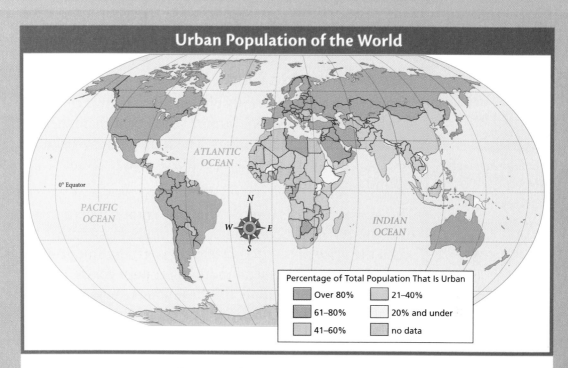

ATLANTIC OCEAN

0° Equator

PACIFIC OCEAN

N
W — E
S

INDIAN OCEAN

**Percentage of Total Population That Is Urban**

- Over 80%
- 61–80%
- 41–60%
- 21–40%
- 20% and under
- no data

*Map Skills*

Perhaps one of the greatest challenges the world will face in the new century is controlling population. The world's population is increasing by 77 million each year. Experts believe that over nine billion people will live on Earth by the year 2050. Unfortunately, the land may not be able to support so many people. Also, many cities around the world are already crowded. This map shows the percentage of people in the world who live in cities.

Study the map and answer the following questions:

**1)** What does this map tell you about the world's urban population?

**2)** Where does the urban population appear to be highest?

**3)** Where does the urban population appear to be lowest?

**4)** What do you think life would be like if everyone in the world lived in large cities?

**5)** What cities do you think will be the largest in the future? Explain why you think so.

## How Is the World a Global Village?

The world seems smaller. Its physical size has not changed, so what has? Today, people around the world share their way of life through technology. The term **global village** describes the sharing of ideas, cultures, and traditions around the world.

This global village is **interdependent.** What happens in one country affects every other country. For example, when the price of Middle Eastern oil goes up, American manufacturers must spend more to produce goods. Consumers then pay more for these goods. A storm that damages the coffee crop in Colombia and Brazil affects coffee drinkers everywhere.

Global village
*The sharing of ideas, cultures, and traditions around the world*

Interdependent
*Dependent on one another; being dependent on what happens somewhere else*

Satellite
*An object that is built to go around Earth in space*

## How Has Technology Affected Geography?

Technology links the whole world together and makes one global village. Better communication and transportation allow us to share our cultures and improve ways of collecting and studying information. For example, hundreds of **satellites** have been sent into Earth's orbit. Satellites send back pictures that show huge dust storms over Africa and large chunks of ice floating in the Arctic Ocean. Some satellites record information about Earth's surface and natural resources. This helps scientists figure out where to mine minerals. Pictures from space show seas, lakes, and rivers. This helps scientists check pollution. Satellites also help weather forecasters track storms.

Computers also affect geography. They store information, look for trends and patterns, and solve hard math problems. With the help of computers, geographers can predict changes in climate, crop failures, hurricanes, and droughts. They can see if polar glaciers are growing or melting. They can find the cause of change and figure out what might happen next.

At age 15, Bill Gates began programming computers. Later, he worked on a programming language for the first personal computer (PC). At that time, not many people used PCs. However, Gates thought they represented the future. Because each computer would need software, Gates and a man named Paul Allen started a computer company in 1975. They began by building an operating system. Gates showed his talent for putting ideas developed by one company with the needs of another. This has been his strength as the chief executive officer of his computer company, which is now the world's leading producer of software for PCs.

**E-mail**
*A tool that allows people to send written messages electronically over the Internet*

**Internet**
*The international computer network*

**Telecommunication**
*Communicating electronically*

Satellites allow us to see events in other parts of the world on television. People use cellular phones to talk to other people. **Telecommunications,** or communicating electronically, is an important way to do business. The **Internet,** the international computer network, connects millions of people around the world. **E-mail** allows us to send written electronic messages to others over the Internet. In June 2000, there were 332.7 million Internet users in the world. About 40 percent of them were in the United States.

New technology has also changed transportation. Japan and France have developed trains that travel over 100 miles per hour. Automobiles and airplanes have given people more freedom. An international air transport system now connects cities and people around the globe.

**WORD BANK**

automobiles

global village

Internet

satellites

technology

**Section 1 Review** On a separate sheet of paper, write the word from the Word bank that completes each sentence.

1) _____ has made the world seem smaller.

2) The _____ is the sharing of ideas around the world.

3) _____ send back pictures of Earth from space.

4) The _____ is the international computer network.

5) _____ give people more freedom to travel.

**What do YOU think?** How has the computer changed your life?

## What Are the Effects of Global Warming?

Ozone layer
*The layer of gas above Earth that protects Earth's atmosphere by filtering out the sun's harmful rays*

Scientists think that gases from cars and factories are heating Earth, causing global warming. Burning wood, coal, oil, or natural gas releases carbon dioxide. Forests and oceans take in some of this gas. However, in many parts of the world, forests and jungles have been cut down to provide farmland and firewood. Also, the ocean currents seem to be warming. As they do, they do not hold as much carbon dioxide.

Global warming could melt the ice caps at both the North and the South Poles. If this happens, water will cover coastal cities on Earth's surface. Then two billion people around the world will have to move inland. Global warming could also increase cloud cover. It could change the rainfall and climate patterns around the world. This would affect people in many ways, especially the world's food production.

## What Are the Effects of Air Pollution?

The burning of fossil fuels, especially from automobiles, causes most air pollution. Pollution is a global problem because air and ocean water are always moving. Heat, moisture, and pollution move around the world with the air and water.

Air pollution might change Earth's climate forever. A helpful layer of gas called the **ozone layer** protects Earth's atmosphere. It filters out the sun's harmful rays. Scientists believe that the ozone layer may be thinning. They have discovered a hole in the ozone layer over Antarctica. Gases in spray cans and refrigeration systems might have caused this damage. People must find ways to prevent this from occurring. Destroying the ozone layer could lead to more skin cancer and crop failure.

## What Are the Effects of Water Pollution and Erosion?

Water covers 70 percent of Earth. People often take water for granted. However, oceans, lakes, and rivers are in trouble. Human pollution has hurt the oceans; farming and industrial waste have hurt lakes and rivers. The problem is most serious in developing countries. Nearly 1.2 billion people in these countries must drink polluted water that carries disease.

People around the world depend on Earth to grow their food. However, billions of tons of topsoil is blowing or washing away. Deforestation, overgrazing, and poor farming methods cause this. Nothing can replace this topsoil. As a result, deserts are growing. Millions of people may starve to death.

## What Are El Niño and La Niña?

**El Niño** is an unusual warming of the tropical Pacific Ocean that occurs about every three to five years. Sometimes El Niño is strong. From 1997 to 1998, El Niño was so strong that it changed weather patterns for much of the world. **La Niña** refers to certain years between El Niño. La Niña and El Niño often have the opposite effects. The ocean currents are colder than usual in La Niña. La Niña is harder to predict and its effects are less severe.

**El Niño**
*The unusual warming of the tropical Pacific Ocean that occurs about every three to five years*

**La Niña**
*A weather pattern in which ocean currents are colder than usual*

---

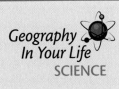

*Geography In Your Life*
SCIENCE

### Research at the South Pole

The United States named the Amundsen-Scott South Pole Station after two explorers. Roald Amundsen, a Norwegian, reached the South Pole in December 1911. A month later, the English explorer Robert Scott reached it.

The South Pole is 9,450 feet above sea level. About 9,000 feet are ice. Antarctica's cold, clear air, its high altitude, and its six months of darkness allow scientists to do research there that they could do nowhere else.

Scientists at the station do many kinds of research. They have discovered that Antarctica has the cleanest air in the world. This dry, clear air allows them to use powerful telescopes. With these, they detect heat that cannot get through the atmosphere anywhere else on Earth. Using technology, scientists track changes in carbon dioxide. They release balloons into the air above Antarctica. The instruments in the balloons measure the amount of ozone there.

**Daylight saving time**
*A way of making better use of daylight by setting clocks one hour ahead in the spring and one hour back in the fall*

**Developed country**
*A country that has already built its economy and has money to provide services for its citizens*

## How Do People Interact with the Environment?

People affect the environment in both good and bad ways. We build dams to bring water to dry areas. We clear land for settlement, farming, and mining. We drain wetlands. In Asia, humans build terraces into hillsides to create more flat land for farming. However, the changes we have made on the physical environment affect wildlife, vegetation, and culture. These changes create garbage, air and water pollution, and harmful waste.

People have always had to adapt to the environment. There are several examples of this. People in Arctic climates had to learn to build shelter out of snow. European explorers introduced the horse to the Americas. The native people quickly learned how to use the horse to hunt buffalo. In places with a hot climate, people have learned to live with the heat by taking a midday rest. They return to work when the weather is cooler. **Daylight saving time** is another way we have adapted to the environment by making better use of daylight. To do this, we set our clocks ahead one hour in the spring. In the fall, we set our clocks back one hour.

## How Do Developing Countries Affect the Environment?

People in developing countries often cut down forests to provide land for farming and livestock. They export wood, coal, and oil to improve their standard of living. They use up their natural resources. These developing countries have only a limited amount of money. Because of this, they depend on industrial countries for the money needed to clean up the environment. However, many rich countries are cutting back on the money they give to poorer countries.

**Developed countries** have already built their economies and have money to provide services for their citizens. Many people in these countries want to save forests. They want to reduce pollution by cutting down on the use of fossil fuels. All of this may help the environment in one country. However, it hurts the economies of developing countries that depend on the sale of natural resources.

If individuals work to care for the environment, pollution like this can be stopped.

## How Can Individuals Protect the Environment?

You and your family can help the environment by reducing, reusing, and recycling. Each of us creates a lot of trash. About 57 percent of everything we throw away ends up buried in a landfill. Reduce the amount of goods, water, and energy you use. Reuse things instead of throwing them away and buying something new.

Recycle things you no longer use. Most cities now collect aluminum cans, plastic containers, glass, and paper. They sell these things to businesses that make new products out of them. For example, one company makes playground equipment from recycled plastic. Another makes new glass bottles from old ones. Some companies even make newspapers, paper towels, and toilet paper from recycled products.

In a global village, all of us share the same problems. We depend on the same Earth to supply us with our needs. In the future. we must improve the quality of life for all people without destroying the environment.

**Section 2 Review** On a separate sheet of paper, write *True* if the statement is true or *False* if the statement is not true. Make each false statement true by changing the underlined word.

1) The burning of wood, coal, oil, or natural gas releases <u>oxygen</u> into the air and causes global warming.

2) Air pollution can affect the <u>ozone layer</u> and change Earth's climate.

3) Because of <u>air</u> pollution, many people drink unsafe water.

4) Deforestation, overgrazing, and poor farming methods cause <u>air</u> erosion.

5) What helps the environment in developed countries may <u>hurt</u> the economies of developing countries.

**What do YOU think?**

What are some ways you can reduce, reuse, or recycle to help the environment?

## What Is the New Global Culture?

The global village is becoming more connected. Because of this, different cultural groups have more contact with one another. People must understand how other groups use land, organize and lay out cities, treat women, educate their young, and celebrate traditional customs and holidays.

The global community is moving toward a global culture. Movies, video cameras, CD players, and television allow people from around the world to share their lives. Technology has helped some businesses become multinational corporations.

Since the end of World War II, the influence of the United States on the new global culture has grown. American television, movies, music, fast food, and clothing styles influence people all over the globe. The global culture has changed the United States, too. Music from Asia, Africa, and Latin America influences American popular music. Americans enjoy foods from all parts of the world.

People need a common language to talk to others around the world. Nearly 25 percent of the world's population now speaks English. It is fast becoming the first global language. It is the official language of more than 75 countries and of international business, science, and government. However, business people know that speaking the same language is not enough. They must also know about the cultures of the people with whom they want to do business.

## What Problems Affect the World?

The new century promises peace, riches, easy travel, and quick communication for some people. For most, it offers little hope. Most of the world's people live in shantytowns around big cities. Millions of people cannot find jobs. In some countries, even small children must work because their families are so poor.

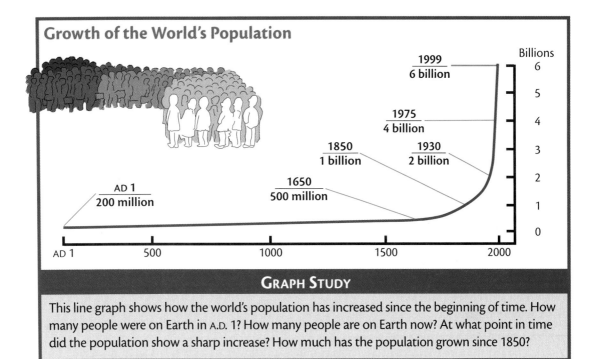

## Growth of the World's Population

Billions

1999
6 billion — 6

1975
4 billion — 4

1850            1930
1 billion       2 billion — 3

                — 2
1650
500 million

AD 1            — 1
200 million

— 0

AD 1        500        1000        1500        2000

### GRAPH STUDY

This line graph shows how the world's population has increased since the beginning of time. How many people were on Earth in A.D. 1? How many people are on Earth now? At what point in time did the population show a sharp increase? How much has the population grown since 1850?

**United Nations (UN)**
*An international organization that tries to settle disagreements, improve the way people live, and keep peace around the world*

War, poverty, disease, and overpopulation affect developing nations, especially Africa. Ethnic and religious violence have killed thousands of people in Africa, Asia, and eastern Europe. There are more poor people today than there were 25 years ago. They do not eat as well as people in developed nations. They live in poor housing and they get sick often. When they get sick, they cannot afford to see a doctor.

Disease is another problem. It affects every country in the world. AIDS affects people in almost every country, especially those in Africa. Alzheimer's disease and heart disease are spreading as the number of older people increases.

## What Organizations Help Solve Problems?

The **United Nations (UN)** is the most important international organization. Countries throughout the world formed it in 1945. The UN tries to settle disagreements, improve the way people live, and keep peace around the world. The UN has several different groups. Each has a special job.

The UN's General Assembly discusses world problems. The Security Council decides what actions the United Nations

UN peacekeeping forces such as this one are sent to troubled areas around the world.

should take to settle international disputes. The International Court of Justice tries to settle arguments between countries. The Economic and Social Council tries to improve the way people live.

The UN also provides troops to act as peacekeepers in troubled areas. The member countries of the UN, such as the United States, provide these troops. The UN has used peacekeepers in Korea, the Middle East, eastern Europe, and Africa. However, the UN has not always been successful in solving problems.

Many other groups deal with problems on an international level. Private individuals, not governments, make up these groups, so they are called **nongovernmental organizations (NGO)**. There are now more than 25,000 international NGOs.

Nongovernmental organization (NGO)
*An organization that is made up of private individuals and that is not run by the government*

**Section 3 Review** Choose the letter of the answer that correctly completes each sentence. Write your answers on a separate sheet of paper.

1) _____ is fast becoming the first global language.
   a. Chinese          c. Arabic
   b. Spanish          d. English

2) War, disease, and overpopulation are most common in _____.
   a. North America    c. England
   b. Africa           d. Canada

3) The _____ is the most important world organization.
   a. United Nations   c. NAFTA
   b. NGO              d. none of the above

4) The _____ of the UN tries to improve the way people live.
   a. General Assembly  c. International Court of Justice
   b. Security Council  d. Economic and Social Council

5) _____ are groups of private individuals.
   a. NGOs             c. NAFTAs
   b. UNs              d. None of the above

**What do YOU think?**

Why do you think the UN has not always been successful?

## How Does Trade Affect the Global Economy?

Most countries must import goods from other countries. For example, the United States depends on other countries for oil, cars, raw materials, and consumer goods. Other countries depend on the U.S. for food products, computers, and machines.

International trade is growing. It allows countries to **specialize.** That is, they work on what they do best. For example, U.S. farmers can grow bananas, but the cost of growing them is high. Other countries can grow them easier and more cheaply. In exchange, farmers in the United States can grow crops like wheat more easily. One country specializes in growing bananas; another country specializes in growing wheat.

Trade has a down side, too. For example, some people in the U.S. buy cars made in Japan. Because of this, U.S. factories might close down and workers might lose jobs. On the other hand, the U.S. can grow some crops more cheaply than farmers in other countries. Exporting these crops and selling them at a lower cost may mean that farmers in other countries cannot sell theirs. They may lose their farms and their way of life.

## What Do Developed Countries Have in Common?

Most people in developed countries live quite well. They usually do not worry about food, clothing, and shelter. Most people in developed countries live longer, can read and write, and are highly skilled. Developed countries have good transportation and communication. Their farmers use a lot of machines. Large farms produce all of the food the people need. Because of this, most people live in urban areas and work in factories, offices, and businesses. These businesses have money to train their workers in computing and other technology. Service jobs are most common.

**Writing About Geography**

If you were wealthy and wanted to help the world solve its economic problems with your money, what things would you do? List at least five ideas. Write why you chose each one.

## What Do Developing Countries Have in Common?

Developing countries are usually much poorer than developed countries. People often do not live as long as people in the developed world. In many rural areas, children must work, so they go to school for only a short while. Because of this, many people cannot read or write. Some farmers migrate to large cities to find better jobs and a better life for themselves and their families. In the cities, they often live in shantytowns with no water, electricity, or bathrooms. Less developed countries often have the highest birthrate, with a population that doubles every 25 years. Many people cannot find work. These countries must import most manufactured goods. However, most people cannot afford to buy these goods. Communication is often poor. Farmers and workers cannot get products to markets because of poor transportation.

## What Are the Economic Trends Today?

One trend, particularly in developed countries, is **globalization.** Globalization is the steady knitting together of all of the world's economies into one. To see how this works, look at the United States. Thirty years ago, events beyond its borders did not greatly affect the American economy. Today, its economy is international, as both imports and exports have increased. World events affect the American economy more than ever before.

Because the international marketplace is interdependent, many countries have joined the **World Trade Organization (WTO).** The 136 members of this global organization deal with rules of trade among nations. The WTO oversees trade agreements. It also handles trade disputes, checks on the trading

**Many people in developing countries are not able to buy the things they want or need.**

**Foreign aid**
*Money, medicine, tools, or machinery given by one country to help another country*

**International Monetary Fund (IMF)**
*An organization that gathers money from 175 members to help countries in need*

**World Bank**
*An organization that loans money to less developed countries at low interest rates*

practices of its members, and provides help and training for developing countries.

Many nations have created free-trade agreements to trade more easily with one another. As you know, free trade means trading without barriers between countries. Free-trade agreements have been reached in Africa, Asia, North America, South America, parts of Europe, Central America, the Caribbean, and among some Arab nations.

## What Is Being Done to Help Poorer Nations?

Many of the world's poorer countries look to developed countries for help. The developed countries give **foreign aid.** That is, they give money, medicine, tools, or machinery to help less developed countries. Sometimes the aid is a gift that does not need to be repaid. Sometimes it is a loan that the poorer country must pay back. Each year, the 21 most industrialized countries give billions of dollars to roughly 182 less developed countries.

The developed countries send their money through two international organizations: the **World Bank** and the **International Monetary Fund (IMF).** The World Bank loans money to less developed countries at low interest rates. The countries use the money to build bridges, dams, roads, and schools and to improve health and the environment. The IMF gathers money from its 175 members to help countries in need.

**Section 4 Review** On a separate sheet of paper, write the answers to these questions.

1) What is one benefit and one harmful effect of international trade?

2) What is foreign aid?

3) What are three things that developed countries have in common?

4) What are three things that developing countries have in common?

5) What is globalization?

**What do YOU think?**

Would it be a good idea to tax people in developed countries to provide money to improve the life of people in developing countries?

# The 100-Person World

Think if it were possible to shrink Earth's population to a village of exactly 100 people. Those people would still represent how the world population is today. What would the village be like? Here are some facts that would describe such a village.

• There would be 57 Asians, 21 Europeans, 14 North and South Americans, and 8 Africans.

• Seventy would be non-white; thirty would be white.

• There would be 26 Christians, 15 Muslims, 10 Hindus, 5 Buddhists, and 5 Chinese folk religion followers. About 12 would be non-religious or atheists. The remaining 27 would each belong to the many smaller religious groups of the world.

• Half of the wealth in the village would be in the hands of six people. All six would be Americans.

• Seventy would not be able to read or write their native language.

• Half would not have enough food to eat.

• Eighty would live in substandard housing.

• Only one would have a college education.

## Spotlight Story Wrap-Up

1) On what continent do most of the world's people live?

2) Are most of the world's people white or people of color?

3) What country is the richest in the world?

4) What shows that most people in the world are poor?

5) How do we know that most people in the world do not receive a good education?

◆ Improved transportation and communication are changing the world into an interdependent global village.

◆ Technology has greatly affected the collecting of information. Satellites provide much of this information.

◆ Technology has helped build the global village, which is moving toward a global culture.

◆ English is fast becoming the world's first global language.

◆ People have changed the environment. Air and water pollution, erosion, and global warming are among the main problems.

◆ People everywhere work to improve the environment. People can protect the environment by reducing waste, reusing things, and recycling.

◆ War, poverty, disease, and overpopulation threaten the future of many people around the world.

◆ The United Nations is the most important international organization dealing with world problems. It helps settle disagreements, improves the way people live, and keeps peace around the world.

◆ The global economy is interdependent. However, people in developed countries tend to be well off. People in developing countries are usually poor.

◆ The developed countries are trying to aid the developing countries. The wealthy countries send money through the World Bank and the International Monetary Fund.

◆ Globalization is the gradual knitting together of all the world's economies.

◆ Many countries have joined the World Trade Organization and made free-trade agreements.

## Comprehension: Identifying Facts

On a separate sheet of paper, use the words from the Word Bank to complete each sentence.

1) The global village is _____ because what happens in one country affects every other country.

2) Scientists believe that high levels of carbon dioxide in the atmosphere cause _____.

3) To help the environment, people can reduce, reuse, and _____.

4) The most important international organization is the _____.

5) The _____ deals with the rules of trade among nations.

## Comprehension: Multiple Choice

On a separate sheet of paper, write the letter of the answer that correctly completes each sentence.

1) The world seems smaller than it used to be because of advances in _____.
   a. geography
   b. technology
   c. industry
   d. medicine

2) _____ gather information about weather, the earth's surface, natural resources, and pollution levels.
   a. Archaeologists
   b. UN peacekeeping forces
   c. Satellites
   d. None of the above

3) War, disease, _____, and overpopulation are some of the worst problems affecting the people of the global village.
   a. wealth
   b. a lower birthrate
   c. small cities
   d. poverty

4) One effect of _____ could be the relocation of two billion people from coastal areas.
   a. technology
   b. communications
   c. the United Nations
   d. global warming

5) The _____ decides what actions the UN should take to settle international disagreements.
   a. International Monetary Fund
   b. World Bank
   c. Security Council
   d. Internet

## Comprehension: Understanding Main Ideas

On a separate sheet of paper, write the answer to each question. Use complete sentences.

1) Why do people sometimes describe the world as a global village?

2) What are two environmental issues that will affect the world in the future?

3) What is one economic trend in the world today?

## Critical Thinking: Write Your Opinion

On a separate sheet of paper, write your opinion to each question. Use complete sentences.

1) How do you think communication will change in the next ten years?

2) What do you think is the greatest threat to the future of our planet—war, disease, overpopulation, pollution, or something else? Explain your choice.

## Applying the Five Themes of Geography

### *Interaction*

How do you affect the geographical environment in which you live? How does your geographical environment affect you?

**Test-Taking Tip** When taking a short-answer test, first answer the questions you know. Then go back to spend time on the questions that you are less sure about. Review all of your answers when you finish the test.

ARCTIC
OCEAN
Beaufort Sea
Baffin Bay
GREENLAND
ICELAND
Bering
Sea
Gulf
of Alaska
Hudson
Bay
Labrador
Sea
U.
K.
IRELA
CANADA
B
of E
NORTH
AMERICA
PORTUG
NORTH
ATLANTIC
OCEAN
NORTH
PACIFIC
OCEAN
UNITED STATES OF AMERICA
CANARY ISLANDS
MOR
MEXICO
Gulf of
Mexico
THE BAHAMAS
WESTERN
SAHARA
CUBA
DOMINICAN
REPUBLIC
MAURITANIA
BELIZE
HAITI
PUERTO RICO (U.S.)
HONDURAS
Caribbean Sea
SENEGAL
GUATEMALA
THE GAMBIA
EL SALVADOR
PANAMA
GUINEA-BISSAU
NICARAGUA
VENEZUELA
GUYANA
GUINEA
COSTA RICA
SURINAME
SIERRA LEONE
FRENCH GUIANA
LIBERIA
COLOMBIA
ECUADOR
SOUTH
AMERICA
PERU
BRAZIL
BOLIVIA
SOUTH
PACIFIC
OCEAN
PARAGUAY
CHILE
SOUT
ATLANT
OCEA
ARGENTINA
URUGUAY
N
W    E
S
FALKLAND ISLANDS (U.K.)
SOUTH GEORGIA ISLAND (U.K.)
160°W    140°W    120°W    100°W    80°W    60°W    40°W    20°W
80°N
60°N
40°N
20°N
0° Equator
20°S
40°S
60°S
80°S

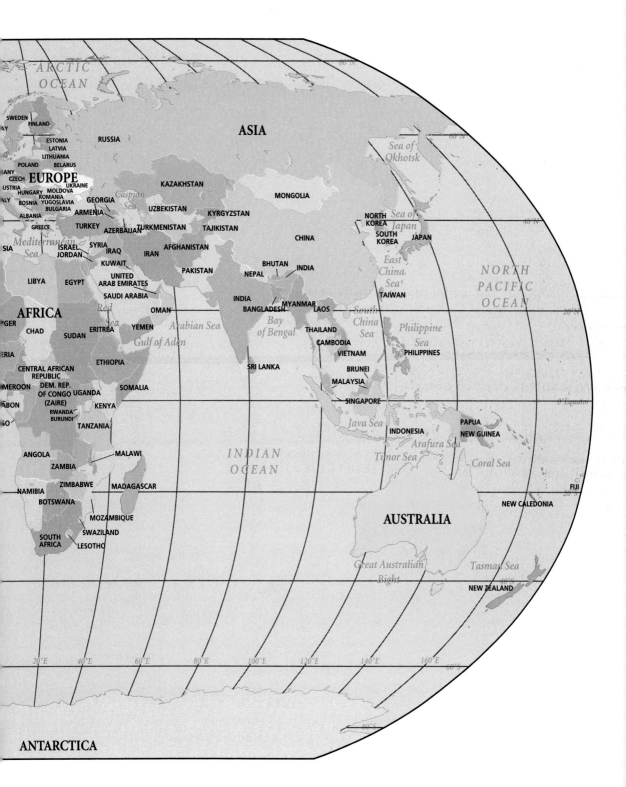

ARCTIC
OCEAN

SWEDEN
FINLAND
AY
ESTONIA
LATVIA
LITHUANIA
POLAND
BELARUS
ANY
CZECH
EUROPE
USTRIA
HUNGARY
MOLDOVA
ALY
BOSNIA
YUGOSLAVIA
BULGARIA
ALBANIA
GREECE
TURKEY

RUSSIA

ASIA

KAZAKHSTAN

MONGOLIA

Caspian
Sea

UZBEKISTAN

KYRGYZSTAN

GEORGIA
ARMENIA
AZERBAIJAN
TURKMENISTAN
TAJIKISTAN

CHINA

Sea of
Okhotsk

80°N

60°N

NORTH
KOREA
SOUTH
KOREA

Sea of
Japan

JAPAN

40°N

Mediterranean
Sea

SIA

ISRAEL
JORDAN
SYRIA
IRAQ
IRAN
KUWAIT

AFGHANISTAN

PAKISTAN

NEPAL
BHUTAN
INDIA

East
China
Sea

NORTH
PACIFIC
OCEAN

LIBYA
EGYPT
UNITED
ARAB EMIRATES
SAUDI ARABIA

TAIWAN

20°N

AFRICA

GER
CHAD
SUDAN

Red
Sea

OMAN

ERITREA
YEMEN

Arabian Sea

INDIA
BANGLADESH
MYANMAR
LAOS

Bay
of Bengal

South
China
Sea

Philippine
Sea

ERIA

Gulf of Aden

THAILAND

CAMBODIA
VIETNAM

PHILIPPINES

CENTRAL AFRICAN
REPUBLIC

ETHIOPIA

SRI LANKA

BRUNEI
MALAYSIA

MEROON
DEM. REP.
OF CONGO UGANDA
(ZAIRE)

SOMALIA

SINGAPORE

0° Equator

ABON
KENYA
RWANDA
BURUNDI
TANZANIA

Java Sea

INDONESIA

PAPUA
NEW GUINEA

GO

Arafura Sea

ANGOLA
MALAWI

Timor Sea

Coral Sea

ZAMBIA

INDIAN
OCEAN

NAMIBIA
ZIMBABWE
MADAGASCAR

BOTSWANA

FIJI

NEW CALEDONIA

20°S

MOZAMBIQUE

SOUTH
AFRICA
SWAZILAND
LESOTHO

AUSTRALIA

Great Australian
Bight

Tasman Sea

NEW ZEALAND

40°S

20°E
40°E
60°E
80°E
100°E
120°E
140°E
160°E

60°S

80°S

ANTARCTICA

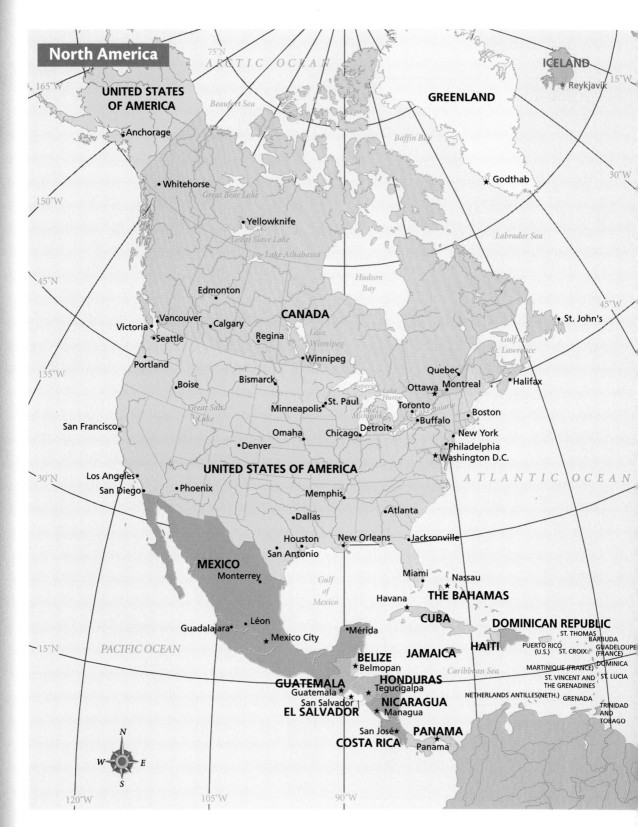

# North America

ARCTIC OCEAN

75°N

165°W

**UNITED STATES OF AMERICA**

Beaufort Sea

150°W

45°N

135°W

30°N

15°N

120°W

105°W

90°W

Anchorage

• Whitehorse

Great Bear Lake

• Yellowknife

Great Slave Lake

Lake Athabasca

Edmonton

**CANADA**

Vancouver • Calgary

Victoria • Regina

Seattle •

• Winnipeg

Portland

Bismarck

Boise •

Minneapolis

San Francisco •

Omaha •

• Denver

• Los Angeles

San Diego •

• Phoenix

**UNITED STATES OF AMERICA**

Memphis •

• Dallas

Houston •

San Antonio •

New Orleans •

Hudson Bay

Lake Winnipeg

Lake Superior

St. Paul •

Lake Michigan

Lake Huron

Chicago •

Detroit •

Lake Ontario

Lake Erie

Atlanta •

Jacksonville •

GREENLAND

ICELAND

15°W

• Reykjavik

Baffin Bay

★ Godthab

30°W

Labrador Sea

45°W

St. John's •

Gulf of St. Lawrence

Quebec •

Ottawa ★ Montreal •

Toronto •

Buffalo •

• Boston

New York •

Philadelphia •

★ Washington D.C.

ATLANTIC OCEAN

Great Salt Lake

**MEXICO**

Monterrey •

Guadalajara •

• Léon

• Mexico City

• Mérida

PACIFIC OCEAN

Gulf of Mexico

Miami •

Havana ★

Nassau ★

**THE BAHAMAS**

**CUBA**

**DOMINICAN REPUBLIC**

ST. THOMAS

BARBUDA

PUERTO RICO (U.S.) ST. CROIX •

GUADELOUPE (FRANCE)

**JAMAICA**

**HAITI**

MARTINIQUE (FRANCE) DOMINICA

**BELIZE**

★ Belmopan

Caribbean Sea

ST. VINCENT AND ST. LUCIA
THE GRENADINES

**GUATEMALA**

Guatemala ★

**HONDURAS**

Tegucigalpa •

NETHERLANDS ANTILLES(NETH.) GRENADA

San Salvador ★

**EL SALVADOR**

**NICARAGUA**

• Managua

TRINIDAD AND TOBAGO

San José ★

**COSTA RICA**

**PANAMA**

★ Panama

N

W   E

S

Caribbean Sea

ST. LUCIA

GRENADA

**South America**

Managua ★

San José

Panama

Barranquilla

Valencia

**Caracas** ★

**VENEZUELA**

Cúcuta

Medellín

**Bogotá** ★

Puerto Ayacucho

Georgetown ★

Paramaribo ★

**GUYANA**

**SURINAME**

★ Cayenne

**FRENCH GUIANA**

**COLOMBIA**

Mitú

Macapá ●

**ECUADOR** ★**Quito**

Guayaquil ●

Santarém

Belém ●

Galápagos
Islands

Talara ●

**PERU**

Fortaleza ●

Teresina ●

Trujillo ●

Porto Velho ●

**BRAZIL**

Recife ●

Maceió ●

Huánuco ●

Barreiras ●

Aracaju ●

Salvador ●

**Lima** ★

Ica ●

Cuzco ●

**BOLIVIA**

La Paz ★

Santa Cruz ●

★ **Sucre**

★ **Brásilia**

Goiânia ●

Iquique ●

**PARAGUAY**

Rio de Janeiro ●

São Paulo ●

**PACIFIC OCEAN**

Antofagasta ●

**CHILE**

★Asunción

Córdoba ●

Rosario ●

★ Santiago

Buenos Aires ★

**URUGUAY**

Montevideo ●

Concepción ●

**ARGENTINA**

**ATLANTIC OCEAN**

Valdivia ●

Puerto Montt ●

N
W ☼ E
S

Comodoro Rivadavia ●

**FALKLAND ISLANDS
(U.K.)**

**SOUTH GEORGIA ISLAND
(U.K.)**

90°W    80°W    70°W    60°W    50°W    40°W

10°N

0°N

0°

10°S

20°S

30°S

40°S

50°S

## Europe

Reykjavik ★ **ICELAND**

*Norwegian Sea*

**Faroe Islands**

**NORTH ATLANTIC OCEAN**

60°N

15°W

0°

15°E

45°E

**SWEDEN**

**FINLAND**

**NORWAY**

*Gulf of Bothnia*

**RUSSIA**

Oslo ★

Stockholm ★

Helsinki ★

★Tallinn

**ESTONIA**

Moscow ★

*Baltic Sea*

*North Sea*

Riga ★

**LATVIA**

**IRELAND**

Belfast ★

Dublin ★

**DENMARK**

★Copenhagen

**LITHUANIA**

Vilnius ★

★ Minsk

**BELARUS**

**U. K.**

**NETHERLANDS**

Amsterdam ★

Berlin ★

Warsaw ★

London ★

*English Channel*

Brussels ★

**BELGIUM**

**LUX.**

**GERMANY**

**POLAND**

★ Kiev

**UKRAIN**

Paris ★

Prague ★

**CZECH REP.**

Ostrava ●

**SLOVAKIA**

**FRANCE**

Bern ★

Vienna ★

★Bratislava

★ Budapest

**MOLDOVA**

Chisinau ●

**SWITZERLAND**

**AUSTRIA**

**HUNGARY**

**ROMANIA**

*Bay of Biscay*

**SLOVENIA**

★Zagreb

Belgrade ●

Bucharest ●

*Black Se*

45°N

Monte Carlo ★

**BOSNIA AND HERZEGOVINA**

**CROATIA**

★Sarajevo

**YUGOSLAVIA**

Varna ●

**MONACO**

**ITALY**

*Adriatic Sea*

**BULGARIA**

Ank

**PORTUGAL**

**ANDORRA**

★ Madrid

*Corsica*

Rome ●

**MACEDONIA**

Sofia ●

★Skopje

Lisbon ●

**SPAIN**

*Sardinia*

Tiranë ●

**ALBANIA**

★ Gibraltar

*Balearic Islands*

*Tyrrhenian Sea*

*Aegean Sea*

**GREECE**

Algiers

★Athens

Rabat

Tunis

*Ionian Sea*

N

W ✦ E

S

★Valletta

**MALTA**

Tripoli

*Mediterranean Sea*

Alexandria

East
Siberian Sea

75°N

RUSSIA

RUSSIA

•Moscow

•Novosibirsk

Sea of Okhotsk

Bering Sea

60°N

Karaganda
KAZAKHSTAN

Ulaanbaatar•
MONGOLIA

AZERBAIJAN
GEORGIA
TURKMENISTAN
UZBEKISTAN

45°N

Black Sea
ARMENIA
Tashkent•

KYRGYZSTAN

TAJIKISTAN

Beijing•

NORTH KOREA
•Pyongyang
•Seoul JAPAN
SOUTH KOREA •Tokyo

TURKEY

CHINA

SYRIA
Baghdad
IRAQ
•Tehran
AFGHANISTAN

East
China
Sea

PACIFIC
OCEAN

30°N

ISRAEL
JORDAN KUWAIT
QATAR
SAUDI ARABIA
U.A.E.

IRAN

PAKISTAN

New Delhi
INDIA
Dhaka
Calcutta•

NEPAL
BHUTAN

Chengdu•

MYANMAR

TAIWAN

Hong Kong•

Red
Sea
•Sanaa YEMEN

OMAN

Bombay•

BANGLADESH
Rangoon
•Vientiane
Bangkok

Hanoi•

LAOS

Manila•

15°N

THAILAND
KAMPUCHEA

VIETNAM
Phnom Penh

PHILIPPINES
•Davao

Colombo•
SRI LANKA

BRUNEI
MALAYSIA
Kuala Lumpur•

0°

INDIAN OCEAN

Jakarta•
Java Sea
I N D O N E S I A

Arafura Sea

PAPUA
NEW GUINEA
Port Moresby•

Timor Sea

Coral Sea

FIJI

NEW CALEDONIA

AUSTRALIA

30°S

N
W E
S

Perth•

Great
Australian Bight

Adelaide•
•Canberra

Auckland•

Tasman
Sea

Wellington•

NEW ZEALAND

30°E 60°E 90°E 120°E 150°E 180°E

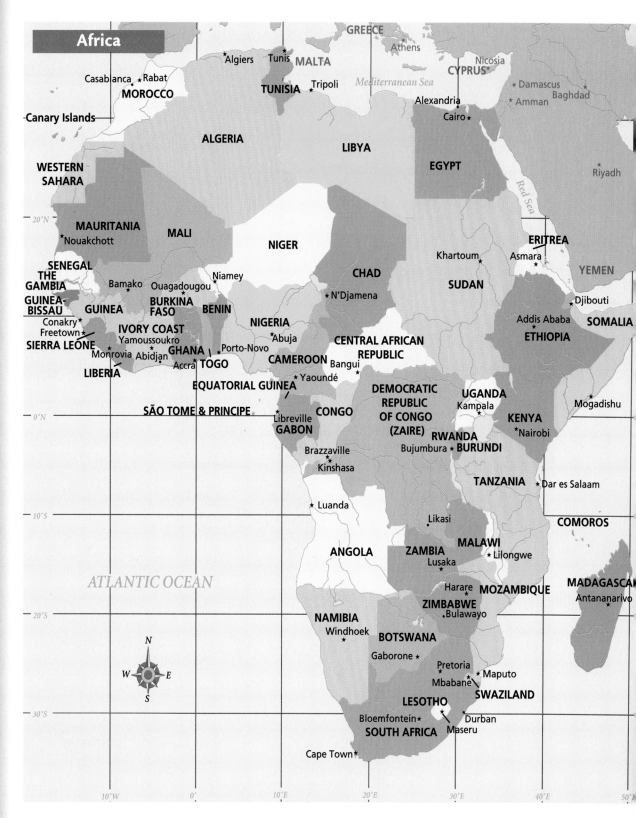

# Africa

GREECE
Athens
MALTA
Algiers ★ Tunis ★
Casablanca ★ Rabat
MOROCCO
TUNISIA
Tripoli
Mediterranean Sea
Nicosia
CYPRUS ★
★ Damascus
Amman ★ Baghdad
Alexandria
Cairo ★
Canary Islands

WESTERN
SAHARA

ALGERIA

LIBYA

EGYPT

Red Sea

Riyadh

20°N

MAURITANIA
★Nouakchott

MALI

NIGER

CHAD

SUDAN

Khartoum
★

ERITREA
Asmara
★

YEMEN

SENEGAL
THE
GAMBIA
Bamako
★
Niamey
Ouagadougou
N'Djamena

Djibouti

GUINEA-
BISSAU
Conakry ★
Freetown ★
SIERRA LEONE
GUINEA
BURKINA
FASO
BENIN
NIGERIA
Abuja
★

CENTRAL AFRICAN
REPUBLIC

Addis Ababa
★
ETHIOPIA

SOMALIA

IVORY COAST
Yamoussoukro
Monrovia ★ Abidjan
LIBERIA
GHANA
Accra ★ TOGO
Porto-Novo
CAMEROON
Bangui
★

Mogadishu

EQUATORIAL GUINEA
★ Yaoundé

0°N

SÃO TOME & PRINCIPE
CONGO
Libreville ★
GABON

DEMOCRATIC
REPUBLIC
OF CONGO
(ZAIRE)

UGANDA
Kampala
★

RWANDA
Bujumbura ★ BURUNDI

KENYA
★ Nairobi

Brazzaville
★
Kinshasa

TANZANIA
★ Dar es Salaam

10°S

Luanda
★

Likasi
★

COMOROS

ATLANTIC OCEAN

ANGOLA

ZAMBIA
Lusaka
★

MALAWI
★ Lilongwe

MADAGASCAR
Antananarivo
★

Harare
★
ZIMBABWE
Bulawayo
★
MOZAMBIQUE

20°S

NAMIBIA
Windhoek
★

BOTSWANA
Gaborone ★

Pretoria
★
Mbabane ★ Maputo
SWAZILAND

N
W ★ E
S

LESOTHO
Bloemfontein ★
SOUTH AFRICA
Maseru ★
Durban

30°S

Cape Town ★

10°W        0°        10°E        20°E        30°E        40°E        50°E

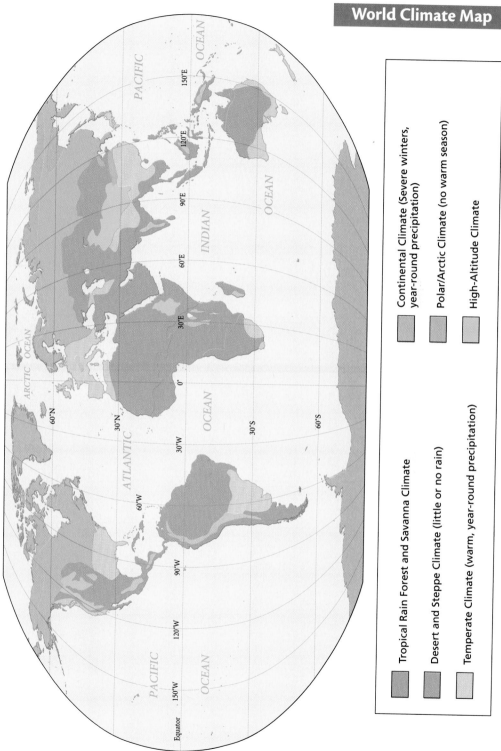

PACIFIC OCEAN

150°E

120°E

90°E

INDIAN

60°E

OCEAN

30°E

0°

ARCTIC OCEAN

ATLANTIC

OCEAN

60°N

30°N

30°W

30°S

60°W

60°S

90°W

120°W

PACIFIC

150°W

OCEAN

Equator

Tropical Rain Forest and Savanna Climate

Desert and Steppe Climate (little or no rain)

Temperate Climate (warm, year-round precipitation)

Continental Climate (Severe winters, year-round precipitation)

Polar/Arctic Climate (no warm season)

High-Altitude Climate

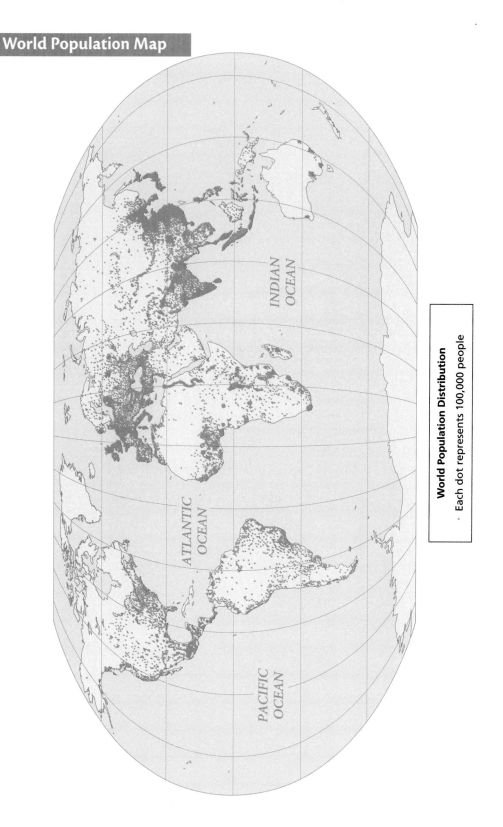

**World Population Distribution**

· Each dot represents 100,000 people

INDIAN OCEAN

ATLANTIC OCEAN

PACIFIC OCEAN

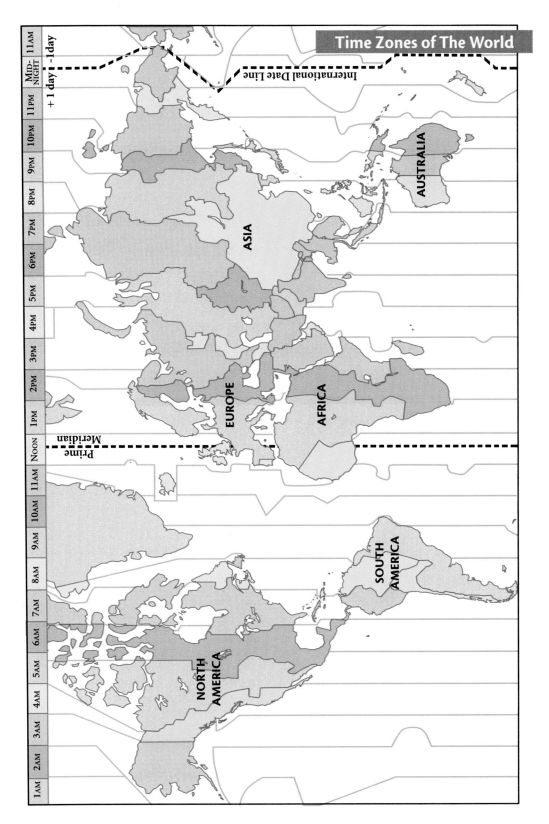

Time Zones of The World

International Date Line

Prime Meridian

NORTH AMERICA

SOUTH AMERICA

EUROPE

AFRICA

ASIA

AUSTRALIA

+1 day    -1day

1AM 2AM 3AM 4AM 5AM 6AM 7AM 8AM 9AM 10AM 11AM NOON 1PM 2PM 3PM 4PM 5PM 6PM 7PM 8PM 9PM 10PM 11PM MID-NIGHT 11AM

# Glossary

## A

**Aborigine** (ab ə rij′ə nē) One of the original people of Australia (p. 448)

**Absolute location** (ab′ sə lüt lō kā′ shən) The exact spot or area of a place (p. 27)

**Accent** (ak′ sent) The unusual way of speaking that occurs when people speak a language other than their first language; a way a person speaks that is common to the person's region (p. 212)

**Acid rain** (as′ id rān) A harmful form of rain that contains acids created when certain materials are released into the air (p. 240)

**Adobe** (ə dō′ bē) A sun-dried brick (p. 362)

**Agribusiness** (ag′ rə biz nis) The business of farming with large farms and lots of machines and chemicals (p. 130)

**Ainu** (ī′ nü) The original people of Japan (p. 384)

**Alluvial** (ə lü′ vē əl) Fertile soil left behind by a river after a flood (p. 403)

**Alms** (ämz) Charity to the poor (p. 342)

**Alpaca** (al pak′ ə) An animal similar to a llama with silky hair (p. 127)

**Altitude** (al′ tə tüd) The height of something above or below sea level (p. 85)

**Ancestor worship** (an′ ses tər wer′ ship) Worshiping members of one's family who lived long ago (p. 280)

**Animist** (an′ ə mist) A person who believes that things in nature contain a spirit and who worships ancestors (p. 280)

**Apartheid** (ə pärt′ hāt) A system that set blacks and other nonwhite South Africans apart from whites (p. 301)

**Aquaculture** (ak′ wə kul chər) Fish farming (p. 216)

**Aquifer** (ak′ wə fər) An underground water source (p. 337)

**Arable land** (ar′ ə bəl land) Land on which farmers can raise crops (p. 370)

**Archipelago** (är chə pel′ ə gō) A group of islands (p. 100)

**Arctic** (ark′ tik) The cold area at the most northern part of Earth (p. 204)

**Arctic Circle** (ark′ tik sėr′ kal) The area of latitude about 66.5° north of the equator (p. 61)

**Assembly line** (ə sem′ blē līn) A group of workers who put parts together to make a product quickly (p. 48)

**Atheist** (ā′ thē ist) A person who does not believe in God (p. 254)

**Atoll** (at′ ol) A chain of islands made up of coral (p. 103)

## B

**Balkanization** (bôl kən ī zā′ shən) The breaking up of a geographical area or a group of people into smaller political groups; these smaller groups often fight with one another (p. 229)

**Bantu** (ban′ tü) An African cultural group that mostly farms for a living (p. 320)

**Basin** (bā′ sn) A low area of land surrounded by higher land, often mountains (p. 37)

**Bedrock** (bed′ rok) The solid rock under the loose material and soil of Earth's surface (p. 56)

**Benelux country** (ben′ ə luks kun′ trē) One of three countries: Belgium, Netherlands, or Luxembourg (p. 176)

**Bilingual** (bī ling′ gwəl) Speaking two languages (p. 64)

**Birthrate** (bėrth′ rāt) The number of births over a given period of time (p. 110)

**Bog** (bôg) A low-lying swampy area that water covers for long periods of time (p. 148)

**Bonsai** (bon′ sī) A small plant or tree (p. 383)

**Boomerang** (bü′ mə rang) A wooden weapon curved so that it returns to the person throwing it (p. 448)

**Brahma** (brä′ mə) A Hindu god; the creative face of God (p. 407)

**Buddhism** (bü′ diz əm) A religion based on the teachings of Buddha and practiced mainly in central and eastern Asia (p. 364)

## C

**Campesino** (käm pā sē′ nō) A poor farmer (p. 88)

**Capitalism** (kap′ ə tə liz əm) An economic system in which people own their own businesses that the government does not control (p. 432)

**Carbon dioxide** (kär′ bən dī ok′ sīd) A gas made up of carbon and oxygen (p. 131)

**Cash crop** (kash krop) A crop raised to be sold by those who grow it (p. 102)

**Caste** (kast) A Hindu social group (p. 408)

**Chinook** (shə nůk′) A hot, dry wind along the eastern slopes of the Rocky Mountains (p. 62)

**Christian** (kris′ chən) A person who accepts the teachings of Jesus (p. 43)

**Christianity** (kris chē an′ ə tē) The religion of Christians (p. 43)

**Civil unrest** (siv′ əl un rest′) A situation in which people rebel because they are unhappy with the conditions in their country (p. 301)

**Civil war** (siv′ əl wôr) A war fought by people within a single country or state against each other (p. 109)

**Clear-cut** (klēr′ kut) To cut down every tree in a forest; an area on which all the trees have been cut down (p. 131)

**Climate** (klī′ mit) The average of weather conditions over a period of time (p. 39)

**Collective farm** (kə lek′ tiv färm) A large, state-owned farm worked by the people (p. 260)

**Command economy** (kə mand′ i kon′ ə mē) An economy in which the government makes the key economic decisions (p. 258)

**Commonwealth of Independent States (CIS)** (kom′ ən welth ov in di pen′ dənt stāts) A group made up of Russia and many of the republics that used to be part of the Soviet Union (p. 248)

**Commonwealth of Nations** (kom′ ən welth ov nā′ shəns) A group of independent nations that were once part of the British Empire and now work together (p. 451)

**Communism** (kom′ yə niz əm) A government system in which there is no private property; the government owns and controls the land and goods (p. 109)

**Concentration camp** (kon sən trā′ shen kamp) A large prison death camp (p. 235)

**Constitution** (kon stə tü′ shən) A nation's written document of rules (p. 248)

**Consumer** (kən sü′ mər) A person who buys and uses goods and services (p. 154)

**Consumer electronics** (kən sü′ mər i lek tron′ iks) Electronic products that people use in their homes (p. 390)

**Consumer goods** (kən sü′ mər gùdz) Things people buy for themselves and for their homes (p. 236)

**Continent** (kon′ tə nənt) One of the seven large areas of land on Earth (p. 34)

**Continental climate** (kon tə nen′ tl klī′ mit) The climate in landlocked areas far from oceans; a climate of short, warm summers and long winters (p. 62)

**Continental drift** (kon tə nen′ tl drift) The theory that one huge piece of land once sat in Earth's ocean and that the land then drifted apart into seven continents (p. 120)

**Coral** (kôr′ əl) A tiny sea animal (p. 103)

**Cordillera** (kôr də lyer′ ə) The Spanish word for mountain range (p. 60)

**Cosmopolitan** (koz mə pol′ ə tən) Having people from all over the world (p. 65)

**Cottage industry** (kot′ ij in′ də strē) The making of a product at home (p. 413)

**Coup** (kü) A sudden overthrow of a government (p. 282)

**Crater** (krā′ tər) The bowl-shaped opening at the mouth of a volcano (p. 381)

**Creole** (krē′ ōl) A mixture of French and African languages (p. 107)

**Cultivator** (kul′ tə vā tər) A farmer who grows crops to sell and to support the family (p. 279)

**Cultural crossroad** (kul′ chər əl kròs′ rōd) A place where different cultures come into contact with one another (p. 234)

**Cultural diffusion** (kul′ chər əl di fyü′ zhən) The borrowing of languages, customs, and religions among cultures (p. 42)

**Culture** (kul′ chər) The languages, religions, customs, art, and dress of a people (p. 26)

**Currency** (kèr′ ən sē) A system of money (p. 173)

**Cyclone** (sī′ klōn) A storm system with strong winds that spin in a circular motion (p. 405)

**Cyrillic alphabet** (si ril′ ik al′ fə bet) An alphabet that began around A.D. 900 and was used to translate the Bible into Slavic languages (p. 234)

---

### D

**Daylight saving time** (dā′ līt sā′ ving tīm) A way of making better use of daylight by setting clocks one hour ahead in the spring and one hour back in the fall (p. 468)

**Death rate** (deth rāt) The number of deaths over a given period of time (p. 128)

**Deciduous** (di sij′ ü əs) A type of tree that drops its leaves (p. 83)

**Deforestation** (de fō rest ā′ shən) The clearing or destruction of forests (p. 68)

| a | hat | e | let | ī | ice | ô | order | ù | put | sh | she | a | in about |
|---|-----|---|-----|---|-----|---|-------|---|-----|----|-----|---|----------|
| ā | age | ē | equal | o | hot | oi | oil | ü | rule | th | thin | e | in taken |
| ä | far | èr | term | ō | open | ou | out | ch | child | ᴛʜ | then | ə ⟨ i | in pencil |
| â | care | i | it | ò | saw | u | cup | ng | long | zh | measure | o | in lemon |
| | | | | | | | | | | | | u | in circus |

**Delta** (del´tə) An area of rich land at the mouth of a river; new land formed by dirt carried downstream by a river (p. 38)

**Descendant** (di sen´dənt) A person who is related to a certain group of people (p. 86)

**Desert** (dez´ərt) A dry area in which few or no people live (p. 36)

**Desertification** (di zėrt ə fə kā´shən) The change from land that produces crops to desert land (p. 275)

**Developed country** (di vel´əped kun´trē) A country that has already built its economy and has money to provide services for its citizens (p. 468)

**Developing country** (di vel´ə ping kun´trē) A country in which people are poor and earn their living mostly by farming (p. 239)

**Dharma** (där´mə) One's duty (p. 408)

**Dialect** (dī´ə lekt) A different form of a language (p. 170)

**Dictator** (dik´tā tər) A person who makes all the laws for a country and rules by force (p. 324)

**Dike** (dīk) A wall that prevents flooding and keeps back the sea (p. 167)

**Diversity** (də vėr´sə tē) A variety of people; differences (p. 65)

**Dormant** (dôr´mənt) The state a volcano is in when it is not likely to erupt (p. 103)

**Dreamtime** (drēm´tīm) The Aboriginal belief that the past, present, and future are part of the now and that spirits of ancestors exist in nature (p. 449)

**Dredge** (drej) To clear away the sand and mud from the bottom of a waterway (p. 276)

**Drought** (drout) A long period of dry weather (p. 62)

## E

**Earthquake** (ėrth´kwāk) The shaking of Earth's surface from plate movement (p. 81)

**Economy** (i kon´ə mē) A system of building, using, and distributing wealth and resources (p. 26)

**Ecotourism** (ē´kō tùr iz əm) A type of tourism in which people come to a country because of its wildlife and the beauty of its land (p. 306)

**El Niño** (el nē´nyō) The unusual warming of the tropical Pacific Ocean that occurs about every three to five years (p. 467)

**Empire** (em´pīr) A nation that rules a large area of land (p. 86)

**E-mail** (ē´māl) A tool that allows people to send written messages electronically over the Internet (p. 465)

**Endangered** (en dān´jerd) An animal or a plant that may become extinct, or cease to exist on Earth (p. 326)

**Epic** (ep´ik) A long poem about ancient heroes (p. 341)

**Equator** (i kwā´tər) An imaginary line that goes around the middle of Earth; it lies halfway between the North and the South Poles (p. 34)

**Erosion** (i rō´zhən) The process by which running water, wind, or ice break down rock or soil (p. 68)

**Erupt** (i rupt´) To burst out of the ground or out of a volcano (p. 209)

**Escarpment** (e skärp´mənt) A line of cliffs or slopes from a plateau to the plains below (p. 276)

**Estuary** (es´chü er ē) A flooded river valley at the mouth of a river where saltwater from a sea mixes with freshwater from a river (p. 124)

**Ethnic group** (eth´nik grüp) A group of people who have a common language, culture, and set of values (p. 234)

**Eurasia** (yùr ā´zhə) The world's largest landmass; the continents of Europe and Asia together (p. 167)

**European Union** (yùr ə pē´ən yü´nyən) A group of European nations that agreed to rid trade barriers and use a common currency (p. 173)

**Evaporate** (i vap´ə rāt) The changing of liquid water into water vapor (p. 317)

**Export** (ek´spôrt) Something sent to another country; to sell something to another country (p. 65)

**Export economy** (ek´spôrt i kon´ə mē) A type of economy in which a country depends on exports for growth (p. 389)

**Extended family** (ek´sten ded fam´ə lē) An entire family, including parents, children, grandparents, aunts, uncles, cousins, godparents, and even close friends (p. 190)

**Extinct** (ek stingkt´) No longer existing anywhere (p. 113)

## F

**Fertile Crescent** (fėr´tl kres´nt) The land between the Tigris and Euphrates Rivers in Iraq and the Jordan River in Israel and Jordan (p. 334)

**Fertilizer** (fėr´tl ī zər) A material that makes crops grow (p. 338)

**Filial piety** (fil´ē əl pī´ə tē) Respect for one's parents and ancestors (p. 363)

**Finance** (fī´nans) The use and management of money by banks, businesses, and corporations (p. 65)

**Fjord** (fyôrd) A long, deep, narrow, ocean inlet that reaches far inland (p. 208)

**Floodplain** (flud´ plān) A level area of land built up by flood deposits (p. 361)

**Foothill** (fut´ hil) A hill at the base of higher hills or a mountain range (p. 123)

**Foreign aid** (fôr´ ən ād) Money, medicine, tools, or machinery given by one country to help another country (p. 475)

**Foreign debt** (fôr´ ən det) The money a country owes to other governments (p. 92)

**Foreigner** (fôr´ ə nər) A person from another country (p. 172)

**Fossil** (fos´ əl) A mold or part of an ancient plant or animal (p. 120)

**Free-market economy** (frē mär´ kit i kon´ ə mē) An economy in which producers compete for the business of consumers (p. 154)

**Free trade** (frē trād) Trading without barriers between countries (p. 91)

**Gale** (gāl) A strong wind (p. 149)

**Gaucho** (gou´ chō) A cowhand of the pampas (p. 128)

**Geography** (jē og´ rə fē) The study of the planet Earth and its people (p. 24)

**Geological fault** (jē ə loj´ ə kel fölt) A break in the earth's crust (p. 316)

**Geologist** (jē ol´ ə jist) A person who studies Earth's physical structure and history (p. 60)

**Geothermal** (jē ō thėr´ məl) Heat from the interior of the earth (p. 103)

**Geyser** (gi´ zər) A hot spring that throws out jets of water and steam (p. 208)

**Glacier** (glā´ shər) A large, slow-moving sheet of ice (p. 38)

**Globalization** (glō bəl i zā´ shən) The steady knitting together of all of the world's economies into one (p. 474)

**Global village** (glō´ bəl vil´ ij) The sharing of ideas, cultures, and traditions around the world (p. 464)

**Global warming** (glō´ bəl wôrm´ ing) A rise in Earth's temperature caused by too much carbon dioxide in the air (p. 132)

**Great Rift Valley** (grāt rift val´ ē) A long valley in Africa that is a geological fault (p. 316)

**Gulf Stream** (gulf strēm) A warm ocean current that begins in the western Caribbean Sea and travels northward through the Atlantic Ocean (p. 149)

**Hacienda** (hä sē en´ də) A large, self-sufficient farm in a Spanish-speaking country (p. 101)

**Hajj** (haj) The pilgrimage to Mecca that is a religious duty of all Muslims, if they can afford it (p. 342)

**Harmattan** (här mət´ tan) The dry, dusty wind on the Atlantic coast of West Africa (p. 277)

**Harmony** (här´ mə nē) The ability to work together and to blend in (p. 383)

**Heavy industry** (hev´ ē in´ də strē) Steel, heavy machinery, and other such industries (p. 154)

**Hemisphere** (hem´ ə sfir) One half of Earth (p. 442)

**Highland climate** (hī´ lənd klī´ mit) The varying climate of a mountainous area (p. 40)

**Hinduism** (hin´ dü iz əm) A religion in which followers worship many gods (p. 407)

**Holocaust** (hol´ ə kȯst) The attempt by Germany's Nazi Party to kill all the Jews in Europe during World War II (p. 235)

**Homogenous** (hō mə jē´ nəs) Belonging to the same group; alike in many ways (p. 211)

**Horn of Africa** (hôrn ov af´ rə kə) The four countries of Djibouti, Eritrea, Ethiopia, and Somalia, which stick out like a rhinoceros horn on the eastern coast of Africa (p. 314)

**Horticulture** (hôr´ tə kul chər) The growing of flowers, fruits, and vegetables for sale (p. 324)

**Human geography** (hyü´ mən jē og´ rə fē) The study of how people live on Earth (p. 25)

**Humid** (hyü´ mid) Very moist (p. 40)

**Humid continental climate** (hyü´ mid kon tə nen´ tl klī´ mit) A climate with long, cold winters and hot, wet summers; a climate with four different seasons (p. 40)

**Hurricane** (hėr´ ə kān) A tropical storm with strong winds, heavy rainfall, and huge waves (p. 105)

**Hydroelectric** (hī drō i lek´ trik) Power created by running water (p. 39)

| a | hat | e | let | ī | ice | ȯ | order | u̇ | put | sh | she | | a | in about |
|---|-----|---|-----|---|-----|---|-------|----|-----|----|-----|---|---|----------|
| ā | age | ē | equal | o | hot | oi | oil | ü | rule | th | thin | ə | e | in taken |
| ä | far | ėr | term | ō | open | ou | out | ch | child | ᴛʜ | then | | i | in pencil |
| â | care | i | it | ȯ | saw | u | cup | ng | long | zh | measure | | o | in lemon |
| | | | | | | | | | | | | | u | in circus |

## I

**Ideogram** (id′ ē ə gram) A picture, symbol, or mark that stands for a thing or an idea in the Chinese language; a character (p. 364)

**Illegal** (i lē′ gəl) Unlawful; against the law (p. 92)

**Immigrant** (im′ ə grənt) A person who leaves one country and goes to live in another (p. 43)

**Import** (im pôrt′) A product from another country; to bring a product from another country into one's own country (p. 47)

**Individuality** (in də vij ü al′ ə tē) The condition in which people act and think for themselves (p. 383)

**Industrial Revolution** (in dus′ trē əl rev ə lü′ shen) A nonviolent change in the late 1700s that included a great increase in the use of iron and steel machines (p. 146)

**Industry** (in′ də strē) A business that makes or puts together things to sell (p. 35)

**Inflation** (in flā′ shən) A period of rising prices (p. 194)

**Interaction** (in tər ak′ shən) How people settle, use, live on, and change the land (p. 27)

**Intercropping** (in′ tər krop ping) Planting different crops in the same field (p. 284)

**Interdependent** (in tər di pen′ dənt) Dependent on one another; being dependent on what happens somewhere else (p. 464)

**International Monetary Fund (IMF)** (in tər nash′ ə nel mon′ ə ter ē fund) An organization that gathers money from 175 members to help countries in need (p. 475)

**International trade** (in tər nash′ ə nel trād) The buying and selling of goods and services between people in different countries (p. 174)

**Internet** (in′ tər net) The international computer network (p. 465)

**Inuit** (in′ ü it) The native people of Canada (p. 58)

**Invader** (in vād′ er) A person who marches into another country in order to overrun it (p. 166)

**Invest** (in vest′) To give or loan money to something in the hope of getting more money back in the future (p. 130)

**Irrigate** (ir′ ə gāt) To pipe in or channel water to fields that get little rain (p. 80)

**Islam** (is′ ləm) The religion that began in Saudi Arabia and that follows the Islamic holy book, the Koran; Muslims are those who follow Islam (p. 342)

**Isolated** (ī′ sə lāt ed) Separated from other areas or people (p. 86)

**Isthmus** (is′ məs) A narrow strip of land connecting two larger land areas (p. 80)

## J

**Jainism** (jī′ niz əm) A religion that began as a protest against the caste system (p. 409)

**Jati** (jät′ ē) A small group within a larger caste (p. 408)

**Judaism** (jü′ dē iz′ əm) The religion of Jews that teaches belief in one God as the creator of the universe (p. 43)

**Jungle** (jung′ gəl) A thick growth of trees and vines (p. 82)

## K

**Karma** (kär′ mə) One's future (p. 408)

## L

**Lagoon** (lə gün′) A shallow body of water separated from the sea (p. 276)

**Landlocked** (land′ lokt) Surrounded by land and little water (p. 62)

**Land reform** (land ri fôrm′) The taking of land from the wealthy and giving it to the poor people who have worked on it (p. 90)

**Landslide** (land′ slīd) The rapid sliding of earth, rocks, or mud down a slope (p. 425)

**La Niña** (lä nē′ nyä) A weather pattern in which ocean currents are colder than usual (p. 467)

**Latitude** (lat′ ə tüd) How far north or south of the equator a place is (p. 34)

**Lava** (lä′ və) Hot, liquid rock (p. 81)

**Leach** (lēch) To wash out minerals from soil (p. 432)

**Leeward** (lē′ wərd) The side away from the wind (p. 40)

**Levant** (lə vant′) The coastal farming region of Syria, Lebanon, and Israel (p. 334)

**Life expectancy** (līf ek spek′ tən sē) The average number of years a person is expected to live (p. 281)

**Light industry** (līt in′ də strē) The making of everyday products that people use (p. 369)

**Llama** (lä′ mə) An animal related to the camel and used to carry things (p. 127)

**Location** (lō kā′ shən) The place on Earth where something is (p. 27)

**Loch** (lok) A Scottish lake (p. 145)

**Loess** (lō′ is) A fine and fertile soil that the wind deposits on the ground (p. 123)

**Longitude** (lon′ jə tüd) How far east or west a place is from the Prime Meridian (p. 34)

**Maghreb nations** (mäg´ reb nä´ shəns) Morocco, Tunisia, and Algeria, which are farthest west in North Africa (p. 334)

**Magma** (mag´ mə) Hot liquid rock (p. 444)

**Mainland** (mān´ land) A continent or part of a continent that is not an island (p. 100)

**Majority** (mə jôr´ ə tē) More than half of a group of people or things (p. 427)

**Mangrove** (mang´ grōv) A tropical tree that grows on swampy, coastal ground (p. 274)

**Manual labor** (man´ yü əl lā´ bər) Physical work that requires little skill (p. 384)

**Maori** (mou´ rē) The native people of New Zealand (p. 449)

**Maquiladora** (mä kē´ lä dō rä) A foreign-owned assembly plant in Mexico (p. 91)

**Marine west coast climate** (mə rēn´ west kōst klī´ mit) A climate from southeast Alaska to California that has mild, cloudy summers and wet winters (p. 41)

**Maritime** (mar´ ə tīm) Bordering on or near the sea (p. 57)

**Maritime climate** (mar´ ə tīm klī´ mit) The type of climate influenced by being close to water (p. 61)

**Market economy** (mär´ kit i kon´ ə mē) An economy in which there are privately-owned businesses (p. 258)

**Marsupial** (mär sü´ pē əl) An animal that carries its young in a pouch (p. 454)

**Mediterranean climate** (med´ ə tə rā nē ən klī´ mit) A climate like that of countries near the Mediterranean Sea: mild, wet winters and hot, dry summers (p. 41)

**Megalopolis** (meg ə lop´ ə lis) A vast city made up of many cities, one right next to another (p. 44)

**Meridian** (mə rid´ ē ən) An imaginary line that circles Earth and runs through the North and South Poles (p. 442)

**Meseta** (mä sā´ tə) The large plateau in Spain that is dry and hot with little vegetation (p. 184)

**Messiah** (mə sī´ ə) A leader who saves others (p. 342)

**Mestizo** (me stē´ zō) A person of mixed native and European ancestry (p. 86)

**Metropolitan area** (met rə pol´ ə tən ar´ ē ə) A city and its suburbs (p. 44)

**Migration** (mī grā´ shən) A large movement of people from one place to another (p. 88)

**Minority** (mə nôr´ ə tē) A small group within a larger group (p. 211)

**Missionary** (mish´ ə ner ē) A member of a church who travels to spread religious beliefs (p. 279)

**Mistral** (mis´ träl) A strong, cold, dry northerly wind from the Alps that blows across southern France (p. 169)

**Moisture** (mois´ chər) Wetness; rain or snow (p. 381)

**Monotheism** (mon´ ə thē iz əm) A belief in only one God (p. 341)

**Monsoon** (mon sün´) Winds that change direction according to the time of year and bring heavy rains in the summer (p. 405)

**Mosque** (mosk) An Islamic house of worship (p. 321)

**Movement** (müv´ mənt) How people, ideas, and products move between places (p. 28)

**Mulatto** (mə lät´ ō) A person whose ancestors were African and European (p. 106)

**Multiculturalism** (mul ti kul´ chər ə liz əm) A blend of many cultures (p. 42)

**Multinational corporation** (mul ti nash´ ə nəl kôr pə rā´ shen) A large company that does business in more than one country (p. 131)

**Muslim** (muz´ ləm) A follower of Islam (p. 235)

**Mutton** (mut´ n) The meat of full-grown sheep (p. 452)

**Narrows** (nar´ ōz) A place where a river becomes narrow; a strait that connects two bodies of water (p. 232)

**Natural resource** (nach´ ər əl rē´ sôrs) A raw material from nature (p. 46)

**Navigable** (nav´ ə gə bəl) A body of water that is deep and wide enough for ships to sail on (p. 104)

**Nilotic** (nī lot´ ik) An African cultural group that mostly herds animals for a living (p. 320)

**Nirvana** (nir vä´ nə) A perfect state of mind (p. 408)

**Nomad** (nō´ mad) A person who moves from place to place (p. 211)

**Nongovernmental organization (NGO)** (non guv´ ərn mən tal ôr gə nə zā´ shən) An organization that is made up of private individuals and that is not run by the government (p. 472)

| a | hat | e | let | ī | ice | ô | order | ů | put | sh | she | ə | a | in about |
|---|-----|---|-----|---|-----|---|-------|---|-----|----|-----|---|---|----------|
| ā | age | ē | equal | o | hot | oi | oil | ü | rule | th | thin | | e | in taken |
| ä | far | ėr | term | ō | open | ou | out | ch | child | ᴛʜ | then | | i | in pencil |
| â | care | i | it | ò | saw | u | cup | ng | long | zh | measure | | o | in lemon |
| | | | | | | | | | | | | | u | in circus |

**North American Free Trade Agreement (NAFTA)** (nôrth ə mer´ ə kən frē trād ə grē´ mənt) An agreement among Canada, the United States, and Mexico that dropped trade barriers and created free trade in North America (p. 91)

**Nuclear waste** (nü´ klē ər wāst) The waste produced by atomic power plants (p. 262)

## O

**Oasis** (ō ā´ sis) An area in the desert with enough freshwater to grow crops or sustain life (p. 337)

**Offshore** (of´ shôr) In water rather than on land (p. 90)

**Organization of Petroleum Exporting Countries (OPEC)** (ôr gə nə zā´ shen ov pə trōl´ lē əm ek spôrt´ ing kun´ trēz) A group of oil producing countries that tries to control the supply of oil by setting production limits (p. 346)

**Outback** (out´ bak) The hot, dry land in the middle of Australia (p. 445)

**Overdevelopment** (ō vər di vel´ əp ment) Developing an area too quickly, without paying attention to the environment (p. 112)

**Overgraze** (ō vər grāz´) To put too many grazing animals on a piece of land (p. 454)

**Ozone layer** (ō´ zōn lā´ ər) The layer of gas above Earth that protects Earth's atmosphere by filtering out the sun's harmful rays (p. 466)

## P

**Paddy** (pad´ ē) A water-covered field (p. 433)

**Palestinian Liberation Organization (PLO)** (pal ə stin´ ē ən lib ə rā´ shən ôr gə nə zā´ shən) An organization of Arabs in Palestine who want their own homeland (p. 345)

**Pampa** (pam´ pə) The grass-covered plain of Argentina (p. 123)

**Pangaea** (pan jē´ ə) The one huge piece of land that once sat in Earth's ocean (p. 120)

**Partition** (pär tish´ ən) To split into different areas; a divided area (p. 410)

**Pass** (pas) An opening in a mountain range (p. 167)

**Pastoralist** (pas´ tər əl ist) A person who looks after animals (p. 279)

**Peak** (pēk) The top of a mountain (p.167)

**Peasant** (pez´ nt) A poor farmer or farmworker (p. 92)

**Peat** (pēt) Decayed plants that have grown in bogs; material burned for heat (p. 148)

**Peninsula** (pə nin´ sə lə) A strip of land surrounded on three sides by water (p. 82)

**Per capita income** (pər kap´ ə tə in´ kum) A way to measure how rich a country is by dividing total income by the number of people (p. 154)

**Permafrost** (pėr´ mə fròst) Permanently frozen ground (p. 61)

**Phosphates** (fos´ fāts) Materials used to make fertilizer (p. 346)

**Physical environment** (fiz´ ə kəl en vī´ rən mənt) The natural world in which a person lives (p. 24)

**Physical geography** (fiz´ ə kəl jē og´ rə fē) The study of Earth itself; the study of the land, water, air, plants, and animals of the natural world (p. 25)

**Place** (plās) The physical and human features that make an area special (p. 27)

**Plain** (plān) Low-lying, usually flat areas (p. 35)

**Plantation** (plan tā´ shən) A large farm on which the owner grows only one crop (p. 102)

**Plateau** (pla tō´) An area of level highland (p. 80)

**Plate tectonics** (plāt tek ton´ iks) The idea that there is slow movement of Earth's plates (p. 81)

**Poaching** (pō´ ching) Hunting illegally in a park or in a place kept for animals (p. 326)

**Polar climate** (pō´ lər klī´ mit) A climate with long, cold winters and short, warm summers (p. 252)

**Polder** (pōl´ dər) A piece of land that was once part of the sea (p. 167)

**Political** (pə lit´ ə kəl) Having to do with government (p. 26)

**Pollute** (pə lüt´) To make something dirty, impure, or unhealthy (p. 48)

**Population density** (pop yə lā´ shen den´ sə tē) The average number of people living in each square mile of an area (p. 108)

**Population distribution** (pop yə lā´ shen dis trə byü´ shən) Where people live (p. 319)

**Poverty** (pov´ ər tē) The condition in which people lack one or more of the basic things needed to live (p. 409)

**Precipitation** (pri sip ə tā´ shən) How much rain, snow, or sleet falls from the sky (p. 39)

**Prejudice** (prej´ ə dis) Forming an opinion about others before getting to know them; looking down on people because of their race, religion, or color (p. 152)

**Prevailing winds** (pri vā´ ling winds) Winds that usually blow from the same direction (p. 297)

**Prime Meridian** (prim mə rid´ ē ən) A fixed point that is zero degrees longitude and runs through Greenwich, England (p. 34)

**Privatization** (prī vit i zā´ shən) Selling state farm land to private owners (p. 260)

**Processing** (pros´ es sing) Preparing a raw material for use or sale (p. 326)

**Producer** (prə dü´ sər) A manufacturer or farmer who makes a product to sell (p. 154)

**Protestant** (prot´ ə stənt) A Christian who does not belong to the Roman Catholic branch of Christianity (p. 43)

**Province** (prov´ əns) A state (p. 56)

**Pulp** (pulp) A wood product used in the making of paper (p. 46)

### Q

**Quebecois** (kā bek wä´) The French-speaking people of Quebec (p. 66)

### R

**Rain forest** (rān´ fôr ist) A thick forest in the Tropics where a great deal of rain falls (p. 83)

**Ramadan** (räm ə dän´) The ninth month of the Muslim calendar; the month is holy to followers of Islam (p. 342)

**Raw material** (rò mə tir´ ē əl) Something that is made into a finished product for sale (p. 285)

**Recycle** (rē sī´ kəl) To make new products from old ones (p. 48)

**Reef** (rēf) A string of rock, sand, or coral close to the surface of a body of water (p. 444)

**Reform** (rē fôrm´) A change in how something is done to make things better (p. 367)

**Refugee** (ref´ yü jē) A person who has left home and gone to another country because of war or political danger (p. 211)

**Region** (rē´ jən) An area on the earth's surface that geographers define by certain similar characteristics (p. 29)

**Regionalism** (rē´ jə nə liz əm) Feeling more loyal to one part of a country than to the whole country (p. 192)

**Reincarnation** (rē in kär nā´ shən) The belief that when people die, their souls are reborn into another living form (p. 386)

**Relative location** (rel´ ə tiv lō kā´ shən) A place described in relationship to another place (p. 27)

**Remote** (ri mōt´) Far away; isolated (p. 426)

**Renewable resource** (ri nü´ ə bəl rē´ sôrs) A resource that can be used but then replanted or replaced (p. 46)

**Republic** (ri pub´ lik) A nation that has a head of state that is not a king or queen (p. 248)

**Resource** (rē´ sôrs) A thing of value, often found in nature, that we can use to do or make something (p. 25)

**Revolution** (rev ə lü´ shən) The overthrowing of a government (p. 90)

**Rift** (rift) A crack in the earth (p. 206)

**Rimland** (rim´ land) The land, often islands and coastal plains, around the edge of an area (p. 101)

**River system** (riv´ ər sis´ təm) A group of rivers that are joined together (p. 38)

**Robotics** (rō bot´ iks) The technology of using machines to do factory work (p. 389)

**Roman Catholic** (rō´ mən kath´ ə lik) A Christian who accepts the pope as head of the largest branch of Christianity (p. 43)

**Romance language** (rō mans´ lang´ gwij) A language that comes from Latin (p. 151)

**Runoff** (run´ ôf) Material mixed with water that washes into rivers and lakes after it rains (p. 306)

**Rural** (rùr´ əl) An area away from the city, such as a farm community (p. 44)

**Rustbelt** (rust´ belt) Industrial states that are growing slowly or losing population (p. 45)

### S

**Safari** (sə fär´ ē) An African hunting trip (p. 324)

**Sahel** (sə hel´) A belt of semiarid land that stretches across Africa from Senegal on the west coast to the highlands of Ethiopia in the east (p. 275)

**Sandbar** (sand´ bär) A ridge of sand built up by ocean waves (p. 276)

**Satellite** (sat´ l īt) An object that is built to go around Earth in space (p. 464)

**Savanna** (sə van´ ə) A flat, grassy plain in the Tropics with few trees (p. 275)

**Scandinavia** (skan´ də nā´ vē ə) The five countries of northern Europe (p. 204)

**Scholar** (skol´ ər) An expert in at least one subject (p. 340)

**Sea level** (sē lev´ əl) The level at the surface of the ocean (p. 38)

| a | hat | e | let | ī | ice | ô | order | ù | put | sh | she | ə | a in about |
|---|---|---|---|---|---|---|---|---|---|---|---|---|---|
| ā | age | ē | equal | o | hot | oi | oil | ü | rule | th | thin | | e in taken |
| ä | far | ėr | term | ō | open | ou | out | ch | child | ᴛʜ | then | | i in pencil |
| â | care | i | it | ò | saw | u | cup | ng | long | zh | measure | | o in lemon |
| | | | | | | | | | | | | | u in circus |

**Sediment** (sed′ ə mənt) Rocks, sand, and dirt carried to a place by wind, water, or glaciers (p. 434)

**Self-sufficient** (self sə fish′ ənt) Able to take care of one's needs without help from someone else (p. 102)

**Service industry** (sėr′ vis in′ də strē) A business that provides a service (p. 48)

**Shantytown** (shan′ tē toun) A slum that surrounds a city and that has shelters made from weak materials (p. 280)

**Shifting agriculture** (shift′ ing ag′ rə kul chər) A type of farming in which farmers move from one plot of land to another (p. 285)

**Shintoism** (shin′ tō iz əm) An ancient Japanese religion in which followers worship spirits in nature (p. 386)

**Shiva** (shiv′ ə) A Hindu god; the destroying face of God (p. 407)

**Shogun** (shō′ gun) A powerful Japanese military leader (p. 379)

**Shortage** (shôr′ tij) Not having enough of something (p. 236)

**Sikhism** (sē′ kiz əm) A religion that combines parts of the Muslim religion with Hinduism (p. 409)

**Silt** (silt) The fertile soil and small rocky pieces carried along by running water (p. 337)

**Sirocco** (sə rok′ ō) A hot, dusty summer wind that sweeps northward from the Sahara (p. 338)

**Slave** (slāv) A person who is held against his or her will and forced to work for free (p. 106)

**Slavic** (slä′ vik) Having to do with people from central Asia who settled in eastern Europe (p. 234)

**Slum** (slum) An overcrowded, poor area in a town or a city (p. 88)

**Socialism** (sō′ shə liz əm) An economic system in which a government controls many of a country's biggest industries (p. 215)

**Specialize** (spesh′ ə līz) To work on what one can do best (p. 473)

**Staple crop** (stā′ pəl krop) A food that people eat most often (p. 284)

**Starvation** (stär vā′ shən) Suffering or dying from lack of food (p. 323)

**Steppe climate** (step klī′ mit) A climate with very hot summers and very cold winters, with little precipitation; the land is covered with wild grasses and few trees (p. 40)

**Strait** (strāt) A narrow passage of water between two larger bodies of water (p. 184)

**Strategic** (strə tē′ jik) Important for military reasons (p. 315)

**Subarctic climate** (sub ärk′ tik klī′ mit) The cold climate of the area immediately outside of the Arctic Circle (p. 61)

**Subcontinent** (sub kon′ tə nənt) A large landmass that is smaller than a continent (p. 402)

**Subsistence farming** (səb sis′ təns fär′ ming) Growing crops mainly to meet the needs of a family (p. 111)

**Subtropical climate** (sub trop′ ə kəl klī ′mit) A climate with hot and humid summers and mild winters (p. 40)

**Suburb** (sub′ ėrb) An area next to a city (p. 44)

**Summer solstice** (sum′ ər sol′ stis) The longest day of the year (p. 209)

**Sunbelt** (sun′ belt) The states of California, Arizona, Texas, and Florida (p. 45)

**Swahili** (swä hē′ lē) An African language that combines African languages with Arabic, Portuguese, Malay, and Persian words and that first developed for the purpose of trade (p. 321)

## T

**Taiga** (tī′ gə) The world's largest forest; contains pine, fir, larch, and other evergreen trees (p. 251)

**Tariff** (tar′ if) A tax that countries put on goods they import (p. 173)

**Tax break** (taks brāk) Being allowed to pay less money to the government for taxes (p. 369)

**Technology** (tek nol′ ə jē) The use of science and machines to improve ways of doing things (p. 90)

**Telecommunication** (tel ə kə myü nə kā′ shən) Communicating electronically (p. 465)

**Temperate climate** (tem′ pər it klī ′mit) A climate that is neither very hot nor very cold and has warm and cool seasons (p. 125)

**Terrace** (ter′ is) A broad, level step dug into a hillside for the growing of crops (p. 360)

**Territory** (ter′ ə tôr ē) An area of land that is part of a country, but is not officially a province or state of a country (p. 56)

**Tide** (tīd) The regular daily rise and fall of ocean waters (p. 174)

**Tierra caliente** (tyār′ ə kol yen′ tā) An area of land in a low altitude with a hot average temperature (p. 85)

**Tierra fría** (tyär′ ə frē′ yä) An area of land in a high altitude with a cold average temperature (p. 85)

**Tierra templada** (tyär′ ə tem plä′ dä) An area of land that is neither too hot nor too cold (p. 85)

**Trade barrier** (trād bar′ ē ər) A law or act that limits imports or puts special taxes on them (p. 92)

**Trade imbalance** (trād im bal´ əns) A situation in which a country pays more for imports than what it can pay for with exports (p. 286)

**Tradition** (trə dish´ ən) The ideas, beliefs, and customs that people pass down to their descendants (p. 191)

**Trend** (trend) A way in which something is headed (p. 44)

**Tributary** (trib´ yə ter ē) A smaller river that flows into a larger one (p. 38)

**Tropic of Cancer** (trop´ ik ov kan´ sər) An imaginary line that lies 23.5° north of the equator (p. 39)

**Tropic of Capricorn** (trop´ ik ov kap´ rə kôrn) An imaginary line that lies 23.5° south of the equator (p. 39)

**Tropical savanna climate** (trop´ ə kəl sə van´ ə klī´ mit) A climate that is hot all year around and has a wet and a dry season (p. 84)

**Tropics** (trop´ iks) The area between the Tropic of Cancer and the Tropic of Capricorn (p. 39)

**Tsunami** (sü nä´ mē) A huge ocean wave produced by underwater Earth movement or volcanic eruption (p. 380)

**Tundra** (tun´ drə) A plain with no trees (p. 56)

**Typhoon** (tī fün´) A tropical windstorm that forms over the ocean (p. 382)

## U

**Underemployment** (un dər em ploi´ mənt) When a person trained for one job must accept another job that often pays less and requires less skills (p. 345)

**Unemployment** (un em ploi´ mənt) The condition of people not being able to find jobs (p. 194)

**Uninhabitable** (un in hab´ ə tə bəl) Not suited for human activity (p. 383)

**United Nations (UN)** (yü nī´ tid nā´ shəns) An international organization that tries to settle disagreements, improve the way people live, and keep peace around the world (p. 471)

**Untouchable** (un tuch´ ə bəl) A Hindu who belongs to no caste and works with death, blood, leather, and dirt (p. 408)

**Urban** (ėr´ bən) Having to do with a city (p. 44)

## V

**Valley** (val´ ē) A stretch of lowlands between mountains (p. 80)

**Veld** (velt) A grassy plain in southern Africa (p. 295)

**Vishnu** (vish´ nü) A Hindu god; the preserving face of God (p. 407)

**Volcano** (vol kā´ nō) A mountain formed when hot liquid rock comes from deep within Earth to its surface (p. 81)

**Voodoo** (vü´ dü) A belief that good and evil spirits influence a person's daily life (p. 107)

## W

**Water table** (wó´ tər tā´ bəl) The level at which underground water can be reached (p. 370)

**Weather** (weth´ ər) The condition of the air at a given time or place (p. 39)

**Welfare** (wel´ fãr) Money or help that a government gives to people who are in need (p. 213)

**Wetland** (wet´ land) Land covered with water some or most of the time, but where plants continue to grow (p. 68)

**Windward** (wind´ wərd) The side from which the wind is blowing (p. 40)

**World Bank** (wėrld bangk) An organization that loans money to less developed countries at low interest rates (p. 475)

**World Trade Organization (WTO)** (wėrld trād ôr gə nə zā´ shen) A global organization that deals with rules of trade among nations (p. 474)

## Y

**Yak** (yak) A large, longhaired ox (p. 363)

## Z

**Zapatistas** (zä pä tē´ stäs) A group of native peasants who rebelled against the Mexican government in 1994 (p. 92)

| | | | | | | | | | |
|---|---|---|---|---|---|---|---|---|---|
| a | hat | e | let | ī | ice | ò | order | ù | put |
| ā | age | ē | equal | o | hot | oi | oil | ü | rule |
| ä | far | ėr | term | ō | open | ou | out | ch | child |
| â | care | i | it | ȯ | saw | u | cup | ng | long |

| | |
|---|---|
| sh | she |
| th | thin |
| ₮H | then |
| zh | measure |

ə { a in about / e in taken / i in pencil / o in lemon / u in circus }

# Index

## A

Aborigines, 448–51, 457, 461
Absolute location, 27
Acapulco, 84, 89
Achelous River, 189
Acid rain, 69, 240, 243, 269, 370
Adobe, 362
Adriatic Sea, 184, 197, 199, 228, 243
Aegean Sea, 184, 199, 228, 243
Afghanistan, 349, 400, 402, 408, 411, 417, 461
Africa, 271–353
Agribusiness, 130
Ainu, 384, 393
Air pollution, 48, 93, 156, 176, 240, 262, 370, 390, 414, 434, 466
Alaska, 36, 46
Albania, 228, 239, 243
Alberta, 58, 67
Alexandria, 344
Algeria, 332, 334, 346, 349
Alluvial, 403
Alms, 342
Alpacas, 127
Alps Mountains, 165, 167, 179, 187
Altitude, 85
Altitudinal zones, 85
Amazonia, 122
Amazon Rain Forest, 132
Amazon River, 122–24, 135
Amsterdam, 171
Amundsen, Roald, 213
Andes Mountains, 122–25, 130, 135, 139
Angel Falls, 125
Angola, 292, 294, 305
Animism, 280, 289, 300, 309
Apartheid, 301
Apennine Mountains, 187
Appalachian Mountains, 37, 46, 51, 56, 71
Aquaculture, 216, 219
Aquifers, 337
Arabian Peninsula, 335
Arabian Sea, 402, 413
Arable land, 370
Arafura Sea, 442

Aral Sea, 261–62, 265
Archipelago, 100, 115, 422
Arctic, 56, 71, 204
Arctic Circle, 61, 204, 209, 219
Arctic Ocean, 56, 248
Argentina, 118, 121, 124, 128–31, 135
Arizona, 45
Armenia, 248, 251, 257, 265, 269
Arno River, 188
Asia, 355–456
Aswan Dam, 338, 347, 349
Atacama Desert, 125
Atheists, 254
Atlantic Ocean, 34, 56, 104, 120, 149, 164, 168, 184, 188, 294
Atlas Mountains, 336
Atolls, 103, 445, 457
Aung San Suu Kyi, 427
Australia, 440, 442–46, 448–55, 457, 461
Australian Alps, 444
Austria, 170, 179, 223
Azerbaijan, 248, 251, 257, 265, 269

## B

Baghdad, 344
Bahamas, 100, 107, 115
Bahrain, 334, 346
Balaton, Lake, 231
Balearic Islands, 188
Balkan countries, 226–45, 269
Balkanization, 229
Balkan Mountains, 231
Balkan Peninsula, 184, 199, 228–29, 231, 243, 269
Baltic Sea, 204, 219, 248
Bangkok, 424, 429, 434–35
Bangladesh, 400, 404–5, 407–8, 410, 413, 417, 461
Bantu, 320
Basins, 37–38, 276
Baykal, Lake, 252, 262, 265
Bay of Bengal, 402
Bay of Biscay, 164, 168, 184, 199
Bedrock, 56
Beijing, 358, 365–66, 370
Belarus, 248, 265

Belgium, 166, 170–71, 173, 176, 179, 223
Belize, 100, 106, 115
Benelux country, 176
Benin, 274
Ben Nevis, 148
Benue River, 277
Bering Sea, 248
Berlin, 171
Bhutan, 400, 406–7, 409, 412–13, 417, 461
Bilingual, 64
Birthrates, 110, 128–29, 153, 213, 281, 344
Biwa, Lake, 381
Black Forest, 165
Black Sea, 228, 243, 265
Blue Nile, 318
Bogotá, 121
Bogs, 148, 159, 209
Bohemian Forest, 165
Bolivia, 122, 125, 127, 135
Bonsai, 383
Bosnia-Herzegovina, 226, 228, 234–36, 243
Botswana, 292, 294, 297, 303–4
Brahma, 407
Brahmaputra River, 404, 417
Brazil, 118, 120–23, 127–31, 135
British Columbia, 58, 60, 64, 67, 71
British Isles, 142–61, 223
Brunei, 422, 434
Brussels, 171
Bucharest, 236
Budapest, 236
Buddhism, 151, 364, 373, 379, 386, 409, 428, 449, 461
Buenos Aires, 129
Bulgaria, 228, 231, 236, 239, 243
Burkina Faso, 274, 282
Burundi, 314, 320

**C**

Cabora Bassa, Lake, 297
Cairo, 344
Calgary, 58
California, 36, 38, 45–46
Cambodia, 422, 424–25, 428
Cameroon, 314, 325
Campesinos, 88
Canada, 54–73, 75
Canadian Rocky Mountains, 60, 71

Canary Islands, 188
Cancun, 84
Cantabrian Mountains, 187
Cape Verde, 274
Capitalism, 432
Caracas, 121
Carbon dioxide, 131–32
Caribbean, 98–117, 139
Caribbean Sea, 100, 115, 120, 149
Carpathian Mountains, 229, 231, 243
Carrier, Willis, 45
Cascade Mountains, 37
Cash crops, 102, 285, 324, 353
Caspian Sea, 251
Caste system, 408, 410, 417
Castro, Fidel, 107
Caucasus Mountains, 251, 265, 269
Central Africa, 312–31, 353
Central African Republic, 314, 324–25
Central America, 98–117, 139
Central Asia, 249, 257, 355–97
Chad, 314
Chao Phraya River, 424, 437, 434
Chapala, Lake, 84
Chechnya, 256
Chernobyl Nuclear Power Plant, 263
Chile, 122, 125, 128, 130–31, 135
China, 356–75, 397
China Sea, 361
Chinook, 62
Christianity, 43, 65, 87, 107, 128, 171, 191, 212, 235, 279, 300, 322, 342, 363–64, 386, 409, 428, 449, 461
Chunnel, 172
Civil unrest, 301, 410–11, 417, 471
Civil war, 109
Clear-cut, 131
Climate, 39–41
Coast Mountains, 60
Collective farming, 260
Colombia, 118, 120–21, 127, 130–31, 135
Command economy, 258
Common Market, 173
Commonwealth of Independent States (CIS), 248, 258, 260
Commonwealth of Nations, 451
Communism, 109, 238–40, 243, 254, 269, 363, 373, 367, 432
Como, Lake, 189

Comoros, 294
Confucius, 363, 373, 379, 397
Congo, 314, 322, 325–26
Congo River and Basin, 315, 318, 329
Consumer electronics, 390
Consumer goods, 236
Consumers, 154
Continent, 34
Continental climate, 62, 71
Continental drift, 120
Corals, 103, 115, 444–45, 457
Cordillera, 60
Cosmopolitan, 65
Costa Brava, 185
Costa del Sol, 185
Costa Rica, 100, 103, 105–6, 109
Côte d'Ivoire (Ivory Coast), 274, 276, 285–86
Cottage industry, 413, 417
Coup, 282
Cousteau, Jacques, 173
Craters, 381
Creoles, 107
Crete, 184, 188
Croatia, 228–29, 243
Cuba, 98, 100, 110
Cultivators, 279, 289
Cultural crossroad, 234
Cultural diffusion, 42
Cultures, 26
Curie, Marie, 230
Cyclones, 405
Cyprus, 334
Cyrillic alphabet, 234
Czech Republic, 228–29, 236, 238–40, 243

**D**

Dalai Lama, 360
Danube River, 168–69, 231–32
Darling River, 445
Daylight saving time, 468
Death rates, 128–29, 281
Death Valley, 38
Deccan Plateau, 404–5, 417
Deciduous trees, 83
Deforestation, 68, 75, 93, 139, 370, 414, 434
Deltas, 38, 289, 337, 353, 437
Democratic Republic of Congo, 314, 325
Deng Xiaoping, 367

Denmark, 202, 204, 206, 208–9, 211–12, 215–16, 219, 223
Descendants, 86
Desertification, 275, 289
Deserts, 36, 82, 249, 253, 295, 336, 338, 359, 361, 446
Developed countries, 468, 473, 475, 477
Developing countries, 239, 467–68, 474–75, 477
Dharma, 408
Dialects, 170
Dictators, 324–25
Dikes, 167
Dinaric Alps, 231
Diversity, 65
Djibouti, 314, 318, 320, 323
Dnieper River, 246, 251
Dolomite Mountains, 187
Dominican Republic, 100
Don River, 251
Dora River, 188
Dormant, 103
Dosanjh, Ujjal, 66
Douro River, 188
Drakensberg Mountains, 295–98, 309, 353
Dreamtime, 449
Drought, 62, 275, 289, 318, 329
Dvina River, 251

**E**

Earthquakes, 81, 206, 336, 444, 457
East Africa, 312–31, 353
East Asia, 355–97
East China Sea, 358
Eastern Europe, 226–45, 269
Ebro River, 188
Ecotourism, 305-6, 309, 353
Ecuador, 120, 122, 127, 132, 135
Edmonton, 58
Egypt, 332, 334, 344–45
Elbe River, 168–69
Elburz Mountains, 336
Ellesmere Island, 56, 60, 71
El Niño, 467
El Salvador, 100, 108–9
E-mail, 465
Endangered, 326
England, 141, 145–46, 148, 150–52, 159
English Channel, 144, 159, 164, 223

Epic, 341
Equator, 34, 120
Equatorial Guinea, 314
Eritrea, 314, 318, 323
Erosion, 68, 93, 197, 370, 414, 467
Escarpments, 276, 296, 309
Estonia, 248
Estuaries, 124
Ethiopia, 312, 314, 320–23, 325
Ethnic groups, 234
Euphrates River, 334, 337, 349
Eurasia, 167
Europe, 141–223
European Economic Community, 173
European Union, 173, 179, 194, 199, 238
Evaporate, 317
Export economy, 389
Extended families, 190
Extinct, 113, 131

Federated States of Micronesia, 440, 443
Fertile Crescent, 334
Fiji Islands, 440, 443
Filial piety, 363
Finland, 202, 204, 207, 209, 211–12, 215–16, 219, 223
Fjords, 208, 219, 223, 445
Floodplain, 361
Florida, 35, 45
Foothills, 123
Foreign aid, 475
Foreign debt, 92
Foreigners, 172
Fossils, 120
France, 162, 166–68, 170–76, 179, 223
Freeman, Cathy, 450
Free-market economy, 154, 159, 173, 179, 219, 223
Freetown, 276
Free trade, 91, 475
French Guiana, 121
French Riviera, 169

Gabon, 314, 325
Galápagos Islands, 134
Gale, 149

Galileo Galilei, 193
Gambia, 274, 279
Gambia River, 277
Ganges River, 400, 403–4, 414, 417
Garda, Lake, 189
Garonne River, 168
Gates, Bill, 465
Gauchos, 128
Geography, 24, 464–65
Geological fault, 316
Geologists, 60
Georgia, 248, 251, 257, 265, 269
Geothermal, 103
Germany, 162, 165–69, 171–72, 174–76, 179, 223
Geysers, 208–9, 219, 444, 457
Ghana, 272, 274, 279, 285–86, 322
Glaciers, 38, 56, 60, 75, 144, 148, 208, 445
Glasgow, 152
Global economy, 473–75, 477
Globalization, 474, 477
Global society, 25
Global village, 464, 470, 477
Global warming, 132, 241, 466, 477
Gobi Desert, 356, 359
Grampian Hills, 148
Great Barrier Reef, 444, 454, 457, 461
Great Basin, 37–38
Great Britain, 145–156, 159, 223
Great Dividing Range, 444–45
Greater Antilles, 100, 103
Great Lakes, 38, 51, 61, 75
Great Lakes-St. Lawrence lowlands, 56, 71
Great Rift Valley, 316–17, 329, 336, 353
Great Wall, 358
Greece, 182, 184–86, 188–91, 194–96, 199, 223
Guadalquivir River, 188
Guatemala, 86, 100, 105–6, 108–9, 111
Guianas, 121, 127, 135
Guinea, 274, 276, 286
Guinea-Bissau, 274
Gulf of Aden, 315
Gulf of Guinea, 274
Gulf of Mexico, 38, 46, 81, 90
Gulf Stream, 149, 159, 169, 179, 209, 219, 223
Guyana, 120

## H

Haciendas, 101–2
Haiti, 98, 100, 107, 110
Hajj, 342
Harmattan, 277, 289
Harmony, 383
Heavy industry, 154, 175–76, 239–40, 262, 413
Hejaz Mountains, 336
Hellas, 190
Hemisphere, 442
Highland climate, 40, 115, 209, 361
Highlands, 121, 145, 185, 295, 336, 359, 406
Himalayas, 360, 373, 402–4, 417, 461
Hinduism, 151, 300, 321, 407–8, 410, 428, 461
Hindu Kush Mountains, 403, 404
Hispaniola, 100
Ho Chi Minh City, 424, 429
Hokkaido, 378
Holocaust, 235
Honduras, 98, 100, 106, 109, 111
Hong Kong, 365
Honshu, 378, 380–81, 397
Horn of Africa, 314
Horticulture, 324
Huang He (Yellow) River, 358, 361, 373, 397
Hudson Bay, 61
Human geography, 25, 470–72
Humid continental climate, 40, 63, 253, 361, 381–82
Humid subtropical climate, 125, 298, 362, 382, 405, 446
Hungary, 226, 228–29, 231, 234–36, 238, 240, 243
Hurricanes, 105
Hydroelectric power, 39, 174–75, 297, 338, 397

## I

Iberian peninsula, 184, 199
Ibrahima, Abd al-Rahman, 281
Iceland, 202, 204, 206, 208–9, 211, 215–16, 219, 223
Iguazú Falls, 77
Illinois, 36, 38, 44, 47
Immigrants, 43, 64, 86, 128, 150, 153, 171–72, 448–50
India, 400, 404–5, 407, 410–14, 416–17, 428, 461
Indian Ocean, 294, 402, 417, 442
Indo-Chinese Peninsula, 422, 424

Indo-Gangetic Plain, 403–4, 417
Indonesia, 420, 422, 424–25, 428, 429, 430, 432, 434
Indus River, 403–4, 406, 417
Industrial Revolution, 146, 171
Industries, 35
Inflation, 194
Interaction, 27
Intercropping, 284–85
International Monetary Fund (IMF), 475, 477
International trade, 174
Internet, 465
Inuit, 58–59, 63–64, 71, 75
Ionian Sea, 184, 199, 243
Iran, 332, 334, 336, 339, 341, 344–46, 349
Iraq, 332, 334, 344–46
Ireland, 145, 148, 150, 159, 223
Irrawaddy River, 424, 437
Irrigation, 80
Islam, 235, 279, 300, 321, 342, 363, 408, 428, 449, 461
Israel, 332, 334, 341, 345, 349
Istanbul, 344
Isthmus of Tehuantepec, 80
Italian peninsula, 184, 199
Italy, 173, 182, 184–85, 188–91, 194, 196–97, 199, 223

## J

Jainism, 409, 461
Jakarta, 429
Jalisco, 84
Jamaica, 100, 107
Japan, 376–95, 397
Japan Current, 382
Japanese Alps, 380
Jati, 408
Java, 429
Johannesburg, 294
Jordan, 334, 345
Jordan River, 334, 349
Jotunheimen Mountains, 208
Judaism, 43, 151, 191, 321, 341
Juruá River, 124
Jutland Peninsula, 204, 219

## K

Kalahari Desert, 295–96, 309, 353
Kamchatka Peninsula, 251
Kanto Plain, 380
Karakoram, 404
Kariba, Lake, 297
Karma, 408
Kasai River, 318
Kazakhstan, 246, 260
Kenya, 312, 314, 316, 320–21, 323–26
Khyber Pass, 402–3
Kiev, 249, 255, 265
Kremlin, 255–56
Kunlun Mountains, 359
Kurdistan, 341
Kuwait, 334, 345–46
Kyoto, 380, 387
Kyushu, 378

## L

Lagoons, 276, 445
Landlocked, 62
Land reform, 90, 95
Landslides, 425
La Niña, 467
Laos, 422, 424, 428
Latin America, 77–139
Latitude, 34, 144, 164, 204, 228, 274, 294, 314, 358
Latvia, 248
Lava, 81, 103
Leach, 432
Lebanon, 334–35, 341, 349
Leeds, 152
Leeward, 40, 62
Lena River, 251
Lesotho, 294, 299, 303
Lesser Antilles, 100
Levant, 334
Liao River, 359
Liberia, 274
Libya, 334, 346
Life expectancy, 281, 289, 387
Light industry, 369
Ligurian Sea, 184, 199
Lithuania, 246, 248
Liverpool, 148
Llamas, 127

Location, 27
Lochs, 145–46
Loess, 123, 359
Loire River, 168
London, 141, 147, 152, 154–55
Longitude, 34
Loroupe, Tegla, 321
Louisiana, 35, 38, 44, 46
Lowlands, 56, 103, 105, 123, 145, 165–66, 171
Luxembourg, 173, 176, 179, 223

## M

Macedonia, 228, 243
Mackenzie River, 61
Madagascar, 294
Maggiore, Lake, 189
Maghreb nations, 334
Magma, 444
Mainland, 100, 103–4, 115
Malawi, 294
Malawi, Lake, 316
Malay Peninsula, 422
Malaysia, 420, 422, 427, 430, 434
Mali, 272, 274, 277, 285
Manchurian Plain, 359, 373
Mandela, Nelson, 302
Mangrove, 274
Manila, 429
Manitoba, 58
Manual labor, 384
Maori, 449, 457, 461
Maquiladora, 91
Maracaibo, Lake, 125
Marine west coast climate, 41, 149, 169, 209, 233
Maritime climate, 61, 298
Maritime Provinces, 57, 71
Market economy, 258
Martinique, 107
Maryland, 35, 44
Massachusetts, 35, 44
Massif Central, 167
Mauritania, 274
Mauritius, 294
Mazatlan, 84
Mediterranean climate, 41, 189, 233, 297, 339, 446
Mediterranean Sea, 164, 168–69, 179, 184, 186, 188, 199, 334–35

Megalopolis, 44
Mekong River, 424, 437
Melanesia, 442–43, 457
Melbourne, 445, 450
Mendes, Chico, 133
Meridian, 442
Meseta, 184–85
Messiah, 342
Mestizos, 86–87, 95, 100, 106, 115, 139
Meteorologists, 40
Metropolitan area, 44
Mexico, 51, 75, 78–97, 139
Mexico City, 80, 83, 88, 93, 95, 370
Michigan, 36, 48
Michoacan, 84
Micronesia, 442–43, 457
Middle East, 332–51, 353
Migrations, 88, 299, 309, 366, 410, 417
Minnesota, 36, 47
Mississippi River, 38, 51, 75
Missouri, 36, 44
Missouri River, 38
Mistral, 169
Mohenjo-Daro, 403
Moldova, 248, 265
Moluccas, 430
Monotheism, 341
Monsoons, 405, 417, 425, 437, 461
Mont Blanc, 167
Montenegro, 228
Montreal, 57, 65
Morita, Akio, 391
Morocco, 334, 349
Moscow, 249, 255–56, 261, 265
Mosque, 321
Mother Teresa, 411
Mount Cook, 445
Mount Everest, 360, 373, 404
Mount Fuji, 380
Mount Hood, 37
Mount Kenya, 317
Mount Kilimanjaro, 316, 329
Mount Kosciusko, 444
Mount Kumgag, 381
Mount Logan, 60
Mount Rainier, 37
Mount Saint Helens, 37
Mount Shasta, 37

Mount Sorak, 381
Movement, 28
Mozambique, 292, 294, 297, 299–300, 303
Mulattos, 106
Multinational corporations, 131, 154
Mumbai (Bombay), 414
Munich, 171
Murray River, 445
Murrumbigee River, 445
Muslims, 151, 191, 235, 279–80, 321, 340, 342, 363, 408
Myanmar, 422, 424, 427–29

## N

Nakuru, Lake, 317
Namib Desert, 295–96, 309, 353
Namibia, 294, 295–96, 301, 304
Nangnim Mountains, 381
Narrows, 232
Nasser, Lake, 338
Nauru, 443
Nebraska, 36
Nepal, 400, 406–7, 412, 417, 461
Netherlands, 162, 167, 171, 173–76, 179, 223
New Brunswick, 57
New Caledonia, 443
Newfoundland, 57, 67
New Orleans, 35, 38, 44
New York City, 35, 44
New Zealand, 440, 442–46, 449–55, 457, 461
Niagara Falls, 61
Nicaragua, 100, 109–10
Nicaragua, Lake, 104
Niger, 272, 274, 286
Nigeria, 272, 274, 276, 279–80, 282, 285–86
Niger River, 274, 276–77, 289, 353
Nile River and Basin, 318, 329, 334–35, 337, 347, 349, 353
Nilotic, 320, 329, 353
Nirvana, 408
Nomads, 211, 275, 346, 349
Nongovernmental Organization (NGO), 472
North Africa, 332–51, 353
North America, 31–70
North American Free Trade Agreement (NAFTA), 91–92, 95
North China Plain, 358–59, 361, 373
Northern Europe, 202–21, 223

Northern Ireland, 145, 151, 159
Northern Poland, 231
North European Plain, 165, 229
North Island, 444–46
North Korea, 376–95
North Pole, 466
North Sea, 144, 156, 159, 164, 168, 179, 204, 215, 223
Northwest Territories, 58, 67
Norway, 202, 204, 206, 208–9, 211, 215–16, 219, 223
Norwegian Sea, 204
Nova Scotia, 57
Nunavut, 58–59, 64

## O

Oasis, 337
Ob River, 251
Ohio, 47
Ohio River, 38
Oman, 334
Ontario, 58, 67, 71
Orange River, 297, 309
Organization of Petroleum Exporting Countries (OPEC), 346
Orinoco River, 125, 135
Osaka, 380, 387
Ottawa, 58
Outback, 445
Overdevelopment, 112, 115
Overgraze, 454
Ozone layer, 466

## P

Pacific Islands, 440–59, 461
Pacific Ocean, 34, 56, 80, 104, 120, 442
Pacific World, 440–59, 461
Paddy, 433
Pakistan, 400, 404–5, 407–8, 412–13, 417, 461
Palestinian Liberation Organization (PLO), 345
Pampas, 123, 128
Panama, 98, 100
Panama Canal, 104, 115
Pangaea, 120
Papua New Guinea, 422, 428–29
Paraguay, 121, 124, 128, 135
Paraguay River, 124
Paraná River, 77, 124

Paris, 162, 166, 168, 171
Parramatta River, 445
Passes, 167
Pastoralists, 279, 289
Patagonia, 125, 135
Pátzcuaro, Lake, 84
Paz, Octavio, 87
Peaks, 167
Peat, 148, 159
Pennine Chain, 145, 148
Pennsylvania, 35, 47
Per capita income, 154, 159
Permafrost, 61
Peru, 118, 122, 124, 127, 135
Philippines, 422–23, 428–30, 432, 434
Phosphates, 346
Physical environment, 24
Physical geography, 25
Pico de Orizaba, 83
Place, 27
Plantations, 102, 112, 130, 324, 433
Plateau of Anatolia, 334
Plateaus, 80–81
Plate Tectonics, 81
Poaching, 326
Poland, 226, 228–29, 231, 234–36, 238–40, 243
Polar climate, 252
Polders, 167, 179
Polynesia, 442–43, 457
Pontic Mountains, 336
Popocatépetl, 83
Population density, 108, 152, 171, 212, 223, 387
Population distribution, 319
Po River, 188
Portugal, 182, 184–86, 188, 190–91, 194–95, 199, 223
Poverty, 92, 95, 115, 135, 281–82, 289, 409–10, 417, 430, 437, 470–71, 477
Prague, 236
Precipitation, 39
Prejudice, 152–53, 159, 172
Prevailing winds, 297–98
Prime Meridian, 34
Princess Basma Bint Ali, 344
Producers, 154
Protestants, 43, 87, 159, 171, 179, 191
Provinces, 56
Puerto Rico, 100, 110
Punjab, 405

Putin, Vladimir, 256
Putumayo River, 124
Pyongyang, 390
Pyrenees Mountains, 167, 187

## Q

Qatar, 334, 346
Qinghai-Tibet Plateau, 359, 361
Quebec, 57, 64, 66–67, 71
Quebec City, 57
Quebecois, 66

## R

Rain forests, 83, 103, 110, 113, 125, 131–32, 315, 325–26
Ramadan, 342
Raw materials, 285
Recycling, 48, 216, 469, 477
Red River, 424, 437
Red Sea, 315–16, 334, 336, 349, 353
Reef, 444
Reform, 367
Refugees, 211, 449
Regionalism, 192
Reincarnation, 386, 408
Relative location, 27
Renewable resource, 46
Republic, 248
Republic of Ireland, 142, 145, 151, 159
Republic of Palau, 443
Republic of South Africa, 294, 299, 301, 303–5
Republic of the Marshall Islands, 443
Rhine River, 168–69, 176
Rhodes, 188
Rhodope Mountains, 231
Rhône River, 168
Richter scale, 406
Rift, 206
Rimland, 101, 103, 115
Río Bravo del Norte (Río Grande), 84
Rio de Janeiro, 121, 129
Rio de la Plata, 124, 135
Río Negro, 124
Rivera, Diego, 89
Rocky Mountains, 36–37, 46, 51, 62
Roddick, Anita Lucia, 157
Romania, 226, 228–29, 231, 234–36, 239, 243
Rome, 191

Rotterdam, 175
Rub' al Khali, 335
Runoff, 144, 306
Rural areas, 44, 108, 115, 129, 135, 139, 280
Russia, 238, 246–67, 269
Rustbelt, 45
Ruwenzori Mountains, 317
Rwanda, 314, 320
Ryukyu Islands, 378

## S

Safari, 324
Sahara Desert, 275, 334–36, 338, 353
Sahel, 275, 289
Sami, 211
Sandbars, 276
San Salvador, 108
São Paulo, 121, 129
São Tomé and Principé, 314
Sardenia, 188
Saskatchewan, 58
Satellites, 464–65, 477
Saudi Arabia, 332, 334, 336, 346
Scafell Peak, 148
Scandinavia, 204–5, 219
Scandinavian Peninsula, 204, 206, 219
Scotland, 145–46, 150, 152, 159
Sea level, 38
Sediment, 434
Seine River, 168
Senegal, 274, 279, 285
Senegal River, 277
Serbia, 228
Serengeti, 271, 325
Serengeti Plain, 315
Service industries, 48, 91, 131, 154, 176, 215, 452
Seychelles, 294
Shanghai, 365
Shannon River, 145
Shantytowns, 280, 287, 323, 329, 470
Shenyang, 365
Shifting agriculture, 285
Shikoku, 378
Shintoism, 386
Shiva, 407
Siberia, 249, 251, 260, 265, 269
Sicily, 188
Sierra Leone, 274, 276, 279, 281, 286

Sierra Madre, 83, 95, 139
Sierra Madre Occidental, 83, 90
Sierra Madre Oriental, 83
Sikhism, 151, 159, 409
Silt, 337, 424
Singapore, 422, 430, 433
Sirocco, 338
Slavic, 234
Slovak Republic (Slovakia), 228, 231, 243
Slovenia, 228, 243
Socialism, 215
Solomon Islands, 443
Somalia, 314, 318, 320–21, 325
Songhai, 288
South Africa, 292
South America, 118–37, 139
South Asia, 400–19, 461
South China Sea, 358
Southeast Asia, 420–39, 461
Southern Africa, 292–311, 353
Southern Alps, 445
Southern Europe, 182–201, 223
South Island, 444–45
South Korea, 376–95
South Pole, 466–67
Spain, 182, 184–86, 188, 190–91, 194–96, 199, 223
Spice Islands, 423
Sri Lanka, 400, 409, 411, 413, 417, 428, 461
Standard of living, 215, 219, 236, 243, 413, 452
Staple crops, 284
St. Elias Mountains, 60
Steppe climate, 40, 84, 253, 298, 318, 339, 361, 406
Steppes, 359, 373
St. Lawrence Seaway, 57, 61, 70
Stockholm, 208, 212
St. Petersburg, 249, 255, 261, 265
Strait of Gibraltar, 184, 199
Subarctic climate, 61, 253
Subcontinent, 402, 417
Subsistence farming, 111, 127, 280, 284, 346, 432
Subtropical climate, 40, 277, 382
Suburb, 44
Sudan, 312, 314, 323
Sudety Mountains, 231
Suez Canal, 338, 349
Summer solstice, 209
Sunbelt, 45
Suriname, 121

Swahili, 321
Swaziland, 294, 303
Sweden, 202, 204, 206–9, 211–12, 215–16, 219, 223
Switzerland, 162, 165, 170, 176, 179, 223
Sydney, 443, 445, 450, 456
Syria, 334, 345, 349

## T

T'aebaek Mountains, 381
Taiga, 251, 265, 269
Taiwan, 366
Tanganyika, Lake, 316–17
Tanzania, 271, 312, 314–15, 320–21, 324–25, 329
Tariffs, 173, 179
Taro River, 188
Tasman Glacier, 445
Tasman Sea, 442
Taupo, Lake, 444–45
Taurus Mountains, 336, 353
Tehran, 344
Temperate climate, 125, 135
Terrace, 360
Texas, 45–46
Thailand, 420, 422, 424, 427–29, 432, 434
Thames, 148
Thar (Great Indian) Desert, 403, 417
Three Gorges Dam, 370–71
Tianjin, 365
Tiber River, 188
Tibet, 360
Tides, 174
Tierra caliente, 85
Tierra fría, 85
Tierra templada, 85, 104
Tigris River, 334, 337, 349
Timor Sea, 442
Titicaca, Lake, 125
Toba, Lake, 425
Toga, 274
Tokyo, 378, 380, 387
Tonle Sap (Great Lake), 425
Toronto, 58, 65
Trade barriers, 92
Trade imbalance, 286
Tributaries, 38, 135
Trinidad, 106
Tropical climate, 105, 125, 277

Tropical monsoon climate, 405
Tropical rain forest climate, 318, 425
Tropical savanna climate, 84, 105, 318, 405, 446
Tropic of Cancer, 39, 100, 358, 402
Tropic of Capricorn, 39, 100
Tropics, 39, 83, 100, 115, 125
Tsunamis, 380
Tundra, 56, 251, 265
Tunisia, 334
Turkey, 334, 336, 339, 344, 349
Typhoons, 382, 425
Tyrrhenian Sea, 184, 199

## U

Ubangi River, 318
Uganda, 314, 320, 323–26
Ukraine, 246, 248–49, 255, 260, 265
Uluru (Ayers Rock), 444, 451, 457
Underemployment, 345
Unemployment, 194, 345
United Arab Emirates, 334, 346
United Kingdom, 142, 159
United Nations (UN), 471–72, 477
United States of America, 32–53, 65, 75, 115
Ural Mountains, 249–50, 265, 269
Urban, 44, 152, 171, 212, 236, 255, 280, 323, 387,
    410, 435
Uruguay, 121, 124, 128, 135
Uruguay River, 124

## V

Valley of Mexico, 80, 86
Valleys, 80, 353, 445
Vancouver, 58, 64–65
Vanern, Lake, 209
Vanuatu, 443
Vatican City, 191
Veld, 295, 309
Venezuela, 120–21, 125, 127, 130–31, 135
Vera Cruz, 89
Victoria Falls, 297
Victoria Island, 60, 71
Victoria, Lake, 316–17, 324, 329
Vietnam, 420, 422, 424, 429, 436
Vishnu, 407
Vistula River, 232
Volcanoes, 81, 100, 103, 139, 206, 208, 251, 319,
    380, 424, 444–45

Volga River, 251, 261, 265
Volta River, 277
Voodoo, 107, 115
Vosges, 167

## W

Waikato River, 445
Wales, 145, 147, 150, 159
Warsaw, 236
Washington, D.C., 35
Water tables, 370
Weather, 39–40, 51
Welfare, 213
West Africa, 272–91, 353
Western Europe, 162–81, 223, 269
Western Samoa, 443
West Indies, 100
Wetlands, 68, 71, 75, 159, 274
White Nile, 318
Windermere, Lake, 148
Windward, 40
Winnipeg, 58
World Bank, 475, 477
World Trade Organization (WTO), 474, 477

## X

Xi Jiang River, 361, 373, 397
Xingu River, 124

## Y

Yangtze River, 361, 370, 373, 397
Yarra River, 445
Yellow Sea, 358, 378
Yemen, 334
Yenisey River, 251
Yokohama, 380, 387
Yucatán Peninsula, 82, 84, 86, 95
Yugoslavia, 228, 239, 243
Yukon Territory, 58, 60

## Z

Zagros Mountains, 336
Zambezi River, 297, 309
Zambia, 294, 304
Zapatistas, 92
Zimbabwe, 292, 294, 301, 303–4

# Acknowledgments

Acknowledgment is made for permission to reprint the following copyrighted images. In the case of any omissions, the publisher will be pleased to make suitable acknowledgments in future editions.

**Cover Image**
© Chris Noble/Stone

**Maps**
Pages 210, 368, 396, and 447 © Hammond World Atlas Corporation, NJ, License Number 12510

**Table of Contents**
Page 3, © SuperStock International; p. 4, © Ron Sanford/Stock Market; p. 5, © Robert Frerck/Stone; p. 6, © James L. Stanfield/National Geographic Image Collection; p. 7, © Daryl Balfour/Stone; p. 9, © Steve Nutt/AP/Wide World Photos; p. 10 by John Edwards; p. 12, © Paul Chesley/Stone

**Introduction**
Page 24, © Steven L. Raymer/National Geographic Image Collection; p. 27, © World Perspectives/Stone; p. 28, © Phil Schermeister/Corbis; p. 29, © Randy Wells/Stone

**Unit 1**
Page 30, © John Edwards/Stone

**Chapter 1**
Page 32, © Toyohiro Yamada/FPG International; p. 35, © Jim Pickerell/Stone; p. 38, © Annie Griffiths/National Geographic Image Collection; p. 42, © Tony Freeman/PhotoEdit; p. 45, © AP/Wide World Photos; p. 48, © Paul S. Howell/Liaison Agency; p. 50, © Paul Chesley/Stone

**Chapter 2**
Page 54, © Tom Bean/Stone; p. 57, © Chris Thomaidis/Stone; p. 62, © SuperStock International; p. 64, © Chris Swartz/Stone; p. 66, © AP/Wide World Photos; p. 67, © Larry Goldstein/Stone; p. 70, © Kenneth Love/National Geographic Image Collection

**Unit 2**
Page 76, © Harvey Lloyd/FPG International

**Chapter 3**
Page 78, © David Hiser/Stone; p. 81, © AP/Wide World Photos; p. 84, © Gavriel Jecan/Stone; p. 87, © Swersey/Liaison Agency; p. 89, © Schalkwijk/Art Resource; p. 91, © Sisse Brimberg/National Geographic Image Collection; p. 94, © Robert Frerck/Odyssey Productions

**Chapter 4**
Page 98, © Tibor Bognar/Stock Market; p. 101, © Stephen Ferry/Liaison Agency; p. 104, © Sarah Stone/Stone; p. 107, © Ferry/Liaison Agency; p. 109, © Coast Guard/Susan Greenwood/Liaison Agency; p. 112, © Chip and Rosa María de la Cueva Peterson; p. 114, © Doug Pensinger/AllSport USA

**Chapter 5**
Page 118, © Telegraph Colour Library/FPG International; p. 121, © VCG/FPG International; p. 123, © John Warden/Stone; p. 128, © Ned Gillette/Stock Market; p. 130, © Francolon J. Claude/Liaison Agency; p. 133, © Sigla/Liaison Agency; p. 134, © Ron Sanford/Stock Market

**Unit 3**
Page 140, © SuperStock International

**Chapter 6**
Page 142, © Joe Cornish/Stone; p. 146, © The Granger Collection; p. 148, © Zefa/Stock Market; p. 150, © Marcus Brooke/Stone; p. 155, © SuperStock International; p. 156, © Stewart Cohen/Stone; p. 157, © Andrew Buurman/FSP/Liaison Agency; p. 158, © Paul Harris/Stone

**Chapter 7**
Page 162, © Shinichi Kanno/FPG International; p. 164, © Anthony Suau/Liaison Agency; p. 167, © Thad Samuels II Abell/National Geographic Image Collection; p. 170, © Adam Woolfitt/National Geographic Image Collection; p. 173, © Rosenfeld/Wallet/Saola/Liaison Agency; p. 176, © Martine Mouchy/Stone; p. 178, © Kenneth Garrett/National Geographic Image Collection

**Chapter 8**
Page 182, © Robert Frerck/Stock Market; p. 185, © John Lamb/Stone; p. 188, © Robert Frerck/Stone; p. 191, © Randy Wells/Stone; p. 193, © Hulton Getty/Stone; p. 195, © Vittoriano Rastelli/Corbis; p. 196, © Kindra Clineff/Stone; p. 198, © Dave Bartruff/Corbis

**Chapter 9**
Page 202, © David Barnes/Stock Market; p. 205, © Hulton Getty/MPI/Stone; p. 206, © SuperStock International; p. 208, © George F. Mobley/National Geographic Image Collection; p. 211, © SuperStock International; p. 213, © Hulton Getty/Stone; p. 216, © Marie-Louise Brimberg/National Geographic Image Collection; p. 218, © Chad Ehlers/Stone

## Unit 4

Page 224, © James Balog/Stone

### Chapter 10

Page 226, © James Stanfield/National Geographic Image Collection; p. 228, © James Stanfield/National Geographic Image Collection; p. 230, © Hulton Getty/Stone; p. 231, © Sylvain Grandadam/Stone; p. 235, © David Turnley/Corbis; p. 239, © James L. Stanfield/National Geographic Image Collection; p. 240, © James P. Blair/National Geographic Image Collection; p. 242, © Kobal Collection

### Chapter 11

Page 246, © Jim Brandenburg/Minden Pictures; p. 249, © Ed Kashi/Ed Kashi; p. 252, © Maria Stenzel/National Geographic Image Collection; p. 255, © George Chan/Stone; p. 256, © AP/Wide World Photos; p. 257, © AP/Wide World Photos; p. 262, © Gerd Ludwig/National Geographic Image Collection; p. 264, © Larry Stein/Black Star Publishing/PictureQuest (PNI)

## Unit 5

Page 270, © Nicholas Parfitt/Stone

### Chapter 12

Page 272, © Victor Englebert/Victor Englebert Photography; p. 277, © The Granger Collection; p. 280, © Andrew Errington/Stone; p. 281, by John Edwards; p. 282, © James L. Stanfield/National Geographic Image Collection; p. 284, © Gerard Del Vecchio/Stone; p. 288, by John Edwards

### Chapter 13

Page 292, © Frans Lanting/Minden Pictures; p. 295, © Chris Harvey/Stone; p. 297, © Ian Murphy/Stone; p. 301, © Mark Peters/Liaison Agency; p. 302, © de Keerle/UK Press/Liaison Agency; p. 303, © Jason Laure'/Laure' Communications; p. 304, © Dave Saunders/Stone; p. 305, © Mitch Kezar/Stone; p. 308, © SuperStock International

### Chapter 14

Page 312, © Art Directors and TRIP Photo Library; p. 314, © Torleif Svensson/Stock Market; p. 316, © Daryl Balfour/Stone; p. 321, © Steve Allen/Liaison Agency; p. 322, © Anthony Suau/Liaison Agency; p. 327, © Pool Raid Gauloise/Liaison Agency; p. 328, © Kenneth Garrett/National Geographic Image Collection

### Chapter 15

Page 332, © Barbara Maurer/Stone; p. 335, © Sylvain Grandadam/Stone; p. 337, © Roger Wood/Corbis; p. 338, © Josef Polleross/Stock Market; p. 342, © Annie Griffiths Belt/National Geographic Image Collection; p. 344, © Scott Peterson/Liaison Agency; p. 345, © Noel Quido/Liaison Agency; p. 348, © Scala/Art Resource

## Unit 6

Page 354 , © Yann Layma/Stone

### Chapter 16

Page 356, © Dean Conger/Corbis; p. 359, © D. E. Cox/Stone; p. 360, © T. Stoddart/Spooner/Liaison Agency; p. 369, © Dean Conger/National Geographic Image Collection; p. 372, © Keren Su/China Span

### Chapter 17

Page 376, © Michael S. Yamashita/Corbis; p. 379, © Hulton Getty/Felice A. Beato/Stone; p. 380, © Orion Press/Stone; p. 382, © AFP Photo/Corbis; p. 385, © SuperStock International; p. 389, © Chad Ehlers/Stone; p. 391, © Kurita/Liaison Agency; p. 392, © SuperStock International

## Unit 7

Page 398, © Index Stock Imagery

### Chapter 18

Page 400, © Miles H. Watson-Cort/Eye Ubiquitous/Corbis; p. 405, © Chip Hires/Liaison Agency; p. 408, © Patrick Frilet/Saola/Liaison Agency; p. 411, © Francois Lochon/Liaison Agency; p. 414, © Tapis and Chales/Liaison Agency; p. 416, © Robert Holmes/Corbis

### Chapter 19

Page 420, © David Hanson/Stone; p. 422, © Oliver Benn/Stone; p. 426, © Christophe Loviny/Liaison Agency; p. 427, © Corbis; p. 429, © Paul Chesley/Stone; p. 432, © Dennis Waugh/Stone; p. 436, © Hulton Getty/Keystone/Stone

### Chapter 20

Page 440, © Paul A. Souders/Corbis; p. 443, © Doug Armand/Stone; p. 444, © Oliver Strewe/Stone; p. 448, © Oliver Strewe/Stone; p. 450, © AFP Worldwide; p. 452, © Jim Erickson/Stock Market; p. 454, © Penny Tweedie/Stone; p. 456, © Steve Nutt/AP/Wide World Photos; p. 460, © Margaret Gowan/Stone

### Chapter 21

Page 462, © World Perspectives/Stone; p. 465, © Jeff Christensen/Liaison Agency; p. 469, © Jeremy Horner/Corbis; p. 472, © Priit J. Vesilind/National Geographic Image Collection; p. 474, © Paul Chesley/Stone